Praise for *The Come Up*

"[Jonathan Abrams] has flexed his oral history muscle before, with *All the Pieces Matter*. This time he turns his attention to the formative days of hip-hop, zipping between times and places and tying it all together with the instincts of a great reporter."

—*The Boston Globe*

"Oral histories rise or fall on reporting and editing. Abrams . . . excels at both. He knows whom to talk to and he knows what questions to ask them. . . . All told, it's an extraordinary tale, the story of how a grassroots culture created itself from the streets and became an international force. To his credit, Abrams doesn't just talk to the architects. He also gets input from the stonemasons, the contractors and the other heavy lifters. It's the oral history hip-hop deserves as its beat goes on."

—*Los Angeles Times*

"When it comes to hip-hop, there are certain all-encompassing histories that give you the entire culture at your fingertips. Jeff Chang's *Can't Stop Won't Stop* and both of Dan Charnas's magnum opuses, *The Big Payback* and *Dilla Time*, set the standard, and now Jonathan Abrams's *The Come Up* raises the stakes to a whole new level. To say this book is incredible simply doesn't do it justice. It's essential. A primary source. It isn't just the fact that you have the voices of the most seminal rap artists who were there from the very beginning; you now have

the perspective of time and reflection. Read this book. Eat this book. Steal this book."

—CHEO HODARI COKER, creator and showrunner of Marvel's *Luke Cage*, co-writer of the biopic *Notorious*, and author of *Unbelievable: The Life, Death, and Afterlife of The Notorious B.I.G.*

"I'm not even sure how Abrams did this, but I'm so grateful he did. It's one thing to say you want to write an oral history on hip-hop. It's another thing to actually do it with a seemingly endless amount of voices who were there on the front lines from the very beginning. Abrams weaves in and out of eras, regions, and decades and does a paramount job of painting a full picture of the world's most influential musical genre. Abrams has always been a phenomenal storyteller, but this is special—even for one of this country's truly legendary storytellers."

—JUSTIN TINSLEY, author of *It Was All a Dream*

"*The Come Up* is as close to Studs Terkel as hip-hop has ever gotten. Jonathan Abrams set out to accomplish a task that sounds absurd on paper: assemble an oral history of hip-hop from the five boroughs to the Bay and from Memphis to Miami, and the ascendance of everyone from G-Funk to G-Unit. But not only does he succeed, he makes it seem effortless and ordained. This book is brilliantly curated, meticulously reported, and will last for decades as a touchstone of scholarship about the most important art form of the last half century. These are the stories that you love to hear again and again and the ones that you can't believe that you never knew."

—JEFF WEISS, founder of Passion of the Weiss

"Hip-hop is a story machine, and Jonathan Abrams is unsurpassed in capturing the best of them. What *Please Kill Me* did for punk rock, *The Come Up* has done for hip-hop—it's something essential, profane, profound, hilarious, tragic, riveting, and real. These are the tales that made a movement."

—JEFF CHANG, author of *Can't Stop Won't Stop*

"Open up practically any page in *The Come Up: An Oral History of the Rise of Hip-Hop*, and a gem drops into your lap.... *The Come Up* is as jam-packed as a Twista song and as weighty as Slick Rick's jewelry.... The total package is a riveting account of how rap carried hip-hop culture from obscurity to ubiquity, from disrespected to winning the Pulitzer Prize—and how it should have been getting that respect all along."

—Andscape

"Cutting through the inherent contradictions that come along with documenting hip-hop history, author and *New York Times* staff writer Jonathan Abrams goes directly to the source(s), conducting over 300 interviews with key players throughout hip-hop's five decade reign.... An ambitious collection of firsthand accounts of hip-hop's birth and ultimate rise as the gravitational center of pop culture."

—Okayplayer

"Monumental and comprehensive . . . Sourced from years of in-depth interviews, *The Come Up: An Oral History of the Rise of Hip-Hop* chronicles the culture from its origins on the playgrounds of the Bronx to its ongoing reign as the most powerful force in popular culture."

—Rock the Bells

"Kaleidoscopic . . . [*The Come Up*] will captivate hip-hop heads."

—*Publishers Weekly*

"Firsthand accounts from more than 300 interviewees provide a vivid picture of how the sound of hip-hop changes with the times and regions in Abrams's essential oral history of the genre. . . . This oral history on the evolution of hip-hop during its first 50 years is a labor of love and respect."

—*Library Journal*

BY JONATHAN ABRAMS

All the Pieces Matter
Boys Among Men
The Come Up

THE COME UP

THE

Come

an ORAL HISTORY of the RISE of HIP-HOP

JONATHAN

abrams

2023 Crown Trade Paperback Edition

Copyright © 2022 by Jonathan Abrams

All rights reserved.

Published in the United States by Crown, an imprint of the Crown Publishing Group, a division of Penguin Random House LLC, New York.

CROWN and the Crown colophon are registered trademarks of Penguin Random House LLC.

Originally published in hardcover in the United States by Crown, an imprint of the Crown Publishing Group, a division of Penguin Random House LLC, in 2022.

Library of Congress Cataloging-in-Publication Data
Names: Abrams, Jonathan P. D., author.
Title: The come up / Jonathan Abrams.
Description: New York: Crown, 2022. | Includes bibliographical references and index.
Identifiers: LCCN 2022016189 (print) | LCCN 2022016190 (ebook) |
ISBN 9781984825155 (paperback) | ISBN 9781984825148 (ebook)
Subjects: LCSH: Rap (Music)—History and criticism. | Hip-hop. | Rap musicians—Interviews. | LCGFT: Oral histories.
Classification: LCC ML3531 .A27 2022 (print) | LCC ML3531 (ebook) | DDC 782.421649—dc23/eng/20220428
LC record available at https://lccn.loc.gov/2022016189
LC ebook record available at https://lccn.loc.gov/2022016190

Printed in the United States of America on acid-free paper

crownpublishing.com

9 8 7 6 5 4 3 2 1

Book design by Anna Kochman

For Aaron and to crafting your own life's beat

CONTENTS

AUTHOR'S NOTE

Every hip-hop music fan has an origin story—when the music ignited those first sparks, grabbing us, shaking us, initiating a lifelong relationship.

Growing up in the suburbs of Los Angeles during the late 1980s, I was too young to appreciate the rebellious explosion of N.W.A, a group that opened millions to the possibilities of the genre. The group's lyrics did not lend themselves to frequent radio play, and my parents didn't openly invite that "hoppity hip" into our home. I was plugged in enough to applaud Dr. Dre when *The Chronic* landed, but could not yet truly appreciate the full evolution of his sonic mastery. *Doggystyle,* Snoop Doggy Dogg's debut album, painted the scenes of an elaborate party that my adolescent mind could only partly imagine.

Instead, for me, the artist who truly stoked those early embers was Tupac Amaru Shakur. As he did for so many people my age, Pac ignited in me a full devotion to hip-hop music.

This was back in the days when the music found you. Long before Spotify and iTunes, I would toggle the radio dial between 92.3 The Beat and Power 106 and record Shakur's songs onto a cassette tape so I could play them back on demand. I got my hands on *Me Against the World,* Shakur's third album, when a teenage employee at Circuit City took pity on my pleading eleven-year-old self. My mom unearthed the cassette, took one look at the Parental Advisory sticker, and marched me back to return it. I discreetly purchased another one, vowing to find a better hiding place. Such was the power and pull of Pac on my young mind.

Pac gifted me a song or lyric for every emotion and feeling. He had a way of making it seem as though he was speaking directly to me, crystallizing thoughts and ideas that were only starting to percolate and form. "Brenda's Got a Baby" illuminated the structural inequities in the world that I sensed people like me faced, but were not being taught in school. "Dear Mama" existed for when I reflected over my mom and witnessed her trudge through setbacks. I reserved "Hit 'Em Up" for those rare and insular moments I wanted to give the world double birds.

Tupac's killing in late 1996 shattered my world. I mourned the death of an artist and poet who transcended his still-young musical genre. I had come to view hip-hop music as a foundational block in my own life and wondered if it would continue evolving, emerging, and influencing after the loss of one of its brightest stars.

The deaths of Shakur and other talented artists gunned down in their prime, like the Notorious B.I.G., were colossal losses. But hip-hop music, above almost anything else, is resilient. The genre's original bricklayers in the Bronx of the 1970s heeded their own flickers of imagination to ignite a musical genre out of decay and neglect. The genre persevered, overcoming every obstacle imaginable—from an older generation who rejected it, to radio stations that did not want to play it, to politicians speaking out against it.

I never found another Pac. But, in the genre, I found a constant ally. I turned to hip-hop music when I needed inspiration or motivation, to zone out or home in, during times of celebration and mourning, for education and enlightenment.

Hip-hop music has now existed for almost half a century—and its origins and evolution are finally beginning to be studied and excavated with the rigor they deserve. But the voices of those who created, innovated, and persevered to propel a musical genre that would one day become the most popular in the United States are still seldom heard from—and some of their stories are at risk of being forever lost. That realization, which I had in 2017, became the catalyst for this project. After publishing my oral history of the groundbreaking TV show *The Wire*, I aimed my next oral history project at a far more ambitious subject: hip-hop's rise and the creative sparks behind its first transcendent moments.

Lyricism, after all, is a form of oral tradition.

This oral history weaves together the sweeping origin, spread, and impact of hip-hop music across generation after generation as it made its dominant march across the country. It starts with the inventiveness of neglected kids amid the Bronx ruins before stretching to New York's other boroughs like the veins on a subway map. It encompasses hip-hop's path from parks onto vinyl, its travels to the West Coast through the rise of gangster rap and G-funk, the Southern surge in cities like Atlanta, Memphis, and New Orleans, and many places and moments beyond and in between. The chapters focus on the artistry, creativeness, and courage of those who made significant impacts, and seek to illuminate the roots of careers that influenced generations of others.

I began this project in the summer of 2018, and over the next four years I would conduct over three hundred interviews. The stories captured on these pages were provided by DJs, artists, producers, label executives, and journalists who lent their time and memories to deliver firsthand accounts. There are people whom I had hoped to talk to for this book and couldn't get to; I hope that these pages still manage to capture their contributions to the music. I also know that there are bricklayers whose influence is *not* documented in this book—but any omissions here are not a judgment on their inroads. Those legacies are eternal. A book dedicated just to listing the names of those who have made positive impacts on hip-hop music could never contain enough space.

People, like hip-hop music, move along on their own schedules, which sometimes didn't align with my reporting timeline. One individual replied to a direct message for an interview more than two years after I first sent the request. Some people whose thoughts I hoped to include in these pages declined requests, preferring to allow a lifetime of work to speak for itself. But many others, including some who have rarely granted interviews, were willing to sit down with me. These conversations—like the late Edward "Duke Bootee" Fletcher describing the origins of "The Message," DMC passionately detailing his groundbreaking efforts, Kool Moe Dee elaborating on his Grammys boycott, and executives like Ann Carli and Monica Lynch detailing their pioneering moves—resulted in a manuscript that, in its initial form, was nearly three times longer than the one you are reading.

In the interest of streamlining and including as many essential viewpoints and anecdotes as possible, the reflections here have been occasionally edited for length and clarity. The minor hitches that arise in natural conversation have been removed. The spirit and intent of every conversation remains. Occasionally, anecdotes conflict. Perspectives of the same event can differ, and memories change and morph over time. I regard all of them as personal and valid.

One challenge of compiling an oral history of a complex subject, one with overlapping chronologies and settings, is how to organize the material. I have sought to tell the story roughly in chronological order, beginning in the Bronx in the early 1970s. As you will see, however, some chapters do backtrack to explore certain figures and events relevant to their theme. Another challenge is how to fairly document complex individuals. It's important to acknowledge that, over the course of decades in the public eye, a few figures have, either in the past or recently, been subject to allegations of wrongdoing, some quite serious. I felt it was nonetheless important to the historical record to include recollections from several such people—Russell Simmons, for example, who made crucial creative and business contributions to the genre—while remaining mindful of and acknowledging their alleged inappropriate conduct.

Each quote is accompanied by that person's professional identity (artist, DJ, producer, etc.); affiliation with musical groups or significant record labels; and sometimes where they are from. Like the chapter introductions and narrative interstitials, this information is meant to provide readers with context. Occasionally a person's title changes as the book progresses, in order to reflect the relevant information for that section. For example, Faith Newman was one of Def Jam's early employees before she later signed Nas to Columbia Records.

Hip-hop music's rise to permeate every strand of popular culture is a winding, tangled, massive story.

And it's one that continues to expand and evolve.

Here's to those next sparks catching fire.

THE COME UP

01 LEMONADE FROM LEMONS

Bronx, New York
1973–1979

Clive Campbell migrated as a child with his family from Jamaica to the United States in the late 1960s, leaving one country roiled by political instability for another. In Kingston, Campbell had become infatuated with the reggae and dub music that blared from giant portable sound systems, and DJs who toasted or talked over instrumental tracks. Campbell arrived in the Bronx during the reign of feel-good disco music, which intersected with the civil rights era and the dire financial straits of a New York City that was facing a declining population and labor unrest. Campbell involved himself in the city's emerging graffiti scene—which had arrived after originating in Philadelphia—and assumed the tag name Kool Herc.

On August 11, 1973, Campbell hosted a back-to-school fundraising party for his sister, Cindy, at 1520 Sedgwick Avenue in the West Bronx—and he is widely credited with birthing hip-hop on that day. By then, the teenage Campbell had assembled his own massive sound system, along with an eclectic record collection that included selections from James Brown and the Incredible Bongo Band. At the party, before an appreciative audience of neighborhood teenagers, DJ Kool Herc performed his "Merry-Go-Round" technique of isolating and prolonging the breakbeat sections of songs (the drum patterns used in interludes—breaks—between sections of melody) by switching between two record players.

DJ Kool Herc became a folk hero in the Bronx as his parties attracted larger and larger crowds. He hosted popular block parties and created Kool Herc & the Herculoids with Clark Kent. Acrobatic dancers known as b-boys, b-girls, and breakers (the media eventually labeled them as breakdancers, a term still in wide circulation today) flocked to DJ Kool Herc's parties to compete in dance circles—no longer having to wait out lengthy songs for a brief moment to get down. DJ Kool Herc enlisted the help of his friend Coke La Rock, regarded as hip-hop's first MC, as La Rock adapted toasting by shouting out the names of friends and encouraging partygoers to dance.

In time, Afrika Bambaataa and Grandmaster Flash joined DJ Kool Herc as Bronx DJs who forged groundbreaking contributions and laid the foundation for hip-hop to flourish, spread, and evolve.

DJ Charlie Chase (Cold Crush Brothers): The Bronx [in the late 1960s and '70s] was the epicenter for poverty, the epicenter for kids who were full of energy, who didn't know what to do with it, didn't have a lot of activities, didn't have role models.

MC Debbie D (artist): The backdrop to the South Bronx is poverty-stricken—crime, gangs, slumlords, abandoned buildings everywhere. So they had coined the Bronx "The Bronx Is Burning." And they wasn't putting money into safe havens for young people. So, with the music outside, you went to a jam, there's a thousand kids standing there. We ain't got nothing else to do.

Easy A.D. (Cold Crush Brothers): We were creating something that took up our time and made us feel good and brought us together. You have to imagine walking out your house every day and seeing abandoned cars burnt up, empty buildings, and you're going to elementary school.

Michael Holman (journalist): A lot of young people are going downtown to see major live acts like [Patti] LaBelle, James Brown, Funkadelic, as well as going to the famous discos, wearing their best clothes, doing the latest dances, and leaving those young punks and all the troubles in the neighborhood behind. What's left behind is an audience of younger people, teenagers who can do all the dances—hell, sometimes they're the originators and are the best dancers.

Kurtis Blow (artist, producer): A big part of hip-hop is breakdancing, b-boying. The dance was around before hip-hop, the actual dance style was developed from playing soul music and that playlist that [Kool Herc used].

Grandmaster Caz (Cold Crush Brothers): Herc was a mythical figure in the neighborhood. You heard about him before you saw him.

Sadat X (artist, Brand Nubian): I remember Herc being this larger-than-life figure, just muscles, with the glasses on. Herc was the commander, putting people in place.

MC Debbie D (artist): When Kool Herc comes out and he starts playing music and then other notable DJs get involved—[Afrika] Bambaataa, [Grandmaster] Flash, L Brothers—and they start playing their music. We're all going to the jams.

Kurtis Blow (artist, producer): He played the music that we wanted to hear. There was a special playlist of b-boy songs, breakdance songs—I can rename right now about ten of them: "Give It Up or Turnit a Loose" by James Brown, "Get Into Something" by the Isley Brothers, "Listen to Me" by Baby Huey, "Melting Pot" by Booker T. & the M.G.'s. You got "Scorpio" by Dennis Coffey and the Detroit Guitar Band. "Shaft in Africa." "Apache" by Michael Viner's Incredible Bongo Band. A couple more James Brown songs you can put in there like "Soul Power" and "Sex Machine" and "Escap-ism," "Make It Funky"—songs like that.

When you playing these songs, this is the time for the b-boys to do their thing, to create circles of people around them. People were competing inside that circle, they were doing acrobatics and flips and twists and all kinds of routines, and going down to the floor doing the splits like James Brown, doing footwork, like the best dancers I've ever seen.

So that was a typical Kool Herc party, and the music was incredible. And of course, he was on the microphone with an echo chamber, "Young ladies, don't hurt nobody-body-body. It's Kool Herc-Herc-Herc. Herculoids-loids-loids. Going down to the last stop-stop-stop-

stop." It was mystical and magical at the same time. It was disco, but it was ghetto disco.

Rahiem (Grandmaster Flash and the Furious Five): It was his playlist that all of the other DJs who aspired to reach his level at the time in the Bronx played. That was Kool Herc's contribution to hip-hop, his playlist.

WHAT WOULD BECOME known as hip-hop sprang from a foundation of DJs with powerful sound systems who operated around the same time as DJ Kool Herc in the early 1970s. Disco King Mario, who lived one floor above Paradise Gray, who would himself go on to help create X Clan, in the Bronxdale Houses projects, threw some of hip-hop's earliest jams with his Chuck Chuck City crew. Disco King Mario and Afrika Bambaataa were both members of the Black Spades gang, and Mario lent equipment for some of Bambaataa's earliest sets.

Pete DJ Jones, a transplant from North Carolina, was popular in Manhattan club circles. He was the first DJ who many, including Kurtis Blow, ever witnessed working two turntables and duplicate copies of the same record, which became the foundation for DJing, extending the breaks of funk and soul songs. Pete DJ Jones also served as a mentor to Grandmaster Flash.

Brooklyn's Grandmaster Flowers is recognized as one of the earliest pioneers of hip-hop for mixing funk and disco records in sequence and throwing massive block parties. Flowers even opened for James Brown at Yankee Stadium in 1969.

They joined others, like Maboya and DJ Plummer, in laying a blueprint for hip-hop to emerge, but never reaping the attention, adulation, or financial windfall that followed.

Daddy-O (artist, producer, Stetsasonic): I think sometimes people think that the first time that equipment came out and people plugged into the streetlamps, it was hip-hop. That's not true. The first time you'd seen the sound systems, it was people playing disco: Grandmaster Flowers, my boy Pete DJ Jones. And it was the reggae guys that was playing all the Lone Ranger stuff, the Sly & Robbie stuff, Bob Marley and the Wailers. Those were the first sound systems you saw on the street, was disco and reggae sound systems.

Paradise Gray (manager of the Latin Quarter, X Clan): I call my mother the Mother of Hip-Hop, because my first crate of records came from my living room. She was the one that introduced me to George Clinton, James Brown, Maceo [Parker], Bootsy [Collins], Sly and the Family Stone. So, a bunch of the breakbeats. When I finally heard Herc and Flowers and Bam and all of these guys playing the breakbeats, I had a whole bunch of those records already.

DJ Mister Cee (producer): That was the time when a lot of DJs was getting into the craft of DJing and buying them big kick-ass speakers— and I'm saying "kick-ass" because there used to be a sticker on the speaker that said "Kick Ass." That was around that time that DJs would play outside and break into a lamppost. Nowadays, there's an outlet in there. Back then, we would break into the lamppost and splice the wires up and connect to an extension cord. That's how we would power up.

Paradise Gray (manager of the Latin Quarter, X Clan): Everything about hip-hop was illegal. Do you know how many laws were broken just to do an average street jam? We broke into the light poles. That's breaking and entering. We cut the wires and we stole the electricity. That's special services. We didn't have no permits to do our jams outside in the streets. We just brought our equipment out and we did it. And we dared the police to try to fuck with us.

Sadat X (artist, Brand Nubian): The whole anticipation of seeing the DJ come; you'd see he'd have about two, three dudes carrying record crates. And just to watch them unfold the tables and put the turntables down and then people start coming and somebody might be making some food. All of a sudden, the music starts. It was like a carnival atmosphere.

DJ Mister Cee (producer): And that all came from Kool Herc from the Bronx and transferred all the way to us in Brooklyn.

Paradise Gray (manager of the Latin Quarter, X Clan): I think that the Bronx narrative of hip-hop is kind of flawed. And when I say it's flawed, I'll say that if the meal is hip-hop, maybe the chef was in the Bronx. But the ingredients existed long before the meal.

For me, [Disco King] Mario was the epitome of swag and style and flavor. He was a living, breathing Super Fly–Shaft that lived in your building. He was the well-dressed dude who had charisma, who knew how to dance. And Pete [DJ Jones] had a bar a block from my house. He was a consummate Black businessman in the community. And that seriousness that he brought to DJing and to just being the example of a Black man, was immeasurable in my life.

Kurtis Blow (artist, producer): Once [Kool Herc] started playing that playlist, that's when he became the father of hip-hop. That's when he became popular, and all the b-boys started flocking to his club because he played the music that we wanted to hear.

Easy A.D. (Cold Crush Brothers): He brought the jams out at the [night-club] Hevalo and all different clubs. So, he brought the rhythm. That's why they call him the father of hip-hop.

Rahiem (Grandmaster Flash and the Furious Five): You went to these jams to get down. And when someone, another opponent, got in the circle with you, if you were a b-boy or b-girl, then it was your intent to burn them. Burning was basically like beating them in a dance battle. And so, b-boy culture was nomadic. Anywhere b-boys and b-girls knew that a DJ was going to be playing the beats, that's where they went. And that was exclusive to the Bronx from about 1973 'til about 1978.

Grandmaster Caz (Cold Crush Brothers): By the time I saw Herc, I was about fifteen. Seeing his sound system and seeing his party for the first time just totally blew me away. And when I first saw him in the club, that pretty much was the selling point for me as far as getting involved in hip-hop.

DJ Charlie Chase (Cold Crush Brothers): The first party I had attended with Herc, he was rocking. He had a big set and that's what intrigued me, the size of his set. And he had Clark Kent [of the Herculoids] playing with him. And they were making announcements on the mic.

Kurtis Blow (artist, producer): He was the man on the microphone, Coke La Rock. He was more like a street dude, a street hustler. So he had the gift of gab and he used to talk a lot of smack. Herc was from Jamaica. He's just getting to the Bronx and he meets Coke La Rock and Coke La Rock has all the lingo. So they became friends and partners.

Michael Holman (journalist): So, you've got DJs experimenting like Herc, like Bambaataa, like Grandmaster Flash, like Jazzy Jay, who are throwing parties in the park at night. In the Bronx River projects, you've got Bambaataa and the Zulu Nation, who reign supreme. In other neighborhoods, like near Sedgwick Avenue, you've got Kool Herc, and they all decide, "Well, since [Patti] LaBelle is playing downtown tonight and everybody's going to be going down there, I'm going to have a party at the same time and all the kids who can't go downtown are going to come to my party in the park."

And people are partying and dancing to the DJs spinning records, and he's playing all these disco hits for these middle school kids who can't go downtown for a myriad of reasons and he has this automatic audience. But he is not being hired by a club downtown and isn't being told what to play and what not to play. He can play what the fuck he wants to play, because it's his party. No one's paying him to do this. It's for fun. It's for love.

So, now they're not tied into only playing disco records, he's throwing in great dance hits like James Brown from ten years before. Oftentimes they would throw down some Caribbean or Jamaican hits, dub hits. Then crazy, wild people like Bambaataa, who was considered "King of Records," would even throw in records that had no business being played at a Black and Brown uptown, urban party, but because there was an element in the song that was so funky you couldn't deny it, he would throw it on, like the TV theme song of *I Dream of Jeannie* or the Monkees' "Mary, Mary."

THE ELEMENTS THAT created hip-hop rose through surrounding blight and institutional neglect in the South Bronx. The costly Cross Bronx Expressway, the vision of urban planner Robert Moses, wrought immense havoc and heartache. Completed in 1963 after fifteen years of construction, the first expressway built through an urban area bifurcated the Bronx, decimating and displacing mostly African American and Puerto Rican communities. Many of the residents who remained in the area relocated to massive public housing projects.

The South Bronx's economy collapsed. Real estate values plummeted. Fires ravaged the area as arson became prevalent. Burned-out, gutted, and abandoned buildings constituted entire blocks. Drug consumption increased. The exodus in population resulted in the reduction of public programs. In October 1975, President Gerald R. Ford decided against offering federal assistance to New York, prompting the New York *Daily News* to run the infamous front-page headline: "FORD TO CITY: DROP DEAD."

Throughout the 1960s, gangs like the Black Spades, Ghetto Brothers, Savage Skulls, and Seven Immortals rose to prominence as the decay in the South Bronx surged. They were comprised mostly of young Blacks and Latinos in search of community and protection. In December 1971, several gangs reached a truce at the Hoe Avenue Peace Meeting following the murder of Cornell "Black Benjy" Benjamin, a member of the Ghetto Brothers who had tried defusing a fight between two gangs. The truce is regarded by many as a vital component of hip-hop's formation. Some leaders of gangs threw block parties as a means to build community and fellowship. While long-standing peace remained elusive, gang members were encouraged to not use violence against one another. Soon, some crews instead engaged in b-boy battles.

Lady B (artist, radio DJ, Philadelphia): It was a terrible time for the Black community. We were gang-stricken, pretty much like it is now, unfortunately. But hip-hop saved lives. We stop fighting with guns and knives and start battling with microphones and turntables.

Paradise Gray (manager of the Latin Quarter, X Clan): When I was a kid and Disco King Mario brought his equipment out and DJ'd in the Bronxdale projects, everybody would come together and cook they food, and drink they beer, listen to the music, dance with the girls. And if you messed up the block party, or you messed up a jam, the gangsters will beat the shit out of you.

The gangs were a part of hip-hop from day one. You had to regulate. If you didn't have that kind of street credibility and juice, you couldn't come out with your equipment, because you wouldn't go home with your equipment.

Rahiem (Grandmaster Flash and the Furious Five): Most of the crews that represented each block were ex–gang members. And so the gang element was still very, very present even though the gangs started to diminish—all they did was, instead of calling themselves a gang, they called themselves a crew. But most of them still behaved the way that a gang behaves.

Like for example, our security, Grandmaster Flash and the Furious Five's security, was called the Casanovas. And the Casanovas were all ex–Black Spades members. Just like the Zulu Nation that secured Bambaataa. Most of those guys were ex–Black Spades.

BORN LANCE TAYLOR, Afrika Bambaataa was a former member of the Black Spades gang who assembled the components of the brewing culture—DJing, MCing, graffiti, and b-boying—and united them within a singular community.

Bambaataa grew up in Soundview's Bronx River Houses and gained inspiration from the indivisibility of the Zulu people of South Africa. Under Bambaataa, former gang members became DJs, MCs, b-boys, b-girls, and graffiti artists within his Zulu Nation. Bambaataa performed at the Bronx River Community Center and at block parties throughout the East Bronx in the mid-to-late 1970s. He developed a reputation as the "Master of Records" by compiling a vast and diverse collection, playing everything from hard rock to funk to classical music. Like DJ

Kool Herc, he kept the source of his breakbeats hidden by blacking-out the names of records. A number of pioneering DJs and two notable crews of artists—the Jazzy Five (Master Ice, Mr. Freeze, Master Bee, Master Dee, and AJ Les) and the Soulsonic Force (Mr. Biggs, Pow Wow, and G.L.O.B.E.)—surfaced from the early days of the Zulu Nation.

MC Shy D (artist, producer): Those was fun days for me, because I was young, and Bambaataa, he used to get the speaker in the window, in the projects, and everybody gathered round the building and we just had good times out there.

Afrika Islam (DJ, Zulu Nation): The record part came in so heavy. [Grand-master] Flash or [Grand Wizzard] Theodore, they might have ten crates of records, but if we came in at forty-two or fifty, we never had to repeat a record. We would just continuously come in and bang you in your head.

But because technique was coming from Theodore, technique was coming from Flash, the sound system was coming from Herc, the sound system was coming from Disco King Mario, music and categories and deepness was coming out of Afrika Bambaataa and the Zulu Kings, that was the formation of what became hip-hop culture.

THE DJS WHO could draw a crowd and, importantly, people who would pay to enter, transitioned from outdoor jams to indoor clubs and advertised their parties through artistic graffiti-inspired flyers. In 1975, DJ Kool Herc began performing at Hevalo, on 180th Street and Jerome Avenue, following an earlier stint at Twilight Zone. The following year, Sal Abbatiello started featuring hip-hop artists at the nearby Disco Fever. Arthur Armstrong, an early hip-hop promoter, ran the Ecstasy Garage Disco on Macombs Road. Ray Chandler operated the Black Door near Boston Road and 170th Street, and the Dixie Club. Afrika Bambaataa routinely performed at Ritchie T's T-Connection.

These clubs joined early hotspots like Club 371, Harlem's Charles Gallery, and the Renaissance Ballroom in Queens, where oftentimes former gang members provided the on-premises security.

Aaron Fuchs (president, Tuff City Records): I went to see Bambaataa at the T-Connection, which really was unforgettable.

I'm already thirty-two and the ferocity of the vibe, the electricity at the T-Connection, was turning me into a kid again. To see Bam and his DJs come to work. He had four guys behind him with record crates on their shoulders. It's like a goddamn caravan, a combination of a caravan and a gang entry.

Afrika Islam (DJ, Zulu Nation): To call yourself a DJ at that time then, you needed vinyl. At that age, thirteen, fourteen, you got to remember this is all new. There were no limits at this stage. So everything we did was creatively new, each and every single time. And you adjusted every single week: that worked, this didn't work.

Aaron Fuchs (president, Tuff City Records): Bambaataa letting me see his record collection . . . [DJ] Red Alert just told me a couple of months ago that that was very rare. It was like being given the Coca-Cola formula.

What it was, was this unprecedented mix of island music along with American Black music and a range of other more segregated American Black music like go-go, little bits of Haitian music, salsa. I knew right then and there I was privy to something important.

Whipper Whip (Fantastic Five): There's only two people that make me stand there and be like, *Wow, I could watch you guys play forever,* and that's Bambaataa and [DJ] Hollywood. 'Cause you never know what they're going to play next.

THE UNIVERSAL ZULU Nation, an international hip-hop awareness group, figured prominently in the domestic and global spread of hip-hop. In the 1980s, the Zulu Nation dispatched members to spread hip-hop and messages of peace and unity. Branches opened around the world, from Japan to South Africa.[*]

---

[*] In 2016, Afrika Bambaataa relinquished his role as head of the Zulu Nation following allegations made by multiple men of sexual abuse.

Afrika Islam (DJ, Zulu Nation): Members of Zulu Nation are mastering their skill, being pulled out and planting seeds in all parts of the planet. As they flew out to Japan and China and Korea and California, they're planting the seed because they were the real deal, how they act, walked, dressed. That's some prophet shit, man. So, if hip-hop is around the world as a music form, then seventy-five percent of it belongs to that Zulu Nation.

Muhammad Islam (Zulu Nation): The greatest impact of Zulu Nation was the spread of hip-hop, not only the rap form, [but] the whole movement [of] the DJing, the graffiti as art, the b-boying, properly known as breakdancing, but also adding that fifth element, which is the thought, intellect, the mind, bringing all this stuff together as a worldwide movement. Certainly the Zulu Nation was paramount in pushing this all over the world, from Brazil to Argentina, to Japan to France and England and Germany. They were pushing the whole idea of hip-hop as a culture and not just a music form.

GRANDMASTER FLASH, BORN Joseph Saddler, evolved the craft that Kool Herc and Afrika Bambaataa had started by inserting finesse and technique into DJing. He moved to the South Bronx from Barbados with his family in the 1960s. He studied his father's extensive (and forbidden) record collection, and learned how electronics worked by taking them apart and reassembling them. He studied DJ Kool Herc, trying to figure out his method for maintaining the beat, and in the 1970s Grandmaster Flash became a DJing partner with DJ Mean Gene Livingston, who advanced to form the L Brothers.

Among Grandmaster Flash's many contributions was his "quick mix" theory, a discovery that served as a backbone for hip-hop music. He found that by using two copies of the same record he could play the breakbeat on one, while searching for the break on the second with his mixer and syncing it to play as soon as the first had finished. He had transformed his turntables into a musical instrument and eventually marked the breaks on the records by hand.

Rahiem (Grandmaster Flash and the Furious Five): Between 1976 and '77, a DJ named Grandmaster Flash created this technique on the turntables. It changed everything.

Right before Grandmaster Flash became notable, there was a time period in which aspiring DJs didn't have two turntables and a mixer, because that was pretty expensive at the time.

Afrika Islam (DJ, Zulu Nation): How many sixteen-year-olds are going to come up with [the money for] a fully made sound system?

Rahiem (Grandmaster Flash and the Furious Five): So, aspiring DJs made these tapes that we called pause-button tapes. When you first pop a cassette in a tape recorder, there was a blank space in which you would just hear white noise. So, pause-button tape DJs would record whatever song that they're recording, they would go past the lead bit of the cassette to where the actual recording started, because they would want the beat to start as soon as the tape started.

So they would do that back and forth and it kind of sounded like a DJ was cutting the record back and forth, almost on beat. Some people who were exceptional at it would be able to catch it on beat a few times, but not as consistently as a DJ who was cutting it back and forth on two turntables. And then these tapes started to circulate of their parties with Flash on the turntables. And that's what actually compelled me to want to go see him, because I needed to see what he was actually doing with my own two eyes on the turntables.

Kurtis Blow (artist, producer): B-boying was the main thing about a Kool Herc party. A Flash party was more about Flash and you standing out in front of a stage watching Flash on those turntables cut it up.

Rahiem (Grandmaster Flash and the Furious Five): The contrasting difference between going to a Kool Herc party and going to the Grandmaster Flash party was that [Kool Herc] didn't cut the records back and forth. He just placed the needle on the record and let the records play, and b-boys and b-girls would go off whenever the breakbeats did play.

Grandmaster Flash would only play what he deemed the dope part of the beat, which was the break. And so, as a result of that, and as a result of his ability to catch the beat back and forth from turntable to turntable, there was never a lull in the activity or the excitement, because he was constantly cutting and scratching records. By that time, b-boys started to be kind of fading out because instead of coming to our parties to dance, they would be more like spectators watching what Flash was doing.

THROUGHOUT THE MID-1970S, a number of innovative, pioneering DJs emerged who would create and increase the popularity of the nascent culture. They included: Grand Wizzard Theodore (credited with discovering scratching), Disco Wiz, Kool DJ AJ, Breakout, Baron, Jazzy Jay, Grand Mixer DXT, and Charlie Chase.

DJ Charlie Chase (Cold Crush Brothers): At the time, everybody was bit by the bug. I was bit early. I became a disco DJ in '75. At the beginning of '76 is when I became a hip-hop DJ.

Bill Stephney (Bomb Squad, Def Jam): The way hip-hop happened in that late '70s period, it was relatively sudden and so distinct from anything else that was going on with the use of the turntables and the extended beats. It relates to the language and the dress and the diversity, too, of the Bronx, especially of having Blacks and Latinos and even a handful of white kids too, all going to parties and not even thinking twice about it, when there were gang wars a year or two before. All of it, in this time, just crystallizes.

DJ Charlie Chase (Cold Crush Brothers): There were a lot of Latino DJs in my neighborhood, and they all started going to jams. We were having battles between us, and we had our own rivalries.

What actually started to introduce Latinos was when I met [DJ] Tony Tone. Tony was already established with Breakout, who was already DJing with Bam and Herc and Islam and everybody in the majors. Tony and I, right off the bat, we hit it off. So he became my crew. He introduced me to Bam. He introduced me to Islam. He introduced me to everybody. That's how I broke into the scene.

When I met these guys, I was already an established DJ. I was making mixtapes. All these people that I met, already knew of me, but hadn't met me. The problem they were having was they thought I was Black, because of the way I was cutting.

WITH DISCO'S POPULARITY reaching its apex, some pioneering DJs and MCs played to the older crowd in a scene separate from the hip-hop music being established in the Bronx. DJ Hollywood, born Anthony Holloway, was influenced by the likes of Jocko Henderson, Pigmeat Markham, Gil Scott-Heron, and Rudy Ray Moore. Hollywood is credited with introducing hip-hop-style rapping through his call-and-response set and syncopated rhyming. He worked the turntables and microphone to become a lucrative earner and a regular at Harlem's famed Apollo Theater throughout the mid to late 1970s.

Russell Simmons, who would advance to help make hip-hop mainstream through the cofounding of Def Jam Recordings, credits Eddie Cheeba—a friend of DJ Hollywood and a popular disco DJ—as being the first person he ever witnessed rapping live. Lovebug Starski, born Kevin Smith, had worked with both Pete DJ Jones and DJ Hollywood, and served as the house DJ at Disco Fever in the Bronx. He merged the styles used by the DJs in the Bronx with the one employed by DJ Hollywood.

Kurtis Blow (artist, producer): He had the golden voice, DJ Hollywood. He just sounded like quality, professional, top of the line, the class of New York. He was a master of the crowd response. And the third thing was his rhythmic rap—he was the first one I saw do [it]. The MCs before him, Coke La Rock and Eddie Cheeba, KC the Prince of Soul, Jay the Disco King—they would just talk on the mic, like, "You're listening to the sounds of New York City's number one DJ, Pete DJ Jones-Jones-Jones," with the echo chamber.

Russell Simmons (cofounder, Def Jam): Eddie Cheeba, I walked in. I just smoked a bag of zootie, which is red-devil angel dust, and I heard it. It was not only hearing him, it was the performance. It was Easy G cutting the records. It was Eddie Cheeba rapping. He had on a plaid jacket from A. J. Lester's, which was the slick shit that we wore in the hood. We sold drugs just so we could get that jacket.

We're talking about a *performance*. . . . It stuck in my head. "On, and on, and on, and on, like hot butter on what?"

The crowd would say, "Popcorn."

They were already ahead of me, like, I missed something.

He wasn't DJing and rapping. He had Easy G cutting and he wasn't echo-chambering his name. His poetry, his showmanship, it was like nothing I'd seen before. And the crowd participation. It was magical.

I wanted to promote parties, and instantly I wanted to promote him. I used to think that I was safe doing what I was doing, considering it was just weed, and then when it wasn't weed it was coca leaf incense. I knew people selling heroin. I wasn't doing that. I was doing what I thought was fairly safe, and here's freedom—here's complete safety and here's something I love.

Kurtis Blow (artist, producer): You were great if you got two hundred dollars a night. But Hollywood started charging five hundred dollars and that was incredible. And this is another thing he also did—if you hired a DJ, the DJ would bring his equipment and play all night. Hollywood, he would just come with his records—you had to have your equipment, your turntables, your sound system, everything together—and he'd come in and just rock the house for a hour, and then go to the next spot. So pretty soon, he's going to about four or five clubs a night on a Friday, Saturday night. And he was making five hundred dollars a night doing this. So that mobile DJ, he put that into play.

Russell Simmons (cofounder, Def Jam): Hollywood would go somewhere and five thousand people would show up. He'd go out to Coney Island or City College and open up for Evelyn "Champagne" King. Hollywood played the Apollo. His name stayed on the awning. He was the star. He would bring the big crowd and he would get them to pay five dollars and fifty cents. Five dollars and fifty cents back then, not a dollar to come to your neighborhood, there's a dramatic difference.

Keith Shocklee (producer, Bomb Squad): Hollywood would be at Broadway International. That's a nightclub. We got to see Maboya and

Flowers, Grandmaster Flowers, and them. You had to go to an event that they were throwing because they had to bring their sound system. And that was different places a lot of time. But Hollywood, when they opened up Broadway International, he was always there. Eddie Cheeba would get down there. That's how we heard them all the time.

Kool Moe Dee (artist, Treacherous Three): There are two different strands of hip-hop: the Hollywood side with the call-and-response, over disco records; and the Herc side is a similar thing, but is old breakbeats and b-boy records. The merging of those two is what really forms what we're calling today's modern hip-hop. Which if you trace further back, you can go until the gospel quartets and see that those styles were around way before we were there, because that's where you got Pigmeat Markham and Jocko [Henderson] and all the guys that were doing it at a time when it just never caught fire and never created the landscape that we did, where everybody that was a teenager at that time, and I'm talking mid to late '70s, everybody was caught up in what we now call hip-hop.

DMC (artist, Run-DMC): If you listen to early rap, everybody would use disco. People minds is blown away how connected disco's presentation was, just a hybrid form or cousin of hip-hop. But people forget the Fat Boys was called the Disco 3 when they first came out. So it was all disco, because it was about the records and the music.

Bill Adler (journalist, Def Jam publicist): It was new, but it wasn't unprecedented. I listened to the Last Poets and I knew about Gil Scott-Heron and I knew about the oral tradition in African American culture. I heard it in the tradition and having heard that, it was remarkable anyways.

Kool Moe Dee (artist, Treacherous Three): Being eight and nine while it's happening, you're aware of it, but you're not really able to participate in it. So, by the time I'm fourteen, I get to hear Lovebug Starski, not only at a block party, but I heard him at a place they called the Renaissance in New York. He was the first, in my opinion, the first DJ/MC, because the DJ had a mic, that would do a combination of the hip-hop breakbeat stuff and the R&B, Hollywood stuff. So he was a combination, in my opinion, of Herc and Hollywood. And I always felt that the two sides were necessary in order to be very functional.

AS THE PROGRAM director of WBLS-FM, legendary DJ Frankie Crocker maintained a sizable influence over popular music and, perhaps, an unwitting one in hip-hop's evolution and growth. Crocker was already known in New York City by the time he arrived at WBLS in the early 1970s. He propelled the station's ratings by introducing the urban contemporary format and playing a wide range of selections, including disco, R&B, and hip-hop music. On air, Crocker defined the charismatic master of ceremonies, delivering imitable rhymes that provided a blueprint for future artists and signing off each night to "Moody's Mood for Love."

Though wary of a changing of the guard, Crocker did not deny hip-hop music's popularity. He broke some of the earliest hip-hop records and hired Mr. Magic, hip-hop's groundbreaking radio DJ, to WBLS.

DJ Mister Cee (producer): If you wanted to get on the radio and you lived in New York City in the late '70s and the '80s, then Frankie Crocker was one of your idols.

Bill Stephney (Bomb Squad, Def Jam): He's not probably hip-hop as we define it today, but there was a point when the culture itself was sort of like the mafia. La Cosa Nostra, I think that the English translation is "This thing of ours," and that's sort of what hip-hop was as it was developing from the Bronx and from Harlem and through the New York area. It was a DJ-driven party culture. And whether you're DJ Hollywood as an MC or even the other rappers, MCs who came up, they're all influenced in terms of tone, phrasing, attitude by Frankie Crocker. The literal term MC, master of ceremony, that's really based on what Frankie Crocker did either on the radio or at parties or at concerts.

DJ Mister Cee (producer): First and foremost, with Frankie Crocker, his voice was very distinctive. At that time, it was just true New York radio. It wasn't called Black radio; it was just radio. So, you would hear Michael Jackson, then you would hear a Madonna record, and then you would hear Prince, and then you would hear Hall & Oates. It wasn't pigeonholed. Whatever the Black community liked, whether the artist was white or wherever they came from, Frankie Crocker was playing the record. That was a big, big deal as well, which is why so many white artists from that era got appreciated by Black people, the Madonnas and the Tears for Fears and the Hall & Oates.

Jeff Sledge (A&R, Jive Records): He was the program director, so he played what he felt. He would go out to a club the night before and hear this new girl, Madonna, who's got this song called "Holiday." He would play it that next day. Like, "Yo, I heard this record in the club. This shit's hot." He was playing test pressings and he was playing records that aren't even affiliated with just major labels. He's just playing the hot shit.

Bill Stephney (Bomb Squad, Def Jam): In many respects, I don't know if hip-hop happens in New York without Frankie Crocker and without the variety of music that Frankie Crocker, as a Black program director, played in devising the most varied music format that any radio station had offered anywhere. Here was a guy who could play "I Got My Mind Made Up" by Instant Funk, into "Stars in Your Eyes" by Herbie Hancock, into "New York, New York" by Frank Sinatra, and fifteen-year-old Black kids in Brooklyn would be into it.

And the parties that we attended in the late '70s, early '80s, in the area, reflected that variety. Bam and Herc and Flash and Spectrum City, Pete DJ Jones, King Charles, the Disco Twins, and Infinity, all these folks who were DJing, generally reflected the nuanced diverse playlist of what Frankie did. You couldn't hear that anywhere else.

NEW YORK CITY teetered on the brink in the summer of 1977. Economic stagnation and soaring unemployment crippled the city. The serial killer known as the Son of Sam stalked victims, while a sweltering heat wave pummeled the five boroughs.

On the evening of July 13, successive lightning strikes strained the area's overburdened power grid and plunged most of the city into pitch-blackness. Confusion and chaos quickly ensued. People took to neighborhood streets and some ransacked stores.

The lights remained off for more than a day. In that time, more than 1,500 businesses had been vandalized. Consolidated Edison, the city's power provider, labeled the outage as an "an act of God." A congressional study estimated that the damages and losses totaled more than $300 million.

While most sought food and domestic necessities, some trained their attention on electronics stores, breaking down doors and snatching equipment. For them, the darkness provided an opportunity to finally build their own audio system or reap the profits from second-hand sales. Overnight and under darkness, new DJs started populating the area. Crews formed after mixing and matching newly gained equipment to form a cohesive system.

Some dismiss the notion that the blackout provided a catalyst for hip-hop's uprising, that the ingredients for the genre were already in circulation and simmering, and the hypothesis of lightning bolts helping to spark the genre is too tidy a narrative. Others who lived in New York City at the time of the blackout insist that the event helped jump-start the early scene.

DJ Charlie Chase (Cold Crush Brothers): The night before [the blackout in] '77, I was in a band and we had a gig in Brooklyn. The next day, I was so exhausted, I did something that I never did in my life and that was go home early. I was home and I was laying in bed and I remember just nodding out and watching television, and all of a sudden: *poof.*

Rahiem (Grandmaster Flash and the Furious Five): I'm in the backyard of the housing complex I grew up in, playing basketball. It was about to get dark outside and the streetlights were just coming on, and I went up for a jump shot, and just as it was going in the basket, one by one, the lights began to go out. We didn't think anything of it at the time, and then we looked up and no lights in any building for as far as the eye could see were on.

MC Debbie D (artist, South Bronx): All of a sudden it was like *click, click, click, click,* and everybody's looking around, like, "What's going on?" But nobody's paying it no mind, because we're all just thinking, *There's some short here, but this is going to come back on.* But it doesn't. And nobody's really going inside, because it's still hot outside. I lived on the nineteenth floor. So it's like, we got to walk upstairs? So people are not really rushing to go upstairs. Everybody's just hanging out outside.

Easy A.D. (Cold Crush Brothers): You didn't realize what was happening. The lights went out, but we didn't understand, like, *The lights, they're not coming back on.*

DJ Charlie Chase (Cold Crush Brothers): It was hot as hell. My windows were open and at first, stillness. At first, everybody's wondering what's going on. You hear a lot of chatter, people screaming, "Apagar las luces. Apagar las luces."

Easy A.D. (Cold Crush Brothers): Everybody froze for a second, and they was like, "Blackout."

MC Debbie D (artist, South Bronx): And then people start opening up the fire hydrant, because it's hot. The reason for the blackout is because it was an eleven-day heat wave. By the time you get to this eleventh day, the electricity is so overused in New York City, that that's what caused the blackout.

DJ Mister Cee (producer): Right in front of my building in my projects [in Brooklyn], we cracked open that fire hydrant. All we did that whole day was, we just had water fights. Throwing water on each other that whole day. We had a blast in my projects.

Easy A.D. (Cold Crush Brothers): Immediately, people started pulling gates up and going into the store. I can honestly say to you that I was immensely afraid of my mom, because if you brought something home that wasn't yours, it was a major problem. So I didn't go into the store.

Whipper Whip (Fantastic Five): When that jumped off, yo, trust, I ain't even step outside. Whip ain't near none of that stuff. I stayed home; I was safe 'cause I was a youngin'. My parents are Puerto Rican. They ain't play that. "You ain't going nowhere." We in the house with candles taking care of the fort.

Grandmaster Caz (Cold Crush Brothers): The blackout was scary as hell. We were DJing with another crew at the park, and all of a sudden the lights started going out and we thought that we had blew out the power, because we were attached to the light pole. But not only did the set go out, the entire block went out, and the whole Bronx went out.

It was pandemonium after that. It was like everybody realized at the same time, "Oh, shit. Blackout. Run for the stores." And everybody just fanned out, all different directions, toward stores.

MC Debbie D (artist, South Bronx): People would go to supermarkets and get shopping carts and then go to the store and pull out a whole TV. And you know Black folks, they didn't have nothing. Because for the most part, and particularly in the South Bronx, it's predominantly Blacks and Puerto Ricans. So we're all poor.

We think hip-hop, we just think of equipment. But people was taking mattresses, couches—and remember, this is the '70s, so they had them big old Cadillac cars. If you had a top-down Cadillac, you know all the stuff you could put in there?

Rahiem (Grandmaster Flash and the Furious Five): We walked to the neighborhood supermarket and looked in the window; we didn't see any employees and the lights were off. So, we picked up a big steel trash can and threw it through the plate-glass window and we all just went in. And it was about maybe thirty of us. We got a sledgehammer and we beat the safe until we unhinged it from the ground. And we walked with the safe up to this tenement building, and took the safe in the basement, and a few OGs [original gangsters] that was down with one of the gangs called the Peacemakers, broke the safe open and they divided up the money and the food stamps. I was fourteen and they gave me, from what I remember, sixteen hundred dollars in food stamps and about twelve hundred in cash. That was my cut.

And so I took the money, the food stamps home, gave my mom some, stashed the rest in my air-conditioner duct, and then went to this store called Sneaker King because I heard that that store had gotten looted, but that if I hurried up I could get myself some free sneakers. When I got to Sneaker King, I walked in there and came out with two tall kitchen trash bags filled with boxes of sneakers all my size.

MC Debbie D (artist, South Bronx): Kids was wilding out. They was just running into stores and seeing what they could get. The alarms are going off. By the time you see it on TV, it's just crazy.

Muhammad Islam (security manager, A Tribe Called Quest): We was poverty like crazy in the hood. You seen an opportunity to take some pants, some TVs, whatever the case may be, it happened.

DJ Charlie Chase (Cold Crush Brothers): GLI is a company [that sells] audio equipment. At the time, they were a very popular company. They had a GLI store on the Concourse, right down the block from my house. And they got hit hard. They smashed the glass, and they took everything. They had some crazy, crazy, crazy equipment in the windows, and that store was completely cleaned out. That's one of the places Caz told me he made a stop at that night.

Grandmaster Caz (Cold Crush Brothers): I didn't get a whole lot of stuff, because I was there trying to protect my own equipment that was in the street, but I did run around the corner to the place I got my first DJ set from. I ran right around the corner to that place, helped pull the gate down, kicked the glass down and everything, and pulled me a mixer out of there.

DJ Charlie Chase (Cold Crush Brothers): A lot of motherfuckers had GLI speakers now.

DJ Clark Kent* (producer): That's when I got my first set of turntables. I was this young boy who was deep with learning how to DJ, and I never had my own set. I just wanted to be equipped. I just wanted my own turntables. If I was smart enough back then I would have thought, *Yeah, you're gonna need an amplifier and some speakers, too.* But it was just me and my cousin, we couldn't take all that.

---

* A different Clark Kent performed with DJ Kool Herc and the Herculoids.

MC Shy D (artist, producer): They was tearing them stores up. Bambaataa had the main equipment in Bronx River, the big stuff, but you had guys fifteen, sixteen, they started coming out with their little mini-sets. Bambaataa influenced everybody, but that blackout, everybody went crazy, man. People got equipment and everything.

DJ Clark Kent (producer): It definitely helped me. I definitely got a turntable and a mixer out of the situation. I'm from an impoverished neighborhood, and we did whatever we could to do whatever we wanted to do. Life in the hood.

MC Debbie D (artist, South Bronx): How else were you going to get it?

Rahiem (Grandmaster Flash and the Furious Five): We used to have after-school programs that we could count on and go play ball and get extra support with your schoolwork. But the federal funding for those programs were all cut. And as a result, most of the kids were left to the streets. So that's why the gang violence became so prevalent. But then, hip-hop gave people options.

In 1977, the blackout is what changed the scope of things, and it really gave the majority of kids who would have probably been victimized or involved in gang violence in some way, it gave them an option. Gang violence began to diminish because being involved in hip-hop culture, it gave latchkey kids something. Their parents weren't home when they got home from school; eventually they're going to be out in the street with no supervision, left to their own devices.

Paradise Gray (manager of the Latin Quarter, X Clan): Before the blackout, people in the Bronx had horrible sound systems. Queens and Brooklyn had the full banging systems at the beginning. But not too many people in the Bronx could afford big sound systems until after the blackout. Then, everybody had sound.

Rahiem (Grandmaster Flash and the Furious Five): The blackout of 1977 is what helped to spawn a multitude of aspiring hip-hop practitioners, because prior to that, the majority of aspiring DJs didn't have two turntables and a mixer or the speakers. So, when the blackout happened, it just seems that everybody got the same idea at the same time. And when the lights came back on in New York City, everybody had DJ equipment.

MC Debbie D (artist, South Bronx): When you get to the blackout, it shifts hip-hop. It's a pivotal moment, because like a week later, everybody was a DJ. Everybody.

> **IN CHICAGO, ON** July 12, 1979, the White Sox hosted Disco Demolition Night; the idea came from a Chicago shock jock who detested the genre of dance music. In New York City, the famed doors of Studio 54 shuttered after its founders, Steve Rubell and Ian Schrager, pleaded guilty to tax evasion.
>
> As fast as disco had risen, its popularity evaporated. The environment that allowed the culture and genre of hip-hop to blossom required dual rejections: the older disco scene rebuffing the younger crowd, and the new generation turning its back on disco in favor of its own creation.

Easy A.D. (Cold Crush Brothers): Disco was prominent. I loved Donna Summer, but I didn't like disco.

DMC (artist, Run-DMC): Disco was so powerful, such a creative, artistic explosion of newness, that the greatest rock and roll bands wanted to get with it. So they got their two cents in because they didn't just make great disco records, they made great records.

Bill Adler (journalist, Def Jam publicist): The disco thing happens—and I don't disparage it because it was formulaic, although I think it was— I think it's because it was very much a producer's music. It didn't build artists. There were some wonderful records, but there were no artists built. So that's not a formula for something that's going to last, and it didn't last.

DMC (artist, Run-DMC): When that statement went nationwide, that "disco sucks," it died. When disco died, hip-hop came alive. Punk rock came alive.

Kurtis Blow (artist, producer): I'm a b-boy and so I used to go out to the Hollywood parties, and I'd start dancing. And if I go down to the floor, they looked at me like I'm crazy. And they didn't like it. "No, no. We don't play that here." Because they were adults. They were wearing shoes and suits and ties and silk dresses, and the b-boys were younger. They were wearing sneakers and jeans and hats backwards, sweat suits. [Grandmaster] Flash used to call them the shoe people and the sneaker people.

Easy A.D. (Cold Crush Brothers): People who wasn't involved in the culture and didn't really have a stake in it just couldn't understand what we were doing, because they didn't relate to something that was young and new and innovative.

Right now, you could say I was just rhyming, but no, you was delivering information that was created by yourself. I just liked the art of being able to express yourself with words and be able to say it on a microphone, and people be in awe of you delivering your rhymes. To be an MC, you had to write your own stuff. You had to be original.

The aspect of hip-hop culture changing, it wasn't just about just playing records. It was about DJing, it was about MCing, so it was more of a show.

MC Debbie D (artist, South Bronx): The DNA of a pioneer MC is your skills on the mic. That's all we want to know. We're not interested in nothing else. That's what made that MC a bonafide MC, because you knew to write those lyrics, you had a whole lot of papers on the floor, because you had to flip it until you got it.

DJ Charlie Chase (Cold Crush Brothers): I came from a neighborhood where we were always playing some kind of sports. We had finished playing a baseball game out in Arthur Park and we was walking home [past] this little park. And there was this one cat who was out there with a little speaker and a microphone, playing some music.

And what caught my attention about him was that he wasn't rhyming or anything like that, but he was just saying things, making people want to stop and take notice and kind of making people feel good about it. He was playing beats, and the audience was engaged. I was pretty impressed with it.

After a few years, I found out that the person who was in the park was Grandmaster Caz.

Grandmaster Caz (Cold Crush Brothers): The difference, to me, is the struggle. Most of the people that you see in hip-hop that got big sound systems and they had this major equipment, they had major money, too. Little ragtime DJs like myself, we took the scraps that were around us and made something out of nothing.

Beat on a car, and then you're saying rhymes to it and then attract a whole crowd around you. We beating in the schools. Beating on the elevator. Just making beats and rhyming to beats until the shit finally made sense.

Easy A.D. (Cold Crush Brothers): We needed something to change the way that we felt. We didn't call it hip-hop at the time, but the music and the rhyming and the creative mind came out. So out of something that would be unattractive came something elegant and phenomenal and groundbreaking.

At every level that you can imagine, it turned the world upside-down. The Bronx went from being decayed into something beautiful. The vibration of the music and the combination of bringing all those elements together, you had to be in there to feel it, because most of the time people only experience the music. But when you have all those elements in one place together, then you understand the essence of the hip-hop culture.

Afrika Islam (DJ, Zulu Nation): We made lemonade from lemons.

I guess we partied from the soul, that's the only word that I can really put it. We partied from the soul and enjoyed music because it was free.

02 THE RIGHT MENU

New York City
1978–1981

By the late 1970s, trailblazing New York City crews—like the Three MC's, the L Brothers, the Funky 4, and the Treacherous Three—were sprouting up. These acts consisted of several MCs typically centered around a DJ.

The crews competed against one another for attention and popularity, sparking the need for originality in their routines. Taking cues from acts like the Temptations and the Jackson 5, whom these groups had grown up watching, they transformed the once DJ-centric sets into concert-like atmospheres. Soon, the MCs had evolved into the main draw at parties.

It would still take a while for the coalescing genre to be known as "hip-hop," but the first use of the term is mostly credited to Keith "Cowboy" Wiggins around 1978, while Lovebug Starski pioneered the use of the phrase in performances, and Afrika Bambaataa adopted the term as a unifying description for the culture.

Rahiem (Funky 4): I wasn't there, but I know that story to be true. Prior to everyone trying to stake a claim and being the first at whatever in hip-hop, Lovebug Starski and Cowboy and Busy Bee Starski used to say "hip-hop, hip-hop." That was a part of the styling of their rhymes. So, according to Cowboy and the other members of the group, he was paying homage to one of his friends who just got recruited to go into the army. On the mic, he started calling cadence as though his friend were marching. And so that's why he did the "hip-hip, hip-hop" thing.

Obviously, he didn't coin the phrase "hip-hop" in the context that the term represented the culture that we are all now practitioners of. He coined the phrase in that it was his way of paying homage to his homeboy. And then I would say that Lovebug Starski made it more popular, and I think it was Afrika Bambaataa who actually called our culture the hip-hop culture.

GRANDMASTER FLASH SHOWED little interest in holding a microphone like other DJs as he worked the turntables. Instead, he offered the microphone to people in the crowd. At one performance Keith "Cowboy" Wiggins commandeered it and showcased a talent for moving the party along and drawing attention away from the performances of the b-boys and b-girls.

Brothers Nathaniel "Kid Creole" and Melvin "Melle Mel" Glover joined him to form the Three MC's. In an effort to outshine Kool Herc's MCs, they introduced expressive rhyming and the element of poetry into the scene, establishing a template for other MCs to follow.

Kurtis Blow (artist, producer): We had stopped breakdancing by then, that was like '77, '78. All the breakdancers became MCs. Everybody wanted to be like the Furious Five and Melle Mel and DJ Hollywood, Eddie Cheeba, Lovebug Starski, people like that. We put up our breakdancing shoes and we became MCs.

Whipper Whip (Fantastic Five): When I saw Flash and the Three MC's and I hear Mel and Creole and Cowboy, that was one hell of a combination of guys, because they each did something different. Mel was a hardcore MC. Fuckin' Kid Creole would tear that echo chamber up and just make music sound beautiful. And Cowboy did all the cadences and had all the crowd responses. You put that together, I was like, *Holy shit*.

Kool Moe Dee (artist, Treacherous Three): I started being known as a guy that would come in and rhyme as a highlight to the show. And I would not only do it at a cadence that's fast, but I would use vocabulary in ways that most people didn't do.

> **THE BROTHERS DISCO** featured DJ Breakout and DJ Baron and their powerful sound system, the "Mighty Mighty Sasquatch." They often performed along with the Funky 4 (eventually known as Funky 4 + 1), a group that included MC Sha-Rock, regarded as the first female MC.

MC Sha-Rock (Funky 4): I started out as a b-girl in 1976. I started rhyming with the Brothers Disco. In the early part of '78, we formed the original Funky 4. It was me, Rahiem, Keith Keith, and K.K. Rockwell.

I became the first female MC as part of an all-male group, and the first female MC to help move the culture forward [with] the style of rhyme and how we created the cadence, the back-and-forth.

I modeled my skills off of Melle Mel, because Melle Mel was an entertainer first. I wanted people to respond to me and be mesmerized by [me] the same way they was with Melle Mel, but on a female level. So now everybody's trying to find also a female to be able to deal with me. The only females that was really on the street that was rocking at the time, that people knew, was the Mercedes Ladies, and it was MC Sha-Rock.

> **WITH THE ADDITION** of Mr. Ness, also known as Scorpio, Grandmaster Flash's Three MC's grew into the Furious Four. Others grappled for attention, and the Furious Four often had to defend their crown. One early pivotal battle occurred between the Furious Four and the up-and-coming Funky 4 MCs. The Furious Four went first, winning that night—and a couple days later, too—by convincing the Funky 4's Rahiem to join their group.

Rahiem (Funky 4): May 11, 1979, at the Webster Avenue PAL [Police Athletic League of New York City] in the Bronx. We had a really, really great performance in store for this battle. Grandmaster Flash and the Furious Four, they were the most popular, and Breakout and Baron and the Funky 4, we were, I guess, the number one contenders because there weren't really a lot of other MC groups out at that time.

MC Sha-Rock (Funky 4): We were going to go on before the Furious Four. We knew that there were other people that were battling, but we were only concerned with the Furious Four because we felt like no one out there was on the level as the Furious Four.

Rahiem (Funky 4): The Cold Crush had not formed yet. In fact, DJ Tony Tone of the Cold Crush Brothers was a member of Breakout and Baron's organization, the Brothers Disco. He was down with us at that time. So, all of the things that we practiced leading up to this battle, when we got to the PAL and it was time for the show to start, Flash and the Furious Four opted to go on before us.

MC Sha-Rock (Funky 4): It's about eleven, twelve at night. People tired because they're hollering and they're screaming. So we knew our position was good, because we were going on before the Furious Four.

Then the guys that put the show together came up to us and said, "Look, we changing stuff up. The Furious are going to go on before you all."

So we were like, *Fuck.*

Rahiem (Funky 4): They were supposed to be the headliner. And when they got on before us, it made sense because they did everything pretty much what *we* rehearsed, like our whole game plan.

MC Sha-Rock (Funky 4): Everything that they did, we were going to do.

Rahiem (Funky 4): It was as if they had a spy sitting in the room with us taking notes about what we intended to do for this battle. The foundation of what they did was basically the foundation of what we were going to do. So when it was our turn to go on stage, it made me not want to do any of what we rehearsed. And it was my call because I created most of our routines.

MC Sha-Rock (Funky 4): Rahiem was like, "My throat hurt," and we was like, "Aw, come on, man, we got to get them."

Rahiem (Grandmaster Flash and the Furious Five): So, when I got on the mic, instead of doing what we planned to do, I just spit my best rhymes and didn't stop until I ran out of words. And that made the audience cheer me on like crazy, and Flash and them were standing in the audience ice-grilling us at first. But then after I was going for like ten, fifteen minutes straight, they started to cheer me on with the audience.

And then a couple of days later, Melle Mel and Mr. Ness showed up at my mom's house and asked me if I would be willing to join their group. And from then on, we called ourselves the Furious Five.

MC Sha-Rock (Funky 4 + 1): I decided to leave [the Funky 4] simply because Rahiem and I was very close. We were like sisters and brothers. I respected his gift of gab on the microphone. Rahiem brought a lot to the game, simply because he was the first person that I knew of that would sing and harmonize at the same time. That was one reason why Melle Mel and Flash wanted him. I left because it was never told to me that Rahiem wanted to go on to some other place, and we were close.

And then when Rahiem went over to the Furious Five, I came back. Now remember, I'm a founding member of the Funky 4, but when I came back, they had two new members, Rodney C and Jazzy Jeff. So it became the +1.

WITH THE REJECTION of disco by an emerging, younger generation complete, hip-hop began its transformation into a dominant art form and culture, sourced and built almost entirely by neglected youth.

DMC (artist, Run-DMC): It was the young hip-hop that was the voice that I related to, because it was the voice of the streets. It was Lil Rodney C and them and Sha-Rock. They were closer to who I was.

The Bronx was burning. It was a fucking war zone. Street gangs up in Harlem, Super Fly, all this shit. And these young brothers and sisters, the Puerto Ricans and the Black people and the youth up there, were making all of these creative rhymes.

The [DJ] Hollywoods and the Kurtis Blows and the Eddie Cheebas and the older dudes that was already doing it in the clubs, they were the men.

But the Funky 4s and the Moe Dees and the Busy Bee Starskis and the Cold Crush and the Jazzy Five MCs and the fuckin' Soulsonic Force and Bambaataa and the Zulu Nation and the fucking Mean Machine, they spoke my language. They was the ones giving the CNN way of life of the streets for the younger kids, because we wasn't in the clubs yet.

It was fucking Moe. It was Caz, it was Mel. It was fuckin' Lil Rodney C. It was Sha-Rock. Those were my influences. The outcasts of this shit.

There was the hip-hop disco thing, which was cool, but it wasn't what Moe and them was doing in Harlem World. If that shit would've been signed back then, that shit would've changed the world. That would've did what Run-DMC did when we came along. Before, it didn't become an art form. The MC was just the voice of the party. And if you could out–master ceremony the next dude, you could create a reputation for yourself.

It wasn't until it was about rocking rhymes that would take it to another whole level.

And the early rhymes were just phrases until guys like Caz and Moe Dee and Mel and Lil Rodney C and K.K. Rockwell and Sha-Rock and LA Sunshine, who's highly overlooked in the history of hip-hop, and dudes like the Crash Crew, they made the rhyme thing part of it. The shit that would make, break, or distinguish you in a huge way. And the rhyme thing also allowed different personalities to be birthed.

IN THOSE EARLY years, groups often mixed and matched members for reasons both creative and practical. DJ Tony Tone had once been a member of the Brothers Disco with DJ Breakout and DJ Baron. DJ Charlie Chase, for a short period, replaced Grandmaster Flash in the Furious Five.

The Cold Crush Brothers went through different lineups until some maneuvering by DJ Charlie Chase landed Grandmaster Caz, formerly DJ Casanova Fly, into the group with DJ Tony Tone, JDL, Easy A.D., and

Almighty Kay Gee. The Cold Crush Brothers evolved into groundbreakers, spreading hip-hop through the global journey of their recorded concerts and directly influenced Run-DMC, among many others.

Easy A.D. (Cold Crush Brothers): Groups were moving around. The L Brothers was Cordie-O, Mean Gene, Kevie Kev, Master Rob, and Busy Bee [Starski]. Then we had us, As Salaam. You had the Infinity Machine. You had Casanova [Grandmaster Caz] and Mighty Mike. But then you had the more established people. You had Grandmaster Flash with Disco Bee and DJ EZ Mike and the Furious Four MCs. You had DJ AJ, and then you had Afrika Islam, which was the son of Afrika Bambaataa over in Bronx River, and the Zulu Nation, Cosmic Force.

Whipper Whip (Fantastic Five): It was just me and DJ Casanova Fly—we grew up together—and Disco Wiz. From there, I needed somebody to help rock with me on the microphone. So I got my man, MC Dot-A-Rock. And he and I became Salt and Pepper. And then Big Bank Hank, every time it comes to doing shows, he's up there talking about, "Yo, man, I gotta pay for the equipment. Gotta pay for this and that." Somewhere, I was getting short on the money. So me and Dot-A left the group. I got down with Kool Herc for a minute, yada yada. And then we got down with Charlie Chase and made up the group called the Cold Crush.

Easy A.D. (Cold Crush Brothers): We all intertwined, until we all just got with the right menu. So you went in and out of groups. I remember when our DJ left and went back home to Jamaica from the As Salaam Brothers, DJ Rashid and I tried out for Islam's group. Donald D made it and I didn't. And I ran into my brother Tony Tone. I said, "I'm an MC."

He said, "I'm starting my own group."

I said, "What's the name going to be?"

He said, "It's going to be the Cold Crush Brothers, and you down."

And that's it. I moved on from there. And he went and got Charlie Chase, and then Whipper Whip, Dot-A-Rock, and Mr. Tee was down at first, and then Whipper Whip and Dot-A-Rock went on to the Fantastic Five.

Whipper Whip (Fantastic Five): Again, me and Dot-A-Rock are Salt and Pepper, so we go to Chase and it's like, "Look, we love Easy A.D. and Kay Gee and all these guys, but yo, it's kind of stagnating our flow."

We went to [Grand Wizzard] Theodore and he was, "Yo, you want to be down with the Fantastic?" 'Cause I think they were just the Fantastic Four: Ruby Dee, [Waterbed] Kev, Master Rob, and Theodore. So they had an audition. We did our little Salt and Pepper routines. Next thing you know, it became Theodore and the Fantastic Five.

Now, when we did that, Grandmaster Caz and JDL took the slot that me and Dot-A-Rock left in the Cold Crush Brothers.

DJ Charlie Chase (Cold Crush Brothers): Tony Tone was the one who came up with the idea for doing the audition at South Bronx High School. I said, "Okay, great. I'm going to tell Caz to meet me because I want him to help me pick my MCs." This is my plan, right?

Grandmaster Caz (Cold Crush Brothers): Charlie Chase and I were good friends because of hip-hop. I happened along a couple of his jams at first and then I became a fan. This guy Chase, he was like the next level.

DJ Charlie Chase (Cold Crush Brothers): All kinds of MCs are lining up to audition. And Kay Gee steps to the mic. He had that voice. I just loved his presence on the stage. He just fucking sounded right, and I was like, "Yeah, this is the motherfucker."

Grandmaster Caz (Cold Crush Brothers): His voice was incredible, and he could follow a rhyme. So I was like, "That dude right there, he's definitely got potential." So then it was Chase, Tone. It was A.D. and now Kay Gee. Now, Chase's idea was like, "Alright, now let me get Caz down here and maybe somebody else."

DJ Charlie Chase (Cold Crush Brothers): And Caz is there with JDL. I wasn't really into the kind of shit that JDL would get into. He was wild. He had a crazy fucking reputation. I just knew I wasn't feeling JDL.

So I said, "Caz, let's do something, man. Get on with A.D. and Kay Gee and rhyme with them. I want to see how it can go as a group."

Caz says, "Sure, sure."

He goes up there. They start rocking. Caz, JDL, Easy A.D., Almighty Kay Gee—it was real fucking good. The chemistry was there.

Grandmaster Caz (Cold Crush Brothers): I'm already all over the place. I'm halfway out of Casanova Fly and halfway into Grandmaster Caz. I'm still doing DJ parties and then I'm doing MC parties as well. And then there were other crews that wanted me to rock with them. Afrika Islam was trying to recruit me to be down with them as well.

DJ Charlie Chase (Cold Crush Brothers): I was like, "Listen, Caz, you know I've been after you for a long time." Word for word, I told him, "I have ideas, and you are just like me. I come from a musical background. I know what it is to put a show on. You're a natural on the stage. You're good at what you do, man. Caz, I'm telling you, you come into my group, I promise you that we're going to make money and we're going to be the biggest thing that ever hit this fucking thing."

And he stopped, and he looked at me because he saw my intensity. I always considered myself to be a good motivational speaker, man. I can motivate a motherfucker to do things.

Grandmaster Caz (Cold Crush Brothers): I finally went to Charlie and I was like, "Yo, listen, man. I'll get down, but JDL got to be down, too." Because they didn't want JDL. JDL was like a wild child. They didn't know what he was going to do from moment to moment, so he was, like, a risk to them. I was like, "Yo, if he don't get down, I'm not down."

DJ Charlie Chase (Cold Crush Brothers): I stopped, and I looked at it and I weighed the options in my mind, and I said, "Okay, fuck it, let's do it."

Easy A.D. (Cold Crush Brothers): Caz convinced him to let JDL join the group, and then that's where what we know now as the Cold Crush Four. Set the hip-hop world on fire as far as our lyrical skills from that point on.

Grandmaster Caz (Cold Crush Brothers): We got on our mission to become a formidable hip-hop group.

DJ Charlie Chase (Cold Crush Brothers): That's how the Cold Crush was birthed. And the rest is history, man. After that, we gelled so fucking good. We were with each other eight to ten to fifteen hours every fuckin' day. We were hanging out. We were going to the movies. We were going to Fordham Road. And if we weren't hanging out, we were practicing. We practiced six, seven, eight hours a day. Every day. For years.

> **THE COLD CRUSH** Brothers were a group ahead of their time in many respects. Beyond their groundbreaking routines, they were pioneers in marketing. They recorded their performances, and used photographs and flyers to grow their name and spread their impact at a time when few others recognized hip-hop music's lasting potential. The documents generated by the group are now viewed as some of hip-hop's earliest artifacts.

Easy A.D. (Cold Crush Brothers): We was our own media, our own flyer distribution, our own sound people, so we did everything.

Flash and Theodore and them had tapes, but it was like, "Shhhh"—you couldn't really hear, you couldn't really feel what was going on. So I asked my friend Elvis Moreno—I named him Tape Master—I was like, "You need to come and record our shows so when people hear our tapes, they can hear what we're saying. They can hear the music."

So he came and he plugged in directly to the system, so our tapes were crisp-clear. That was important to me and also our photographer, Joey.

Joe Conzo (photographer): I went to South Bronx High School. A.D., Adrian Harris, and Angelo King, also known as Tony Tone, went to school there also. So we became friends. A.D. was a star basketball player at South Bronx High School, and I was the school photographer. He invited me one day to take pictures of his group that he was joining.

I landed at the T-Connection one Friday night. I took pictures of the Cold Crush Brothers playing music that I'd never heard played that way. Charlie Chase was playing Aretha Franklin and James Brown, all this music that I grew up on from my parents, but he wasn't playing it the way I was used to hearing it played. I tell people, that's the night I was kidnapped by the culture of hip-hop.

Easy A.D. (Cold Crush Brothers): I had a concept because I loved history in school. I wanted to make sure I had our history.

Joe Conzo (photographer): They had the foresight to: (a) have a photographer shooting their jams, (b) Tape Master, Elvis, recording all their shows, and (c) Buddy Esquire doing these flyers. It was a stage performance for the Cold Crush Brothers. We could sit here all day and talk about their four-part harmony and this, that, and the other, but their performances were documented for a reason, because they had the foresight to do that.

Easy A.D. (Cold Crush Brothers): One of the things that I really like about what we did is our tapes went from New York City to Florida to Germany to Japan, so it went to all the military bases around the world where people had their brothers and sisters in the military. One of the other things people used to say: "Don't never lend your Cold Crush tape out, because you ain't going to get it back."

DMC (artist, Run-DMC): I talked to [Easy A.D.]. He was like, "Yo, whether or not this shit was going to be commercial, this shit is historic." And it is. But see, that was the thing: He cared. He wanted the clarity. He wanted the tape to feel good.

Easy A.D. (Cold Crush Brothers): Run and D from Run-DMC said that Russell [Simmons] made them listen to our tapes every day, and he said, "You've got to be better than them." That's why they knew all our routines and rhymes.

Daddy-O (artist, producer, Stetsasonic): Flash and them seemed like they was always headed for the pop charts. When I heard the Cold Crush, none of that was in the music. It was just pure street stuff.

GRAND WIZZARD THEODORE had already etched his name in history by experimenting with the equipment owned by his brother Mean Gene, and inventing the scratching technique for DJs. After forming the L Brothers with his siblings, Grand Wizzard Theodore eventually headed the Fantastic Five, a group that came to consist of Theodore, Whipper Whip, Dot-A-Rock, Waterbed Kevie Kev, Ruby Dee, and Master Rob.

A rivalry between the Cold Crush Brothers and the Fantastic Five culminated in a showoff at Harlem World on the evening of July 3, 1981. The Cold Crush came equipped in stylish suits, fedoras, and plastic handguns. That night, the crowd's applause crowned the Fantastic Five as the victors, awarding them a $1,000 prize. Soon, recordings of the matchup were disseminated in the streets, and while they may have lost the battle against the Fantastic Five, the Cold Crush Brothers developed a reputation as the city's most elite hip-hop group.

Easy A.D. (Cold Crush Brothers): One of my favorite memories is us walking towards the stage at Harlem World [before the battle] and seeing all the floors were packed. And us having on our gangster suits with our lyrical machine guns, it was incredible. I've never experienced that euphoria inside my body ever again.

DJ Charlie Chase (Cold Crush Brothers): What sticks out to me about the rivalry was that the MCs were always at each other's throats. But me and Theodore were always cool with each other. Me and Theodore never had a fucking grudge. We were always good friends. To this day, we're still good friends.

The other thing that stood out to me was how ferocious we were towards each other [as groups]. That shit sticks out to me, because we had it out for each other. It didn't matter where we were, if we bumped into them before the night of the battle, it was a fucking scene. Almost fistfights and all kinds of shit. We really took that seriously.

DMC (artist, Run-DMC): When I first heard the Cold Crush, it was different hip-hop because it was the first time where the MCs were actually going at the other MCs with a destroying attitude. They made it all about the performance and presentation of the DJ and MC. All the beats that Charlie Chase and Tony Tone was choosing precisely fit the attitude and the vibe of each routine. What I liked about Cold Crush, they didn't need to have successful records because they kept hip-hop to its rawest form.

Easy A.D. (Cold Crush Brothers): We mastered the performance level of entertainment and hip-hop. We just had that thing, that energy, and understood the vibration of our audience, and we delivered it properly.

03 WHAT IN THE WORLD IS THIS?

Englewood, New Jersey; New York City
1979–1982

Sylvia Robinson engineered a varied and influential music career long before she was dubbed "the Mother of Hip-Hop" for having the epiphany to bottle the new music and transfer it to vinyl. As a teenager in the 1950s, she recorded R&B singles as Little Sylvia. A few years later, she joined her guitar teacher, McHouston "Mickey" Baker, to form the guitar-and-vocal duo Mickey & Sylvia. In 1956, their single "Love Is Strange" leaped to the top of the R&B charts.

Later, Robinson made a mark as a producer and also played an instrumental role in Ike & Tina Turner's gigantic single "It's Gonna Work Out Fine." Robinson did not receive the compensation or credit she likely deserved for her role, which became a recurring complaint of some of the artists and musicians who later worked for her.

By the mid-1960s, Robinson had moved to New Jersey and started All Platinum Records with her husband, Joe Robinson, who owned nightclubs in Harlem, and whom many suspected of having mob ties. When Al Green passed on a demo tape that Sylvia Robinson delivered to him, she opted to record the song herself. The effort resulted in 1973's racy hit "Pillow Talk," which rose to third on the Billboard Hot 100 and earned a Grammy nomination.

But a few years later, the hits had dried up. All Platinum and its subsidiary labels faced bankruptcy by the time Robinson agreed to attend a party at Harlem World in 1979. There, Robinson witnessed Lovebug

Starski work the turntables and the crowd into a frenzy with his call-and-responses.

Robinson wanted to capture the music and release it commercially. When Lovebug Starski declined the arrangement, Robinson went on a hunt for other artists. Meanwhile, Joe Robinson partnered with Morris "Mo" Levy, an acquaintance from his club-owning days and a music executive with alleged mob ties, to form Sugar Hill Records, named after a historic section of Harlem.

The search for talent, piloted by their son, Joey Robinson Jr., eventually led Sylvia Robinson to a New Jersey pizza parlor. Before long, Henry Jackson, who worked at the pizzeria and helped manage the Cold Crush Brothers, sat in Robinson's car for an impromptu audition. Guy O'Brien and Michael Wright happened upon the car and showcased their skills as well, and Robinson christened them a group. Big Bank Hank, Master Gee, and Wonder Mike became the Sugarhill Gang.

Robinson's house band re-created a loop from Chic's disco smash "Good Times" (Nile Rodgers and Bernard Edwards were not credited for their song and later threatened to sue for copyright infringement, before receiving credit as co-writers) and the group met for a session. They produced a charismatic and catchy fifteen-minute song where they traded verses, boasted, rhymed, and even defined the form: "Now, what you hear is not a test, I'm rapping to the beat / And me, the groove, and my friends are gonna try to move your feet."

New York City radio stations initially dismissed the song, but the Robinsons had a connection with WESL out of St. Louis, which agreed to play it. In the fall of 1979, "Rapper's Delight" flooded the airwaves and the streets. The song's success relegated the Fatback Band's "King Tim III (Personality Jock)"—hip-hop's first commercially released song, which had debuted just a few months earlier—to the status of historical trivia.

FOR SOME OF the genre's Bronx pioneers, "Rapper's Delight" sounded like a sanitized imitation of what they had created. The song even included phrases and lines taken from better-known practitioners. Most egregiously, one of Grandmaster Caz's monikers, Casanova

Fly—is spelled outright by Big Bank Hank. Few in the Bronx took the song or the group seriously.

But the dam had been broken. A phenomenon was born. In becoming the first label to specialize in hip-hop music, Sugar Hill Records proved it was financially viable. Robinson became known as a rainmaker, and many held her in high regard, while others questioned Sugar Hill's business practices.

And the commercial door for hip-hop music, once opened, would never close again.

Russell Simmons (cofounder, Def Jam): [Sylvia] was everybody's mother. She was nice to me. Like those singing niggas to her. She was very sweet to all of them, but she didn't pay 'em. They was kind of gangster too, because they had the gangsters behind 'em, right?

Duke Bootee (producer, Sugar Hill): My father's frat brother was Joe Robinson's lawyer, and he said, "Son, you working for gangsters. I was Joe Robinson's lawyer when he was buying bars in New York with cache cases full of money, so just know who you're dealing with."

So, I knew who I was dealing with.

Russell Simmons (cofounder, Def Jam): [Sugar Hill Records] didn't see the artists the same way. . . . Every one of them deserved the opportunity to be a brand. They had spent their whole life as artists. They were not disposable singers out of their church, they were people who had their own personalities that could have exuded their own charisma that could have been branded and built out bigger. And they didn't get that opportunity at Sugar Hill or anywhere. The white guys who bought into the companies, they didn't give a fuck neither.

Lady B (artist, radio DJ, Philadelphia): Before her and Mr. Joe [Robinson], may they both rest in peace, decided to do "Rapper's Delight," they had their label. She was always a very classy, very opinionated lady. She was like my Aunt Sylvia, in my head. She was always so brave, and I never saw her fearful as a woman. I was impressed with that—to see a woman go even toe-to-toe with her husband sometimes.

Russell Simmons (cofounder, Def Jam): She stood up in the Fever and sniffed coke with me—in the front. Everybody had to go to the back. We would sniff at the bar in the front. Because she was Sylvia.

Edie B. Anderson (radio DJ, WESL, St. Louis): I worked at a radio station called WESL. On Tuesdays, we played the oldies-but-goodies. On the last hour, I would call it the "Ladies' Concert Half Hour," where I would play the ladies back-to-back—like the Billie Holidays, Dinah Washingtons—and I had a real nice following.

Jim Gates, my program director and general manager, walks into the control room and he's carrying this album. He handed it to me, I put it on the turntable, and I dropped the needle on it, and all of a sudden it's like, "I said a hip-hop, the hippie the hippie." I'm like, *What in the world is this?*

But the minute I did that, the phones lit up. And from what I learned, Sylvia Robinson was their manager, she and Jim Gates were friends, and she wanted the record played on air. At the time that I dropped the needle on the record and start hearing the hippity-hop and all that, it went for like fourteen minutes. I said to Jim, "This is going to be the end of R&B as we know it."

Bill Adler (journalist, Def Jam publicist): With rock [and] R&B running out of gas, and the pop music universe segregated by race, it was a perfect moment for this new rap music to emerge. And unlike punk rock—the revolution that failed—rap was going to be the revolution that succeeded.

DMC (artist, Run-DMC): The two things that changed the world creatively, artistically, and even in an educational-mindset way simultaneously was punk rock and hip-hop. The punk rockers came along, anti-government, "Fuck this. We going to make our music, say what we want to say." So, when hip-hop came along, it validated what the punk rockers was already doing.

Bill Adler (journalist, Def Jam publicist): Punk rock electrified the critics. The everyday music lover at home did not pretend to care about it. But "Rapper's Delight" comes out in the fall of 1979: It's fifteen minutes long; it's on an independent label; it's Black artists in a moment where supposedly white folks aren't listening to Black artists.

It not only does very, very well in America, but it charts in a dozen countries worldwide.

It had everything that you would really want from rock and roll. It had sex and humor and aggression, and it's right-up-to-the-moment and it looked different. And the way it looked was super cool. It just rang a bunch of bells at that moment.

Cory Robbins (cofounder, Profile Records): It was a phenomenon. I used to go to a record store at lunch every day around the corner from where I worked and the line for the cash register was to the back of the store, and everybody had a copy of "Rapper's Delight."

Al Kapone (artist, Memphis): My aunt at the time was dating a DJ. I used to listen to the radio station to catch him when he was DJing, and that was the first time I heard "Rapper's Delight." And I memorized it. Every word, every line in reverse, I just fell in love with it.

Dupré "DoItAll" Kelly (artist, Lords of the Underground): There was the relatable lines. If you talking about fried chicken in the Black and Brown neighborhood, when you talking about it tastes like wood, you know that there's somebody's mama that couldn't cook. Everybody's mother in the Black and Brown neighborhoods can cook some fried chicken.

Cormega (artist, Queensbridge): I remember hip-hop being fun when I first heard Sugarhill Gang and they said something about a chicken tastes like wood. My father was laughing, he said his sister's chicken tastes like [that]. The song was cool to us, 'cause we was young and it was cool to the adults.

Mike Gee (artist, Jungle Brothers): Grandmaster Caz, he is my top, he is like my number one. He is my G.O.A.T. He is that dude to me.

DJ Clark Kent (producer): The guy who I would say was the best in that beginning-of-rap era, it's definitely Grandmaster Caz. He had everything. He had bars, he had stories, he had style, he had flair, he had stage presence. He was the true first definition of pure rapper.

Mike Gee (artist, Jungle Brothers): Those late '70s, early '80s mixtapes, Caz was dropping verses, dropping stories. He was top-notch, and there were only really a handful. Him, G.L.O.B.E. [of Soulsonic Force], Kool Moe Dee. There are probably like two more, but if it was top five, Caz was number one. He had rhymes, all solid content. He was ahead of his time.

Whipper Whip (Fantastic Five): When you first heard ["Rapper's Delight"], it's like, *Holy crap.* The city was like, *What is that?* "Yo, Caz, that don't sound like you, but it's your shit." Everybody knows Caz's shit.

Grandmaster Caz (Cold Crush Brothers): When I first heard "Rapper's Delight," I thought it sucked, because I heard it in my house on the turntables. [Big Bank] Hank came over, and at first I was shocked that he was serious, he had really made a record. But then when I heard it on the radio and I heard other people listening to it, I was like, "Oh, wow. That's me. That's my rhymes on a record."

Whipper Whip (Fantastic Five): Well, some of it was my rhymes. Me and Dot-A-Rock. [Hank] was our manager and he had that opportunity. Caz gave him a book and he did his thing.

Grandmaster Caz (Cold Crush Brothers): He didn't have to look through my rhyme book. Hank was down with me. He knew my rhymes. These are rhymes that were on tapes and that we used to do at jams and at parties. Of course he knew my rhymes. He knew which ones to say, and he knew the fill-ins to use as well.

Sometimes I've been misquoted, and then sometimes I've made the mistake myself of saying I wrote all of Big Bank Hank's lyrics for "Rapper's Delight." What I meant is his verses. I meant his rhymes. But the little bridges, the hook, that's DJ Hollywood. That, "Imp the Dimp, the ladies' pimp. The women fight for my . . . ," that's Rahiem from Grandmaster Flash and the Furious Five. Those two things, I didn't write, but the full rhymes he says, "I'm the C-A-S-AN, the O-V-A from the time I was only six years old" and then the Superman and Lois Lane, I wrote all of that.

DMC (artist, Run-DMC): When "Rapper's Delight" came out, the only reason that I liked [it] was because of Big Bank Hank's rhyme, which happened to be Grandmaster Caz's rhyme about Superman. I related to it, because all I did as a kid was read comic books.

Caz's rhymes about "Oh, he's a sucker flying through the air in his pantyhose." Even that rhyme had attitude. Caz is dissing Superman. I'd never experienced this before.

Rahiem (Grandmaster Flash and the Furious Five): When I heard my line, I guess I was just as pissed off as Grandmaster Caz was when he heard his lines. But the difference between Caz and I, as far as the Sugarhill Gang is concerned, I never gave Hank a book of my rhymes or permission to use them. He used my rhyme because it was popular, and he wasn't the first one to bite that rhyme. Busy Bee Starski was the first one. And I guess as a result of him biting it, other people bit it.

My reaction was pretty much the standard reaction from every Bronx MC who heard "Rapper's Delight" when it first came out. And that is: "Yo, who the fuck is this? They ain't no real MCs. We never heard of them. They ain't no real rap group. They ain't never did no park jams. Ain't nobody ever paid no money to see them perform at the club. They didn't establish a street following." So we just bombarded them with all kinds of "What the fuck?"

Grandmaster Caz (Cold Crush Brothers): We hadn't accepted the fact that hip-hop had started to spread to other places. We were still under this veil of *Yeah, this is the Bronx.*

Rahiem (Grandmaster Flash and the Furious Five): So, I heard Hank use [my line] and, prior to me learning of how much of a commercial success "Rapper's Delight" was at that time, to me he sounded very corny saying my rhyme. They all sounded really corny to me. And at first when we got signed to Sugar Hill Records, Sugarhill Gang was our archenemy. And every time we toured together, we relished in the thought of spanking them on stage.

Whipper Whip (Fantastic Five): It was actually great. After a while, it became the phenomenon that set up a whole new genre. It showed the whole world what hip-hop was.

Rahiem (Grandmaster Flash and the Furious Five): I've known Hank for many years, and Hank was not an apologetic kind of a person. If he knew he wronged you in some way and he had to face you, he'd probably buy you dinner or get you high or something like that. Never say sorry, though.

Grandmaster Caz (Cold Crush Brothers): When I heard my lyrics, I thought it was dope. I always joke when I tell people the story, "I thought the song sucked." But I never gave the song a chance. I never really gave it a good listen. I was mortified by it, and then after a while, I thought I should've been on that shit. I'm Casanova Fly. If they came to Hank and they were looking for an MC, that was supposed to be me. I was so entrenched trying to succeed in the street that I didn't really pursue that, I guess, as vehemently as other people would have.

DJ Charlie Chase (Cold Crush Brothers): When "Rapper's Delight" came out [in '79], it set hip-hop back five years. Hip-hop started in '73. In '77, that shit was preschool for us at that point. We were already rhyming.

Easy A.D. (Cold Crush Brothers): We heard the song. We just thought it was whack. We looked at it like, "What? They not even MCs."

DJ Charlie Chase (Cold Crush Brothers): The hood was rocking at that point. We were already at another level. But when that shit came out, that was brand-spanking-new to them. Then everybody wanted to hear more of that shit. So now we had to back up a few years, retrain ourselves to sound like that shit, so we could start making records, which was an insult to us.

DMC (artist, Run-DMC): Chase is one hundred percent right. It set it back because that was that "hip-hop hippity" shit. Motherfuckers was writing rhymes and doing dope shit by that time.

Whipper Whip (Fantastic Five): Yeah, you could say that, but even though Chase feels that way, it's being played today and still making money today.

DJ Charlie Chase (Cold Crush Brothers): The Treacherous Three ended [up] coming out with "The New Rap Language" and Spoonie Gee, which was more of the times. Them motherfuckers were machines. They were rhyming like nobody else was doing at the time. There was no spaces when they were handing off to each other. That was fucking next-level shit right there.

But nobody was going to catch that shit. It was just too advanced. Too complicated. You have to train your listener, give it to them in small doses. And that's why we found ourselves having to go back and do over what we did. And for some of us—and that includes Cold Crush—we were like, "We ain't going back to that shit. That's a fucking insult to us."

Easy A.D. (Cold Crush Brothers): The record is what it is. It's established, we understand that, but they would be like the Milli Vanilli of hip-hop.

Bill Stephney (Bomb Squad, Def Jam): There's no way to convey how popular "Rapper's Delight" was as a song. It was like it was everywhere. To the point where you had to say to yourself, *This is revolutionary. This is not just a new art; this is not funk. This is not just even James Brown. This is larger than that.*

Kool Moe Dee (artist, Treacherous Three): I understood why there was a lot of MCs at the time that didn't like it, because I just think the social construct of oppression puts us against each other in many ways. In my opinion, many African Americans have a hard time giving other African Americans credit for achieving because so much of white America accepted that record and they started to define it from their perspective. And we're saying we've already been here; it's not new. So a backlash was on Sugar Hill that wasn't deserved because they didn't ask for it.

But I'm not saying America does this intentionally. I'm just saying the infrastructure of racism, that plate is already set. So, usually if you come out and "do something" and it's Black and we feel it from an African American standpoint, we're very happy. As soon as white America embraces it, it separates us. And then you get the resentment.

So it was never not really hip-hop. We had just gotten more lyrically sophisticated at that time and the record was a great record. And looking back, if it wasn't for Sugar Hill, we might not have an industry as prominent as we have because of the success of "Rapper's Delight."

Bill Stephney (Bomb Squad, Def Jam): It was a party culture. "Rapper's Delight" converts it now to a recording culture with the emphasis on the rapper, and it's completely different. We lose the ability of a DJ to search the globe far and wide for the perfect beat and to soak the label off of that vinyl, because you want to be the only one who's now found that perfect beat that's going to rock the party. What does that even have to do with anything that's going on today? That's like coming from the days of the pyramids with how far away and distinct that period was.

DMC (artist, Run-DMC): Hip-hop was always about Cold Crush gotta out-rhyme the Force MCs. And if Cold Crush out-rhymed the Force MCs, next week the Force MCs was going to come back and out-rhyme the Cold Crush, which is going to cause the Cold Crush to come back next week and out-rhyme them. We would always be elevating ourselves.

It was young people being creative and innovative with what we had available to us. My claim to fame was "Yo, nobody is making rock-beat jams." So we did "Rock Box," "King of Rock," and then eventually we did "Walk This Way," which was full circle. It's not new. Because like Chase said, "Rapper's Delight" sent us back five years. What they was doing in 1978 and '79 was so futuristic, beyond comprehension of this current music industry.

Grandmaster Caz (Cold Crush Brothers): I appreciated the notoriety from being attached to one of the most important rap songs of all time. On the flip side of the coin, I'm the asshole who got jerked from Sugar Hill Records and Big Bank Hank and didn't do nothing about it, so it was like a double-edged sword for me. To me, it was more important just to move on to the next thing that I was going to do.

Kool Moe Dee (artist, Treacherous Three): I personally thought it was a one-off. I didn't think they were ever going to turn hip-hop into an industry because, quite frankly, it was just African American teenagers. We were the last generation that was consciously bred to not believe in ourselves. Putting a rhyme together and then going out and saying the rhyme and seeing if people respond was a huge boost of self-esteem.

But we also had an older generation telling us that this isn't real music: *It's not going to last. Who's going to pay to hear people talk over records that already came out, that you don't play any instruments, and who's going to sit there and watch a DJ scratch records?* Because that whole paradigm was absolutely judging it from the thing that they came up, and every generation does it. We're doing it right now, quite frankly, for the new generation of hip-hop.

AS ONE OF the first journalists to document hip-hop, Robert "Rocky" Ford foresaw a future in the emerging genre and culture. He had the vision to collaborate with J. B. Moore, his former colleague at *Billboard* magazine, to create a hip-hop-centric holiday single in 1979.

His search for an artist to work with led him to a young and exuberant party promoter in Queens named Russell Simmons, and to Kurtis Blow, who became hip-hop's first solo star.

Robert "Rocky" Ford (journalist, producer): I knew [hip-hop] was going to be something. I didn't know how big a thing. But I knew it was going to happen. I'm somewhat surprised how big it became.

Russell Simmons (cofounder, Def Jam): Robert Ford was a guy who really inspired me to be in the music business.

I booked my first party at Renaissance. I looked at the models that inspired me to promote the shows, and I wanted to make a living by giving everybody hip-hop. I looked at Jerry Roebuck. He used to promote DJ Hollywood at the Hotel Diplomat. It was Martin Hall and another guy named Winston Sanders. They were just older guys who had promoted the Black concerts [that] came to New York, whether it'd be the Apollo or the Garden. They would then partner with young promoters. They'd book the venue, and they'd get the venue cheaper and they would be partners on these shows with us. So I was inspired by Martin Hall, but especially Jerry Roebuck.

Robert "Rocky" Ford (journalist, producer): I saw his brother [Simmons's brother, Joey "Run" Simmons] putting up posters for a party he had coming up. I had a *Billboard* card. And I gave him my card, I said, "Tell your brother to call me." And his brother did, and we've been friends ever since.

Russell Simmons (cofounder, Def Jam): He did an interview with me and wrote a story for *Billboard* magazine about DJ Hollywood and this emerging scene that was happening in Harlem and in the Bronx.

Robert "Rocky" Ford (journalist, producer): Rappers wanted to be covered in *Billboard*. I remember DJ Hollywood coming in my office. I remember DJ Starski, early on, came up to my office. And they all want to be national. For all intents and purposes, even though I am Black, I was the white media. I exposed them to that. And I was able to do that at a time when nobody knew anything about anybody.

Russell Simmons (cofounder, Def Jam): I took Flash to Queens, to Brooklyn, and to the Hotel Diplomat. I brought him to the Diplomat last because he had never been there. He and Eddie Cheeba had never shared a stage, but I did that the first time he got there.

When I brought Flash to Hotel Diplomat, that's when Robert Ford saw him, and he saw Kurtis Blow. Flash, when he played the Fantasia or somewhere in Queens, he would just bring Kurtis Blow because that was my man, that was "Queens #1." Even though he's from Harlem, I named him Queens #1 and it kind of stuck, just like we named him "King of Rap" and it stuck. I was a little bit of a branding person. I learned what I did learn about branding from Robert Ford.

Kurtis Blow (artist, producer): Russell was a sociology major, and I was a communications major, and I learned in one of my broadcasting classes that the way you make it in this competitive industry is go out to the boondocks or the secondary markets and create a track record, a name for yourself, then come back to the big city. And then you can say, "Well, I'm number one in this small town here, so give me a job here."

I told Russell about this, I said, "Man, we need to open up a club out in your hood, out in Hollis, Queens." And we did. We opened this club called Night Fever Disco. I played there for about two years and all around Queens, and Russell was the promoter. And that's how I got good, and I owe that to Russell.

Russell Simmons (cofounder, Def Jam): Robert came to see Eddie Cheeba. It was Eddie Cheeba and it was Grandmaster Flash. Kurtis Blow rapped for Flash instead of the Furious Five, for me. And it was so different from Eddie Cheeba, who was rapping over "Good Times." It was Bob James's "[Take Me to the] Mardi Gras," and it wasn't sped up like we did on [Run-DMC's] "Peter Piper." It was slow. It was like dust music.

Even though Kurtis Blow was more of a party rapper, we did have a mix. A lot of kids who had never been to the Diplomat showed up because of Flash. A lot of kids didn't want to go to the Diplomat because of Flash, like the college kids, who would go to see Hollywood and Cheeba. So it was a mix. The first time these kids were mixed, we had a shoot-out ultimately that night. But it was a huge turnout and [Ford] saw Kurtis Blow and he decided.

Robert "Rocky" Ford (journalist, producer): I had worked with a man named Mickey Addy, who lived his life being able to take vacations and cruises based on one obscure, very minor Christmas song that he wrote. And so, I'd already figured out, the first record I did was going to be about Christmas, because it came back every year. I'd already told Russell I wanted to make a record, and he brought me Kurtis Blow and everything came off from there. And "Christmas Rappin' " was just an obvious idea for a record to me.

Kurtis Blow (artist, producer): J. B. Moore came up with the concept and the actual witty lyrics that we still listen to today—the first half of the song. I wrote the second half of the song. All of the party stuff. It's about Santa Claus visiting a house in Harlem and he comes down the chimney and then he parties with the family and then he gives everybody presents and then he leaves.

When he parties with everyone, that's the part I wrote. I remember going over to J. B. Moore's house and meeting him for the first time. I was sitting there with Larry Smith, who's our young bass player, and Denzil Miller, who is our concert pianist, and between those three, they came up with the track. That was the most incredible track.

Russell Simmons (cofounder, Def Jam): They had the vision, and they were much more in tune with commercial taste, and they wrote an amazing bassline, which Queen later stole [for "Another One Bites the Dust"].

Kurtis Blow (artist, producer): [Larry Smith asked,] "Who's your favorite artist?" I said, "James Brown." And then I thought about it, and the number one music out during that time was a band called Chic, so we wanted to make a style, a sound that was right in between James Brown and that of Chic.

We came up with "Christmas Rappin'" with those James Brown guitars, and the Fender Rhodes, the keyboards, and bassline was inspired by the song "Good Times." So I wouldn't want to say a rip-off, but we kind of changed it up and made it simpler instead of the runny, runny bassline. And that's when I found out less is best.

I was nineteen years old. It was the most incredible time of my life. Just being around those musicians and producers and going into the studio for the first time, it was just like a dream come true in a dream world.

THE DEMO OF "Christmas Rappin'" caught the attention of Cory Robbins, who soon thought he had closed on a deal for the single. Instead, Kurtis Blow became the first hip-hop artist to sign with a major label when he joined Mercury Records. The success of "Christmas Rappin'" allowed Blow to record "The Breaks," hip-hop's first song to be certified gold by the Recording Industry Association of America.

Robbins recovered by releasing "Genius Rap" by Dr. Jeckyll & Mr. Hyde (Andre Harrell and Alonzo Brown) and later signing Run-DMC to Profile Records.

Cory Robbins (cofounder, Profile Records): J. B. Moore came in. He was one of the producers and played it for me. It was getting close to Christmas time, so we didn't have a lot of time to waste. We had to get the record out.

Back then, you had to get press records up and get them in the stores and ship them. And it was weeks of work to get a record out, especially with a Christmas record, because you really didn't have a second shot at it once Christmas is over. That's it until next Christmas. So we were rushing, and we have a handshake deal on it. We mastered the record and we're about to start pressing it, and he calls up and says he made a deal with Mercury. And that was that.

I was upset. I thought it wasn't right, but it went to Mercury, and it was a huge hit.

Neal H. Pogue (engineer, producer): Back in those days, you were so used to Christmas songs being Nat King Cole and all the greats, and hearing it come from a rapper, it was different. And you knew something like that was going to appeal to everybody. But you never thought about it appealing to any other culture but Black culture. It felt like that was something for us.

Bill Adler (journalist, Def Jam publicist): It was charming, and it was such a hit. Rap was still so novel, and that record was so electrifying that local radio continued to play it until fuckin' February.

Kurtis Blow (artist, producer): It played all the way into the springtime, summertime of the next year, and I was performing live outside of New York for the first time in my life and that was the most incredible thing—just seeing audiences who didn't know anything about hip-hop and were experiencing it for the first time.

And the great thing about it was the Christmas rap song had an instrumental on the B-side and it was eight minutes long, so a lot of the DJs would throw on that instrumental and just play that music without the rap, and it was the most incredible track that everyone could dance to.

And the other magnificent thing about the record was, there's a whole crowd response section. Little did we know that the crowds in the clubs would respond—and I wasn't even singing it live. It doesn't get any better than that—a thousand people screaming, you can hear that from miles around.

[Russell Simmons] took a leave of absence [from college] and they wanted me to take a leave of absence, but I was like, "Oh no, I am not taking a leave of absence yet. We've got to have a couple of these hit records." And so, when "Christmas Rappin'" came out, I had this crazy record deal.

Russell Simmons (cofounder, Def Jam): They used to feel that 12-inch records were for disposable artists. All of the disco records that were so great were sang by one person, and owned by another, and performed by another. They were disposable.

I believed in the artists as artists. Putting Kurtis Blow's picture on a 12-inch cover was probably the best thing that I ever did from a branding perspective. It was so unheard of. And I did it with the help of Robert Ford and J. B. Moore, of course. We'd wait, build up the excitement, the anticipation, and here comes the album.

The whole branding thing was because I believed in them. Because I was from the generation. I was in love with the culture. And because of that, I wanted an album. Because of that, I wanted to be treated like a star. And because of that, I wanted to create things that were sticky, and lasting, about each artist.

Kurtis Blow (artist, producer): It was a dream world, and I was a special commodity for all the promoters because it was just one DJ and one rapper. We had turntables, we could put them on a plane, no problem. A mixer and a microphone, two turntables and a microphone, and that's all we needed. Just give us some water and some juice and we're good.

So, I worked all the time. I did so many concerts, so many live shows, and promoters just wanted me to be a part of that situation. I was a hot, hot, hot commodity.

Russell Simmons (cofounder, Def Jam): Larry Levan [the DJ at SoHo's Paradise Garage] still was responsible for breaking all the Black music.

He would play these records when they were ready to get played on Black radio. And Frankie Crocker would stand over Larry and picked his records. He played "Christmas Rappin' " about a week before Christmas, and Frankie Crocker heard it and played it Christmas Eve. And the B-side played all that whole next year. And Frankie Crocker added "The Breaks" the week it came out.

Kurtis Blow (artist, producer): "Christmas Rappin' " sold over three hundred and seventy thousand copies, so I got the opportunity to do the next song, which was "The Breaks."

Bill Adler (journalist, Def Jam publicist): I moved to New York in 1980 and I start freelancing to the *Daily News,* among some other places. At that time, Kurt had his follow-up single. It was called "The Breaks." It charted nationally. I was able to talk to my editors at the paper and say, "Listen, you've got a young rapper. This rap stuff seems to be taking off a little bit. It so happens he lives in Harlem. Maybe we should do something about him. He's a local guy." And they said, "Go ahead and do the story."

Kool Moe Dee (artist, Treacherous Three): I always say we understood songwriting and we understood how to put a hook on a record because of Kurtis Blow. When you listen to "Rapper's Delight," it's just a fifteen-minute song of people rhyming. There's really no hook. And then most of the records that we made at that time, even Grandmaster Flash and the Furious Five, Funky 4, Treacherous Three, none of us had hooks.

Kurtis Blow was the first one to bring the hook into the equation, and that's when I truly understood this was going to be more prominent than I thought it would be. Because hip-hop was not an industry yet. It's just something we're doing in the street. It's not a real art form yet. It's just what we are doing because we love it and we're passionate and we're kids and we're making names doing it.

Kurtis Blow (artist, producer): Actually, I think the Sequence girls did a hook on a song called "Funk You Up" before "The Breaks" came out as well. But I was with musicians and songwriters, professional producers who understood what hip-hop was, and they wanted to take that next step to the next level and make it an art form. And I understood that in order for this thing to be successful, we need it to fuse with different forms of music, and we had different styles of rapping. And of course, the incredible musicians, Larry Smith and J. B. Moore and Denzil Miller came up with the style of music, and they also wanted to fuse with different forms of music. So I was always trying new stuff.

My life, when I think back in those days, it was like a whole dream world. Just so many miracles and blessings and good times happening during those days.

> **BOBBY ROBINSON, WHO** ran the independent Enjoy Records out of Harlem, witnessed the quick success of Sugar Hill Records and joined in on the action by signing groups like Grandmaster Flash and the Furious Five, the Funky 4 + 1, and the Treacherous Three.
>
> Through Enjoy, Grandmaster Flash and the Furious Five released "Superrappin'" before joining Sugar Hill and dropping "The Adventures of Grandmaster Flash on the Wheels of Steel," the influential single that introduced many future DJs to the turntables.
>
> In the summer of 1982, Grandmaster Flash and the Furious Five debuted "The Message," one of the first hip-hop songs that provided social commentary, articulating the stresses and indignities of inner-city poverty: "Broken glass everywhere / People pissing on the stairs, you know, they just don't care."
>
> The song was mostly written by Duke Bootee, a member of Sugar Hill Records' house band with Skip Alexander, Jiggs Chase, and Doug Wimbish, and included some of Melle Mel's lines from "Superrappin'."
>
> "The Message" was such a turn from most of the popular party raps in circulation that most of the group originally hesitated to record it. But it is a song that has maintained its relevancy and impact throughout each passing generation.

Duke Bootee (producer, Sugar Hill): I came up and auditioned, and Doug [Wimbish] and Skip [Alexander] were like, "Well, we're giving you a three-to-five." I'm like, "What's that?" Said, "You'll be with us at least four years." I was like, "Cool." And I wound up staying with them for four years. That's pretty clairvoyant.

I was a percussionist playing on all of those records and I used to tell them guys, "You better hope I don't never do this shit, because y'all ain't talking about nothing." [Melle] Mel would say, "Well, how do you come up with this?" I'm like, "I read five papers a day. What do you do?"

It's about making yourself aware of what's going on in the world and then trying to mirror it. Everybody used to try to make me political, but I'm social. I'm just trying to show what people are going through. It was about trying to mirror what I was seeing around me.

I had made the track and did the reference vocal. Sylvia was having [members of Grandmaster Flash and the Furious Five] try it. They didn't like it. They were like, "Don't nobody want to bring their problems to the disco. That's a downer." And then they got all mad and walked out the studio. But then, Mel, before the cab service came, came back to me, and says, "Look, I like that shit, and I got a verse from a record called 'Superrappin'' and I think it'll go right with it." I said, "Well, spit it." And he did and I said, "Well, that's the shit. Sylvia, you've got to hear this verse he's got." She heard it. She liked it. We put it on, and she bought the rights to it from Enjoy Records.

Rahiem (Grandmaster Flash and the Furious Five): That's actually not the way that it happened and Fletcher [Duke Bootee] is mistaken. His memory is failing him. And you could tell him I said that with love.

Actually, the way that Mel got on "The Message" was, I went into the booth and instead of spitting one of my own rhymes, to me, Mel's rhyme, "A child is born . . ." from "Superrappin'" fit the song. So when I went in the booth for my audition, I spit Mel's rhyme, and Sylvia loved it and she was going to keep my recording of it. But then I said to her, "Oh nah, Ms. Rob. That's Mel's verse from 'Superrappin'.' I just spit that verse because it fit the song."

She was like, "That's a great call. Mel, go in the booth and do your verse, baby." And that's how Mel got on the song.

Duke Bootee (producer, Sugar Hill): About a week after the first time I heard it on the radio, sales were knocking through the roof. It was kind of providential because Sylvia's into numerology. The actual length of the song was seven minutes, eleven seconds, without altering or doctoring. It just came out to that. She was like, "Damn. We've got to get this on the radio right now, because that number is this, that, and the other."

And then about a week after, it had done so well and had been picked up by so many stations, I figured, *Well, I guess this is going to do a little something.* That was all like a training for the real business of music, like the Harvard of how things really go. Joe [Robinson] said, "Whenever things get that big, it changes people's attitude, and it changes their expectations." And that's exactly what happened.

Rahiem (Grandmaster Flash and the Furious Five): We were at this club in Manhattan called the Savoy, the old jazz club, and there was an event there called the Urban Contemporary Awards. And I believe Frankie Crocker, very popular radio personality with WBLS in New York, was the host, and so we're sitting there. Lionel Richie, Luther Vandross, and Quincy Jones came up to me to congratulate me on our song success, and I'm like, "What?" I couldn't believe that these three giants were even speaking to me, let alone acknowledging anything good that we did. And that definitely gave me an idea of the magnitude of how that song hit.

Schoolly D (artist, Philadelphia): "The Message" was more than just hip-hop. The Funky 4 + 1 already put me on the right edge. And Prince. And Rick James put me on the right edge, but "The Message" was something different because it was on AM radio, FM radio, and television—it was right in your face every day.

I think "The Message" gave all of us who were on the fringe a voice. I don't have to just talk about partying, I can talk about exactly what the fuck was going on. I think it gave us all hope, that we can just do that, just be ourselves.

Ant Banks (producer, Dangerous Crew): He broke down what any Black kid would go through in any type of poverty, or neighborhood, or growing up in that type of situation. That was the first rap song to me that actually hit home.

Cormega (artist, Queensbridge): That's taking you into turmoil and life in the urban communities. And to this day, I think that's one of the best-written rap songs in history.

Dupré "DoItAll" Kelly (artist, Lords of the Underground): We didn't recognize the power of it being a mainstream thing. We did understand that it brought our communities together. We did understand that it gave us a voice. When you hear people like Melle Mel with "The Message," written by Duke Bootee and Melle Mel, it was a way of sending messages to our culture. We knew that the mainstream—disco, R&B, jazz—we weren't going to get those same type of mainstream success with radio, so we took the best part and turned nothing into something.

Afrika Baby Bam (artist, producer, Jungle Brothers): That record still works to this day. That one just put the smack down. It's so real. You can't argue with it. You can't say you don't understand, even though it comes from one person's situation, from one person's neighborhood. The whole world should be able to relate to that. And they did. So Melle Mel was the first dude I heard that could go party battle and be socially conscious.

Duke Bootee (producer, Sugar Hill): Mel had a way of telling the truth. He'd catch you very unsuspecting. I'll give you an example. At one point, Reverend [Al] Sharpton had come over, I think with James Brown or somebody, and he was talking about leadership. Mel looked at him and said, "If you're as big a leader as you thought, you would've been shot by now." Mel would just say shit.

DMC (artist, Run-DMC): "The Message" came out, everybody started making message records. But it wasn't until later that individual personalities depicted how the story would be told. "Mind Playing Tricks on Me" [by the Geto Boys] was a baby of "The Message." All of [Kool] G Rap's music.

Duke Bootee (producer, Sugar Hill): It's honest and it strikes a chord. And it tells a story that people are going through. As a producer, having done a lot of records, it's got to be the right song with the right act with the right label at the right time. That's what makes records big.

Kool Moe Dee (artist, Treacherous Three): We are living in a culture that is money over humanity at every turn. Once hip-hop became a business, we completely lost the social aspect that we had. I got the first taste of it when Melle Mel came out with "The Message." And I saw the impact. At some point we wanted to effect social change, and I still think there's a side of us as African Americans that absolutely want to be told something, to be motivated to move socially.

04 A REAL MIX

New York City
1979–1983

By the early 1980s, through a smattering of songs like "Rapper's Delight," more people were becoming aware of the burgeoning genre emerging from the Bronx. But few living outside of the Bronx—as well as pockets of Manhattan, Brooklyn, and Queens—had seen hip-hop music performed live. That started changing once Fab 5 Freddy, born Fred Brathwaite, began playing a key role in connecting hip-hop with downtown Manhattan's music and art scene.

Growing up in Brooklyn, Fab 5 Freddy was a member of the Fabulous 5, a graffiti group that included Lee Quiñones and was known for affixing subway trains with colorful murals. In 1979, *The Village Voice* featured Fab 5 Freddy and Quiñones in a tiny article where they pitched their artistic services and offered a phone number. Fab 5 Freddy collaborated with Michael Holman in fashioning 1979's Canal Zone Party, which displayed the elements of hip-hop for the downtown scene and included Jean-Michel Basquiat (then part of the graffiti duo SAMO), who became one of the most influential artists of all time.

Figures like Afrika Bambaataa and the Zulu Nation and the Funky 4 + 1 started migrating to downtown Manhattan, ingratiating themselves at landmark venues like the Ritz, the Mudd Club, Negril, and the Roxy (the last two run by Kool Lady Blue). Fab 5 Freddy was able to connect hip-hop acts with the club owners and bookers, and helped conceive—as well as starred in—Charlie Ahearn's *Wild Style,* a seminal 1982 film that recorded hip-hop in its authentic infancy.

Michael Holman (journalist/filmmaker/creator, *Graffiti Rock*): Fab 5 Freddy is my first introduction to hip-hop. He was the one who turned me on to the game. I met him through an article that was in *The Village Voice* about this graffiti crew called the Fabulous 5 [that] would come to your place of business or your home and do giant graffiti burners for a fee. Providing this service was revolutionary. At this stage, graffiti was still pretty much relegated to illegal vandalism, namely on trains.

So I called him up and invited him over, and now Freddy and I and my friend Stan Peskett, who's from London, an artist, would hang out on the weekend, talking art, and we came up with a plan to have a party for the Fabulous 5, in which we would invite all the downtown art scene, and everybody came, including Jean-Michel Basquiat. We didn't know who he was, and we found out that night at that party that he was one half of SAMO [with Al Diaz].

Then Freddy would bring Bambaataa down to the Mudd Club to perform, and from that moment on, I became in my own right a hip-hop pioneer, impresario, bringing hip-hop artists downtown, setting up performances, setting up events like Freddy. But you have to also give [photographer and videographer] Henry Chalfant respect and credit for bringing hip-hop artists downtown, as well as Charlie Ahearn and some other early downtown people who were involved with exposing hip-hop artists to the rest of the world.

MC Sha-Rock (Funky 4 + 1): We were the major group that took hip-hop around to the places like the Mudd Club or the Ritz, where the Beastie Boys used to come watch us. So we knew that we had touched down on something different, because what the Funky 4 did is we combined punk rock and hip-hop together as MCs. That's what we did for hip-hop.

Michael Holman (journalist/filmmaker/creator, *Graffiti Rock*): So, at that gig in '81 for Bow Wow Wow, Ruza Blue [also known as Kool Lady Blue] knew Malcolm McLaren. Kosmo Vinyl, who was the manager of the

Clash, he was given Thursday night at a little club in the East Village called Negril, a Jamaican reggae club, to do whatever he wanted. He's too busy, so he gives it to Ruza Blue. She sees my hip-hop revue opening up for Bow Wow Wow and asked me to bring that to her club at Negril. Now, for the first time, there is a hip-hop club where all the elements of hip-hop—writing, dancing, turntablism, and spitting rhymes—happens. Arguably, it's the first hip-hop club in history for that reason, Negril.

THE ROXY EXPANDED on the scene that had started at Club Negril, enabling an inclusive environment that included those from all colors and musical backgrounds. Pioneering DJs like Afrika Bambaataa, Afrika Islam, and Grand Mixer DXT made the journey from the Bronx to West Eighteenth Street to rock the roller skating rink–turned–club, where artists like Madonna, LL Cool J, and Run-DMC performed before they were household names.

Monica Lynch (A&R, Tommy Boy Records): You already had places like Negril where Kool Lady Blue was presenting Freddy and emerging hip-hop talent from uptown. There was already an uptown-meets-downtown vibe. The same thing at the Mudd Club, the same thing at Danceteria, the same thing at Roxy.

A lot of those big DJs were getting their vinyls downtown, but so was Afrika Bambaataa. They'd get imports from overseas, as well as hip-hop records and whatever the hot dance tracks were in the post-disco years of the early '80s, [which] were, to me, a golden era in New York, just because it was a real mix of all these sorts of nascent cultures coming together and vibing with each other.

Afrika Islam (DJ, producer): It just seemed like a natural progression, because I was versed in those records because of Bambaataa. Bambaataa was playing the Clash. He had played the Beatles. We had this in our repertoire. That's one of the results of having all of those crates of records.

Dante Ross (A&R, producer): If you went to the Roxy, you learned how to do the Smurf [dance] pretty quickly. Another thing was that the mix of all different cultures—Black, white, hip-hop, new wave—the cultural exchange that was going on. All the colors, creeds, races, shapes, and sizes of this one group of people that were all grooving to this one kind of music.

Afrika Islam (DJ, producer): It was freedom. Musical freedom, no segregation, no color lines. Rich, poor. Bianca Jagger to Andy Warhol to the Rock Steady Crew to Grandmaster Flash to Hall & Oates to Herbie Hancock to Madonna to Afrika Islam. Kool Lady Blue put together a melting pot.

Dante Ross (A&R, producer): It was a living example in that time period of cultural exchange at the highest level I may have ever seen—at least in a musical/cultural exchange. Unfortunately, I feel like Black people get shortchanged. They got skinny pants and opiates. White people got all this fucking amazing culture.

A PARTICIPANT IN that cultural exchange, Debbie Harry strung together a number of hits as the new wave lead vocalist for Blondie. In the late 1970s, Harry and Chris Stein, Blondie's cofounder and guitarist, became friends with Fab 5 Freddy and Grandmaster Flash, among other early hip-hop pioneers.

Harry vowed to shout out Grandmaster Flash in a future song, which resulted in 1981's genre-bending "Rapture." The song mixed elements of disco and punk and featured an extended rap verse from Harry, where she shouted out foundational hip-hop figures who, to that point, were unknown outside of New York City.

Fab 5 Freddy, Lee Quiñones, and Jean-Michel Basquiat, subbing for Grandmaster Flash on the turntables, all made appearances in the song's video, which became the first rap song to top the Billboard singles chart.

Michael Holman (journalist/filmmaker/creator, *Graffiti Rock*): I always had one foot in the uptown world of hip-hop and I always had one foot in the downtown world, new wave, art world, Mudd Club. Fab 5 Freddy was that way. He was involved in avant-garde downtown as much as he was in the uptown world. Vincent Gallo was. Debi Mazar was. There were a lot of people who straddled those two universes, people like David Bowie, Andy Warhol, Johnny Lydon from the Sex Pistols.

So, when ["Rapture"] came out, it had Debbie Harry from Blondie, who was just a part of the downtown scene. When she came out with this record that shouted out Freddy, and that had a video that had Basquiat in it, it just felt like an everyday thing. I didn't think of it in terms of its global impact. Because we were the cool kids. It was no surprise to us, and later on it started to dawn on us, *Oh, yeah, that's a big hit.*

I'm willing to wager that if hip-hop had depended only on the Sugarhill Gang's breakout song, and it had not come downtown and experienced the cultural and media embrace and explosion, it would not have happened the way it did. What put rap music on the map was when the culture was encapsulated as a multifaceted diamond of dance, writing, song, music, lyrics, visuals, graffiti, and then presented to the world.

DEBBIE HARRY WAS scheduled to host and perform on *Saturday Night Live* for Valentine's Day, 1981. The show allowed her to pick a guest to perform with her. Harry, with Blondie guitarist Chris Stein, asked the Funky 4 + 1 to perform their single "That's the Joint." Their inclusion marked the first time that a hip-hop group had performed on live national television, offering a wide audience a vibrant introduction to what young New Yorkers had originated.

MC Sha-Rock (Funky 4 + 1): We were the first [hip-hop] group on national television, *Saturday Night Live.* We knew that we were already celebrities in New York City. We knew that our friends and family were sitting at home watching. But I did not know at the time, as the first female MC and a founding member of the culture, that we were making history.

AMONG THE TRIUMVIRATE of founding DJs—Afrika Bambaataa, DJ Kool Herc, and Grandmaster Flash—Bambaataa had the most impact upon hip-hop music's transition to vinyl. In the early 1980s, he signed a singles deal with Tom Silverman, publisher of the biweekly *Dance Music Report,* who had created Tommy Boy Music with a loan from his parents.

The deal led to the timeless "Jazzy Sensation," which featured Bambaataa with the Jazzy Five and an overhauled chorus of Gwen McCrae's "Funky Sensation." It was a sharp departure from the direction in which Sugar Hill Records was taking hip-hop. The song's success allowed Silverman to hire another employee, Monica Lynch, who would go on to become a visionary executive.

Following "Jazzy Sensation," Bambaataa and Arthur Baker, a former club DJ in Boston, decided to make another song in honor of their appreciation of Kraftwerk, the German band and electronic music innovators. In 1982, Bambaataa joined with the Soulsonic Force and DJ Jazzy Jay for "Planet Rock." The song represented a landmark moment: Bambaataa helped introduce the Roland TR-808 drum machine to hip-hop, thus melding hip-hop with electronic music. The dynamic, futuristic sound opened new horizons for the young genre.

The success of "Planet Rock" allowed Tommy Boy Records to assert itself as one of hip-hop's earliest independent labels. Tommy Boy later partnered with Warner Bros. Records, and signed influential and groundbreaking artists and groups like Stetsasonic, Queen Latifah, Coolio, De La Soul, and Digital Underground.

Afrika Islam (DJ, producer): Bambaataa took it from Kraftwerk—Germans, who look like neo-Nazis, ain't got no funky shit in their body at all, no soul at all—and adapted it in the Bronx, where it's completely the opposite. And then, for it to be regurgitated, along with the funkiness of Bambaataa and the beats that were put down, which was more of soca, calypso beat, [the] drumbeat that's put under it, and then the technology from [guitarist and synthesizer player] John Robie and Arthur Baker putting it together, then you had the minds that came together to put out something new. Technology meets creativity.

"Planet Rock" is a hodgepodge between [Kraftwerk's] "Numbers" and a calypso beat. And then with the greatness of the Soulsonic Force doing the rhyme style that they did, Mr. Biggs, Pow Wow, and G.L.O.B.E. putting it together, that's what made it a complete thing.

Monica Lynch (A&R, Tommy Boy Records): It was about March of '82 that I accompanied Tom [Silverman] over to WHBI's studio on Riverside Drive, which is where [Mr.] Magic and Marley [Marl] were doing their hip-hop show. We delivered the plate of "Planet Rock" and as soon as it got played on Magic's show, there was just something you felt. I think it was even more significant back then, because people were on the street with their boom boxes. They were driving in cars with their windows down, the radio was blasting. It just wafted. It started getting played in all the right clubs.

Muhammad Islam (security manager, A Tribe Called Quest): It gave life to more than just hip-hop. "Planet Rock" also gave life to electric funk. It was punk rockish, hip-hoppish, electric funk, so we was spreading through all the genres that were what we would consider underground at that time.

Monica Lynch (A&R, Tommy Boy Records): It was the first huge hit at Tommy Boy, and all of a sudden we were getting calls from all over the country for orders of this record in markets where we had never had distribution. It really exploded.

Afrika Baby Bam (artist, producer, Jungle Brothers): A lot of the music back then had a futuristic sound to it. It was like, "Okay, we got these drum machines and we got these synth sounds and we got special effects like an echo chamber." That was the biggest part of the sound. "Planet Rock" represented that to the fullest. Plus, it had a socially conscious message, which I think, apart from Melle Mel's "The Message," other records didn't have that. This was like a spiritually conscious record. So that just went with the whole mode of what youths were going in at the time with breakdancing and popping and locking. Everything was futuristic.

A YOUNG FILMMAKER named Charlie Ahearn screened his debut film, *The Deadly Art of Survival,* at 1980's seminal art exhibit, the Times Square Show. During the exhibit, Ahearn met Fab 5 Freddy and the two concocted the seeds of *Wild Style.*

In the film, Ahearn sought to show all the branches of hip-hop—graffiti, DJing, MCing, and b-boying. He fought for Lee Quiñones and Lady Pink, leading graffiti artists, to have large parts, while Fab 5 Freddy played a significant role as the hip-hop artist and club promoter Phade.

The film was released in the fall of 1982. Over the years, it developed a large cult following as a time capsule that carefully and artfully documented hip-hop's beginnings.

Charlie Ahearn (director, *Wild Style*): It's like this movie was pent-up inside of me waiting to be made. And bringing Lee to the Times Square Show to do this mural was going to be proof of coupon. I gave him fifty dollars to buy spray paint, and they did this mural in about three hours in broad daylight in Times Square with no permission from anyone. The police seemed to ignore us.

And the most amazing thing was, I had brought Fred and Lee to this place in the Bronx that was a tiny amphitheater with a stage, and I brought Lee up there to show him some retaining walls on the side, and I said, "You can spray-paint something on these retaining walls, and this will be the climax of the movie."

And Lee said, "I've got to show you something that I think you're going to like," and he brought me to the amphitheater which was in the far Lower East Side, and he said, "This is where I used to play when I was a child, and there'd be kids shooting up drugs here and I practiced graffiti on this building here."

And the amphitheater was so vast. It could easily hold two thousand people. As soon as I saw it, I said, "This is it. This is going to be the end of the movie."

THE FILM MADE up for a thin plotline by providing something that resembled more of a documentary than a dramatic feature film. *Wild Style* excelled in capturing the hip-hop pioneers in their true environment before anyone had a clue about the gargantuan business the music would become. *Wild Style* featured Grandmaster Flash performing in his kitchen; the true rivalry between the Cold Crush Brothers and the Fantastic Five, depicted simultaneously through a basketball game and an MC battle; and Lil Rodney C and K.K. Rockwell trading rhymes on a stoop.

Charlie Ahearn (director, *Wild Style*): I was very close to Grandmaster Caz, and Caz invited me to come up to his house and he brought me up to his little room. And he pulled out this stack of those schoolbooks that had those black-and-white marbly covers. He spread them out on his bed, and each page was a song. He had gorgeous penmanship, and he wrote in each page the complete rhyme that he was thinking of, which indicated that that's how MCs worked—that they worked on it and worked on it, and then wrote it down after the fact, when it was complete. And I thought that was such a beautiful way to make poetry. And we were right next to the basketball court where he used to go to practice his rhymes. I'm like, *This is the movie right here.*

And I was later at West Fourth Street one time, and that's probably one of the best streetball game spots in all of New York. And there was a DJ on the other side of the court practicing records, and that combined with this whole thing of Grandmaster Caz writing his rhymes while he's playing basketball, it was maybe one of my favorite inspirations of making the film.

DJ Charlie Chase (Cold Crush Brothers): Our role in *Wild Style* was dope. Charlie Ahearn took the concept of the battle and also did capitalize on the fact that we were rivals with [Grand Wizzard] Theodore and them. He took that, and instead of putting it as a club thing, he took it to a sport thing, where people could associate with it better. It was just well-thought-out, where now you got all of us going head-to-head against each other. We're actually barking off what we feel about us or the next motherfucker before we actually take it to the fucking court.

DJ Mister Cee (producer): I became a fan of Flash and [Grand Mixer] DXT once I watched the movie *Wild Style*. When I saw Flash cutting up "Mardi Gras" in his kitchen with Fab 5 Freddy watching, I was just amazed. Same thing with DXT. He was cutting up "Good Times" at the end of the movie. That's a moment that I'll never ever forget.

CHARLIE AHEARN'S VISION of closing the film at the amphitheater in East River Park came to fruition in a fashion true to hip-hop. Ahearn never asked for permission or obtained a permit to hold a massive outdoor concert, which was punctuated by performances by Busy Bee Starski, Kool Moe Dee, and others.

Charlie Ahearn (director, *Wild Style*): Special K [of the Treacherous Three], who I love, he jumped off the bus as we were going down to the amphitheater because he had to speak to his girlfriend. And I said, "But you have to come down to be in the show," and he said, "Don't worry. I know where it is. I'll be there."

And when he didn't show up, it sort of pissed me off, because on the flyer they were the headliners. And in a way, they could've been the headliners for the movie. I did love them as a group. And of course, they were all super talented.

So I basically said, "You guys can perform, but we're not running cameras on you," which is so fucking cheap and stupid to say. Kool Moe Dee was fuming on stage, and he was watching Busy Bee, and you could see him like, *Man, I could crush this guy,* with his arms folded. And then it was getting late in the film. You could see that the party was almost over, and he just grabbed a microphone and started pogo-ing across the stage, saying "Jump, jump!" And I think his attitude of like, *I'm going to get mine* was infectious, because as soon as he started to do that, everyone else poured right out onto the front of the stage to get their attention. And it was absolutely hip-hop chaos, which was heaven for the film.

WILD STYLE PLAYED a prominent role in hip-hop's international expansion. The film premiered in Japan in 1983 before it opened in New York. Nearly forty members of the cast and crew traveled to Tokyo for a series of exhibitions to promote the film and showcase their talents.

Other hip-hop-centric films, like *Beat Street* and *Breakin',* soon followed *Wild Style*. But no other early film so closely captured hip-hop's early beginnings.

DJ Charlie Chase (Cold Crush Brothers): We're in Tokyo. We had already done major TV, all this kind of shit. This kid walks up, he's got a boom box—didn't speak a fucking drop of English—and he's got a fucking Cold Crush tape in his box. He's rocking for us. That fucked up my mind, the fact that this non–English speaking motherfucker was rhyming all the rhymes on the tape. Fucking bananas.

Monie Love (artist, London): [Hip-hop] was just something brand-new. As a kid growing up in the inner city in London, it was refreshing. It really first came along in the form of videotapes that people had gotten ahold of and movies like *Wild Style*. So those were the first visuals that we got of breaking and b-boy culture. That's really what came first, before the music. So we all became breakers, poppers, lockers. We all dived into the dance form of hip-hop culture.

Grandmaster Caz (Cold Crush Brothers): *Wild Style* sort of validated hip-hop in the eyes of a lot of people. We were never really encouraged to do hip-hop, except for like-minded youth like us that were down with us as well. So *Wild Style*, people coming from another place, another culture, embracing ours, kind of validated it for us. Like, "Yeah, we are doing the right thing. This is cool. This is dope. People do like this. We can get somewhere doing this."

DJ Charlie Chase (Cold Crush Brothers): *Wild Style* is the reason why hip-hop even exists around the planet. That little fuckin' one-hundred-thousand-dollar bullshit movie right there.

AS HIP-HOP SPREAD beyond New York City, the role of the MC continued gaining more prominence in the culture, an elevation accelerated through production advancements and a new crop of sophisticated lyricists.

Of hip-hop's foundational elements—DJing, MCing, breaking, and graffiti art—it was the MC who wielded the most financial marketability and viability. By the mid-1980s, with the genre's new stars on the brink of breaking through, many of hip-hop's originators found themselves with little way to capitalize on a genre they had built.

Michael Holman (journalist/filmmaker/creator, *Graffiti Rock*): The New York City Breakers, which was a [b-boy] crew I created in the process of running Negril, they were the stars of *Beat Street.* They had performed all over the world, for kings and queens and presidents. But by '88, for me anyway, and for other impresarios and for other artists in hip-hop, things started to wind down. My phone started to not ring so much, and this was true for a lot of the early cats, the Grandmaster Cazzes, the Treacherous Threes.

Joe Conzo (photographer): The crack epidemic came and pretty much wiped out a lot of us. It took out a whole generation of pioneers. But most of us bounced back and picked up where we left off.

Michael Holman (journalist/filmmaker/creator, *Graffiti Rock*): A lot of things started to wind down in '88 as the new artists like Run-DMC, and the West Coast sound and the Southern sound—when all these artists were coming, and the focus on rap, the focus on music started happening, the DJs who were the kings of hip-hop started to lose their prominence and importance unless they became producers.

05 NEVER BEEN THE SAME

New York City
1983–2000

Russell Simmons wanted to be a party promoter. Instead, his belief in hip-hop's crossover appeal helped usher the genre into popular culture and, to the chagrin of purists, revealed its ripeness for commercialization. Simmons managed Run-DMC, a groundbreaking group comprised of his younger brother, Joseph "Run" Simmons; Darryl "DMC" McDaniels; and DJ Jason "Jam Master Jay" Mizell. Run-DMC was signed to the fledgling Profile Records and their stripped-down music produced by Larry Smith, couplet trade-offs, b-boy roots, and cutting-edge fashion nearly single-handedly propelled hip-hop far from its partially inspired disco roots.

Simmons and Rick Rubin, then a twenty-one-year-old student at New York University, joined to launch Def Jam Recordings from a boutique label into one that ushered hip-hop music from the parks and the streets onto the radio and MTV. The onetime outsiders transformed the genre as Def Jam evolved into hip-hop music's preeminent label. Simmons and Rubin showcased shrewd business acumen in arranging a distribution deal with CBS Records through Columbia Records, and signed diverse and influential artists and groups who shaped hip-hop's new school, including LL Cool J, Beastie Boys, Slick Rick, and later, Public Enemy and EPMD.

Russell Simmons (cofounder, Def Jam): Joey became a DJ because he was excited about Kurtis Blow, and Davy D, I guess, was one of his inspirations. He got so good, so quick. I remember when "Good Times" first came out, he cut the "good" so fast and it just cut the air. "Good times, good times, good, goo, goo." Air, cutting back and forth.

I was like, "Oh shit." I had never seen that from nobody. Cutting air. So he then became Kurtis Blow's DJ.

Kurtis Blow (artist, producer): Joey was incredible. He was so very fast. I rank him right up there with the best. His accuracy, there's only one DJ that's better, I think, with accuracy—well, two, [DJ] Junebug and Davy DMX, and maybe Flash. But Joey, I put him up there with any of them in a battle. He was incredible.

Russell Simmons (cofounder, Def Jam): Eventually, he broke his arm. He couldn't go on the road with Kurtis.

Kurtis Blow (artist, producer): I was devastated because we had so many shows we had performed before that, and we had this routine, and it was great. We were getting ready to tear up the world, and so he's playing basketball down the block with his friend, this guy named Jason Mizell, and broke his arm. We're going on a Commodores tour, an All Platinum tour, about a hundred shows.

Russell Simmons (cofounder, Def Jam): Davy D took over. Davy D never gave that job back.

Kurtis Blow (artist, producer): When I came back from tour using Davy DMX, like three months later, Joey had started this rap group with Jason Mizell and this other kid named Darryl McDaniels called Run-DMC. I was devastated again, I was like, "What happened?" And we wanted him to be a solo artist.

DMC (artist, Run-DMC): Run came to me. We wasn't friends. We just went to the same school. He found out in eighth grade this guy, Darryl McDaniels, could write some rhymes. We started hanging out. He saw that I could DJ like Flash and I could write rhymes like Melle Mel. We just became friends. He was the son of Kurtis Blow. So he would come over all throughout the summertime and play me tapes of the shows he was going to.

He was always asking Russell, "Yo, Russell, let me make a record. Let me make a record."

Russell was like, "No, Joey. You're fucking fifteen years old. You're too fucking young." And then Run was so persistent that Russell said, "Okay, here's the deal. You show me a high school diploma, I'll let you make a record. Because if your music career doesn't work out, at least you'll have something to fall back on."

Fast-forward, Joe get his diploma. Me and Run, we teamed up. He wrote his rhymes. I wrote my rhymes. Boom. Russell let us go record "It's Like That."

Now it's time for the B-side. Originally, [producer] Larry Smith was going to do something that was very funky and R&B-ish. I said, "Nobody's making beat jams, man. You all got to make a beat jam."

"Fuck is a beat jam, D?"

"Just a fuckin' beat and you rhyming like the Cold Crush do. Just the beat and the music."

He was like, "Yo, that's a great idea."

So, Larry made the "Sucker M.C.'s" track. But I said, "Make that shit sound hard, like a Bambaataa beat. Drop it on them, one of the fucking Bam tapes. Zulu Nation tapes." So he did that.

Run goes to the booth and lays all three of his verses. And Run kept telling Russell, "Yo, let D get on this record, too. D can rhyme."

Russell was like, "No, no, no, no, no." He said, "D could write, he's creative, but he's not you, Run. He's not Kurtis Blow. He's not Hollywood. He's not Busy Bee Starski. He don't do this. He just can write really good because he's a smart motherfucker." I was a straight-A student.

So Joe convinces Russell. "Yo, just let him kick one rhyme. If you don't like it, take it off the record."

So I went in there and when Run passes me the mic, "You're drivin' big cars, get your gas from Getty." My newest rhyme was a rhyme that I wrote when I came home from high school one day and opened up the letter and I got accepted to St. John's University. I just put that rhyme down on the record. And then Russell went crazy. "Yo, this motherfucker talking about St. John's University and fuckin' chicken and collard greens."

Afrika Islam (DJ, producer): That was at the Roxy [where Run-DMC first performed "Sucker M.C.'s"]. We played it and it was right for the dance floor. When they performed, it was [like] looking at the Cold Crush—I can't say 2.0, but it was looking at the facsimile of the Cold Crush as an act. The routines, same with the Beastie Boys, were based upon the different pieces they took from hours of routines done by the Cold Crush, done by the Funky 4 + 1, done by the Furious Five.

Cory Robbins (cofounder, Profile Records): We were putting out rap records and we had a little office on Fifty-seventh Street. And [Russell Simmons] started coming around and he started bringing tapes with him of things he was chopping, and they were pretty good, and we wound up signing Run-DMC.

"It's Like That" was really different, because it wasn't like all the other rap records that were out. It only had a bass and drums. It didn't have any guitar or keyboard or anything. It was really very sparse. It took a little getting used to. I played it and I said, "Alright, let me keep this overnight and I'll call you tomorrow. I want to play this some more."

I remember driving around that night with the cassette and playing it over and over again, and I got used to it and how different it was. And then I called him up the next day and made him an offer and we made a deal.

They did "Sucker M.C.'s" in the studio. We gave him two thousand dollars to make the record and they made "It's Like That." So, we put that on the same record, [and] they wound up having a double hit. Both songs became huge.

DMC (artist, Run-DMC): I never told my parents that I went and made a record. They found out I made a record when "It's Like That" and "Sucker M.C.'s" started blowing up in the streets. I had to go tell them, "Oh, Mom. Remember that night I came home at two in the morning last year? Yeah. I actually made a record."

Cory Robbins (cofounder, Profile Records): Then, after six weeks, it just exploded. I think people got used to it. All of a sudden, it was everywhere. We had three stations in New York—BLS, KISS, and KTU—and they were all playing it.

Russell Simmons (cofounder, Def Jam): Bill [Stephney] did a lot of good college work and groundwork to get records on the radio.

Bill Stephney (Bomb Squad, Def Jam): A big R&B radio station that in those years would have played Whitney Houston and Freddie Jackson and Luther Vandross and Atlantic Starr, they're not going to play our stuff. But there are college stations in that same town. Or there may be what we referred to back then as time-broker stations, stations where there are people who went and paid to become DJs on those signals, those FM signals, and have their own shows. So we'll get our music on those stations.

And then there's always the premise, an opportunity from that era of what we called street music. It's the time of the boom box, of the ghetto blaster, of young folks walking through Hollis, Queens, literally with living room stereo systems held by their hand. You had a boom box, there were thirty, forty other people listening to it because that's how loud and booming it was.

So, if you figured out a way to get your music to those kids, you were in heavy rotation on the street radio. And we were lucky enough to be young and connected to the culture where it was just second nature. As Chuck [D] said, we just went around them.

Russell Simmons (cofounder, Def Jam): The only other place you might get [your record] played would be in Danceteria or the Mudd Club, and the World and the Ritz, because punk rockers really gave us our press. They had the Critics Poll at *The Village Voice*. Rap records would flood those year-end polls. They loved hip-hop like it was the new punk rock. They gave us our due, more than we would have ever expected to get from anywhere, and certainly nobody Black would ever think about us. They didn't like it because they knew it smelled like the hood. Those niggas escaped the hood. They like their polish.

Paris (artist, producer, San Francisco): There was a kind of haughty, holier-than-thou attitude that they had toward hip-hop. That's always the case when it's something that's a radical departure from what people have come to expect. That's what I had come to expect from the older Black generation anyways.

Russell Simmons (cofounder, Def Jam): You realize that all these cultural phenomena—jazz, blues, rock and roll—[spring from] just [being] sick of white people telling us what to play. And they'd destroyed what we built, so now we start to build something new. That's the experiences of blues and what they did to it, and jazz and what they did to it, and R&B and what they turned it into—pop music.

DMC (artist, Run-DMC): I got tired of that record ["It's Like That"/"Sucker M.C.'s"] six months after it dropped, and it's my record. Everywhere I went, I would hear it. And I'm talking about all day, twenty-four hours, somebody's coming by in the car with their system on. Somebody with a boom box, it's all over the radio.

The thing that made Run-DMC so successful is we did what we was doing before we [knew we] was doing it. The reason why our records worked—even "Tricky"—"Tricky" is not a rap rock song. "Tricky" is a rhyme routine that we learned from Treacherous Three, Cold Crush, and the Force MCs. The thing that was taught to us: You take a beat, you take the beat jam, and you say some dope rhyme, and you find a melody, instead of taking the actual song.

Dante Ross (A&R, producer): Early rap music, it had like a disco feel to it. Musically, it had the aesthetic of Black punk rock, do-it-yourself music. I think a culmination of that was Run-DMC. They're yelling at you and there's no music, just drums, a stab and yelling. Rapping super-aggressive. It was so punk rock to me. It was the record that made me go, "Punk rock's over. This is so much more punk than punk."

Rahiem (Grandmaster Flash and the Furious Five): The issue that Bronx MCs had with Run-DMC, initially, was their style. For lack of a better term, their style was extremely elementary. And so, to us, they simplified MCing; and to us, they gave the secret away.

DJ Charlie Chase (Cold Crush Brothers): There were a lot of people already emulating us. We were another crew just doing what we was doing. We didn't know that the Cold Crush influence was that strong.

[Run DMC] were mad, mad cool with us. To be honest, we weren't really receptive of them. It wasn't because it was them. We just weren't very receptive with anybody because we took everything really fucking seriously, to the point where we're a motherfuckin' battle crew. So we kind of treated them—not bad—but we just weren't very friendly with them.

DMC (artist, Run-DMC): When Run put me in the group, I knew we had to be serious with this shit, especially after "Sucker M.C.'s" was tearing the streets up. I said, "Yo, if we ain't bringing it like the Cold Crush, I'm not doing this shit." Even if we're making a record that's going on the radio—that's why I think our music was so loved—it's got to be something that we're doing in the park. We learned a lot from Cold Crush, Furious Five, and the Zulu Nation, Soulsonic Force.

Grandmaster Caz (Cold Crush Brothers): I wasn't impressed by Run-DMC, but I was impressed by the fact that they were the next generation. What happened was that we took hip-hop in a direction that was kind of getting away from hip-hop. The Furious Five, because of their early success, started going on tours with rock stars, with Cameo and Rick James and all of these guys, and they had to have that rock star mentality.

We kind of followed suit, but it was more local. We did what the Furious Five were out there doing on tour. They stepped up the game for what MCs are supposed to do, so when they left that void, it was up to the next set of crews to step up and take their place.

DMC (artist, Run-DMC): One of the main things of Run-DMC's existence was to never let nobody forget the core essence and purpose of this hip-hop shit. It's about the DJs and MCs. That's the fucking foundation.

So, this hip-hop thing became our music. It became our voice, but it also gave us a place in the world where we felt that we could fit in.

Rahiem (Grandmaster Flash and the Furious Five): To us, Run-DMC helped white people figure out how to rap. And that was a good thing and a bad thing to us at that time. It was necessary in order to push the culture forward and develop its growth. But when you have something organic, as soon as the corporate world puts two dollars into it, it changes the nature of what that thing was forever.

Ice Cube (artist, N.W.A): "Sucker M.C.'s" was, to me, the most unique hip-hop song of the time that I had heard, because it was all drums. Wasn't a lot of music. I was just like, *That's how rap's supposed to be presented.* Raw like that. Anything Run-DMC would do, I'd get my hands on it. Those dudes were our examples on how to do it on a high level.

Bill Adler (journalist, Def Jam publicist): Run-DMC and Larry Smith, with Russell, are making records with a beat machine, a beatbox, a drum machine. That was closer to the sound of the music that you'd get in the clubs than what Sylvia [Robinson] was doing at Sugar Hill. It's much more of the moment.

And then the way the guys dressed—the Sugarhill Gang were basically disco-era guys, in terms of their attire. Grandmaster Flash and them were like refugees from Parliament-Funkadelic. Bambaataa is certainly in the lineage of George Clinton. As appealing as any of that might be, it wasn't new. Run-DMC, taking their cue from Jam Master Jay, who basically took his cue from his older brother Marvin [Thompson], ten years older, [who] was dressing like a Queens street hustler, which is stylish, cool criminal.

DMC (artist, Run-DMC): Our shit was "Man, we are not costume characters. We are what the streets are." Now, that being said, you've got to understand: The first rappers, the first DJs and MCs are the greatest DJs and MCs ever. Not Eminem, not DMC, not Chuck D, not Jay-Z. Fuck us. The greatest MCs and DJs are the first ever. Why? They were the first.

The first MCs and DJs, when they came into show business, had no MCs and DJs to look up to. They had no source to pour from except what they'd been seeing in the industry and musically and commercially all their lives—the Rolling Stones, Parliament-Funkadelic, and Rick James.

Melle Mel wore Adidas and fucking Lee jeans and nylons and Kangols. When they got into show business, they said, "Oh, we need outfits." So, who did they look to? Their idols. Up until that time, there was nobody representing the streets, styling themselves like the streets.

Bill Adler (journalist, Def Jam publicist): Run-DMC, they're wearing Stetson hats and Kangols. I can buy those down the block. They're wearing Lee jeans. Not a problem. Adidas sneakers? Well, they're a little old-fashioned now, but we're going to end up writing a song that makes them new again. You can say, in effect, sonically, Run-DMC was the punk rock of hip-hop.

Cory Robbins (cofounder, Profile Records): When I first signed them in 1983, they came to the office and we did a signing photo. They have their arms crossed in that Run-DMC stance. They weren't famous yet. They were just a couple of kids. Nobody heard of them, and they weren't on the radio yet and they pose like that. Who would do that? But they knew who they were.

Bill Adler (journalist, Def Jam publicist): The appeal of the early groups was cross-racial, cross-cultural. What Run-DMC had going for them was that they were transitioning out of an earlier era of rap, unlike, say, the Sugarhill Gang; those groups were building on their immediate predecessors, noticeably disco and funk. They're transitional in that way. Run-DMC are transitional because, in effect, they were born into rap, and I think they were seen as more native to rap, just more of the moment, more authentic, and also different.

DMC (artist, Run-DMC): We held [the original generation of hip-hop artists] in such a high place. For us, it would've been disrespectful to even dress like they dress on stage.

For us in Queens, when I was hearing the tapes, I didn't know what Bam looked like. I didn't know what MC G.L.O.B.E. looked like. All I could picture them was in some fucking Pumas or some Adidas on and some Kangols and shit like that. That was the image we wanted to bring to the stage. We made it acceptable for you to be you and still exist in show business.

WITH A HANDFUL of bona fide hits already in circulation, Cory Robbins sought to capitalize on Run-DMC's nascent popularity by releasing an entire album. The group, thinking there was little financial incentive to complete an entire album, reluctantly rounded out their self-titled debut and released it in March 1984.

Run-D.M.C. became the first hip-hop album to be certified gold, and cemented the group's status as hip-hop's new heirs. It included "Rock Box," a track produced by Larry Smith that fused rap with rock by including Eddie Martinez's guitar riff. Profile green-lit a small budget to film a music video for the song, which Steve Kahn directed at the nightclub Danceteria. The video showcased Run-DMC and Jam Master Jay in leather suits and Adidas sneakers. For years, Black artists had denounced MTV for the cable network's refusal to play Black artists. MTV had played Blondie's "Rapture," but had not put a song by a hip-hop group on regular rotation until "Rock Box."

Cory Robbins (cofounder, Profile Records): "It's Like That," "Sucker M.C.'s," "Hard Times," "Jam-Master Jay"—that's four hits already. Then I had asked them to make an album. They did not want to do it. Big arguments about that. And I said, "Give me five more songs, we got an album."

"No, rap albums don't sell."

I'm like, "Just do it. We'll sell at least thirty thousand of them. It's worth doing." So they finally did. We obviously sold, like, a million of them.

DMC (artist, Run-DMC): One of the most powerful moments for me in hip-hop: When I heard [Kool] Moe Dee and the Treacherous Three, they was doing that routine over "The Big Beat." Because when we made "Rock Box," we was trying to make Billy Squier's "Big Beat," but we didn't want to bite the actual arrangement. But it was Larry Smith who put all the bells and the music and shit and the guitars to take it to another level.

Bill Adler (journalist, Def Jam publicist): Larry Smith, he's a music lover. He kind of dipped into R&B, but he loves rock and roll as well. Run-DMC are in the studio, and they're making their album. And down the hall in another studio, there's a band playing some rock and roll and everybody's ear kind of picked up, and Larry says, "What the fuck? We can make some rock and roll, too."

So, they make "Rock Box" in 1984—not "Rap Box."

Larry said, "Blacks play rock and roll, too. We're not going to be bound by genre restrictions and we're not going to be bound by racial restrictions. We're going to make rock and roll too, because we feel it too."

Cory Robbins (cofounder, Profile Records): Larry Smith was really a great producer. I wish he was better remembered because he was a really talented guy and a great musician. And he had a few years where he was just the hottest guy around.

Bill Adler (journalist, Def Jam publicist): This might sound cynical, but to the extent that MTV was feeling some pressure to integrate, Run-DMC made it very easy for them, because they're some Black folks playing rock, and in case you don't know, it's called "Rock Box."

Russell Simmons (cofounder, Def Jam): It was hard [to get "Rock Box" on MTV]. It was a lot of begging. And Rick James opened the door for us, because he fought for us. He called them niggas all kinds of racist everything and then eventually Michael [Jackson] came in. But Michael didn't open the door, really, because he was just so big. But the idea [that] somebody could be Black and could have something culturally that matters, that door opened from when Rick James got in it.

DMC (artist, Run-DMC): When MTV came out, we didn't have MTV in Queens until, like, a year later. "Rock Box" was in hot rotation on MTV, it wasn't in Queens yet.

The record originally was nothing that Bam didn't do already, was nothing that Charlie Chase and Flash didn't do already. They were rhyming over rock records. "Tom Sawyer" by Rush, Queen, Aerosmith, Rolling Stones, and the list goes on. So the thing that made "Rock Box" do what it would do, it was just perfect timing, like the perfect storm.

MTV was getting slack even from David Bowie. He's the rock king of the world and, in the middle of his own interview on MTV, looked over and the guy just started stuttering. He said, "Why don't you play more Black people? Why are there no Black people on there?"

Another thing about us, we were safe. We wasn't "The Message." We wasn't "Planet Rock." We wasn't despair and we wasn't hope. We were just some crazy "What the fuck? What are these motherfuckers doing?"

That's the thing that made [it] "Okay, this is safe to play, because if it don't work, it don't make MTV bad. And if it does work, it makes MTV look good."

Bill Adler (journalist, Def Jam publicist): They start to play it, and not only does it benefit Run-DMC, of course, but it's huge for MTV.

Cory Robbins (cofounder, Profile Records): By the second album, the *King of Rock* album, I think we realized that white people were buying the album too. 'Cause we were getting a lot of reports from record stores. But we weren't getting pop airplay. It was just white kids were finding it. But then the third album, then we knew, because then "Walk This Way" was on every Top 40 and rock station.

Dante Ross (A&R, producer): Bad Brains and Run-DMC were my two favorite groups. Totally disconnected musically, but the same end result: cathartic explosion. And for a disenfranchised, young, working-class white kid, those were things I needed. I was angry and aggressive and full of energy and creative and trying to figure it out, and that was what those bands both symbolized.

Russell opened the door for Run-DMC to take over white America. And now [with Beastie Boys], white America had their own white boys. And he knew that that shit was going to go big.

Bill Adler (journalist, Def Jam publicist): Russell's idea was, "We do not have to crossover. We're going to pull the mainstream in our direction. We're going to produce recordings that are full-strength rap, and we have enough faith in the intrinsic power of this music to communicate directly and effectively with listeners, that we're just going to let it be."

We're going to take the creative expressions of this particular community, and we're going to introduce it uncut, uncompromised, to the listening public. We believe: (a) that's the respectful thing to do vis-à-vis the culture, and (b) it's going to end up more popular that way, not less popular.

Ann Carli (senior VP, Jive Records): The artists themselves didn't take it as a fad. And I'm so grateful for that time when nobody even knew what it was going to be. I think there are people that get into hip-hop now that see it as a good way to make money, but back then it was about saying something. Because we couldn't get records on radio.

I worked with Russell Simmons because he managed some of our groups, and if you were involved in hip-hop, you knew Russell. He drew those comparisons to rock and roll, punk rock, heavy metal. Like he always said, "Don't try to narrow-cast this form. This is teenage music. This is about rebellion."

Dante Ross (A&R, producer): He opened that door with Run-DMC "Rock Box" and fucking slammed the Mack truck through. And white America's never been the same.

AARON FUCHS, A former journalist who started Tuff City Records and secured a short-lived distribution deal with CBS Associated Records, recalled advising Rick Rubin to seek out Russell Simmons to help with his publicity efforts. Rubin had started Def Jam Recordings from his New York University dorm room, producing T La Rock & Jazzy Jay's "It's Yours."

Stories vary on when Rubin and Simmons initially met. Most pinpoint a party for the pilot of Michael Holman's *Graffiti Rock*. Their business partnership would transform not only hip-hop, but the entire music industry.

Cormega (artist, Queensbridge): One of the songs that really made me think, *Wow, this is amazing,* like when I really learned the difference between rap and lyrics, is unsung hero T La Rock. He was a big influence on people's styles. He was the first single released on Def Jam and after that came LL, but even if you listen to some of LL, you can see that T La Rock was an influence on him as well. That other rap was fun rap. But this is like you could be smart and articulate in music. This is a whole other level.

Aaron Fuchs (president, Tuff City Records): We both used to work out of Power Play [Studios]. I was a baby boomer. He was in his twenties. I had some gravitas, and he was very aggressive in wanting to learn in the business. That's what I did. I did it for Rick, really. I did more running around with Russell back then. I just thought that because they were such different kinds of personalities, that there'd be a synergy. Each had a value. Russell was real, real aggressive and tremendous in thinking on his feet. Rick was more inside. I saw the way he was taking to the studio.

Russell Simmons (cofounder, Def Jam): Danceteria and the Mudd Club, the World, the Ritz, and all the punk rock clubs when we were downtown. That's where Madonna came from. That's where I found the Beastie Boys and Rick Rubin, in that world.

Bill Adler (journalist, Def Jam publicist): Russell Simmons, what he always had going for him, is huge charisma and intelligence and creativity. In any given gathering, Russell was going to be the most interesting person in the room. He was magnetic.

Also, he's obviously a very early champion of rap music. He understood and appreciated it not just as music, but also he understood its sociology and its history. His father, and this is probably true of his mom too, his father was an activist in the civil rights movement in the '6os, when Russ is growing up. So he's going to move around in the world with a sense of Black pride. And also, when he went to college, he studied sociology. So, he had a sociological perspective on rap. That led him to respect this thing called hip-hop, not just as a musical form, but as an expression of a community. Young folks of color made something new, and he was going to champion it and do what he could also to protect it—he and Rick.

Rick is not a Black man. But he was a fan of rap music. As an aspiring record producer, he thought there was a gulf between the excitement of a rap on record versus the excitement of live rap. Rick's whole idea was, *Might there be a way for us to capture the excitement of live rap on a record?* Rick believed that rap was rock. It was all rock to him.

Russell Simmons (cofounder, Def Jam): Rick liked rock and roll. He heard "Rock Box," one of the things that attracted him to me and to our music, and "King of Rock." When we made *Raising Hell* [Run-DMC's third album] together, it was a meeting of the minds. We were kids. We weren't businesspeople, even though we had to do business.

ADAM "AD-ROCK" HOROVITZ, Adam "MCA" Yauch, and Mike "Mike D" Diamond were products of the same diverse downtown music scene that had inspired Rick Rubin. Beastie Boys were hardcore punk rockers influenced by hip-hop's emergence. Rubin served as an early DJ for the group, which released its debut single, 1983's "Cooky Puss," through Rat Cage Records.

Beastie Boys were among Def Jam's first signees, and Rubin served as the producer of 1984's "Rock Hard." The group, at that time, revolved around juvenile antics and brash lyrics. They gained a name touring with Madonna in 1985, leading to their debut album, *Licensed to III*.

The Rubin-produced album melded rock with hip-hop. The single "(You Gotta) Fight for Your Right (to Party!)" became one of the country's most requested songs. *Licensed to III* was the first hip-hop album to top the Billboard charts, a reflection of Def Jam's quickly widening influence and the ability for a white rap group to gain mainstream marketability.

Russell Simmons (cofounder, Def Jam): Meeting the Beastie Boys, who so much wanted to be rap, I saw 'em the same, but I saw the cultural elements as very different. The Beastie Boys came to me with red, shiny Puma sweatsuits and red Pumas, trying to be Run-DMC, or their own version. They were inspired. But then I saw them as the Young and the Useless, their punk rock band, and I saw them dressed as the Beastie Boys, and I thought, *There you are. That's you, nigga.*

The same as dressing Run-DMC and Jay. It was the Hollis Avenue uniform when they put that leather suit on and the little hat and the shell toes. They were just hood uniforms. The Beastie Boys' uniform was holey jeans and dirty sneakers.

They had an affinity for hip-hop, Black music. But they also had an affinity for the alternative music they played. I think by dressing them that way, we gave them freedom to actually be themselves and take all the elements that inspired them and make their career what it became.

Robert "Rocky" Ford (journalist, producer): They used to ride across the Brooklyn Bridge on skateboards to get to our office.

Bill Adler (journalist, Def Jam publicist): What [Russell Simmons] said was, "We're going to break them Black and cross them over white."

Russell Simmons (cofounder, Def Jam): They made "Hold It Now, Hit It." Adam Yauch made that by himself. That's one of the best records ever made.

Dante Ross (A&R, producer): I saw them perform at the Apollo and win over a Black audience and I knew it was on. When "Hold It Now, Hit It" came out, I was like, "Oh, they got it." They paid enough dues doing punk rock downtown shows and getting booed by Black audiences. I had no doubt in my mind after I saw them in the Apollo Theater do two shows with Run-DMC, they were going to be famous. It was a confirmation that all the stuff that we thought, was right.

Bill Adler (journalist, Def Jam publicist): They put up their first singles in the fall of '84. Come summer of '85, they're still putting out singles. Madonna's manager goes to Russell and says, "We want Run-DMC to open for Madonna on her *Like a Virgin* tour."

Russ says, "Sorry. Run-DMC's too big. They're headliners now. They're not opening for anybody. But I've got this other band, the Beastie Boys, maybe you might want them."

She had played with them downtown. She knew them a little bit. So she said, "Okay."

It's to Madonna's credit that she let it happen, but then again, it's not a threat to her. It's not some slightly younger female artist who's going to be the next Madonna. These are three bratty white boys who jump on stage grabbing their crotch.

Then come early '87, they put out the video and the single for "Fight for Your Right" and it's a gigantic pop hit. What they would say afterwards is they did it as sort of a joke. They were comedians.

First, they were very excited this record is doing so well and they're playing to bigger and bigger crowds. But then they start to see kids in the front row, a bunch of beer-swilling white guys. It's like [Brett] Kavanaugh and his fraternity brothers at a Beastie Boys show and they're just buffoons and they've embraced this song—and the Beasties, who are some New York hipsters, are appalled. They can't fucking believe it. So they start to have second thoughts about their whole career, even in the middle of this success of "Fight for Your Right."

BEYOND KURTIS BLOW, hip-hop had yet to birth many solo stars. That changed when the demo of a brash kid from Queens made its way to Rick Rubin's dorm. Born James Todd Smith, LL Cool J signed to Def Jam Recordings.

In 1984, the boastful teenager recorded a forceful 12-inch single, "I Need a Beat," which sold well, paving the way for his debut album, 1985's *Radio*. The platinum-selling album solidified LL Cool J as a new breed of dynamic hip-hop superstar, and Rubin as a minimalist marquee producer.

In 1987, LL Cool J released his second album, *Bigger and Deffer*. The L.A. Posse produced the second single, "I Need Love," providing one of hip-hop's first love ballads and reflecting a vulnerability seldom seen to that point from hip-hop artists.

Robert "Rocky" Ford (journalist, producer): I remember when LL Cool J was a young boy. All he wanted to do was rap and look cool. Obviously, he did that.

Bill Stephney (Bomb Squad, Def Jam): When I heard "I Need a Beat," he sounded like Run to me. LL was, at that point, sixteen years old;

his command of the language was just insane. There's an extended remix of "Rock the Bells" that he made with Rick that is just a tour de force. I think he may have been sixteen or seventeen when he did the remix. Just his command of the dictionary. So LL, to me, is underrated. LL did stuff, not only in the studio; there's a whole component that we miss in terms of live performing and MCing and the ability to command a stage and a crowd.

Al Kapone (artist, Memphis): LL to me, his aggressive energy, it embodied how I felt as a youth. It was that aggressive *I'm the best, and I'm gonna spit that aggression and represent this youthful vibe.* That's what captivated me with LL, it was just that youthful, no-holds-barred energy.

Murs (artist, Los Angeles): The fact he dissed Oreos [in "I'm Bad"] was the craziest shit in the world. As a kid, that appealed. He said, "So forget Oreos, eat Cool J cookies." We couldn't afford Oreos; I never had an Oreo until I was an adult. They were like ninety-nine cents then. *This guy was shitting on this fucking Ferrari of cookies? He must be the fucking greatest guy ever.*

Russell Simmons (cofounder, Def Jam): Rick had a strong love for alternative rock and roll, but I liked the alternative side of hip-hop equally as much as he did, I would say.

Rick will tell you today that he liked [LL Cool J's] "I Need Love."

He didn't like "I Need Love."

I'll go to my grave thinking it kind of broke his heart. He wanted LL to wait for him to record. Because he was busy, just like I was busy. We were making our childhood fantasies [come true]. Rick made a bunch of rock and roll records and had to pay attention to the shop on top of it. I got the L.A. Posse and made LL's second album. "I Need Love," I understood it. It was LL Cool J's honest expression.

Lady B (artist, radio DJ, Philadelphia): Russell was so eager to get his stuff on the air, he would literally come to Philly with a cassette, like, "Play this." Those were such great days. We just had so much freedom and creativity and it was just such a pleasure to be there when, "Should LL do a slow song? Is hip-hop ready for a love song?"

"Yeah, let's do it."

RUSSELL SIMMONS ORIGINALLY did not know what, if anything, to make of Lyor Cohen. Cohen, whose parents had immigrated from Israel, was born in New York and grew up in Los Angeles. He promoted his own shows in Los Angeles and booked Run-DMC to perform at the Mix Club in Hollywood in 1984. Through either a mix-up in communication or a forgotten promise, a twenty-four-year-old Cohen flew to New York shortly after, expecting a job from Simmons at Rush Artist Management (which steered the careers of many of hip-hop's earliest stars, like Whodini, Run-DMC, and Jimmy Spicer). Simmons did not remember having made the offer, but kept Cohen around once he ingratiated himself with Run-DMC, becoming the group's road manager.

Eventually, Cohen brokered a landmark deal for Run-DMC. Cohen ensured that executives from Adidas, the German athletic apparel company, were in attendance when Run-DMC performed "My Adidas," the group's lead single from 1986's *Raising Hell.* The executives took note of the many raised shoes in the air, and an endorsement contract followed shortly after, the first of many partnerships between hip-hop and corporate entities.

Cohen advanced to play a pivotal role at Def Jam. When Simmons and Rick Rubin separated in 1988, Rubin formed Def American Recordings and Cohen became president of Def Jam.

Russell Simmons (cofounder, Def Jam): Lyor always tells the stories, and he has different memories than me. That motherfucker.

Dante Ross (A&R, producer): Russell's good cop. Lyor's bad cop. He's Cohen the Barbarian. Russell's the guy you want to hang out with.

Russell Simmons (cofounder, Def Jam): We always tried to make inspired records that were true, something to brag about, but we were doing something good. My Adidas, where'd they go? They left Hollis Avenue. They went everywhere. "We started in the alley, now we chill in Cali." It was all Lyor, who actually got the deal.

Faith Newman (Def Jam): Being in Madison Square Garden when they performed "My Adidas" and people took off their Adidas and raised them in the air, I think that's when you knew the power of hip-hop, the power of what the future of branding is going to look like. That was a big turning point.

> **BY 1987, DEF** Jam and Rush Artist Management had moved into a building on Elizabeth Street in lower Manhattan. For the first time, Russell Simmons and Rick Rubin had space outside of Rubin's cramped dorm room. Early employees included Dave Funken-Klein, Andre Harrell, Faith Newman, and Bill Stephney, all of whom would make important impacts on hip-hop. Def Jam upheld many of its free-wheeling roots as it evolved into a conglomerate.

Bill Stephney (Bomb Squad, Def Jam): Russell and Rick get a ton of money as an advance from CBS Records, which gives them the financial wherewithal to start building their own version of the Chung King Studios that everyone worked out of.

Faith Newman (Def Jam): We were out on Elizabeth Street and the building was three floors. The second floor was this little shitty office with five desks crammed in it, or four desks for five people actually. And that was Def Jam. And then the third floor was where Rick Rubin lived. And we basically shared desks, shared phones. Bill Stephney had his own little corner in his space. And it was me, George Sommers, Dave Funken-Klein, Lindsay Williams, and Bill, and we had this closet-sized space where the accountant worked.

Bill Stephney (Bomb Squad, Def Jam): And on the other side of that floor were squatters who would not leave. They were in the building previous to Rick and Russell buying the building. They couldn't get them out. So we could not expand beyond that small space. Now, there are two additional floors, which turn out to be a duplex for Rick. And he hooked it up nicely.

Faith Newman (Def Jam): When I got there [in 1987], there was no structure to the company, businesswise. There were no agreements. There was no system worked out in terms of invoicing. It was just a mess. That's what I did for a year, was clean shit up and put systems in place and learn from lawyers, learn from other admin people at labels, how to do that stuff.

I had to get all the writers signed up with ASCAP or BMI. None of them had done that. Copyright forms, which used to be manual, weren't being sent out. I remember working with [Public Enemy] on that stuff and having [Flavor] Flav come to the office, because you need to attach lyric sheets to the stuff that you send out and I needed lyrics to "Don't Believe the Hype." He sat down at the typewriter and started typing them out using his index finger, typing one letter at a time. I love that moment. He was so funny. I was like, "Flav, it's cool. I'll do it. You just dictate and I'll do it." So yeah, somehow we managed to pull it together.

Russell Simmons (cofounder, Def Jam): Lyor would get it done, in the same way that [future president of Def Jam] Kevin Liles would get it done. And by making other people better is how he got better—he's the greatest mentor. He was a mentor as an underling, and he was a mentor as a leader.

Look what he did with Julie Greenwald, and with Michael Kyser, and with Kevin Liles, and with Chris Lighty. He brought them along for the ride, but they were also mentored to the point where, if they did leave, they could be valuable elsewhere. Too many other companies, they brought people along, and they didn't really train them.

Julie Greenwald's the biggest woman, maybe in the history of the record business, most powerful ever. Her and Sylvia Rhone. She was empowered by Lyor. Michael Kyser's the president of music at Atlantic. Kevin Liles, president of Def Jam for a long time and still now runs 300 [Entertainment]. [Music executive] Todd Moscowitz can act like he ain't part of our family, but everything he learned, and all of his experience that brought him to whatever he's doing now, came from working with us.

PROPELLED BY THE gargantuan sales of artists like Jay-Z and DMX, Russell Simmons sold his remaining stake in Def Jam to Uni-

versal Music Group for a reported $100 million in 1999. Lyor Cohen
remained to head Island Def Jam Music Group.

    Simmons had believed in hip-hop's marketability since its begin-
ning, and expanded the genre into outlets like fashion (Phat Farm) and
humor (*Def Comedy Jam*).

Russell Simmons[*] **(cofounder, Def Jam):** I had a time in 1990 where Car-
men Ashhurst was the president, where Faith Newman was the head
of A&R. Women ran Def Jam, every facet of it. That would only happen in hip-hop. Never would it happen in rock and roll.

    Rappers are not more sexist than the firemen. They're not more
sexist than the policemen, or the rabbi, or the preacher who won't let
the woman in the pulpit. They're more compassionate. Poets have
always been more compassionate. Rappers are the first to point out
when things are hurtful and bad, because they're poets. Artists look
inside for answers and for their creativity. That's where the truth
comes out, from inside. They're our truth-tellers.

Duke Bootee (producer, Sugar Hill): Russell was the genius of this shit.
He was one of the hardest-working people I've ever met. Him and
Tom Silverman, the president of Tommy Boy Records, are actually
the two hardest-working people I've ever been around.

Paul Stewart (producer, promoter): I'm going be real with you. Lyor
Cohen was not an A&R source. They had a lot of bricks. It was before
Jay-Z. It was before DMX. It was after Public Enemy, Beastie Boys,
LL Cool J, that whole era. Wu-Tang had come out.

    I remember when they got Method Man. I already had my deal
over there. Obviously, they were a legacy, but they were pretty cold
as far as a lot of the groups that were over there. I was a hip-hop fan.

---

[*] In recent years, Simmons has been accused of sexual assault and/or sexual misconduct in more than a dozen cases. "The second he agreed to work with me, my
budget increased, the label was paying more attention to me," Tina Baker, a singer
who accused Simmons of rape in the early 1990s, when he managed her, told
The New York Times in 2017. After the alleged assault, Baker said: "I went into
oblivion." While apologizing for being "thoughtless and insensitive," Simmons
has denied accusations of non-consensual sexual encounters.

I was just enamored to be working with such a legendary company, and they were also very good at the record business and smart, and they knew what to do to market and promote. If they got a hit, they knew what the fuck to do. They also, at that time, still really understood the culture. Most of the bigger companies didn't, so they were in a unique place where they had the might of a bigger company but they understood the culture. There was really nothing like that, 'cause the smaller companies, none of them really amassed the promotion, marketing strength, power that Def Jam did.

It was a unique time where Def Jam was really powerful. If you look at the history of Def Jam, and you look at the acts that Rick Rubin, Chris Lighty, Irv Gotti, myself brought there, and you take all those groups out, you got a bunch of old-school hip-hop. Russell and Lyor were great at running a record label, but they were never really the guys that found the talent per se.

06 COMPLETELY DIFFERENT NATIONS

Los Angeles
1983–1986

Recordings of early hip-hop performances slowly spread across the country, mostly by people who had relatives elsewhere or by those who served on military bases and were returning home. On the West Coast, Duffy Hooks recorded Disco Daddy and Captain Rapp after being influenced by the success of Sugar Hill Records. Their 1981 single, "The Gigolo Rapp," received only sporadic radio play.

Afrika Bambaataa and electronic music were the brand of hip-hop music that developed from Los Angeles's bubbling mobile DJ scene of the late 1970s. Radio DJ Greg Mack introduced New York hip-hop artists to West Coast listeners on KDAY 1580-AM in 1983, and soon acts like Kurtis Blow and Run-DMC were performing in Los Angeles.

But it only took a short time for Los Angeles to place its own stamp on hip-hop. How much did the music tide shift in a few short years? The man who laid the foundation for N.W.A's rise, Alonzo Williams, originally went by the stage name of Disco Lonzo.

Williams grew up in Compton, a city just south of downtown Los Angeles, during an era of turmoil. The nearby Watts rebellion of 1965—nearly a week of unrest sparked by police abuse, which caused over $40 million in property damage—was seared in residents' memories. By the 1970s, "blockbusting," a predatory practice used by real estate agents to scare white homeowners into selling their property for fear of

living next to Black residents, had eroded the city's tax base and transformed the nearly all-white suburb into a predominantly Black one.

Williams shifted his approach with the changing of popular music.
He departed the mobile DJ scene for a stationary home at the L.A.
nightclub Eve After Dark, where he organized the World Class Wreckin'
Cru. Other units, like Uncle Jamm's Army—headed by Williams's former partner, Rodger Clayton—continued incubating talent through DJ-
centric parties that would come to define early West Coast hip-hop.

Both Eve After Dark and Uncle Jamm's Army invited acts from New
York to perform in the mid-1980s, and the impression left by those like
Kurtis Blow, Run-DMC, and Davy DMX had an outsized impact on the
West Coast.

Other venues played integral roles in the development and spread
of hip-hop in Los Angeles, including clubs like Radio, where DJ Chris
"The Glove" Taylor made his name, and skating rinks such as Skateland
and World on Wheels.

Alonzo Williams (DJ, World Class Wreckin' Cru): Being a mobile DJ back
in the day was my love, my passion. I learned some tricks early in the
game, how to secure gigs, which kept me very busy. One, my partner's
dad owned a print shop. So usually I'd go to get my flyers done and I'd
walk around the print shop, and I'd see different jobs that his dad had
done. People getting married, baby showers, or whatever the case may
be. I'd call them up and see if they wanted a DJ and a lot of times,
"Yeah. Oh, I hadn't thought about that." Wedding receptions, baby
showers, birthday parties. I sold myself cheap for a couple of years,
until I developed the clientele. I stayed booked.

Now, I come from the disco era. My first name as a DJ was Disco
Lonzo. I'm transitioning from Temptations stuff as a DJ in '75. I get to
'76, we doing the disco thing. By '77, '78, we transitioning into funk.
So, in a six-, seven-year period, we've had three major music segues.

Now, here comes this hip-hop situation, and at that time, we
thought it was cool, but nobody knew it was going to be what it was.
You only had two real rap records, that was Kurtis Blow "Christmas
Rappin'," then you had "Rapper's Delight." Hip-hop hadn't established itself sufficiently on the West Coast yet.

Chris "The Glove" Taylor (DJ, producer): The East Coast and the West Coast are completely different nations at this time. Records took forever to migrate across the United States. So, I get my hands on a record called "The Adventures of Grandmaster Flash on the Wheels of Steel." I'm hearing these sounds. Turns out, it's scratching. I had no idea of what this was, but I was just into it.

So I told my dad I want to be a DJ. I said, "I want to take my student loans, fuck those books, I want to buy some turntables." He said, "Okay, let's go."

So, he took me. I got two [Technics] SL-B1 turntables and a Gemini mixer, I got speakers, everything. So I take this gear home, set it up in the garage. Now, a few months before, I started working at this place called Delicious Records, 'cause I wanted to get records. I got the student loan to get the gear and I got the job at the record store to get records.

And so, I got my hands on all those records that Grandmaster Flash was using and I tried to figure out how he put them together, and I got that [Chic's] "Good Times" and this dude is playing turntables like bongos. So it was percussive moves. That's how I scratch. I scratch like a drummer.

Alonzo Williams (DJ, World Class Wreckin' Cru): Eve After Dark was a unique situation that I was blessed with at the age of twenty-two. My dad and the owner were best friends, and his friend had just built a second floor to his nightclub. My dad came out and saw me at another venue having a very successful night, and thought it might be a good idea for his friend to have that conversation with me about me running his top floor.

That was June 22, 1979. I cut the deal when I was twenty-one. We opened about a week after my birthday.

I was actually going to work with Rodger Clayton at Uncle Jamm's Army, but he wasn't familiar with the area and his attitude was there was too many shermheads* and it was a rough area. But I'm from the area. So everybody knew me, and I knew all the shermheads and all the shermhead dealers, so I'm home.

---

*A "sherm" is a cigarette or joint dipped in PCP.

After about five months, maybe six months of struggling, I had the opportunity to bring [the soul-influenced funk group] Cameo in when they were hot as fish grease. They had just dropped "Shake Your Pants" or one of them songs. From that point on, the Eve After Dark became the place to be in the hood for everybody eighteen and over.

We had a hell of a ride, and in doing the Eve, I had pop-locking contests, breakdancing contests, rapping contests. That's how I met Cli-N-Tel, at a rap contest, and we were right there on the cusp of hip-hop.

Cli-N-Tel (artist, World Class Wreckin' Cru): [West Coast hip-hop pioneer] Joe Cooley and I were still in high school. I think the first song we'd ever heard, really as far as hip-hop was concerned, was "Rapper's Delight," because that was blasting everywhere, like the late '70s. So we started our own little DJ crew. I was basically a DJ and a rapper and Joe Cooley was on the mix up in Compton. At that time, it was just something fun for us to do, kept us out of trouble. It wasn't a real serious gang issue then, but it was growing. You could kind of feel it in the neighborhoods.

So, we wanted to go the other route and just stay out of trouble. We started looking up to cats like Sugarhill Gang and Kurtis Blow. Then we started going over to the Eve After Dark, which was Lonzo's club, because we'd see these little DJ crews cropping up. So we started going to dances with Uncle Jamm's Army.

We'd see DJ Yella [and] DJ Egyptian Lover mixing, and we like, "Yo, that's what we want to do." So we started organizing. Got our money together, bought some turntables, flyers, business cards, and we just started doing our own gigs, neighborhood parties, whatever we could get. We'd have parties that sometimes were so packed that by the time the party was over, you'd see blue jean stains all on the walls. It was that serious. So we're like, "Man, we might have something here."

Alonzo Williams (DJ, World Class Wreckin' Cru): When we first opened the Eve, hip-hop was not really in existence on the West Coast, not at all. When hip-hop finally took root on the West Coast, I was the one that dug the hole for the root.

Most people don't know that me and [Dr.] Dre grew up on the same

street, and although we didn't play together—I was much older than
him—I knew of him. When he came to the club trying to get in, he
reminded me who he was [and] got into the club. At some point, Dre
made his way to my turntables. He had this mix he was doing; it was
[the Marvelettes' 1961 single] "Please Mr. Postman" and a breakbeat
that was just so unique. Shortly after that, I talked to him and got a
little deeper into who he was.

I'm [also] the one that brought in Kurtis Blow to Eve After Dark.
His DJ, Davy DMX, taught DJ Yella how to scratch.

Cli-N-Tel (artist, World Class Wreckin' Cru): Yella was very technical, in
terms of learning how to be a sound engineer. He was a big influence
on Dre's early understanding of sound engineering, because he had
an ear for drums. Yella wasn't necessarily a good scratch DJ, but he
was a really good blend DJ. He could pick tempos and cadences and
breakdowns in songs that would match really well, so his blending
was really, really good. So, what I think made him significant was his
ear for drums and his ear for beats and being able to just beat-match
really well.

Davy DMX (DJ): We did a show there. Then, the next day, it was like a
rap contest with Kurtis Blow as a judge. I think Ice-T won.

Kurtis Blow (artist, producer): He did very, very, very well. He was talking like a pimp—"bitch better have my money" and "motherfucker"
and all this profanity—but the crowd loved it and they went crazy.

So, me being a long way from home, I said, "Look, I think I better
give him a ten because he really did well by the crowd, but personally
I don't agree with that kind of rap profanity." I made my stance about
that, but I gave a ten and he won.

That contest was a big inspiration for Ice-T. I've heard him quote
this in magazines, that it inspired him, winning the contest, so he went
on to pursue his rap career and become an MC.

Davy DMX (DJ): I was in the crowd. My turntables were still there. So,
after the party, they was like, "Yo, we like what you're doing." I'm
like, "I'll show you."

Kurtis Blow (artist, producer): Alonzo Williams, it was his office, and we were doing a show, and Davy D had set up in the back of the office and he showed them how to DJ. Dave and I used to do a thing called quick mix where he would go from one turntable to the other, very fast with blinding speed, and then he would go faster, and then even faster than that, and that would always mesmerize the crowd. Dave was showing a lot of people how to do that and also how to scratch, how to cut.

Davy DMX (DJ): I taught Yella. Dre could've been standing there. I don't even know.

Cli-N-Tel (artist, World Class Wreckin' Cru): As DJs on the West Coast, we started watching DJ Yella, so in essence Davy DMX taught all of us. Because he taught Yella, and then Yella taught Dre and subsequently me, and Joe Cooley. We just started watching Yella and studying him and that's how we learned.

> **ALONZO WILLIAMS STARTED** N.W.A's precursor, the World Class Wreckin' Cru, for performances at Eve After Dark. The electro-rap group often dressed in sequined jumpsuits and featured members including DJ Yella, Cli-N-Tel, and Dr. Dre.
>
> Williams created Kru-Cut Records and released the group's debut singles, "Slice" and "Surgery," through the independent Macola Records before landing a deal with CBS/Epic Records.

Alonzo Williams (DJ, World Class Wreckin' Cru): World Class Wreckin' Cru came about after I had booked Run-DMC at the club. I listened to ["Sucker M.C.'s"] and I'm like, "That ain't shit. That's a record? That ain't no big deal." A buddy of mine had a drum machine and we made this record called "Slice" sound just like that record.

As a mobile DJ, my production company was called Disco Construction 'cause we would build you a party anywhere: backyard, hall, bathroom. As long as you got electricity, we'd make it happen. I had a couple of guys that rolled with me that would help me carry my equipment, because back in the day, being a mobile DJ, you were literally moving a one-bedroom apartment every time you loaded your truck up. All the speakers and the amps and the records. I had to have help.

My buddy, one night, we were out in Alpine Village in Torrance and my boys were tearing my stuff down and he says, "Oh, you're Disco Construction? Who are they? The wrecking crew?"

He started laughing, and it stuck. If you were a part of the Wrecking Crew, you were a part of an elite group of folks that worked at Eve After Dark, and when I started making records, I used that name, Wrecking Crew, to promote the records.

[Dr. Dre] didn't originally start with Wrecking Cru. He started with Unknown DJ, [but] Dre was disappointed with the financial arrangement [so] he came and worked for me. Shortly after that he joined the Wrecking Cru.

Then I found out there was a group out of Chicago called the Wrecking Crew and they were like the Motown group. I got a cease-and-desist letter saying you can't use the name, so I added World Class. It was about '84 by this time, and it was the Olympics [in Los Angeles] and every time I look around, on the radio or the television, I hear, "He's a world-class sprinter. World-class swimmer." So we became the World Class Wreckin' Cru.

Cli-N-Tel (artist, World Class Wreckin' Cru): We are true hip-hop heads, and Dre, Yella, and I learned to have a work ethic that if we wanted to do something right, to work at it, and we became perfectionists at whatever it was that we did, and we were self-aware of the role we played, even back then. Because at that time, real musicians were saying, "This is not going to last. It's a fad. That's not even real music. These kids are just taking everybody else's stuff and remaking it. They just stealing." We heard all the stories and all the comments, but we just keep pushing along, and when other people started doing it, it just kind of grew out of all of that tension.

GREG MACK MOVED to Los Angeles from Houston in 1983 with the unenviable task of revitalizing the radio station KDAY 1580-AM.

Mack focused on the music that he found to be most popular in the neighborhoods he frequented and brought hip-hop to the station's forefront.

Before Mack, you could catch a song by the Fat Boys or Whodini here and there if you tuned in to a station long enough. Mack devoted the station to hip-hop on a larger scale, providing the music a voice and outlet in Los Angeles. He played popular East Coast stars, while breaking nearly every significant West Coast hip-hop act that emerged in the 1980s. His "Mack Attack Mixmasters" show put local club and party DJs on the radio, helping to propel the careers of those like Dr. Dre, DJ Yella, and N.W.A.

Greg Mack (music director, KDAY): When I got to Majic 102 [in Houston], I really got into it and started learning how to program the music. I just liked rap at that time, although it was kind of built as a novelty situation. Then, when I got to Los Angeles, 1580 KDAY, they had asked me to try and figure it out. Out of the five Black stations at that time in Los Angeles, they were in last place. They were trying to figure out a new direction.

I said, "Let me listen to what's going on in the city," because I didn't really know the city that well yet. I was living with my mom. She had a rental house behind her house in South Central L.A. It didn't take long to figure out just by opening your window what everybody was listening to, which was rap music. Everywhere. You'd hear cars bumping through the neighborhood playing Run-DMC or Kurtis Blow.

I said, "Why is nobody playing that on the radio?"

"Oh, it's just novelty shit."

I said, "I think we should put some in."

And we did. I think within the first book, we were number two out of the five. It just exploded. I felt like, in order to win, we needed to win in the streets. Then, my sister had invited me to a dance. She said, "Come go with me to the Uncle Jamm's Army dance."

RODGER CLAYTON AND Gid Martin formed Unique Dreams Entertainment in the late 1970s. The promoters started small, throwing parties at banquet halls, and became shaped by electro sounds. They changed their name to Uncle Jamm's Army, and their mobile DJ unit attracted thousands of revelers for booming get-downs at venues like the Los Angeles Convention Center and Los Angeles Memorial Sports Arena. Uncle Jamm's Army became a rival of Alonzo Williams and World Class Wreckin' Cru, nurturing the career beginnings of Ice-T, DJ Pooh, Egyptian Lover (a pioneer of the Los Angeles hip-hop and electro scene), and many others.

Arabian Prince (artist, producer, N.W.A): Uncle Jamm's Army, it was a phenomenon. You had this big battle on the West Coast. You had Uncle Jamm's Army. You had Disco Construction, which was the Wreckin' Cru. You had all these DJ crews that used to battle each other. I was maybe fifteen, sixteen years old at the time.

Deadly Threat (artist, Los Angeles): We used to have to sneak into some of them. That's how young we were. Man, those were some real, real wild and crazy days. DJ Pooh, that's like my big brother, he was a part of the Uncle Jamm's Army with the California Cat Crew and all of these guys. So I was exposed to that lifestyle from a pretty early age.

We used to actually steal cars to go to the dance. So, that's how powerful and how much of a magnification it was to actually be present at some of these parties and dances. It was a must. Diversity was at an all-time high. It was fun.

There was only a handful of crews that were really actually leading the march. Uncle Jamm's Army was definitely one of the head ones. Wherever they went, we all followed. They basically were setting the tone for rap as it is today.

Cli-N-Tel (artist, World Class Wreckin' Cru): Wreckin' Cru was more marketing- and business-minded with a tighter organization, whereas Uncle Jamm's Army was sort of a bigger, kind of loosely organized DJ crew. They were ran by two people who actually started out as friends, Lonzo and Rodger Clayton. They were actually DJs together; met at a record company they both worked at. And so, when they split, Lonzo started Disco Construction and Rodger started Uncle Jamm's Army, and they had their own territory and we had our own territory, and we sort of understood the rules of not crossing the lines.

Arabian Prince (artist, producer, N.W.A): We would go to the early Uncle Jamm's Army dances before they started doing the bigger stuff. I was friends with Egyptian Lover at the time, like right when he became one of the main DJs for them. I would go and hang out with him and eventually got to rock with them a little bit.

Rodger was a genius at finding the hit records, because a lot of the stuff that Uncle Jamm's Army played were B-sides. He just knew where to find that beat, and then later on it would be a mix and the DJs would play it.

Cli-N-Tel (artist, World Class Wreckin' Cru): Once the competition became a little more fierce, we started putting a bounty on their posters and they started putting a bounty on our posters. So, it's like every poster you snatched down and bring as proof of concept, you get five dollars for. Lonzo would pay us every time we'd see an Uncle Jamm's Army poster riding through the neighborhoods and take it down.

So that wasn't cool, because that cut in their market and then they cut in our market, so we marked our own territories and sort of stayed there, and every time they'd make a record, we'd make a record. Or every time they'd do a big dance, we'd do a big dance. So it was always back and forth. And then sometimes when Rodger heard about us bringing in a certain act, he would contact that act and go, "Yo, since you guys are gonna be in town, why don't you stop by my spot first?" And so he would basically cut us off at the knees—we'd fly the act out, but then he'd get them on the cheap because he wouldn't have to pay for a hotel and flights.

Sometimes folks would call the fire marshal. Shit like that went on all the time. It was mostly friendly, but there was some competition there. But that competition really pushed us, all the crews, to be innovative and be better, so in a roundabout way I guess it was a good thing to experience that.

Greg Mack (music director, KDAY): Uncle Jamm's Army was the hottest thing in the streets. These guys would have shows at the L.A. Sports

Arena, have ten thousand kids there partying with just DJs. I'd never seen such a thing. I was just blown away.

I immediately decided that if those guys have that kind of control in the streets, I want to be a part of that. I met with Rodger Clayton and I asked him if we could tie in with it. Rodger looked at the crowd, pointed to all those kids, and he says, "Does it look like I need fucking radio?"

He had a point.

What he didn't know is that you can't shut me out, it's just another hurdle. In my weekly meetings that I had with all the record labels, one of the guys that I met with one week was Lonzo. He was trying to get a group going called World Class Wreckin' Cru. He had a club going. I told him what happened with me at Sports Arena.

Alonzo Williams (DJ, World Class Wreckin' Cru): When Greg Mack first came to Los Angeles, I was one of the first people he met. I had just shut the Eve After Dark [club] and I had just cut the deal to go to Doodo's, but I was concerned about Doodo's because it was so much bigger than Eve After Dark.

Doodo's holds two thousand people. It was an auditorium. I had talked to my sales rep at KDAY, a lady by the name of Rochelle Lucas, and she says, "Well, you ought to talk to our new DJ. He's going to be our program director. Maybe I can work out something," and I did.

Greg ain't been there about three weeks and we met. Took him over to Doodo's and, when he got it, he's like, "Oh, my God."

Greg Mack (music director, KDAY): I said, "I've got this idea for this thing I want to do called Traffic Jam. I need a DJ just to mix for me when I'm on the air in the afternoons."

He said, "You can use my guys, man." He brought them up to the station and it was Dr. Dre and DJ Yella.

I listened to their mix. I was blown away. I was like, "Oh my God." Because it wasn't just two turntables. Dre actually made it a production. It was like an eight-track, a mix. Dre would actually lay a beat down for thirty minutes, then he'd come back and layer some other music over that, layer some other music over that. I'd never heard nothing like it.

Ice Cube (artist, N.W.A): [KDAY] was so big that all we dreamed of was to have a song playing on KDAY. It was what everybody Black listened to. It was everything for us.

When we were still locals, they had something called the Best Rapper of the West contest. We joined it and we went all the way to the finals. We came in runner-up.

You had the Wreckin' Cru trying to get a record played on KDAY, and they couldn't, but what they could get played was Dre's Traffic Jams. Dre would do these four-track mixtapes that lasted maybe twenty-five, thirty minutes, called the Traffic Jam, where they would do rhymes and they would rap, and he would cut stuff up and make it sound crazy. Nobody was four-tracking back then, so it sounded like he had seven turntables. It was amazing. Shit we had never heard before. They were delivering that every day for the Traffic Jam.

Greg Mack (music director, KDAY): I put it on my show, and it took off so fast that they started selling those mixes at the Roadium Swap Meet and made so much money that they just got too busy with being in the studio making those mixes. It just kind of took off from there.

Sir Jinx (producer): Greg Mack is a really, really good friend of mine. I went up there as a runt. And I end up getting to know him. Greg Mack played my mixes and they were terrible. Fucking terrible. But the dope part is, he let me shine. And what we end up doing, Yo-Yo, [Ice] Cube went up there. We got it straight off the press and we took Yo-Yo straight up there to Greg Mack.

Deadly Threat (artist, Los Angeles): Yo-Yo was the queen [of battling in high school]. There was some other girls, but they were in groups. Yo-Yo was one of the only girls that rapped by herself, but they would never battle her, because she was a little more advanced than theirs and shit. But they were all kind of nice. They really had good raps, even back then.

Greg Mack (music director, KDAY): One thing I was very proud of with what I did then is, I never took payola. I just had an open-door policy. If you had a good record—sometimes it wasn't that good—but you knew that you'd have a local radio station that would play it.

Sir Jinx (producer): Even if he didn't know your name, he'd listen to your stuff. He'd be like, "Sit back, sit back." And he'd burn it right there on the air for you. If it wasn't for Greg Mack, a lot of people wouldn't have the confidence that they had to hear their music behind other successful artists.

Greg Mack (music director, KDAY): [Uncle Jamm's Army] had the L.A. Sports Arena on lockdown. I decided that I wanted to start doing dances. There was a club that Lonzo and Dre and all of them were doing called Doodo's in Compton. We started doing Doodo's.

The first event I did, I called in my friends, the group New Edition. We had to turn away so many people. I said, "God, I gotta find a bigger spot."

The skating rink was right next door, called Skateland, which held probably a couple thousand people. We decided we were going to do Skateland.

> **ACROSS THE UNITED** States, skating rinks played an important role in the spread of hip-hop music. The venues drew large youth gatherings at a time when most radio stations refused to play the young genre. In Southern California, Skateland and World on Wheels became early, integral hip-hop venues by linking with mobile DJ crews and hosting KDAY broadcasts and visiting artists.

Alonzo Williams (DJ, World Class Wreckin' Cru): Skateland was a piece of cake. I'm doing Doodo's and Craig Schweisinger, the owner of Skateland, asked me to come over and promote. That was even better, because all the promotions were no effort. I used to get them in Fridays at Doodo's and I just would advertise on the microphone, "Tomorrow night, we going to be next door." It was probably the best promotional deal arrangement I ever had, and he only took twenty percent and I got the rest of the door.

Hip-hop, as it started to grow, the people who owned the theaters didn't understand the impact. The standard skating rink can hold two or three thousand people. If you got a hot act—and most of these acts came from underground at that time—a promoter can get a skating rink a lot cheaper than you can get a theater. People want to dance anyway. So you got a huge dance floor, big space, and most of them had great sound systems, and it just was the capacity and the economics makes sense overall.

Sir Jinx (producer): The crazy thing about Skateland is it's in a full Blood area. The street next to it is called Parmelee. When people wanted to go there and heard it on the radio, they had no clue that it was in the heart of Compton. I saw a lot of stuff.

The gangsters used to line the whole driveway and look into the window and see if you looked like anybody that they wanted to fuck with. And I done seen a lot of people get drug out of their car in that driveway. But it was a lot of good memories with Chuck D, and Salt-N-Pepa, and LL Cool J.

When we had all this stuff going on, you had another group across the city that was doing something else. Rodger Clayton. Rodger had the Coliseum and all this stuff, the World on Wheels [in Mid-City]. I was too young to go to Uncle Jamm's Army, so I was always over there dealing with Dre and them at Skateland.

That's the first place I learned how to party. That was my first time looking for records and playing them without no supervision. I was probably sixteen. So I was DJing in a full skating rink, crazy place.

All these old clubs, it was a little rugged. So yeah, Skateland was a real hot place. And if you wanted to perform there, you had to have your way in and way out.

Alonzo Williams (DJ, World Class Wreckin' Cru): Greg would give me acts. 'Cause a lot of times, part of the deal, radio stations, they get promotions for different record companies, and so, as acts would come to town, Greg would give them to me. "Hey, man, here's LL Cool J. Here's New Edition. Put them at Doodo's." So, because I got Doodo's and Skateland on lock, I'm the man. Greg was on the radio. I'm making records, I'm promoting clubs, I'm promoting events, so we had a trifecta.

Greg Mack (music director, KDAY): What the gangs and rappers really found interesting about me is that, coming from Texas—I still have that Texas accent—I wasn't afraid to go into any neighborhood. They had picked up on the fact that I was naïve. They gave me a pass. There were a few shootings here and there at our events, outside. They showed me respect and didn't shoot anybody inside. It became such that when there was a drive-by in Los Angeles, most of the time the gang members that did the drive-bys would call me at the radio station and tell me why they did it. Back then, they had a reason for doing a drive-by. They didn't just do it.

With Skateland, I started to realize that that was a Blood area. So we were missing a lot of people. I started doing them at World on Wheels because that's where the Crips were. We started doing Sherman Square out in the Valley because that's where the Latin gangs were. We would rotate from week to week from the Bloods, to the Crips, the Sureños, to make sure that we were down with everybody.

Then we started doing a club in the middle of downtown called the Casa Camino Real, which was neutral territory. All of the gangs would come there, as well as normal people. Then we started doing a venue out in Santa Monica called the 321 Club, which was where all the white kids went that wouldn't go to any of the other places. We just rotated. Every now and then we would veer off into something in Pasadena and other places, Radiotron.

Alonzo Williams (DJ, World Class Wreckin' Cru): Later, Greg expanded his market to bring in some of the East Coast cats.

Russell Simmons (cofounder, Def Jam): We came out to L.A., and I went to see him. Greg Mack was always an ally—a good set of ears, give the best advice he could give, loved hip-hop. A lot of people made a lot of money, but he is a true pioneer in that he dedicated his life to it. He gave a lot to the culture, just the courage to do what he did.

Greg Mack (music director, KDAY): There was a lot of backlash when I started doing what I was doing at KDAY, and record stores wouldn't even carry rap music at that time. The mom-and-pops, they were coming up big-time in the Roadium Swap Meet. They were making crazy money. But the major stores wouldn't carry [it], the major record labels wouldn't pick it up. And the community was really against it. They thought we were a bad influence on kids.

But the thing is, we were not an all-rap station at that time. We also created the music they call freestyle. I was the first DJ to play many of those artists. Also, we played R&B. We played Luther [Vandross] and Teddy [Pendergrass], Patti LaBelle. It was an interesting mixture, which you just don't hear on the radio nowadays.

Murs (artist, Los Angeles): It was a godsend. They'd broadcast the Ten Commandments every day. Religiously listening, taping, especially for someone like me—there was no other way that I was getting rap music into my house. My mom would throw away my tapes. And as a child from a low-income family with no income, it was almost impossible for me to get rap music. I wouldn't be who I am without KDAY.

Greg Mack (music director, KDAY): All I wanted to do was play the hits. As a program director, you can't shy away from playing a song because it's not politically correct. If people like it, they like it.

I've always felt like if you play the hits, you just can't lose. Plus, you gotta remember, nobody believed in rap music but me at that time, as far as radio. It was just like, if it's a good song, it's got a good beat, kids will like it, because I was out there with them all the time. They always kept me up to date as to what was going on with the streets.

IN THE EARLY 1980s, the elements of West Coast hip-hop culture fused in L.A.'s MacArthur Park at a club called Radio, later renamed Radiotron; in 1984, director Joel Silberg released *Breakin'*, a comedy-drama inspired by the club and the scene. The previous year had witnessed Ice-T's film debut, in writer/director Topper Carew's documentary about Los Angeles hip-hop called *Breakin' 'N' Enterin'*. The soundtrack for *Breakin'* also marked Ice-T's first appearance on an album, in "Reckless," produced by Chris "The Glove" Taylor and David Storrs.

Chris "The Glove" Taylor (DJ, producer): I was DJing at a club called Radio. There wasn't no hip-hop place in L.A. but there. So that's where I met Egyptian Lover. We used to practice in the backyard of the Uncle Jamm's Army dude [Edwin Vaultz].

He didn't really scratch, but he could move fast, and he was cutting. When I started scratching, people watched like, *What is this dude doing?* And Radio was that kind of club. People would come and watch. They wouldn't just dance. They came to watch. It was a trip.

Ice-T (artist, Rhyme Syndicate): It was more like a punk rock club. People like Malcolm McLaren were there, Adam Ant. I met Madonna there for the first time. It was just a place you could go on a Friday or Saturday night and get on a stage and really practice your shit, because the audience didn't know whether you were good or bad. Hip-hop was too new. But it was like the first L.A. hip-hop club. Then came the Rhythm Lounge, but it was definitely started at the Radio.

Chris "The Glove" Taylor (DJ, producer): When I [first] got to Radio, I was delivering speakers and the guy, my boss, was introducing me to everybody 'cause, you know, I was a hot DJ. He was like, "This guy's dope. Trust me." He had faith in me.

So, I'm putting the speakers in, I had to wear these big-ass gardening gloves, and they're talking to me. They're like, "Oh hey, I heard you're a DJ."

I'm a hotshot. So I'm like, "Yeah, I'm the best DJ you know."

I'm talking shit and they're like, "Okay, hot DJ, what's your DJ name?"

And I was like, "I don't have no DJ name, bro." I said, "Chris, DJ Chris." Like it was the shit. I tried to be tough.

They laugh. "Looky here, monkey boy. We got something for you. When you come back, we'll have a name for you. We want to see what you do. Come at eleven."

I got there at eleven. They had a marquee: Shake City at nine. The Glove at eleven. So I said, "Okay, I'm The Glove."

Lately I've been telling people, it could've been some other dude whose name was The Glove that was supposed to be there, but I just went for it. There's some dude who's tied up somewhere going, "No, it was me."

First time I got my name, it was up in lights. I met Ice-T at the club that same night. He was like, "Check this DJ out. This nigga's good." He's telling everybody. He worked at the club as the MC.

This is how I got on *Breakin'*. I was the DJ, right? They were saying, "Man, we got to get something like 'Planet Rock,' blah blah blah." They only knew that title, but there's all these other songs. So I was like, "Yo, I do that music. Why would you go to New York to get something about what we're talking about right here?"

And he was like, "Okay, hotshot, can you score film?"

I was like, "Yeah."

"Okay, cool. We're going to give you all the club scenes. We want you to put music to them."

So, I went to the studio, met this guy named Dave Storrs, [and] we figured out how to do that. We had to do not only scoring, but I was like the technical director of scratching. I was like, "You're not going to fuck this up. I'm doing it."

And then they said, "Okay, this is great. We love the music. Can we get a rap song from one of the pieces out of the club? We want to put that on the soundtrack." This is at the midnight hour. Not even the eleventh hour. They just decided at the last minute, "Hey, can you make a rap?"

I called Ice-T; it was two in the morning. I went and picked him up. "Reckless" was the beat from the first scene of the club.

07 ATOMS SMASHING

Long Island, New York
1985–1992

While other hip-hop groups and artists have sold countless records, received extensive radio airplay, and spawned myriad imitators, none can claim the degree of social impact and mastery of their craft as much as Public Enemy.

At its peak, the group redefined hip-hop's potential as a means of stirring consciousness and awakening minds. Listeners were forced into a tug-of-war over where to place their attention: the profound voice of Chuck D shedding light on social and racial disparities, or the masterful soundscapes created through a dizzying array of samples used by the Bomb Squad, the group's in-house production team. Ultimately, audiences heeded both, as Public Enemy redefined hip-hop's place in contemporary culture in the same way that the voices of Martin Luther King Jr. and Malcolm X penetrated ideologies.

It took decades for the group to receive its flowers, as is usual for revolutionaries. In 2013, Public Enemy was inducted into the Rock and Roll Hall of Fame, and the group received a Grammy Lifetime Achievement Award in 2020.

The seeds for the group coalesced in New York's Long Island when Chuck D joined Spectrum City, a group of popular mobile DJs. He studied graphic design at Adelphi University, where his thirst for knowledge joined other hungry minds inside the classroom of Andrei Strobert, a jazz drummer and African American studies professor, and at WBAU, the campus radio station.

The young students became linked to the nascent culture through visits into the city, from where the new sights and sounds were spreading to neighboring suburbs via public transportation.

Bill Stephney (Bomb Squad, Def Jam): I can use me and Chuck [D] probably as best examples. Both of our families migrated from Harlem and from the Bronx to Hempstead and Roosevelt. So, even though we're living in Nassau County, grandma, grandpa, aunts, uncles, cousins are all back in Harlem and in the Bronx.

My mother wanted to be near her parents as she was raising kids. During my formative years, during the week, I'm living in Hempstead, but during the weekends my paternal grandmother lived in the projects in the Northeast Bronx, where we would then spend Sunday evening. So I got the best of both worlds of being the suburban kid during the week, but I'm Co-op City and Soundview Houses Billy on Saturdays, and being exposed to everything that was going on during that time.

Keith Shocklee (producer, Bomb Squad): [Spectrum City] started in our youth center—we used to have community parties in the basement and we used to DJ. I used to be there and my brother [Hank Shocklee] would be there. As we became more local in the community, everybody wanted to hire us. And to really make a bigger noise, we started promoting our own parties. And that's when it became big-time serious.

Chuck came into the picture, like, '79. I was going into my senior year in high school. Chuck was already at Adelphi, and Adelphi had these parties called the Thursday Night Throwdowns. My brother heard Chuck when he did a PSA for some announcement [and] when Hank heard his voice, Hank was like, "Yo, I heard this kid with this incredible voice. He said he's from Roosevelt."

Hank approached him to be in the group, and Chuck, his first instinct was like, "Nah, man." Hank kind of convinced him to be an MC. He had the original golden voice for our generation.

Bill Stephney (Bomb Squad, Def Jam): So, I am on the Adelphi campus my sophomore year. I'm already one of the folks helping to run the campus station, BAU. We did interviews with newsmakers. We'd have someone like Kwame Ture, Stokely Carmichael, then we'd play bits and pieces of an interview from him and then we're playing break-beats and whatever rap records were coming out on Sugar Hill and Enjoy, or any independent label. We'd play those and I'd play some alternative imports coming from punk music.

I began that show. And one day I happened to see this guy wearing a silk Spectrum City DJ jacket. And Spectrum City was the preeminent mobile DJ hip-hop crew on Long Island for the late '70s, early '80s. They threw the best parties. They had the best, almost like city club sound system speakers—which just goes to the advantage of being the suburban kid, is that we had access to more resources. So we could get better equipment. We could do what the city kids did, but we could do it, we thought, with a little more polish and a little more technical proficiency.

So, I see this guy in the Spectrum City jacket, and as it turns out, this guy's a graphics student, who's two years older than me, but who was also MC Chuckie D. And I said, "Hey, man, I'm the biggest fan of Spectrum City. I'd love to have you and the crew up to BAU to my show, *The Mr. Bill Show.*"

He said, "Yeah, we know about *The Mr. Bill Show.* Yeah, you're good. Yes, absolutely."

It was at that moment that everything really starts to connect for me, and that partnership, alliance, and friendship now exists to this minute.

André "Doctor Dré" Brown[*] **(DJ, artist, Original Concept):** I got a scholarship to go to Adelphi University, and I always tell the story, "I fell for the big butt and the smile." I was dating a young lady who happened to go to Adelphi. But I also had a scholarship to Cornell University, so my mother was like, "You're giving up Cornell for Adelphi?"

So, I went there and I signed up for History of Black Music in

---

[*] A different Dr. Dre (Andre Young) found fame with N.W.A.

America, Professor Andrei Strobert. So in attendance was myself; another gentleman named Harold McGregor, a.k.a. Harry Allen; another gentleman named Carlton Ridenhour, a.k.a. Chuck D; and, of course, Mr. Bill Stephney was in that class.

Bill Stephney (Bomb Squad, Def Jam): It was magical in that we had four guys, all thinking they're the smartest guy on the planet—probably why we were all friends. And we had a professor who was a wonderful jazz musician, who could see within us that we were serious about our appreciation and our expression of music, that we were young, and that we needed an adult in the room to provide that necessary academic and artistic guidance. Andrei Strobert was without question that guy.

André "Doctor Dré" Brown (DJ, artist, Original Concept): We would go back and forth about a lot of different things in that class. And I would always bring up things about Earth, Wind & Fire, Parliament-Funkadelic, and all these different things, and they kept turning and looking at me, *Who is this kid?*

We were all cool, and one day Bill took me to BAU and he said, "What do you think? I do my show on Monday, and Chuck and them have a show on Saturday night."

I said, "Wow. Can I come by?"

He said, "Sure, come on up."

Bill Stephney (Bomb Squad, Def Jam): I wanted to be a radio DJ and my radio idol was Frankie Crocker. He was the program director of WBLS, 107.5 in New York. If there is a collection of Black men of that era who were just the epitome of cool, he's on the list along with Clyde Frazier, Dr. J—just style, debonair, sophistication.

André "Doctor Dré" Brown (DJ, artist, Original Concept): I started to meet all these different people—Butch [Cassidy], Hank [Shocklee], Keith [Shocklee]. And I said, "This is what I've always wanted to do, but I've never had a place like this or a group of people who are like-minded."

So, we built a great relationship and eventually, being there at BAU, I was trained as an engineer. We would do a Thursday night party at Adelphi. They hooked me up with Keith Shocklee, and we just took it by storm. When we threw a park jam through BAU, we would have thousands of people there.

Eric "Vietnam" Sadler (producer, Bomb Squad): I had a band, and we would rehearse in my basement, and my parents were really getting tired of it and so were the neighbors. My dentist, who lived across the street from me, Dr. [Raymond] Gant, I talked to him and he said he would rent me some space. So, using the equipment from my friends in the band, my friend Charles and I moved down there and opened up the studio. I got some cork from the local hardware store and put cork up. And that was it. It was like, "Alright. We're going to have a rehearsal studio and we're going to charge seven bucks an hour for bands to come in and rehearse."

Professor Griff (Minister of Information, Public Enemy): Eric had a studio in the basement of 510 South Franklin. We just called it 510.

Eric "Vietnam" Sadler (producer, Bomb Squad): We were casual friends—me, Hank, Keith, Chuck. Griff would always be playing percussion with a different band and working on his martial arts. Even though we were in different towns, we would see each other all the time.

One day, I get a call. It was Hank. He's like, "Hey, I heard you had some space. Do you think you could help me get into where you are?"

I'm like, "Alright, I'll talk to the doctor and put in a good word and try to get you in."

Dr. Gant said fine, but I'm responsible for them. And that was it; that's how they got into the building.

André "Doctor Dré" Brown (DJ, artist, Original Concept): We all went in there and we did a lot of creative things. Security of the First World came out there doing the parties with us. We always had to have security at our parties, because we gathered quite a crowd.

Professor Griff (Minister of Information, Public Enemy): Security of the First World came about as a result of the work I was doing in the community. It was at a time in New York where almost at every party, someone was getting shot, beat up, robbed. You took your chance on going out to some of these parties. I got tired of it, and I put together a crew and we actually secured parties. Prior to that, I was training them in martial arts. I had thirty, forty students at a time. I set up study groups and we started studying together and training in martial arts.

Keith Shocklee (producer, Bomb Squad): When Chuck told his dad that he was going to pursue a music career, parents went crazy. My mom was looking at us like, *What are y'all gonna do with your lives? You can't keep doing this music.* And we knew there was something there, but we didn't know what it would be. The whole world was saying this is a fad, while, on the bottom note, we understand that independent record labels are making money.

André "Doctor Dré" Brown (DJ, artist, Original Concept): For us, this was a lifestyle. This is what we have to do. We did not treat it as a fad. We treated it like we could really make this happen.

PEOPLE NOTICED WILLIAM Drayton's eccentric personality first, followed closely by his deep knowledge of music. Drayton took the name of MC DJ Flavor, hosted a show at WBAU, and quickly ingratiated himself with the rest of the group.

Bill Stephney (Bomb Squad, Def Jam): We didn't take Flavor seriously at all. Flavor was this guy who always had a smile on his face, hat to the side, sunglasses on even though it's twelve midnight. Has a suitcase full of cassettes of all the music that he was working on, and this ranged from R&B to soulful blues ballads to everything else. You hear him coming because you heard the shaking of the cassettes in the suitcase.

You know the Marx Brothers? Now, Harpo Marx was the complete, thorough, silly fool of the brothers. But then he would become serious, and he'd sit down with a harp and play just the most intricate of classical pieces and he's a virtuoso. Flavor was kind of like that. He would be this jokester clown all the time, but then, when he would become serious, especially when it came to his music, you realized that this guy can play ten instruments.

André "Doctor Dré" Brown (DJ, artist, Original Concept): Chuck was really the bombastic MC because he had the voice. He had the cadence. Flavor was more the comic relief.

Professor Griff (Minister of Information, Public Enemy): I'm like, "You need a hype dude to keep the party going, so people won't think about robbing somebody or fighting." Flavor was that dude, and it worked.

André "Doctor Dré" Brown (DJ, artist, Original Concept): Flavor was like a love-to-hate guy. You loved him, but you hated him sometimes because he became annoying. But his annoyance was just in making sure that the music got out there, and he drummed up his own little personal fan club and he would do his own personal little song, and eventually he got the hour and a half before the *Super Spectrum Mixx Show.*

WBAU BECAME A hotbed of early hip-hop and the exchange of energy and ideas. Before becoming Public Enemy, the hosts cut and scratched records on the station and participated in record pools. Run-DMC conducted one of its first radio interviews at the station, and a synergy developed between Spectrum City and the group. Because of a lack of hip-hop available to play, Spectrum City rounded out their show by cutting their own demo.

André "Doctor Dré" Brown (DJ, artist, Original Concept): With Chuck, we did a party somewhere and some dude tried to stick it up and was trying to shut down us doing these parties. So, Chuck was getting angry like he does, he went and wrote a song called "Public Enemy No. 1," which was trying to tell everybody, "You guys try to imitate what we do and you can't do it, so why don't you leave it alone. If you want to know, we'll teach you how to do it, but don't come here and mess it up, so we can't go back there."

I had been talking with Russell Simmons and Rush [Artist Management] on the phone and he told me, "Well, you want to fix the music, you need to see Rick Rubin."

He gave me Rick's number and I go see him at Def Jam. For us, Def

Jam, at the time, was brand-new. The only song that we ever heard from Def Jam was "It's Yours" by Jazzy Jay and T La Rock.

I met with Rick Rubin and I played him some stuff. I played him "It's Great to Be Here," "Can You Feel It," and "Knowledge Me."

He went crazy. He said, "This is insane! Who did this?"

I said, "Well, I did."

He said, "Get out of here. I've got to sign you."

I started DJing for Rick [with Beastie Boys], because Rick was like, "Yo, Dré, I'm getting real busy. We're about to make this big deal at Columbia. I can't DJ with them all the time, would you mind taking over and DJing for me?"

So, I went in the studio with Rick and [Original Concept member] T Money and Keith Shocklee and my man Eric McIntosh, and we actually recorded the first single and changed the group.

ORIGINAL CONCEPT RELEASED the underground hits "Can You Feel It?"/"Knowledge Me" in 1986. Soon afterward, Doctor Dré brought Public Enemy's demo to the attention of Rick Rubin; Russell Simmons recalls DMC alerting him to the group.

By that time, Bill Stephney, the former program director at WBAU, worked for Simmons and Rubin at their young label.

One of his first assignments? Convincing Chuck D to sign to Def Jam.

Chuck D initially ducked Rubin's overtures to sign him as a solo MC, adamant that he had aged out of the role (he was twenty-six). Rubin's persistence eventually paid off. He signed Chuck D and Flavor Flav—about whom Rubin, as a hype man, remained uncertain. Public Enemy also formed a management company, Rhythm Method Enterprises.

André "Doctor Dré" Brown (DJ, artist, Original Concept): I'm on the road with the Beasties and I've got tapes of BAU. Then here comes "Public Enemy No. 1." They hear Chuck and they say, "You got to play this for Rick." They're telling Rick about it.

Rick says, "I've heard about this group. Come play it for me."

So, I go to Rick's dorm and Russell Simmons is laying on a futon, and I put it in the tape machine, and I press the button and Russell wakes up, goes over to the cassette player, takes the tape, and throws it out the window.

I say, "Yo, what the fuck are you doing?"

He goes, "Yo, man. That's nothing but a bunch of noise. That'll never, never sell."

Russell Simmons (cofounder, Def Jam): DMC brought it to us. I thought it was alternative and I thought it was cool as shit. But Rick was in love with them.

The argument that I didn't like them—it's not true. I thought they were cool as shit, and they were alternative, and they were very street. It was a record that hip-hop people would love. Public Enemy was b-boy. Rick liked it more than anything and did everything he could every day to sign Public Enemy.

Professor Griff (Minister of Information, Public Enemy): When Def Jam offered Chuck D a deal, Russell was the one that threw our fucking demo tape in the garbage. You can quote me on that, right. He threw our shit in the garbage.

So we stopped looking for him to be that go-to type of person at the label. We started relying on Rick and Bill and other people. Russell was into R&B and cocaine. He ain't into no Public Enemy. Ain't a radical bone in Russell Simmons's body.

Bill Stephney (Bomb Squad, Def Jam): Chuck was working for a photographic printing firm in Hempstead. He's a college graduate, graphic arts degree. Super, super-duper smart guy. He wanted to be Frankie Crocker or to develop a show on a major station, a different version of what Mr. Magic did on WBLS. And he knew that it was just a matter of time before he would get that opportunity.

We had so much popularity with the shows that we did on BAU. I'm MCing and hosting many of those parties. Our competition, if you wanted to call it that, was what Frankie Crocker was doing on WBLS. So we had a free lane to combine all those assets to develop popularity. And that popularity was the basis for opportunity.

And so Chuck is like, "Why should I become the next rapper whose 12-inch winds up being in the fifty-cent bin at a record store when I have the possibility of being the next Frankie Crocker?"

It's still the early '80s. Our shiniest, biggest example of Black stardom is Eddie [Murphy], who is growing up with, of course, Chuck and Hank in Roosevelt. But there's no Michael Jordan yet. There's no Spike Lee yet. There's no Oprah yet. All this stuff is about to happen. So the big star is whoever the big guy is on the local Black radio station.

André "Doctor Dré" Brown (DJ, artist, Original Concept): Rick Rubin signed Public Enemy to Def Jam, and Bill Stephney became vice president of Def Jam at the time.

Bill Stephney (Bomb Squad, Def Jam): I think it was a collective [effort that convinced Chuck to sign]. I think of Rick and his respect and desire to have Chuck as part of Def Jam. And our ability— me, Hank, and Chuck—to come up with a compelling concept and rationale for Chuck to become an MC and a recording star on the label.

Professor Griff (Minister of Information, Public Enemy): Every single thing that we were doing was a component that made up PE—it kind of all morphed together from 510 South Franklin. It morphed together from WBAU at Adelphi University. It morphed together from the stuff at the parties and the gigs and the jams. So, the show that Flavor had at WBAU, Chuck's show on BAU, what I was doing in the community, all that came together under one umbrella.

PUBLIC ENEMY RELEASED their debut, *Yo! Bum Rush the Show,* in February 1987, an album that officially introduced Chuck D, Flavor Flav, and the Bomb Squad and showed the potential of hip-hop music as an energizing force.

Even the group's logo—the silhouette of a man in the crosshairs of a rifle—showed the album's ambition of shocking the status quo. Initially, however, the group struggled to receive radio airplay.

Eric "Vietnam" Sadler (producer, Bomb Squad): Hank [Shocklee] and Chuck are the main focus of the ideas of what Public Enemy wanted to be. They had the majority of ideas and different things that they wanted to do, and since they didn't know basically almost how to even turn on equipment, they brought me in to take their ideas and make it into something.

I was R&B. I wasn't really hip-hop. I was a straight 64th/triplet note, grew up on soul and Earth, Wind & Fire. The hip-hop thing I liked, because my mentor was Larry Smith, who had done Whodini, Run-DMC. I was a fan of "The Message" and all of those early songs and bands.

So, when Hank and Chuck were coming to me with "Alright, we want to just take this little piece here and we want to . . . ," I started to get into the flow of what it was they were talking about. And from that point on, I started to write and I was extremely prolific at it. But the thought process originally came from Hank and Chuck. They didn't want something musical. They wanted aggressive noise.

I'm like, "Alright, fine. No problem. I can do all of that." But still, being a musician, I had to make it sonically resolve somewhere. Although we've been called noise and a bunch of different things, musically, things are relatable and technically sound and resolve somewhere in the record.

Ron Skoler (attorney, Rhythm Method Enterprises): Everything they did was very focused, from the logo that they had in the sights of the gun, to Chuck's voice and Flavor playing off of it—to add a little bit of humor to offset some of the harshness, the sugarcoating around the bitter pill.

Flavor, I thought, was really from the heart. He really did walk around with a clock around his neck. He really did say all of those things to people in the street. He was always joking—I can't say [he was] "in character," because I think that's really who Flavor was.

Eric "Vietnam" Sadler (producer, Bomb Squad): Me, Hank, and Chuck were basically in the studio for the first album maybe a week or two laying everything down, and then Chuck and Hank brought in Flavor for, like, two days, three tops, to do all of his parts, even his songs. He was always prepared, so it was easy, because during all of our sessions it was business. No drinking, no smoking, no women. Nothing, zero, whenever we were in the studio.

After Flav had his stuff, now it's time for the DJ's stuff. Norm [Rogers], at that time, Terminator X, wasn't really a studio DJ. He was for live blending and mixing. He hadn't become who he later on turned out to be. We needed to bring in Johnny Juice.

Johnny "Juice" Rosado was a technician who was hanging around the studio. Whatever we needed him to do, an idea, he could come in and just knock it out and give you ideas at the same time. So he came in and did the majority of scratching.

When Juice wasn't there, or Terminator wasn't there, Chuck would do some scratching. It was fucked-up scratching, but he has a rhythm that creates a whole other entity, a whole other feeling that you never felt before. So the combination of DJ Johnny Juice's technical aspect, Norman's regular rubbing, and Chuck's fucked-up style, that combination of all of us together is what made the sound. It's like atoms smashing into each other to create something else.

Professor Griff (Minister of Information, Public Enemy): It was really some raw type of shit that happened early Public Enemy times. It wasn't cute. Somebody had to establish that, and I just so happened to be the one. But nobody talks about that. They talk about the other stuff, the narrative that Def Jam wanted to put out there in reference to how Public Enemy got started. It's like, "Come on, man. Tell the truth."

Chuck wasn't no street dude. Flavor was a street dude, but Flavor wasn't a drug-dealing thief. But the conscious stuff—the martial arts, the studying, all the things that we did in the street to establish Public Enemy—reflected in what happened with Public Enemy. Those violent little altercations we had on the road—we had to put Terminator, Chuck, and Flavor, lock them on the tour bus and go handle that business. It was kind of ugly in the beginning, but we established it.

Russell Simmons (cofounder, Def Jam): It is totally false that I didn't like them from the beginning. When they came out with their record and there was criticism, they were talking about conscious things in a rough way, and it was kind of like they were becoming the Public

Enemy they became in their second album. Back then, there was no gangster rap per se and so they were perceived as the closest thing to gangster rap, and they were everything but that.

Bill Stephney (Bomb Squad, Def Jam): The fact that we were able to create something that started to draw some energy, it was definitely satisfying. But it was hard to appreciate because there was just so much going on.

André "Doctor Dré" Brown (DJ, artist, Original Concept): Mr. Magic had went after Chuck and Public Enemy [on WBLS], saying, "No more music by the suckers," and he would criticize what we were doing at BAU.

I was like, "Yo, what did he say? Is he crazy?"

And Chuck went and wrote "Rebel Without a Pause" and the rest is history.

He was so pissed off. That's what he'd do. Chuck would get mad, or we would get mad, we didn't come at you and get physical. We said, "Okay, we gonna out-think you. We're gonna out-promote you. We're gonna out-market you. You can't mess with our energy." And that's what BAU was. It was that energy. That thought process.

And even when things went bad, we found ways to make it work, and I credit it to our fellowship, our brotherhood. We just wanted to be treated legitimately. That's all we cared about.

Ron Skoler (attorney, Rhythm Method Enterprises): The B-side was "Rebel Without a Pause." And "Rebel Without a Pause" just blew up on the underground, and DJs like Red Alert were blasting it on the radio and it picked up nationwide, and that became their first record to get real radio play.

Bill Stephney (Bomb Squad, Def Jam): "Rebel Without a Pause" really gave the group more solid grounding with the established hip-hop audience that *Yo! Bum Rush the Show* didn't do. It was one thing to sample and loop beats, but it was another thing to have musicians making sure things are in key and in specific time signatures and everything else. It was just a different musical experience to combine the DJ experience with the musician experience.

Russell Simmons (cofounder, Def Jam): I loved that first album and the second album. "Rebel Without a Pause" was their birth. That was my favorite record.

PUBLIC ENEMY RELEASED its masterpiece, *It Takes a Nation of Millions to Hold Us Back,* in the summer of 1988. The album exudes boundless energy and pounding urgency through Chuck D's political and social commentary, with his many references to activist parties like the Black Panthers and the Nation of Islam; Flavor Flav's role as a timely foil; and the Bomb Squad's mix of dissonant and poignant production, featuring a diverse selection of samples.

On tracks like "Don't Believe the Hype," "Night of the Living Base-heads," and "Black Steel in the Hour of Chaos," the group's revolutionary spirit was on full display.

Eric "Vietnam" Sadler (producer, Bomb Squad): *Nation* was the only album we ever worked on as the Bomb Squad—that all four of us worked on together. Every other [album], whether it was Ice Cube or Slick Rick or Doug E. Fresh or LL Cool J or whatever it was, it was always bits and pieces of us, but never all together.

Keith Shocklee (producer, Bomb Squad): Records are based on feel, what feels good at this point in time. When you're rocking a party, you're going to play a certain record that's going to make the crowd go crazy. So it's always about that. And we didn't care if it was in key or not because rapping wasn't about being in key. It was about how dope you was and how big your drums were. We would break the rules and Eric would shape what we broke, so it can be musically in time.

Bill Adler (publicist, Def Jam): They're fans of Run-DMC and even so, as time goes on, they become critical not just of Run-DMC, but the culture at large. They're guys who are asking you to pay attention to the news. They're not going to live in a little youthful bubble. Racial politics in New York, mid-'80s into the late '80s, are pretty fraught. Public Enemy are paying attention to it.

Keith Shocklee (producer, Bomb Squad): When we did Spectrum City, we did "Lies" and "Check Out the Radio." Both songs were based off a Run-DMC bite.

Bill Stephney (Bomb Squad, Def Jam): Our expressions were more, I think, to the general condition of Black folks. We had our own versions of what we thought were challenges and difficulties that we felt were general. And we also thought we could take advantage of additional resources, and probably our ability to have more comfortable lives gave us the room to be political.

So, if you're from a difficult everyday circumstance in Harlem, in the Bronx, in South L.A., that every-moment struggle, we didn't have that, which allowed us to then tap into the education that we get from an Andrei Strobert. And instead of us treating our experience from an elite standpoint, we felt that we had an extra responsibility, because we had advantages, to express and to impact socially.

Professor Griff (Minister of Information, Public Enemy): In order to get popular and famous in this new art form, people were just kind of pulling from what they saw around them. So if you wanted to make a whole damn song about a sneaker, then do that. That's just not what we do. If you want to talk about "Latoya" and "Renee" and all these songs about women and the way you do it, that's just not what we do. We just had a different insight and we dared to go against the grain and speak truth to power.

Keith Shocklee (producer, Bomb Squad): It was Marley Marl doing everything [for the Juice Crew's production]. With us, it was me, Eric, Hank, Chuck, Flav. So everybody's taking different parts, so we can go deeper.

The greatest thing I thought we had, we all heard things differently in records that we already owned. Eric would sample a part from a record, and I would be like, "Oh shit, I would have never thought about taking that part." But that's the uniqueness of Eric.

Professor Griff (Minister of Information, Public Enemy): Eric was probably one of the most instrumental individuals in the Bomb Squad, because Eric knew how to play different instruments, and Eric was a dynamic producer and engineer.

Keith Shocklee (producer, Bomb Squad): When rap was coming up and it was getting hot, our parents were like, "What's all that noise you're listening to?" To us, it was music. It's just the parts that you wouldn't think of, or you wouldn't hear constantly over and over. Whether the pitch is off, we like the feel of it, because we played it in a way where it felt like it was in key.

Professor Griff (Minister of Information, Public Enemy): We had a determined idea and we had a studio and we had eight people around us—myself, Keith, Hank, Chuck, Bill, Harry Allen, Eric, Johnny Juice, Terminator X. The energy was flowing. But the idea that kind of fueled that was the fact that we were going to get in the industry, we were going to shock them, and we were going to get out.

Eric "Vietnam" Sadler (producer, Bomb Squad): The only thing I knew that we would have a little bit different was nobody was going to be able to re-create what we did. A lot of DJs would make a four-bar pattern, maybe have a roll, then another pattern. They'd have about three or four patterns. I'd have thirty or forty patterns in a song.

Because an actual drummer never plays the same thing, even if he's playing the same beat. There's a variation that creates a whole movie of a song. The hi-hat on this verse is going to be just a little bit different on the next verse, and you can't do that unless you have a real drummer, and if you don't have a real drummer, then you have to program not just four-bar patterns, but you have to make it into a whole stretch of a song.

Bill Adler (publicist, Def Jam): Public Enemy split the culture off in a whole new direction. PE puts out their first record in 1987. It makes some noise. Actually, it makes more noise in England. They're embraced more heavily in England because of their politics. By late '87 into '88—there's a production change. They get into sampling. They were fucked up by the sample Eric B. and Rakim used for "Eric B. Is President." You sample James Brown, how do you lose?

Paris (artist, producer, San Francisco): Chuck is supremely influenced by James Brown. A lot of his vocal cadences come directly from that.

Bill Adler (publicist, Def Jam): Come '88, *It Takes a Nation of Millions,* that blows up, because it was this magnificent marriage. It's not just the expression of Black pride in these lyrics, but the music is killing.

Keith Shocklee (producer, Bomb Squad): We saw people trying to replicate it, but they didn't come close. We were DJs, and everything we did had to have a reason. We knew music from a musician standpoint, but we took it from a sampling perspective, which people couldn't understand. [Dr.] Dre comes close to trying to replicate it.

And then you had like five people on a song. Everybody's putting in to the point where before you hear the final sample, we done tried six, maybe eight different samples for one part, and found the right one. We knew parts of records better than anybody.

Bill Adler (publicist, Def Jam): Two of the secrets to Public Enemy's success were: Hank Shocklee as the chief producer and Flavor Flav as comic relief. Nobody should underestimate the importance of their contributions, because if it had just been Chuck and a more average producer, it wouldn't have been as compelling. It would have sounded hectoring after a while—eat-your-spinach kind of stuff.

That record, *Nation of Millions,* which may be the greatest record to my taste in the history of hip-hop, came together, and it's really a very unique combination of talents. And it includes not just Chuck as writer and lead voice, but it includes Flavor as comic relief and a whole production squad, the aptly named Bomb Squad, and it's Hank at the head of it. But it includes Bill Stephney and Eric Sadler and Keith as well.

That's an astonishing array of talent, and they gelled long enough to produce this one magnificent album. The record drops in '88, and before the year is out there are cracks in that coalition and it's a terrible shame. And all you can do now is be grateful that they managed to hold themselves together and work fruitfully for as long as they did.

THE MOMENTUM GAINED from the work of *It Takes a Nation of Millions to Hold Us Back* was short-lived.

The group became ensnarled in controversy when Professor Griff encountered David Mills, then a reporter at *The Washington Times.*

> Griff made anti-Semitic remarks to the reporter in the summer of 1989,
> unaware that Mills intended to publish their conversation. In response,
> the Jewish Defense League in New York called for a boycott of Spike
> Lee's *Do the Right Thing,* which featured the group's anthem, "Fight
> the Power." The JDL distributed pamphlets castigating Public Enemy,
> even though the controversial words hadn't been spoken by Chuck D
> or Flavor Flav, the group's most public-facing members.
>
> A series of press conferences and public statements followed.
> The accounts varied: Griff had left Public Enemy, or he was fired, or
> Def Jam had disbanded the entire group. Griff expressed remorse for
> the remarks in 1990, following a meeting with the National Holocaust
> Awareness Student Organization.

Ron Skoler (attorney, Rhythm Method Enterprises): My experiences with Griff were always good. What he told me was it was after a show in Washington, D.C. They were in the lounge of the hotel. He was approached by a Black journalist for *The Washington Times,* which is a right-wing newspaper, if I am correct. And he started asking some questions and Griff thought the guy was friendly, and cooperated, and I think he was kidding around with him on a lot of stuff.

Professor Griff (Minister of Information, Public Enemy): The thing about it, somebody asked me recently, if you had the chance to do it all over again, would you go back and apologize?

I was like, "I can't apologize for the truth." I didn't make that stuff up. I'm a researcher. I'm well-read and I studied. I just pulled the quotes from wherever I could find them. It wasn't done in a malicious way. It wasn't vile. It wasn't mean-spirited. It was just a conversation. So, to see that turn up in the paper, I'm like, "Wow. Come on, bruh. Stop that. That conversation didn't go on like that. No, no, no."

Ron Skoler (attorney, Rhythm Method Enterprises): He didn't realize that this was all going to be quoted—quoted or misquoted, I'm not sure— and he came across in a really hateful way, so that if you didn't know him, you would feel like, *Oh, this is a horrible human being.*

It was a stupid thing to say. I know that he's not a hateful person, but I can understand how he'd be portrayed that way.

Professor Griff (Minister of Information, Public Enemy): To be honest with you, I thought I was going to die during that period. I had to move my family out of town, my children, to make sure they was safe. It wasn't as insulting as people was picturing it to be. None of the quotes were my quotes. They were all quotes that I lifted from Jewish people and authors and writers.

There's the story about the Jewish guy shooting at Def Jam, thinking I was in the building. That's the reason why I got a divorce; I moved out of New York; I went to Miami. So it was a very critical time for me. But my main thing was to protect my children.

Ron Skoler (attorney, Rhythm Method Enterprises): I always found Griff to be a nice person. I found him to be funny in a humorous, witty way. He was always polite. My experiences with him were good. I understand that he had certain political beliefs. Maybe he meant some of those things. Other things, I think he was kidding, and it came across in a twisted way. But knowing him as I have, I just do not believe that he's a hateful person, and I think that's what happened after this article came out and people started protesting against him. I think the industry put pressure on Public Enemy, on Chuck and Hank, to do something, and I think he was pretty much sacrificed so that they could go on in the industry. And then later on, they brought him back.

Professor Griff (Minister of Information, Public Enemy): That's the reason why I've got to tell my story. That stuff affects me to this day. I'm going to New Mexico tomorrow. They said they can't put my name on the flyer to promote the lecture in the Black history event. They can't even put my name on the flyer. Can you imagine that? Thirty years later. It's like, "Wooow."

DESPITE THE INTERNAL and external controversy, "Fight the Power" still pushed Public Enemy and hip-hop into a different realm, as Chuck D's voice reached more corners of the world and record executives took note of the potential for hip-hop's reach.

Professor Griff (Minister of Information, Public Enemy): We started to see people change. The nasty-ass, fake gold-rope chains that people used to wear, turn they neck green, they started taking them off and started wearing African medallions, pointing people toward organizations that were out there. People started joining study groups.

We would make one trip around; everybody would be wilding out. By the time Public Enemy came back around, the people were studying. We started to change the conversation. Even the people in the music industry are trying to make more uplifting songs.

Khujo (artist, Goodie Mob): When I first heard Chuck D's voice, I was like, "Whoa, man." It sounded like he was doing it effortless, like that was his real voice. So, I wanted my voice to sound like his. Public Enemy really influenced me to really say something in my raps, along with incorporating the strength of street knowledge.

Mr. Serv-On (artist, No Limit): When Public Enemy came along . . . it was the education of learning who I am. I was growing up in the South and from a civil rights city [New Orleans], so I knew the things I needed to know. My grandmother was caught in that, beaten trying to eat at Woolworth's and things like that. But the awareness that hip-hop talked about with the Furious Five and that song "The Message," it was everything. It was like your integrity, where I'm saying to myself, *Look at the power they've got.*

Bun B (artist, UGK): I think it all came together with "Fight the Power," just to be able to see hip-hop's voice, speaking of something larger than itself, something deeper than itself. It wasn't about radio or placement or sales or anything. It was about really getting a message out, which is the original concept of what hip-hop was meant to be as a culture, right? It was all about advancement. It was all about reinforcing and engaging, and I think when it's done at the highest level, people like Chuck D and Public Enemy, it can inspire a nation.

Kool Moe Dee (artist, Treacherous Three): Public Enemy is what I call the paradigm shift in hip-hop that kind of draws the line. By the time we get to 1989, a perfect storm happens where Public Enemy becomes popular on the street, very underground. They're not getting any mainstream radio play. Spike Lee taps them to do the main theme song for *Do the Right Thing*.

So, when they get the lead song on that movie and it's the opening theme on the credits and you see Rosie [Perez] dancing, and before the movie drops to have this synergy where everything's hitting at one time—it's very rare that you get Hollywood in line with the music industry, in line with the socially conscious [hip-hop] group. I don't think it's ever happened before.

Spike Lee was the new hot kid on the up-and-coming Black film side, and he tapped into Public Enemy and they do the video and "Fight the Power" is the lead single and we get to the line—"Elvis was a hero to most / But he never meant shit to me you see / Straight up racist that sucker was / Simple and plain / Mother fuck him and John Wayne"—when he says that, the crowd organically erupts, and that visceral reaction was caught on film. And you saw people looking at each other and shaking their head like, *I can't believe Public Enemy just said that*.

But we all feel that. That was the key to Public Enemy's success, the fact that they would say things that Black people felt but didn't have the heart to say or didn't think would be received well. They were absolutely proud of Public Enemy being who they were and saying what they were saying unabashedly with no apologies. So when Public Enemy did that video and that moment happened, I said white America just got served notice that we are here, this is what we feel.

And [the artists] put the profanity in there because they didn't have any ambitions of being on the radio. N.W.A was trying to be anti. They didn't want to be pop. And because Public Enemy did what they did, the powers that be said, "We have a vested interest in gangster being popular. So we'll bleep the profanity out and put it on mainstream radio," which hadn't ever happened before in hip-hop. So now you have N.W.A. You have Ice Cube and then Snoop and Dre coming right out on the heels of all of that stuff being mainstream, because that is where the money is at now. "We want you to focus on gangster as opposed to social consciousness or anything political."

Ice Cube (artist, N.W.A): Listen to *Nation of Millions*. Listen to *Straight Outta Compton*. Got a lot of the same breakbeats in there. It was a period of maybe four or five years where breakbeats made up most of hip-hop.

It was a thing where me and [MC] Ren—Dre was a Chuck D, Public Enemy fan—but me and Ren was fanatics. We loved Public Enemy. Everything they was delivering was fire to us. "Straight Outta Compton," "Fuck Tha Police," we was hoping that we would create the same kind of energy that "Rebel Without a Pause" had, "Don't Believe the Hype," or "Bring the Noise." I was hoping to get that kind of energy going, and we did. Dre, why he's a genius, he was able to take that and make it our own thing and not just copy what we liked.

Bill Adler (publicist, Def Jam): Before that year is out, here comes N.W.A with *Straight Outta Compton*. Each of them defined the culture and it split the culture. Street rap turned out to be more popular. Conscience rap had an impact. Public Enemy had a career for twenty-five or thirty years. Chuck stayed true to his beliefs. He continued to make wonderful records. I don't think there was ever a conscience rapper that came after PE that topped PE in terms of the power of the music, but they were tremendously influential.

DJ EFN (Crazy Hood Productions, Miami): When N.W.A came and Public Enemy, they're equally as important to me, I had never heard emotions transcend that way through music. It hit me, like I'm either scared of these dudes or scared of Compton, or fuck, these guys are angry. I felt their emotion and it changed how I viewed hip-hop. And then I realized how important hip-hop was, how it was the music of my generation, so I felt like, *Shit, this is my generation's music. I got to get involved.* I had never felt the emotion that I had felt in other hip-hop artists until N.W.A and Public Enemy.

Big Gipp (artist, Goodie Mob): I learned everything from Chuck D. I didn't know about [Louis] Farrakhan until I heard it come out of

Chuck D's mouth. I didn't know about a lot of stuff until I learned about Chuck D. Chuck D is my everything. He is so much of the real deal that they killed them off the radio for twenty years, thirty years.

Once he dropped "Burn Hollywood Burn," you didn't see no more videos. After he did that video, and I think there was another one ["By the Time I Get to Arizona"], they took Chuck and Public Enemy off the TV. As soon as Bob Johnson sold BET to Viacom [in 2000], you didn't see Public Enemy anymore.

08 A GUMBO OF MAGNIFICENCE

New York City
1979–1988

By the close of the 1970s, just a handful of songs that would be retroactively labeled as hip-hop had made it to the radio. The percolating culture and genre still possessed no steady on-air outlet. That changed in 1979 when Mr. Magic started purchasing airtime on the tiny New York station WHBI for his show, *The Mr. Magic Disco Showcase.* Mr. Magic played breakbeats twice a week starting at 2:00 A.M., and is widely credited as the first to play hip-hop on the radio.

Mr. Magic had gained his start as John Rivas, a Brooklyn DJ who worked as Lucky the Magician and moonlit at an electronics store. Sal Abbatiello, owner of the South Bronx club Disco Fever, was one of Mr. Magic's show sponsors. Magic spent long nights at Disco Fever, where the group who hung out into the early mornings came to anoint themselves the Juice Crew, and Mr. Magic became Sir Juice.

Inspired by Frankie Crocker, Mr. Magic joined with him to bring a hip-hop show, *Rap Attack,* to WBLS. Because of Mr. Magic, hip-hop was no longer confined to block parties and cassette tapes, but wafted throughout the city.

Led by Mr. Magic, the Juice Crew became hip-hop's first collective of legitimate all-stars, introducing groundbreaking artists like Big Daddy Kane, Biz Markie, and Roxanne Shanté, who were backed by the innovative production genius of Marley Marl.

As Def Jam Recordings spread hip-hop across the country and

brought it into the mainstream, the Juice Crew stayed tethered to their New York City roots. Over time, feuds, both artistic and destructive, became a defining feature of hip-hop. The Juice Crew's feud with the Bronx's Boogie Down Productions marks one of hip-hop's most notable early rivalries.

Afrika Islam (DJ, producer): When myself, Jazzy Jay, others—I'm just talking about the Bronx—[were] going down to Chambers Street, there was a person that was working at the [electronics] store by the name of John Rivas. And John Rivas is Mr. Magic. So that's where that connection was made. He was selling parts to us and every other mobile DJ in the city. We were doing this way before he jumped on the radio.

EARLY IN HIS radio career, Mr. Magic formed a relationship with the members of what would become the legendary group Whodini. The group broke through with "Magic's Wand," a shout-out to Mr. Magic.

Barry Weiss (president, Jive Records): I was telling [Jive founder] Clive [Calder] that we should do some rap stuff here at Jive. I was very close with Mr. Magic, who was the big DJ at WHBI, which was the community radio station, and they were breaking all these rap records.

Clive was like, "Listen, why don't we have [English musician and producer] Thomas Dolby produce a record, because he's really funky? He's got a really great bottom end"—like, bass and drum sounds.

I didn't fucking know rappers. So I was like, "Let's go get this guy Mr. Magic to rap on the record."

This would be the equivalent of getting Ryan Seacrest to sing on a record. I mean, if you look back on it now, it's kind of a cheesy idea, like [getting] Charlamagne from the Hot 97 *Breakfast Club* to rap on the record. But I didn't know really where to go. So I contacted Mr. Magic, who I was close with, and he was like, "Yeah, I'm down. . . . I never really rapped before."

And I'm thinking, *Fuck it. Anybody could rap. Right?*

So, we get it all set up and Thomas Dolby comes up with a track called "Magic's Wand." And it's basically a double entendre for his dick, right? Like, he's the magic man with the magic dick. We get it all set up and then the day of the recording session, I get a call from Mr. Magic saying, "Listen, I can't do this. I just got hired by WBLS to have a prime-time slot on the radio—I'm hitting the big time now. And my advisers and my lawyer is telling me I can't be on WBLS and have a record out."

It's a conflict, right? It was like twelve noon, for a five o'clock session we had booked for him to come in and rap. So I'm like, "You put me in a really bad spot here, man. What are we going to do?"

And he's like, "Listen, I got this guy named Jalil [Hutchins]. He's a really good writer. He's the guy that mans the vibe line for me." The vibe line was like the request line on the radio station. So he's like, "What about if we have him do it? I think he can rap and he's the one that's been writing the verses for me anyway."

We go to the studio, and I have fifteen hundred cash in my pocket for Jalil to basically rap the record. All of a sudden, he brings with him some other guy, and I'm like, "Who is this guy?"

And he's like, "Oh, that's my rhyming partner. That's Ecstasy."

I'm like, "Who the fuck is Ecstasy? I don't have money for this dude."

So he's like, "No, no, man. He's a great rapper. We're going to both be on the record."

I'm fucking just going apoplectic. I'm like, "What the F? I don't have money for this guy. I don't know how I'm going to pay him."

He's like, "Don't worry about it."

So I'm like, "Fuck it. We're here. Let's go. Guys, you ready to rhyme?"

They're like, "Oh, no, we haven't written the verse yet."

I'm like, "What the fuck do you mean you haven't written it yet? I'm paying for studio time here."

We spent, like, eight hours. I'm watching them standing over a fucking piano in the control room writing the verses and I'm thinking I'm going to get fired. So I'm like, "Guys, look, we're never going to get this done today. Why don't we just come back tomorrow and knock it out?"

Come back the next day and they actually knock it out. And the record sounds pretty fucking good. I think Jalil got fifteen hundred and like a one-percent or a two-percent royalty, and Ecstasy, to this day, never got paid a dime for the record.

Clive had this whole idea. He starts telling me all about this British group where they had interchangeable members. This preceded Menudo, where the members of the group were salaried employees. And he's like, "Let's just come up with a name. We'll own the name and the rights and everything, and then we'll figure out who's the actual members later if it gets past this one single."

So we're like, "Okay, what are we going to call it?"

Clive goes, "Barry, I think I've got the name. The record's called 'Magic's Wand.' Why don't we call them Houdinis?"

So I'm like, "You know what, Clive? That's a fucking great idea, but we shouldn't just spell it like H-O-U-D-I-N-I." I came up with the spelling, W-H-O-D-I-N-I.

So, Clive came up with the name, and I came up with the spelling, and that was the beginning of Whodini, which went on to have two platinum albums for us.

AS MR. MAGIC became a pioneering force, his future "Engineer All-Star" began discovering his passion and talent for music. Queensbridge native Marley Marl interned at a recording studio as a teenager. Around 1985, while working on Captain Rock's "Cosmic Blast," he stumbled into the realization that he could take the snares from vinyl records, insert them into drum machines, and craft his own sounds. This discovery would change the sound of hip-hop.

DJ Marley Marl (producer, Juice Crew): I was actually in Unique Recording [Studios] and I wanted something off of a record and just before we [cut off the excess material] I was like, "Yo, hold on. Don't truncate it. Turn the other snare down." And I started playing the snare alone. Then it hit me, I was like, *I can take any kick, any snare that I get from any record that I get a good response from, and tap out my own beats.*

I told the engineer to turn the other snare down. I played the snare alone with it, and the rest is history. Actually, I left the studio that day, bought a little bullshit sampler, and went home and started playing.

MR. MAGIC HAD heard of Marley Marl's precocious skills. Marley Marl had heard of Mr. Magic's braggadocio—so he was hesitant when Mr. Magic asked him to swing by the radio station. Yet Mr. Magic talked him into it, and when he heard Marley Marl perform a remix of Malcolm McLaren's "Buffalo Gals," an alliance was born.

DJ Marley Marl (producer, Juice Crew): One day, Mr. Magic came and he saw me DJing and he was like, "Wow. Yo, what you doing on the weekends?"

At that point, I was already a club DJ in the city, but I was about seventeen years old. I said, "Well, I do this on the weekends."

He said, "How much do they pay you?"

I was like, "They pay me this."

He said, "Well, I'll double it if you come to the radio station and do that."

I was like, "Okay."

So, the first day I went up there is when he threw on one of my remixes from the reel that I mixed in. He was going for the records and I was like, "Nah, that doesn't mix with it."

He said, "What you mean? Show me what you mean."

So I went and found a record that mixed with it. It was a seamless mix. He was like, "Yo." That was it from there.

FOR A SHORT stint, Mr. Magic and his manager, Tyrone "Fly Ty" Williams, operated their show from Philadelphia's WDAS-FM. While there, the trio U.T.F.O. stood them up for a promotional visit. Mr. Magic took offense. U.T.F.O. had a track, "Roxanne, Roxanne," in which the members alternate trying to catch a woman's attention. In response to being stood up, Marley Marl and a fourteen-year-old girl who lived in Queensbridge, Lolita Shanté Gooden, made "Roxanne's Revenge."

DJ Marley Marl (producer, Juice Crew): "Roxanne's Revenge" was never supposed to be a record. That was my special version of "Roxanne, Roxanne." Shanté was a girl rapper from the block. Her, [MC] Shan, and this guy named Infinite used to have all these battles on the block when I used to be coming home, and one day I stopped by. I was like, "Wow, that's intense and shit." Shanté, she was one of the best out there at that time. Now you guys [U.T.F.O.] are talking about trying to get Roxanne. I got the girl y'all trying to get.

PHILADELPHIA'S POP ART Records released "Roxanne's Revenge" as a 12-inch. This early "diss record," a song that verbally attacks a target, quickly became a sensation, bringing immediate cachet to Gooden (who started going by "Roxanne Shanté"), Mr. Magic, and Marley Marl. At a young age, Shanté became one of the first female artists to break out, allowing countless others to follow in her footsteps.

Eventually, answer records—songs created in response to previous songs—flooded in from everywhere: "The Parents of Roxanne," "Yo, My Little Sister (Roxanne's Brothers)," "I'm Lil Roxanne," "The Final Word—No More Roxanne (Please)."

Chris Schwartz (cofounder, Ruffhouse): I did the video for Roxanne Shanté, "Roxanne's Revenge." We shot that video at my house in West Philly. Mr. Magic and Marley Marl spent the night, and I got up in the morning, came down, and they're in my living room, on my couch, covered in blankets, eating cereal, watching cartoons.

Lady B (artist, radio DJ, Philadelphia): Roxanne Shanté was like a little sister to me. [I] loved her to death. I also had relationships with all the ladies that were coming out with the Roxanne songs. I gave a fair spin to all of the Roxannes. I played Shanté, I played the Real Roxanne. It was a fun time, because it was all about the battling.

MC Shan (Juice Crew, Queensbridge): We used to do it on the benches for fun, but then when I got on tour with Shanté and seen that I could make money, I'm not going back to work. My grandfather used to yell at me and say, "You got to come back to work." I'm like, "I'm making four hundred dollars for twenty minutes. I'm working all week for a hundred and twenty dollars. You've got to be crazy. I'm not going back to work."

MC SHAN LENT his vocals for 1985's "Marley Marl Scratch." Marl made the track by using a four-track cassette player, and its bass drum and snare signified the beginnings of Marl's turn toward his signature "boom bap" production. Around the same time, Marl also worked with a young Queens artist, Craig G, on the single "Shout."

MC Shan (Juice Crew, Queensbridge): That's the way I got in, by making a song about my DJ. I did the "Marley Marl Scratch." It was about the DJ, but then it became about the artist, which made the DJs kind of mad because they wanted half the money and we wasn't having it.

Cormega (artist, Queensbridge): Shan is an unsung hero. He doesn't get the credit he deserves. Shan has one of the best voices I've ever heard. There's people who have stronger voices, but I'm talking about his cadence. He had a dope voice, then he had that flow and then he was just smooth with it.

Craig G (Juice Crew, Queensbridge): Marley Marl lived in my building, and he knew who all the neighborhood MCs were. I don't know if Pop Art or Marley had the idea to do the rap version of "Shout," but they wanted a younger person and Marley asked me to do it. I went to the studio to record it and I rhymed for like six minutes straight, and Shan happened to be at the session and he had to show me how to break the rhymes up into verses. I mean, I was twelve years old. What the hell do I know?

AS MC SHAN started making a name for himself, another Queens MC began his climb to stardom: LL Cool J.

To Shan, LL Cool J had violated one of hip-hop's foundational tenets. Shan accused him and Rick Rubin of using bits of "Marley Marl Scratch" for "Rock the Bells," and in response, Shan recorded "Beat Biter."

MC Shan (Juice Crew, Queensbridge): At that point, we were still on our original thing. If we was writing a rhyme and that one word was close to yours, we wouldn't use it, we'd change the whole set. So, to take my beat while we're on tour—it probably wasn't his idea, it was probably Rick Rubin's or whatever. But then, "Oh, you out with Shan and that 'Marley Scratch' beat is hot." So they took and did the pattern. If anybody plays "Rock the Bells" and "Marley Marl Scratch" back-to-back, you'll see it's the same beat.

A RIVALRY BETWEEN MC Shan and LL Cool J never fully materialized. Instead, it was the B-side to "Beat Biter"—"The Bridge"—that helped spark hip-hop's largest lyrical rivalry to that point, bringing KRS-One, Scott La Rock, and Boogie Down Productions to prominence and deepening the burgeoning on-air duel between Mr. Magic and DJ Red Alert, who by then hosted his own rap show.

DJ Red Alert is a foundational figure in hip-hop who came up through Afrika Bambaataa's Zulu Nation. He started his radio career as part of the highly influential *Zulu Beat Show* on WHBI 105.9 FM. Red spun at clubs like the Roxy, where he first met Barry Mayo, the program director of WRKS 98.7 Kiss FM. Mayo hired him for his *Dance Mix Party*. While staying close to his hip-hop roots, DJ Red Alert is also credited with fostering and launching hip-hop's succeeding generation of talent.

Afrika Baby Bam (artist, producer, Jungle Brothers): He had one of the first shows that had a concept, with the whole "Red Alert Goes Berserk" [a Saturday Night Mastermix]. But I remember his shows before it got to that point, and it sounded like a real sound system throwdown: carefully curated, the right breaks at the right time, the right rap records at the right time, and everything mixed together, so that even if you didn't know a record in between, it fit with the other records you knew and it just made for a good tape. He was the DJ on the radio that was turning it over to our generation. Red was the guy that was bridging it.

Dante Ross (A&R, producer): He was the one who was from the old school, started playing all the new stuff, as he calls it. He stopped playing the drum machine records, the beatbox records, and started playing the sample records. He's the first guy to ever play Eric B. and Rakim, and he was the first person to play De La Soul. He's the official changing of the guard DJ. He's the older guy who embraced the youth. He's the first guy to play Public Enemy, first guy to play 3rd Bass, [A] Tribe [Called Quest], Jungle Brothers, Ultramagnetics, all that.

DJ Mister Cee (producer): We were just happy to have Red Alert and Chuck Chillout and Mr. Magic and Marley Marl be on Fridays and Saturdays. If you loved hip-hop in the '80s, all of New York City was listening to them. And that's all we had, was Friday and Saturday nights. Nobody was thinking that we would have a twenty-four-hour hip-hop radio station [in New York City with Hot 97].

Just Blaze (producer): In the early '80s, you didn't really hear rap music on the radio. You had Red Alert and Chuck Chillout on 98.7 on the weekends, and then on 107.5 you had Mr. Magic and Marley Marl during the same time slot. I was maybe only six years old at the time, but I had an older cousin who's around seven years older than me. He had two boom boxes. So I used to spend my weekends at his house, and he would have both boom boxes set up, one recording 98.7 and one recording 107.5. We were kids at the time, so it's not like we had a plethora of blank tapes. So we would record the shows for that week, listen to them all week, and then tape over those shows the following week.

J-Live (artist, New York): It was just constant four-hour sessions of all the latest, greatest hip-hop, and there was so much contrast.

MARLEY MARL HAD originally asked MC Shan to record "The Bridge" as an ode to some of Queensbridge's early DJs and artists, not thinking that anyone outside the neighborhood would ever pay much attention to it.

MC Shan (Juice Crew, Queensbridge): Before ["The Bridge"] was actually a record, Marley and them was on the radio playing it all the time. "The Bridge" was the first real record repping the hood instead of repping Queens, repping Brooklyn, repping the Bronx, that it actually represented our actual six-block territory in Queens.

OUT IN THE Bronx, Kris Parker was a child when his mother moved to an area adjacent to 1520 Sedgwick Avenue and the domain of Kool Herc. Parker soaked in the atmosphere of the block parties and later lived at the Bronx's Franklin Avenue Armory men's shelter on 166th Street as a teenager, when he came across Scott Sterling. Sterling had landed a job as a social worker at the shelter. The two originally butted heads before discovering their mutual passion for hip-hop.

Parker eventually assumed the moniker KRS-One—Knowledge Reigns Supreme Over Nearly Everyone—and Sterling became DJ Scott La Rock. The pair formed the backbone of the Boogie Down Crew and, later, Boogie Down Productions. They were still looking to break through when they happened upon Mr. Magic at Power Play Studios in Queens one night and eagerly attempted to play the influential radio host their demo.

DJ Marley Marl (producer, Juice Crew): I was in the studio recording with Roxanne Shanté. BDP was in the other room. They was excited to meet Mr. Magic. Mr. Magic said, "Hey, Marley, come in the room with me. They want me to hear their demo."

I was like, "Uh-oh," because I already knew how Mr. Magic was.

Craig G (Juice Crew, Queensbridge): Magic spoke his mind. And even if it was offensive, it was his truth. So it was kind of entertaining to me, to see him talk to people and tell them their music was trash.

Mike Gee (artist, Jungle Brothers): I liked Mr. Magic. I did not like the arrogance.

DJ Marley Marl (producer, Juice Crew): We go in the room. They played the fucking demo, jumping around like it's the shit. Mr. Magic looking at everybody like they crazy. All of a sudden he's like, "Hold up, man." He goes over to the fucking knob and turns it down. "That ain't real hip-hop. You want real hip-hop? Marley Marl, Roxanne Shanté, MC Shan, Mr. Magic. That's real hip-hop."

So now he walks out the room and leaves me with these fucking guys. They're upset. We're wrapping up. I get the fuck out of there.

Mr. Magic is my ride back to the hood, so I'm rushing to get everything out of the studio before we leave. In my rush, I forgot my [drum] reel. I didn't notice for a few days, I was like, *Damn, where is my fucking reel?*

About two months later I go back to Power Play, I saw my reel on the desk, I said, "Oh, shit. Who had this? Yo, this where it was at?"

I pick it up, snatch it off of the desk, and leave.

AFTER BEING DISMISSED by Mr. Magic—and already simmering over the notion that hip-hop had started in Queens, as some took "The Bridge" to imply—Boogie Down Productions hunkered down and wrote. Their response was "South Bronx." On the track, KRS-One took aim at MC Shan while crediting the Bronx's Kool Herc, Grandmaster Flash, Afrika Bambaataa, and other borough natives as hip-hop's architects. DJ Red Alert, already in a rivalry with Mr. Magic, eagerly amplified "South Bronx" over radio airwaves.

Paradise Gray (manager of the Latin Quarter, X Clan): First time "South Bronx" played in a club, I played it. Scott La Rock came before the club opened with KRS-One and Ms. Melodie. He introduced me to them, and he handed me the test press. He said, "Look, man, this is my new shit. You think you can get Red Alert to play it?"

And I was like, "I don't know. Let's see what it sound like."

I put it on the turntable and I turned it up, and good lord, it banged crazy on our sound system at Latin Quarter. I was like, "Damn, Scott. This shit is a hit."

He was like, "Word?"

So, when the club opened, I played it again and the early crowd blew up. And so when my house DJs came, they played it four or five times before Red Alert even came to the club. So by the time Red got there, that shit was busting crazy. The crowd blew up. And the rest was history. Red played it four more times that night. That record played like nine times in one night, and the crowd went bananas every fucking time. From the first time it ever spun, we knew it was a mega-hit.

Carlos "Six July" Broady (producer, Hitmen): Probably around [the mid-80s], I heard a Chuck Chillout mixtape, and it had "South Bronx" on it. And just the way that record was put together, that was the spark [that birthed my interest in hip-hop]. But the second moment was probably in '86 when I heard "Eric B. Is President." I remember hearing it and I lost my mind. I had to find that record.

You hear "Rapper's Delight," and I knew that was "Good Times" replayed. But the way the record "South Bronx" sounded, I'd never heard nothing sounding like that. Just imagine being a kid hearing some shit like that.

THE JUICE CREW answered with MC Shan's "Kill That Noise."

"Yo, Shan, I didn't hear you say hip-hop started in the Bridge on your record," Marley Marl said on the track.

"I didn't, they wanted to get on the bandwagon," Shan responded.

Boogie Down Productions delivered a knockout rebuttal with "The Bridge Is Over": "Manhattan keeps on making it, Brooklyn keeps on taking it / Bronx keeps creating it, and Queens keeps on faking it," KRS-One declared over the boom bap and reggae–inspired track. Marley Marl later discovered that his own misplaced drum reel was used to produce the track with the help of Ced-Gee, an associate of Boogie Down Productions and a member of the Ultramagnetic MCs.

DJ Marley Marl (producer, Juice Crew): All of a sudden, here comes "The Bridge Is Over." And the funny thing about it, I never really listened to that song, because if I would've really listened, I would've been like, *Oh, that's my fucking drum sounds pitched up*. But I never even paid attention to it.

One day, one of the engineers from Power Play told me, "Yo, Marley. You know Ced-Gee had your reel?"

I was, "Fuck outta here. What you mean?"

He said, "When you left your reel that time, they went in the studio and picked your reel up."

I was like, "Get the fuck outta here. They're the ones that stole the reel and resampled all my shit off the reel and put it back?"

So now, with him telling me that, I'm going back through Ced-Gee's productions and I'm noticing my kicks and my snares on his shit. I'm hearing Ultramagnetic records, some of them, some BDP joints with my drum sounds on it and shit. That was the golden reel.

Mike Gee (artist, Jungle Brothers): At that time, it was all about Red. I would fight for Red all day, until my last breath. I think when KRS did "The Bridge Is Over," it was like alright, this is the anthem, this is the war call.

Dante Ross (A&R, producer): I rocked with Kris. I've known him a long time. I know all those guys. They were Latin Quarter dudes. They were known to shut people down. And I thought it was admirable, these two cats from the Bronx took on everybody and they won. Shan was a much lesser rapper. And I preferred what KRS-One and them did. I prefer Boogie Down Productions' music to Shan and basically all of the Juice Crew, except Biz [Markie] and [Big Daddy] Kane.

Cormega (artist, Queensbridge): "The Bridge Is Over," that was a perfect record, [and] people in the Bridge played it. I think that's one of the things that makes Queensbridge so dope. It's really a hip-hop hub. They embraced it. Like, you can make a song dissing Queensbridge and if it's dope, people from Queensbridge will tell you it's dope.

Craig G (Juice Crew, Queensbridge): Listen, you have two choices. Somebody says, "Hey, man. Get that outta here. That music's trash," and you can go home and cry about it, or you could use that energy and create something, and that's what Boogie Down Productions did, and that was dope.

Cormega (artist, Queensbridge): The song "The Bridge" was amazing to me, and then "South Bronx" came out. That was okay. Then "Kill That Noise" came out. I was feeling that. Then "The Bridge Is Over" came out and I was like, *Whoa*. That was the exclamation point. It was just lessons learned and history being absorbed.

MC Shan (Juice Crew, Queensbridge): That's what we did back then. That was the whole entertainment portion of what we did. It wasn't always about preaching a message. We did this for sport.

Cormega (artist, Queensbridge): There's a thing about battling and there's the thing about being friends with somebody. So, people that I am real close with, I wouldn't want to battle with them. Me and Craig G were friends for a very long time. So I wouldn't want to battle him. There was a lot of rappers that I was cool with. That's why we didn't battle, because we were friends and we have respect for each other. Mutual respect. After a while, when you get to a certain point and your name just starts being so dominant, then everybody wants you to battle people. You might not even want it to be a rivalry, but the public demands it, then before you know it, you're defending yourself.

Easy Mo Bee (producer): Witnessing the beef between KRS-One and MC Shan, which turned into a Bronx/Queens thing, I think that was a better example of a beef because it wasn't violent, not to the point where anybody actually got hurt. Hip-hop has always been a sport of competition. So it's only natural that one MC is going to spar with the other. It's just that we never expected it to travel to the point of violence [in the following decade].

A CHARISMATIC BIZ Markie, innovative Big Daddy Kane, and lyrically precise Kool G Rap joined the likes of Roxanne Shanté, MC Shan, Craig G, and Masta Ace to form the crux of the Juice Crew. Most eventually signed with Tyrone "Fly Ty" Williams and Len Fichtelberg's Cold Chillin' Records, which was distributed by Warner Bros. Records.

DJ Mister Cee (producer): When I first met Kane, we in high school, in Brooklyn. He pulled out an old-school ELI-mic out of his inside pocket of his leather jacket and was battling the kid. The mic is not hooked up to nothing. He just pulled it out of his pocket. I'm like, "Holy shit."

MC Shan (Juice Crew, Queensbridge): Biz bring Kane in, but Kane had to earn his way up through the ranks like everybody else did. Like Biz did. If you wasn't the shit, you couldn't get down with the Juice Crew. We was already established. Shanté was already established. Shanté established me. We looking to establish the next one. So if you wasn't good, you wasn't getting down, period.

Masta Ace (Juice Crew, Brooklyn): I won this contest, and this first prize was six hours of studio time with Marley. I was given a phone number and the skating rink, which is where I won the contest, they had prepaid him for the time, so I called that number for the entire winter into spring. His sister would answer; she'd be like, "He's not here." And that would be the end of it.

I was calling every week or so and it got to the point where she knew my voice and she knew my name, so she would answer the phone, "Hi, Ace. My brother's not here." And then, one day, I don't know if she just started to feel sorry for me or maybe we had built a little bit of a rapport over the phone, one day she was just like, "You know what, Ace? This is not his number. He don't stay here no more. Here's his real number."

And I called him, and I'm like, "Yo, my name is Masta Ace. I won this contest last winter, and you owe me six hours of studio time." I was real indignant about it.

And he was like, "Alright, well, meet me such and such day in Queensbridge projects."

Me and my DJ at the time, Steady Pace, we jumped on a train from Brooklyn. We rode all the way out to Queens to this project, and we got out there early, and we're sitting on the bench in front of his building. Then, after a couple of hours, Craig G comes walking up. He was like, "Y'all waiting for Marley, right?"

I was like, "How did you know?"

He was like, "Yeah, he's always got people on this bench waiting for him."

And so he sat there with us, and we talked a couple hours, probably. We got there at, like, eleven-thirty. Marley pulled up at, like, five. But I'm like, "We're not leaving."

And, he pulled up, he had just bought a new car. He was at the dealership, I guess it took longer than expected or whatever, but he probably didn't even remember that he told me to meet him there. And we went into his studio, which was actually his sister's apartment in Queensbridge, and I started the process of recording my first demo.

DJ Marley Marl (producer, Juice Crew): I was just making tracks and just passing them out, like, "Here, you get this, Kane. You get this, G Rap. This for Shanté."

But Kane had ideas, too. Kane would bring me a loop and say, "Yo, I want you to chop this up." And I'm like, "Yo, it doesn't go." And he was like, "Yo, make it go."

That's how Kane really opened me up wider in production, because he started bringing me little loops and saying, "Hey, put this in there. Hey, I want to do a record off this." And he opened me up to faster beats.

MC Shan (Juice Crew, Queensbridge): At that time, we were the only voice for the hood. The news only would bring light to the negative situations in our hood and not really put any light on the plights of our people.

Masta Ace (Juice Crew, Brooklyn): [The Juice Crew] had all of the bases covered in terms of different types of artists—nobody was the same; everybody had their own thing, their own flow, their own style, their own image.

It's unfortunate that we were stuck on a label [Cold Chillin' Records] that didn't have respect for their artists and was more in the business of robbing their artists than taking care of them, because everybody could've done a lot more, put out more projects, potentially had more success if the label had been more of a stand-up label.

MARLEY MARL'S SAMPLING and use of James Brown samples forever changed the sound of hip-hop, revolutionizing the genre and providing the sonic template of the golden age. His work paved a lane for super-producers like Pete Rock, DJ Premier, Large Professor, and RZA.

DJ Marley Marl (producer, Juice Crew): James Brown is the first b-boy. James Brown's music you were always able to dance to and, every time we would throw these songs on at a party, would always result in something great. I already knew that James Brown was a catalyst. It was something dope already.

Masta Ace (Juice Crew, Brooklyn): [Marley Marl] took this James Brown thing and did some weird stuff to it, and I didn't really understand it. It sounded so different than everything that I was like, "I don't know if this is going to work."

Looking back years later, [he's] definitely one of the innovators. From a production standpoint, he did some really new and different things. I asked a lot of questions. "Why'd you do that? Where'd you get that sound from? What does this machine do?" I just really tried to soak in everything that I could.

DJ Mister Cee (producer): Everything before Marley was the Linn-Drum* and stuff like that. Marley changed everything. Unofficially, he's the first person to sample James Brown. That alone, you got to give Marley one hundred percent, two hundred percent credit for what he did, what he brought into his production style. Once Marley started indulging with the samples, it just spread like wildfire.

Easy Mo Bee (producer): In my opinion, pause tapes were my original teaching. But when I saw Marley Marl come out with the Juice Crew—that is Big Daddy Kane, Roxanne Shanté, Biz Markie, Kool G Rap, Masta Ace, that whole movement right there—I'm listening to what Marley was doing and also to Hurby "Luv Bug" [Azor]. Huge influence on me. I'm listening to what they're doing and I'm like, *Yo, that's not too*

---

*The LinnDrum is an affordable drum machine that features high-quality samples, released in 1982.

different from what you doing with the pause tapes and the overdubbing. So I guess it was just something that was meant to happen.

"THE SYMPHONY," FROM Marley Marl's *In Control, Volume 1,* came about organically. The 1988 track featured Juice Crew members Masta Ace, Craig G, Kool G Rap, and Big Daddy Kane all trying to one-up each other through lively verses. The lengthy track was one of the first examples of a posse cut in displaying the solo artists engaging in verbal sparring.

In 2017, *Rolling Stone* ranked "The Symphony" as the forty-eighth greatest hip-hop song of all time.

Marley Marl (producer, Juice Crew): We was doing a photo shoot for the back of the album cover and I wanted to re-create Kane and G Rap, [how] they rapped on "Raw." When we was going back to the studio after the photo shoot, Kane suggested, "Yo, let's re-create that today." So, G Rap happened to be there [with] Kane, Masta Ace, and Craig G.

We decided to do the record. I had a beat. I played it. They was like, "Yeah, that's a hot one." Those two were sitting over there ready to rhyme and G Rap didn't want to go first. Kane didn't want to go first.

Craig G (Juice Crew, Queensbridge): So, Kane came up with the transition, "And next up, I believe that's me." And then he left because he has some shows or whatever. So it's me, Ace, and G Rap sitting there, and we're all taking our time writing—me and G. And Marley was getting impatient, so he let Ace get up there, and he killed it.

DJ Marley Marl (producer, Juice Crew): We was going to throw Shan on the record with them, actually, and Shan didn't show up. And it became the biggest record in the Juice Crew.

MC Shan (Juice Crew, Queensbridge): I just knew that "The Symphony" was a Marley trick. I had been there before. Marley would say, "Let's go make a tape," right? And the next thing you know, the tape becomes a record. So I knew this already.

There's no regrets of me not being on "The Symphony." I get many questions asked of why I'm not on it. They said they were going to do a tape. This happened the same day that we did that picture for Marley Marl, *In Control*. They went to the studio, and I went home. And there you have it. "The Symphony" with Masta Ace. Ace's spot would have been my spot if I would've went.

Masta Ace (Juice Crew, Brooklyn): I wasn't even that fond of the beat, initially, to be honest. Like, it was cool, [but] it wasn't that dope to me. I felt like Marley had done doper stuff. And, since I wasn't intended to rap on it, I wasn't really even thinking about anything, I was just in there, chilling, watching G Rap and Craig and Kane write their rhymes. And, when it came time for somebody to spit, they were all kind of passing the buck. Craig was like, "Yo, let Kane go." Kane was like, "Let G go." G was like, "Let Craig go." And they were just going around and around.

DJ Marley Marl (producer, Juice Crew): I said, "Masta Ace, go on the front." Because I wasn't even going to keep his vocals. I just wanted to have something there to erase. He can go first, then Craig G can go second, then whoever is going to go can go.

Masta Ace (Juice Crew, Brooklyn): I always got something. They were like, "Go in the booth, show these guys. They're acting scared. Go in there and warm up the booth." So, I went in and I spit a rhyme that I had from memory. It wasn't something I wrote to that beat. It was just something I walked around with. And I laid my verse down, and then everybody got comfortable, and then everybody went in order. And that's how that wound up on the song.

DJ Marley Marl (producer, Juice Crew): [Masta Ace's] verse came out so hot, everybody was looking around. I was like, "Yo, that sounds like a keeper to me." So now we move on. Craig goes down.

Masta Ace (Juice Crew, Brooklyn): I heard Craig's verse, I was like, "Okay, his verse was cool. It's dope." You know, me and Craig was cool.

DJ Marley Marl (producer, Juice Crew): G Rap goes, he rhymes all the way to the end. He didn't leave no space for Kane.

Masta Ace (Juice Crew, Brooklyn): And then G Rap rhymed I don't know how many bars, sixty bars or something. He rhymed so far that the two-inch tape ended, like it went off the reel.

Craig G (Juice Crew, Queensbridge): He rhymed until the spool came off the tape. So there's like a whole other half of G Rap's verse on "The Symphony" that people never heard. This was before Pro Tools, so you have to have enough space on the tape.

Masta Ace (Juice Crew, Brooklyn): He left no room for Kane, and Marley was like, "Yo, you've got to shorten that, because Kane's got to still go. You've got to leave some space for Kane."

DJ Marley Marl (producer, Juice Crew): I had to cut his vocals down and give Kane some love on the record and that's how "The Symphony" was made.

Masta Ace (Juice Crew, Brooklyn): [Kool G Rap] was like, "Alright, I'll just say something different." He had another one. Like, he said this sixty-bar verse, I don't even remember what the rhyme was, but he had another one, so he left room for Kane.

When I heard G Rap's verse, I was just like, "Man, I should've said something different." Like, I started thinking about: *I could've said this verse, I could've said that verse.* I was questioning everything because G Rap was just on another level with the rhymes.

FOLLOWING THE ATTENTION gained from the Bridge Wars, Boogie Down Productions crafted their debut studio album, *Criminal Minded,* released through B-Boy Records in the spring of 1987. The album's cover featured KRS-One and DJ Scott La Rock posing with weapons. KRS-One provided poetical teachings on top of Scott La Rock's crisp production. Soon the group was in negotiations for a deal with Jive.

Less than six months after the release of *Criminal Minded,* La Rock acted as a mediator for an altercation between Boogie Down Productions' Derrick "D-Nice" Jones and an adversary. La Rock was shot while leaving the South Bronx's Highbridge Gardens projects and died hours later at Lincoln Hospital. Two people were arrested for the murder the following year, but were acquitted.

Barry Weiss (president, Jive Records): They were buzzing off of the *Criminal Minded* album, which was a classic album. And then Scott La Rock tragically got killed.

All the other labels ran for the hills. Scott La Rock had the bigger name at the time because he was a DJ and made music. But the rapper was KRS-One, and he was the writer, the lyricist. So I was like, "Fuck it, let's keep going."

And so, I had the conviction to continue with the deal, despite the fact that one of the primary members of the group was deceased. KRS-One is one of the greatest ever, one of the greatest live artists, one of the greatest lyricists. He was an amazing artist to work with.

> **MORE SONGS FOLLOWED** in the Bridge Wars, but after "The Bridge Is Over" and Scott La Rock's murder, the rivalry between the Juice Crew and Boogie Down Productions lost most of its steam.

MC Shan (Juice Crew, Queensbridge): The only reason why I didn't make another record behind what Kris did is because Marley didn't produce it. In a different day and time, I would have went to my computer and made my own beat and did my own rhymes.

> **KRS-ONE AUTHORED A** pioneering and influential legacy in safe-guarding hip-hop's cultures and traditions. He dropped a number of classic albums and was one of the first artists to frequent college campuses. He and MC Shan once filmed a Sprite commercial in which they mimicked a rap battle while in a boxing ring, but according to Shan, the two have never lyrically confronted each other. Decades after the Bridge Wars, KRS-One and Marley Marl joined forces on a collaborative album: 2007's *Hip Hop Lives*.

MC Shan (Juice Crew, Queensbridge): [KRS-One] also perpetuates the story of "how I took Shan out." Me and Kris have never battled. We've done many shows together and the closest thing we ever had to a real battle, face-to-face like that, was the Sprite commercial. I always be on some "Got to stop telling the people that you took me out."

He knows the rules of hip-hop more than anybody I know. All this "Well, I've sold more records than you did" is bullshit. That's that new battle shit. The old battling way is "Nigga, I'll go face-to-face with you, and one stage, one mic, and that's the end of it." We never did that.

AS HIP-HOP CONTINUED to evolve and expand, few states—let alone another six blocks—continually impacted and influenced the genre as much as Queensbridge. Those ninety-six buildings of public housing development produced the likes of Marley Marl, Roxanne Shanté, Craig G, Blaq Poet, Cormega, Havoc, Tragedy Khadafi, Capone, and Nas.

DJ Marley Marl (producer, Juice Crew): Queensbridge is so close to Manhattan. You're looking across the water. You're seeing the lights come up every night, and a lot of people from Queensbridge was looking at Manhattan like, "Hey, we want to be over there." If Manhattan wasn't that close, where you could literally just walk across the bridge and get to where everything was at, that [ambition] wouldn't have been there.

Cormega (artist, Queensbridge): Queensbridge is the biggest housing projects in America. Every single block is big enough to be its own projects. So, there is six big blocks like that inside one project.

You heard stories of rappers going from neighborhoods to neighborhoods to battle people or for competition. Queensbridge has talented people in every block. So I think it's the competitive nature that makes Queensbridge so good. Because if you suck, you wasn't going to make it out of there.

Queensbridge is like Rome. Rome was cultural epicenter. You had Rome, going to Egypt, picking up some of their culture. They was getting some of their culture from Greece. And that is how Queensbridge is. It was a place of renaissance. It was a place of inner bickering. That's why I used to call it Rome, too—the inner bickering caused it to fall.

So, Queensbridge is in a middle of everything, so it picks up everything. Queensbridge is Brooklyn and Manhattan and all of that shit meshed into one. It is a gumbo of magnificence.

DJ Marley Marl (producer, Juice Crew): Before rap, there was a lot of people making records in Queensbridge and those were the people that I looked up to. Mr. Darryl Payne [a post-disco record producer and songwriter] lived on my block. Andre Booth [an early hip-hop producer] lived in Queensbridge. A whole slew of musicians were in Queensbridge and were making records already before hip-hop was even here. We was on the map already.

Cormega (artist, Queensbridge): You were able to see some of the top gladiators often and early. I started eating fish sandwiches because MC Shan used to be on the block eating a fish sandwich. And that was my favorite rapper. I wanted to be just like Shan. I got to see Biz Markie's debut. Got to see Marley Marl. Seeing those guys on a regular, I was in awe of pretty much all of them.

I started rapping as a joke. You know how people roast people? I'd be like, "You got bummy gear, nappy hair, your mother's on welfare, your father robbed the liquor store and all he took was beer." That was one of my first raps. Shit like that. I was playing around with it.

And then seeing MC Shan perform live at a park jam, the grace and the way he put the words together—hearing the songs is one thing but seeing somebody—it was a big difference. That's when I was like, *I want to do that.* Then, from people challenging me and me winning, that's when I started realizing, *Wow, I can really rap.* But Far Rock taught me how to be a battle rapper because Far Rockaway is an aggressive place. I called Queensbridge Rome, but Far Rockaway could easily be called Sparta. That made me tough as a rapper.

It's like a fight. Sometimes when you're having a fight, you might be intimidated by the guy, but when he hits you, the adrenaline just goes up, or he hits you and you're like, *Oh my God, that's the best he could do?* And that's how I was with raps. Sometimes I would hear people rap and I'd be like, *Word? This the guy that everybody was saying was so good?* And I'll say a rhyme and it's over after that, and then people would just be in awe.

09 REINVENTING THE WHEEL

New York City and New Jersey
1986–1996

The success of Run-DMC and Def Jam, which proved hip-hop's gargantuan commercial viability, would usher in what is now known as the golden age, during which a wave of innovation, competition, and diversity swept across the genre. The music's pioneers, having established hip-hop, had left a canvas for another generation to take it wherever their imagination landed, and to master its capabilities and influence. While New York remained hip-hop's heartbeat and epicenter, the genre started spreading outside the boroughs as Philadelphia artists like Schoolly D and West Coast artists like Ice-T and N.W.A gained a following.

During this period, wordsmiths like Rakim, Big Daddy Kane, Slick Rick, KRS-One, and Kool G Rap elevated the artistry of lyricism. Artists such as MC Lyte, Queen Latifah, and Salt-N-Pepa broke down doors for female artists. Producers influenced by Marley Marl, like Pete Rock and Gang Starr's DJ Premier, began establishing New York's sonic template. And the Native Tongues provided a bohemian alternative.

The divisive policies of the Reagan administration, and the havoc that the crack epidemic wreaked on urban communities, served as much of the golden age's backdrop. The gap between the rich and the impoverished became more pronounced during this time, as wealthy people and big business received tax cuts and social benefits were stripped. Much of hip-hop music reflected the desperate conditions of

the era. Public Enemy continued to document societal ills, while consciousness groups came of age, offering pro-Black messages and dis-
patches of Afrocentrism. Meanwhile, the genre faced a backlash that
permeated most mainstream media outlets, which often blamed hip-
hop music for violent incidents at concerts.

Afrika Baby Bam (artist, producer, Jungle Brothers): There was the initial impact with the breakbeat days and the sound system up in the
Bronx and the drum machines. . . . Cats would be having ideas, getting
together, freestyling, and using a bit of the records for the call-and-
response action that you heard on the tapes, mixed in with your own
story, and it was kind of like it was in your blood. 'Cause you connected
with it and you could relate to it so strongly.

Even if you didn't have a drum machine or access to a studio, you
go through some joints and beats, records you would take off the radio,
that you think would work, make a little pause tape. Or you pull out
your notepad and you start writing some lyrics and you create that
magic that you heard.

And that's why groups like Run-DMC were the forerunners of taking it different places and through different mediums. It was like, "Yo,
see look, they was just on MTV. Look, they was just on the radio over
here. Look, now they at Madison Square Garden." It's not like they're
only in their neighborhood at a jam. "Oh, they're in this magazine,
now they're in this newspaper." That was the little telltales.

DMC (artist, Run-DMC): It wasn't a thing of being accepted, trying to be
famous. We became famous because of the brilliant things we were
creating.

Afrika Baby Bam (artist, producer, Jungle Brothers): There's so much more
creativity to come that could get it to where it is today, or where it
was in the '90s when they had a full hip-hop radio format from Hot
97 to the Baka Boyz, to Sway & Tech. It was like, "Yeah, this genre
can hold down a whole station twenty-four hours, because there's so
many variations and offshoots of the rudiments that still isn't here
yet, that could be."

You saw that when the Fat Boys had a beatbox. Doug E. Fresh was

beatboxing with Slick Rick's storytelling. You had Biz Markie beatboxing, but doing comical stuff, then you had the female rapper. Then the
drum machine with Davy D just making instrumentals. A lot of those
rap records had one instrumental cut on the album for DJs. So, there
was lots of different techniques that we knew right away, but again it
was like all this ground is uncovered.

> **RAKIM ALLAH, BORN** William Griffin, grew up in Long Island's Wy-
> andanch, surrounded by music. His aunt was the R&B great Ruth
> Brown. In 1985, another rapper had stood up Eric B., a DJ who had
> established a relationship with Marley Marl. Eric B. was now on the
> hunt for an artist to align himself with. A promoter recommended Ra-
> kim, and eventually the new DJ/MC pair headed over to Marley Marl's
> place to cut their demo.
>
> For many, there is Rakim followed by every other artist who has ever
> touched a microphone.

Marley Marl (producer, Juice Crew): When I first heard Rakim, I knew
there was something special. He wanted to rhyme off of slower beats,
so we did the slow "My Melody" first, and then we picked the tempo
up on the second song, which was, "Eric B. Is President."

MC Shan (Juice Crew, Queensbridge): I recorded the vocals. Rakim had
a funny style. His style was laid-back—and I can't say nothing, I'm
like the main creator of laid-back styles—but his was laid, laid-back.
So me and Marley laughed at him.

Marley would say, "Tell him to change the style."

Ra say to me, he'd go: "Yo, Shan, come on. Nobody don't tell you
how to rhyme. How you going to tell me how to rhyme?"

And I just had to look at the nigga and say, "You know what? He's
right like a motherfucker. Do your thing."

Marley Marl (producer, Juice Crew): I figured that we was just making a
demo that I didn't know if it would have even seen the light of day. I
didn't know what Eric was going to do with the tapes from the studio.

THE PAIR DROPPED "Eric B. Is President" and "My Melody" in 1986. Their debut album, the following year's *Paid in Full,* from 4th & B'way Records, served as a challenge to all other artists and producers: The craft had advanced, and it was time to modernize.

Rakim's complex flow harmonized with the soundscapes Eric B. provided using sampling. Nowhere was the sync more complete than in "I Know You Got Soul," which helped to popularize the use of James Brown samples in hip-hop.

Dante Ross (A&R, producer): We watched the change right in front of us. When we first heard that shit, no one heard nothing like that. And then when he followed up with "I Ain't No Joke," "I Know You Got Soul," and other big records, it was like forget it. We knew it wasn't a one-time-only thing.

You got to remember, too, "My Melody" and "Eric B. Is President" are both hit songs, not just one. That record was like the longest-living hip-hop 12-inch of all time, probably. He reinvented the wheel right in front of us. But he's not the only one reinventing the wheel. At that time period, rap music grows in leaps and bounds.

RAKIM IS REVERED for his imprint upon legions of lyricists who followed him. Before Rakim, most artists followed rhyming schemes popularized by the likes of Run-DMC and LL Cool J. Rakim's flow was built on more intricate rhyme patterns; he challenged other artists to up their skills, and provided a figure for a younger generation— including Nas and Jay-Z—to study and emulate.

Dante Ross (A&R, producer): Rakim is very interesting, because he's from Brooklyn but grew up in the suburbs. I always feel like there's this wave of guys who were suburban rappers, De La Soul included. They had the ability to hone their craft in their basement with two turntables and a microphone—even Run-DMC were suburban kids, kind of. It no longer was the Bronx and Harlem. It's this wave of guys from around the way, out in Queens and Long Island

and other places, who were allowed to hone their craft within the house.

Skillz (artist, Virginia): Rakim was super cool; he always just seemed calm.

DJ Clark Kent (producer): It's almost like you never, ever saw him sweat. I don't think I ever saw him in any mood but "I'm a god of rap."

I will say this, he *is* the god. He's got one of the best sense of humors. He's funnier than hell. He's just a regular dude. He just can out-rap everybody.

Deadly Threat (artist, Los Angeles): We were used to a certain style, a certain type of finesse, and he was just a breath of fresh air.

DJ Clark Kent (producer): I always say Grandmaster Caz is the first best MC. The next best MC was Rakim. But Rakim was the most important MC ever. And I say that because everybody was rapping before Rakim. Then Rakim comes and everybody starts rhyming.

It was about "I take seven MCs, put 'em in a line. / And add seven more brothers who think they can rhyme. / Well, it'll take seven more before I go for mine / Now that's twenty-one MCs ate up at the same time."

It was about saying dope rhymes and saying them well. Not singy-songy rapping shit. We're not at a party no more. We're in a booth and we're going to show you that you have to be fuckin' amazing. Rakim changed the way MCs rapped. Dude jacked them right out the gate.

Skillz (artist, Virginia): Rakim was probably the first rapper where what he was saying was good enough. He captivated you enough with his voice and what he was saying. And that super-cool demeanor just struck me as something special. He could say one thing, and let's say we got three people listening. We all could interpret that one thing different ways. And I never knew whether or not it was voluntary or involuntary. That just made him genius to me.

Deadly Threat (artist, Los Angeles): He really turned it on, to where it was not just rhyme-like but a totally different style of music. And that was refreshing to not just a lot of the MCs, but as well as to society.

Bun B (artist, UGK): The way that people were able to express themselves, the way people were able to present themselves [in hip-hop at the time], it was a new way of looking at young Black men. The confidence, the swagger, the jewelry. Particularly, for me, Rakim.

Rakim's prose and Rakim's discipline to his craft, his level of confidence was really unmatched, and I think it all came together for me with "Microphone Fiend." Just the way the video was shot, the way they moved. I want to walk in a world like that. I want to be the man like that. And that's when I went from probably just looking at hip-hop and embracing the culture, to actually wanting to be an active part of it.

Capital D (artist, Chicago): Rakim is the difference between, say, military music and jazz. When you listen to Run-DMC it was, "dat, dat, dat" with the patterns. And then Rakim, everything is: "Follow me into a flow." Everything is just a lot more rhythmic.

It's a before-and-after. He basically kind of broke everybody's mind. Rakim had enough of a message, but he wouldn't beat it over the head. Every MC after him had some remnant, and owed something to him for breaking that mold.

Deadly Threat (artist, Los Angeles): I think everybody at the time could agree, he really, really brought us into a new era and style of rap. If it wasn't for him, a lot of people wouldn't have even attempted to go in different other directions.

Styles P (artist, the Lox): It shifted the culture. He sped it up. It's kind of like he was the computer of rap. It's like the introduction of something more advanced.

THE LATIN QUARTER, a Times Square nightclub originally opened in 1942, became an incubator of talent during the golden age. The club served as a beacon for those in the surrounding boroughs who wanted to listen and dance to the latest and newest hip-hop offerings. To ascend in the culture, artists had to prove themselves at the Latin Quarter by performing in front of a combustible crowd in a raucous atmosphere, while earning the approval of DJ Red Alert. Artists like

> Big Daddy Kane, Biz Markie, Queen Latifah, Salt-N-Pepa, and Public
> Enemy started making noise for themselves by appearing at the club.
>
> The air pulsated with a mix of menace and excitement. Public
> Enemy once argued with club security over a batch of fake weapons
> they intended to use as stage props. On any given night, chains were
> snatched. Fights erupted. Real gangsters mingled with the crowd.
>
> A generation of stars was born.

Paradise Gray (manager of the Latin Quarter, X Clan): I went to the Latin Quarter with the Awesome Two. They got an opportunity to do Celebrity Tuesdays, [which] was basically like Showtime at the Apollo for rappers, where they had a bunch of unsigned rappers competing like *American Idol*. The Awesome Two asked me if I would be a celebrity judge.

At that time, remember, it was no hip-hop clubs. All of the clubs would play rap music for an hour on a Friday and Saturday, but the rest of the night they would play R&B, and funk, and dance music, and salsa, and reggae. But [owner] Mike Goldberg gave me an opportunity after I smooth-talked him into making Friday and Saturday nights strictly hip-hop, from opening to close, and it worked.

Faith Newman (Def Jam, Columbia): Latin Quarter was the best. I saw so many early shows there. Public Enemy did their first show there.

Paradise Gray (manager of the Latin Quarter, X Clan): That whole night was crazy. It started out with my security force pulling guns on Public Enemy in the lobby when the S1Ws [Security of the First World, the group's security team] had those plastic Uzis in their suitcases with their wardrobe.

And then, to have Melle Mel—he was the star when we got there at Latin Quarter, he was the man—him and Busy Bee used to walk around the club, dissing everybody that was rapping: "The champs are here. The champs are here. All y'all bums, you can't get no crumbs. You all ain't getting no pussy tonight, no money tonight, because the champs are here."

Melle Mel, he was the Deebo onstage. Dudes would be performing their song and the crowd would be standing there looking at them.

Then, all of a sudden, they would hear a giant cheer. And they would get all smiley-faced, thinking they was rocking and shit, and look to the side, and Melle Mel is standing there with no shirt on. And then he's doing fifty push-ups while they're performing. And then he gets up, all swole up. He was calling himself Muscle Simmons. And he would go and snatch the mic from you, and be like, "Alright. Well, enough of this bullshit. Put my shit on." Right in the middle of your show.

Faith Newman (Def Jam, Columbia): Latin Quarter, as far as breaking records went, was the place to be. Red Alert would DJ. Biz Markie, Just-Ice, Schoolly D came through. The energy there was amazing.

Schoolly D (artist, Philadelphia): My stage show was, like, fucking raw. For the first ten minutes I'm fucking just drinking and smoking. It was weird as shit. Then I got to the music.

Back then, it was the real motherfuckers who got up at midnight to go out. It was Queen Latifah and Heavy D at nine o'clock. It was Ice-T, Schoolly D, and Just-Ice at two in the morning.

AT THE LATIN QUARTER, Melle Mel faced off against KRS-One, Kool Moe Dee battled LL Cool J, while, infamously, MC Hammer was booed off the stage during an early performance. The club instituted a changing of the guard, from the genre's pioneering stars to a new generation of icons.

Paradise Gray (manager of the Latin Quarter, X Clan): The first shot across the bow was LL Cool J. LL was the first newer artist to hold his own against a legendary old-school artist, which was Kool Moe Dee. When LL didn't back down from Moe Dee, it gave the new rappers the idea that "Look, we can compete with these motherfuckers." LL didn't exactly knock Moe Dee out of the box, but he did show you the changing of the guard was coming.

But I think the Melle Mel, KRS-One moment solidified it—when KRS-One stood up to Melle Mel and he had years of hype that he had to defeat. And it was obvious that people were ready for something new and a change.

At that time, hip-hop at the Latin Quarter was participatory. When those records come on, the IOU and the JAC dancers are running to the stage and start dancing. The whole crowd followed. Whodini was one of the groups that introduced the element of dance, probably better than anybody else in that era. They were the bridge between breakdancing, popping and locking, electric boogie, and what became known as freestyle hip-hop dancing.

It was like a live *Soul Train* for hip-hop. You needed beats that could bounce, and you needed dancers that knew how to rock. And if you didn't have the dancers, there was no way in hell you could compete with Heavy D, Salt-N-Pepa, Kid 'n Play, Big Daddy Kane. Because now they had all the elements of an extremely entertaining show.

[MC] Hammer is the epitome of what I tried to do at the Latin Quarter, that if you wasn't honed, if you wasn't ready, you got booed. But I love an artist that comes in and ain't ready, and then come back hard. Hammer came back after that performance with "Turn This Mutha Out." And, like the consummate professional that he is, he came back right and he proved us wrong. And I really respect and love MC Hammer as an artist, a performer, and as a man.

Thirstin Howl III (Lo Life, Brooklyn): Latin Quarter, that was dangerous. That was when Brooklyn was dominating the club scene. Especially within hip-hop, violence and aggression and things like that.

Sadat X (artist, Brand Nubian): Latin Quarter was basically a madhouse. You definitely had dudes from uptown, but the majority was Brooklyn, and you already knew what you was going to get when you went there.

Thirstin Howl III (Lo Life, Brooklyn): The Brooklyn aggression was on a whole 'nother level. The role of Brooklyn was like, "We're coming to take your shit."

The one thing I learned in these clubs was how numbers dominated, how you overpower everything with the amount of people you come with. I learned that from Latin Quarter. I would go there with a few people from my projects and run into other people from my same neighborhood and we would link together. So I'm standing outside of the club with fifty dudes, and by the time I walked in, another twenty to thirty of them gathered up with me. So this was a big Brooklyn thing.

Sadat X (artist, Brand Nubian): I saw countless people get robbed in Latin Quarter, get their jewelry taken. I've seen girls get their earrings snatched. I've seen people get their gold teeth knocked out, all while the party kept going. It wasn't so much about shooting back then. You might go somewhere and just get beat up.

Paradise Gray (manager of the Latin Quarter, X Clan): You got to remember what time it was in New York. This was New Crack City. During the time of the Latin Quarter was when Larry Davis had the shoot-out with the twenty-five cops in the Bronx.

Ice-T (artist, Rhyme Syndicate): I was hanging in the South Bronx, working on music, and we performed ["6 'N the Mornin'"] at Prospect Theatre and we also performed it at Latin Quarter and Union Square. The funny thing is, New Yorkers thought that song was about Larry Davis, the guy who had ran from the cops in New York, actually had a shoot-out with the cops. So the timing couldn't have been more perfect for a song called "6 'N the Mornin'"—they thought I made a song about Larry Davis, so they really rockin' with it.

Paradise Gray (manager of the Latin Quarter, X Clan): During the time of the Latin Quarter, Alpo [Martinez] was in Harlem doing his thing. And Fat Cat and all of those guys was in Queens. It was a real crack-driven thing. Remember, during those times, all the rappers was bringing out the fat gold chains and the big cars and shit.

That wasn't crack dealers trying to look like rappers. That was rappers trying to look like crack dealers. So the ghetto superstars in the hood was the thugs and the gangsters and the crack dealers. They had the money. They had the cars. They had gold. They had the women. It was like the new, same-old pimp. The new Super Fly, the new Shaft.

Once that image started popping, now all the drug dealers and gangsters, "Hey, these niggas are just like us. These niggas are down with us." So, we had 50 Cent, and the A-Team, and the Brooklyn Zoo, and the Hollis Crew all hanging out in the same club, and that was a recipe for disaster.

Sadat X (artist, Brand Nubian): When Latin Quarter was going on, it was run by young people, for young people. So an element of that was a fear element inside. You didn't know what you were going to get from week to week, but you went back the next week because you knew that was the spot, and you knew certain songs was heat-up songs. You know, "Here I Go Brooklyn," Audio Two, somebody might get robbed on that song. You hear Kane, "Let It Roll, Get Bold," or "Warm It Up, Kane," you knew that the wolves was going to be out when that song came on. Some of Biz Markie's songs, there was a nervous anticipation of something could happen, but that nervous anticipation brought you right back the next week.

Faith Newman (Def Jam, Columbia): It's ultimately what closed it down. It was this total melee at the end that closed it down forever where a bunch of people got stabbed.

Paradise Gray (manager of the Latin Quarter, X Clan): When I went into the Latin Quarter, the big stars that was on stage was Melle Mel and Busy Bee. When we left Latin Quarter, it was Big Daddy Kane, Rakim, and KRS-One. A whole new generation of hip-hop stars were incubated there—MC Lyte, EPMD, Stetsasonic. We just totally changed the face of hip-hop.

THE GOLDEN AGE featured lyricists like Rakim, Big Daddy Kane, KRS-One, and Kool G Rap at the height of their abilities. They studied hip-hop's history, rhyme patterns, and wordplay, elevating the ingenuity of lyricism and lifting it into a competitive art.

Dante Ross (A&R, producer): It takes a fast-forward ten years in [those] one to two years, where there's KRS-One or Rakim or Big Daddy Kane. They're changing the game. So was [the Ultramagnetic MCs].

Things are jumping leaps and bounds in a short period of time, 'cause KRS-One is rapping off-beat, on-beat, and he's embracing metaphysics and all this other shit that no one did. And Rakim is expansive with his lyrical vocabulary and also his rhyme pattern. Big Daddy Kane is just a machine gun. No one's ever rhymed that rapid-fire before. These guys in an eighteen-month period are reinventing the wheel.

DJ Mister Cee (producer): In particular, Kane, Rakim, KRS-One, those three guys, the way they changed the music industry, lyrically, nobody was rhyming like them three. You got to throw [Kool] G Rap in there as well. Nobody was really making records at that fast a pace until Kane came around.

Styles P (artist, the Lox): As far as Kool G, Kane, Rakim, and KRS, I think they brought a shift to music that was more advanced than what came before them. They were saying things wittier, more clever, had wordplay and patterns to the beat that weren't stereotypical of what rapping or rhyming was before that.

DMC (artist, Run-DMC): We think we killing, and this guy Big Daddy Kane comes along. We think we're killing, this guy named Rakim comes along. This guy named Kool G Rap comes along. This guy named Ice Cube comes along. This guy named LL comes along. This group named Public Enemy comes along. This guy named Chuck D comes along. And this group called Cypress Hill comes along. This motherfucker named Phife Dawg and Q-Tip comes along. So that made us go back and find ourselves so we could fucking maintain and participate. But what that would do is, it elevated us all.

Dante Ross (A&R, producer): These guys come out and they're light-years beyond that. And then Public Enemy. Not rhythmically, not rap-wise changing the game, but sonically. We get this one period where everything's changed so quickly and the amount of growth in that short period of time [is] unparalleled, has never been surpassed.

Matt Sonzala (journalist, Houston): In the '80s, when crack was taking over, drug laws were changing, gang wars, Reagan/Bush—there was a lot of frustration, a lot of anger, and a lot of that came out in the music. When people get comfortable and complacent, the music is not as exciting.

Think about some of the jazz music that came out of the civil rights movement. Think about the blues music that came out of the turn of the last century, literally out of slavery. That's American music—hip-hop, blues, and jazz—that's American music to the core. All that shit came out of hardship, all that shit came out of struggle, came from pain, and they turned the pain into art.

DJ Mister Cee (producer): Everybody was in they own zone trying to create the best music possible. Myself and Kane, we really wasn't paying attention to what Rakim and KRS-One was doing. I'm sure they probably wasn't paying attention to us. We listened to their album, but we wasn't saying that we need to top what they're doing. We was just creating our own sound, our own movement, our own lane. If you really listen to the three rappers—Kane, Rakim, and KRS-One—it's three different deliveries, three different styles. It's hard to find two artists from that era that was successful that sounded the same.

BARRY WEISS WAS born into the music industry. His father, Hy, had built his own label, Old Town Records, in the 1950s. While a college student at Cornell, Barry worked part-time promoting songs to radio stations. Soon he met Clive Calder and became one of Jive Records' first employees in the United States, as the company started a distribution deal with Clive Davis's Arista Records.

Weiss may have lucked into aligning with Whodini. But he had his finger on the pulse of what people wanted to hear. Whodini's success facilitated Jive's ability to explore more hip-hop artists ignored by other labels. Weiss's efforts were aided by the addition of record executive Ann Carli, who cultivated relationships with artists and was an early recognizer of the genre's sustainability.

Throughout the 1980s and 1990s, Jive assembled a hip-hop empire by signing DJ Jazzy Jeff & the Fresh Prince, one of hip-hop's first significant mainstream crossovers; Boogie Down Productions; A Tribe Called Quest; Too $hort; and Schoolly D, among others.

Barry Weiss (president, Jive Records): I was the first employee for Jive Records in America. Jive was a company that was started by Clive Calder, a South African expatriate who moved to London and started the label. We had a distribution deal in America through Arista Records, and in Canada through Quality Records.

So, when he did the deal with Clive Davis for Jive at Arista, I got ensconced in the New York hip-hop scene, which I was in anyway before Clive hired me. I put out a record on my own with my dad. I grew up in the business, and I was very, very deep in the whole club scene. I was in my early twenties and into rap and New York, the Roxy and Afrika Bambaataa, "Planet Rock."

Ann Carli (senior VP, Jive Records): Arista Records, in the early days, considered hip-hop and rap records as novelty records. But these weren't novelty records. What the rappers were talking about in hip-hop, a lot of the subjects were timeless, whether it was a party record to a social record. The most important thing is story, because it links to everything. Whether it's a painting or something written, music, it's story that connects with other human beings emotionally.

Barry Weiss (president, Jive Records): We saw the fact that we had a competitive edge because the major labels were nowhere near this. The price of entry was not crazy, and we were an independent label trying to hit the ball where they ain't, so to speak.

ARTISTS AND GROUPS often caravanned together for hip-hop's early concert tours, fostering an atmosphere of camaraderie, kinship, and competition at sold-out amphitheaters, arenas, and coliseums. One notable example was 1987's Def Jam Tour, which spread hip-hop domestically and internationally and featured Eric B. and Rakim, LL Cool J, Whodini, Public Enemy, and several other influential acts.

Daddy-O (artist, producer, Stetsasonic): It's this big-ass tour, right? LL Cool J and Whodini are the headliners. Jazzy Jeff & the Fresh Prince is on that tour because they just starting to blow. They actually used to switch out with Doug E. Fresh on the weekends, because he had his own gig that he was doing. EPMD's on that bill. Eric B. and Rakim is on that bill, and Stetsasonic and Public Enemy.

LL Cool J's got with him [DJs] Bobcat and Cut Creator. Whodini, it's Jeff, Will, and [beatbox pioneer] Ready Rock [C]. Doug E. had [DJ] Barry Bee and [Chill] Will. It's six members in Stet. It's six members in Public Enemy. We shared a bus. It was cool because there was just so much talking, so much dialogue, so much learning. Prince Paul is basically putting together *3 Feet High and Rising* in his head, and I think he brought his drum machine.

My most fond memory is Chuck D and I bringing "Dope Man" on the bus, the N.W.A record, and everybody from Public Enemy cursing him out, and everybody from Stetsasonic, except for Wise, cursing me out. And we're like, "No, this is dope." And they're like, "No, it's not dope." We're like, "Listen, man, hip-hop is not just going to always just be New York. This is their expression of it."

DEF JAM HAD the opportunity to sign Jeff Townes and Will Smith, a pair from Philadelphia who had met in 1985 and released their independent debut single, "Girls Ain't Nothing but Trouble." But Russell Simmons was initially skeptical of the duo's appeal. (Eventually they would join Simmons at Rush Artist Management.)

Meanwhile, the pair signed to Jive Records. DJ Jazzy Jeff & the Fresh Prince gained mainstream popularity in creating a lighthearted brand of hip-hop. Although it was Smith who would become the Hollywood A-lister, it was Townes as DJ Jazzy Jeff who landed the greater impact on hip-hop culture. He proved himself a masterful technician on the turntables, and was one of the first influential DJs to come from outside New York.

The duo's first album, *Rock the House,* was released by Jive in March 1987. The next year's follow-up, *He's the DJ, I'm the Rapper,* was hip-hop's first double album, and included the mega-hit "Parents Just Don't Understand"; it went multiplatinum.

Lady B (artist, radio DJ, Philadelphia): The key that made Will as good as he was, was the fact that Jeff was so good. I know people laugh that I'm so biased. I will give the birth of hip-hop to New York every day— you can't take that history away—but when it comes to turntablism, Philadelphia stands alone. We did then and we still do now.

It is a real art. It's like playing an instrument. You can be an okay sax player, or you can be Miles Davis. Jeff is the Miles Davis of turntablism.

I remember the first day I put Jeff on radio to spin, the audience went frigging bananas. All those World Supremacy conferences they used to have, I remember the first year when Jeff won, and he took a basketball out and he scratched with a basketball. It was amazing. We all lost our minds.

DJ Jaycee (the Aphilliates): I had a friend in the neighborhood who was from Philadelphia. And he would have tapes, like little block party, house party tapes, third- or fourth-generation recordings that would feature DJs like Jazzy Jeff and Cash Money and Grandmaster Nell and Cosmic Kev. And the type of DJing that they were doing was very scratch-intensive, and the shit on these tapes from Philadelphia was way, way more advanced than anything that I had ever fucking heard in my life.

Hearing Jazzy Jeff and Cash Money do DJ routines with records like [Herman Kelly & Life's] "Dance to the Drummer's Beat" and "Pump Me Up" by Trouble Funk, that shit changed my fucking life. So, now I want to learn how to do what I'm hearing on these tapes. I put the practice in, and it took me a while, but we can say I learned.

Lady B (artist, radio DJ, Philadelphia): I just felt like [Will Smith and Jazzy Jeff] had something else. They were special. I remember calling Russell Simmons and asking for his assistance in getting them a real contract with a real label, and we got them that deal with Jive Records. The rest is history.

Will and Jeff had crossover appeal. They had the look, the boy-next-door kind of thing. They were very polished. Their beats were so dope, and the DJ is everything in hip-hop, and with Jeff being so friggin' amazing on those turntables, it was just a perfect mixture.

Him and Will, they just really went together like peanut butter and jelly. And back then is when we had all the battles on the turntables. So you have a DJ like Jeff who had started to master the artistry of turntablism, and you had this cute little boy who was from West Philly up there saying stuff that made you laugh.

Just Blaze (producer): When *He's the DJ, I'm the Rapper* came out, that was the first hip-hop double album, and one was like a rap album, and one was a DJ album. It was a Jeff album and a Will album. On Jeff's record, they had a track called "Rhythm Trax (House Party Style)" and it was just Jeff and Will re-creating routines they used to do when they were kids. And it was all very DJ-centric, and Fresh Prince was more so like the hype man.

FOLLOWING ROXANNE SHANTÉ'S breakthrough, female hip-hop artists like MC Lyte, Salt-N-Pepa, and Queen Latifah brought original-ity, talent, and charisma to hip-hop's golden age, more than holding their own against their male counterparts.

At the age of sixteen, Lyte, a native of Brooklyn, released her debut single, "I Cram to Understand U (Sam)," one of the first songs to address the crippling crack epidemic—discussing it through the lens of a romantic relationship. She released her foundational debut album a year later with 1988's *Lyte as a Rock*. Lyte became a cultural icon and constantly broke new ground. She was the first female rapper nomi-nated for a Grammy, and one of the first to put out a diss record.

Around the same time that Lyte started crafting "I Cram to Under-stand U (Sam)," Cheryl James and Sandra Denton met as nursing stu-dents at Queensborough Community College, becoming close while working together at Sears. The pair linked with Hurby "Luv Bug" Azor, an up-and-coming producer, who was soon working out of Queens with James and Denton, Kid 'n Play, Kwamé, and many others.

Debuting as Super Nature, the pair changed their name to Salt-N-Pepa. Their debut album, 1986's *Hot, Cool & Vicious,* was one of the first to challenge hip-hop's male sovereignty. Salt-N-Pepa, who in 1987 were joined by DJ Spinderella [Deidra Roper], expressed unabashed confidence in tackling topics others wouldn't or couldn't, and became the first female hip-hop artists to go platinum.

Janette Beckman (documentary photographer): I just loved the spirit of Salt-N-Pepa and the fact that they were really some of the first women in hip-hop to answer back to the guys.

Kwamé (artist, producer, New York): Salt-N-Pepa got on stage the way they were as women. They were just themselves. They didn't do anything different than how they were as normal everyday people. That's what I think resonates with Salt-N-Pepa. Women immediately connected with them.

WHILE AT NEW Jersey's Irvington High School, Dana Owens formed the group Ladies Fresh with her friends Tangy B and Landy D. Charging that all women were queens, Owens assumed the name of Queen Latifah. Her mother, Rita Owens, worked as an art instructor at Irvington and invited a local DJ, Mark the 45 King, to work at a school dance. Mark the 45 King produced Latifah's demo, which found its way to Monica Lynch at Tommy Boy Records.

Queen Latifah would advance to become the leading feminist voice in hip-hop, advocating for women empowerment beginning with her debut, 1989's *All Hail the Queen*.

Monica Lynch (A&R, Tommy Boy Records): There are three people who I credit bringing Latifah to my attention. Those three people would be Dante Ross, a very young A&R guy that I had just hired—he was formerly Lyor Cohen's assistant at Rush Management; Fab 5 Freddy, who was in my ear about Dana at the same time; and of course, Mark the 45 King. All three of those people were really buzzing at me about this chick, Dana Owens.

She wasn't Queen Latifah at that point. She came to the office and she probably just turned eighteen. She's wearing a sweatshirt, jeans, no makeup. She just looked like an around-the-way girl just hanging out. But we really clicked. She had a very strong presence. You could tell that she was very smart, very personable. She was very shy, but she also was engaging. She had a real warmth, a great sense of humor.

There weren't a lot of female MCs out there at that point. Of course, Salt-N-Pepa sort of wrote their own book as far as it's R&B, it's hip-hop, sexy type of thing. But save for Lyte, there weren't too many in the female hip-hop category that was taking it from this sort of hard, cool, "I can hang with the guys and get respect from the guys, and you can put me up with any of them." She had that going on, too.

Dante Ross (A&R, producer): With Dana, when she walked in the room, she looked a million bucks. And they played "Wrath of My Madness" and "Princess of the Posse" and I was like, "She's the one."

KURTIS BLOW HAD broken new ground by performing "The Breaks" on *Soul Train,* the syndicated television showcase for Black culture and art, in 1980. The show's host, Don Cornelius, conceded that he did not really understand the emerging genre when he interviewed Blow during the broadcast. Soon after, the Funky 4 + 1 appeared on *Saturday Night Live.* Those appearances represented anomalies. Hip-hop had remained a mostly underground phenomenon without much visual representation on television.

That started changing in the mid-1980s. Michael Holman, a veteran of downtown New York's music and art scene, opened television up to hip-hop across the country when his pilot for *Graffiti Rock* aired in June 1984 on New York City's WPIX-TV and in nearly one hundred markets around the country. The nationally syndicated show featured artists like Run-DMC, Kool Moe Dee, and the New York City Breakers, a b-boy crew. Despite strong ratings, *Graffiti Rock* was not picked up as a regular series and instead gained cult status over time as one of hip-hop's earliest visual gems.

Michael Holman (journalist/filmmaker/creator, *Graffiti Rock*): When I first was trying to get *Graffiti Rock* off the ground, it took me two years to raise the money, to design the show, and it finally aired in '84. I was very conscious of that paradigm of middle school kids being the engine that drove hip-hop, and I wanted to design a show that was for young people, so that I could plant those seeds so that when those kids grew up, they would grow up on this movement.

DJ Mister Cee (producer): I became a fan of Jam Master Jay watching *Graffiti Rock.* It was a TV show that came on locally here in New York. It was Run-DMC and the artist Shannon and the Treacherous Three. They was all on the show. Jam Master Jay, the way he was cutting up

"Sucker M.C.'s," he made it sound totally different from the record during the live performance.

Michael Holman (journalist/filmmaker/creator, *Graffiti Rock*): I'll never forget back in the early 2000s, Q-Tip approached me and he said, "Man, I just always wanted to thank you and tell you how much I appreciated *Graffiti Rock*. I was that twelve-year-old kid who when I saw this show, I wanted to be a rapper because I saw Kool Moe Dee and Run-DMC."

If I only inspired Q-Tip, then *Graffiti Rock* was a huge success. It was only on a pilot for one episode. It aired in eighty-eight markets all around the country, had great Nielsen ratings, but we couldn't sell it because the station managers, mostly all middle-class white men, didn't understand. The big pushback was "Rap is a fad. It won't last."

So I had Trendheimer's disease. That's kind of a joke term meaning I was five years ahead of my time, and I suffered for it. Timing is everything. It's great to be the first with something, but it usually is the kiss of death. You want to be there when everyone else has made the mistakes. The people who do things first, they've made all the mistakes, and now you come in and clean up.

IN NEW YORK, Ralph McDaniels was an engineer at WNYC-TV when he pitched a show that would play some of the videos he was receiving from record companies. In 1983, New York City kids began hustling home after school to catch the latest episode of *Video Music Box*. The hip-hop videos it aired were true to the atmosphere that the city's children were now born into. McDaniels hosted the show with Lionel "Vid Kid" Martin, and after a while started directing many of the videos himself, to supplement the short supply. The long-running *Video Music Box* became an educational stimulant for hip-hop and helped fuel the early careers of Jay-Z, Nas, and many, many others. Several years later, MTV belatedly created *Yo! MTV Raps,* a show that helped usher hip-hop into the mainstream.

A generation of kids who had grown up with hip-hop pulsating around them were now coming of age in New York City with the genre firmly established. They heard the music on the radio, riding subways, playing at the park, and could see it increasingly on television. It permeated the air and coursed through their veins.

Sadat X (artist, Brand Nubian): [*Video Music Box*] was the one, even better than MTV, because now this was coming on every day. And on Fridays they would play the new videos, and you'd race home to see those, and then watch it again, the recast next morning.

Just Blaze (producer, New Jersey): The advent of the music video: There were two video shows that ended up coming out on network TV all around the same time. One was called *New York Hot Tracks*, and then you had *Friday Night Videos*. And then, during the day, you were able to watch *Video Music Box*, and Ralph McDaniels, Lionel Martin, they were kind of the pioneers of the rap videos.

So, me being surrounded by all of that, plus my dad was a jazz organist, so there were always keyboards around the house, some of which had little drum machines built into them. So I'm mimicking the stuff that I'm hearing on the radio with the drum machines.

Fast-forward a little bit and now I have one of those Casios, and my mom had bought me the Radio Shack DJ Mixer that a lot of early DJs from that era had. And as I'm becoming more fascinated with the culture, I'm asking for records and it's the same records that I'm hearing on these mix shows, whether they're Kool G Rap and [DJ] Polo's "Poison" or Chuck Chillout and Kool Chip.

And then getting into my mom's attic and finding a box of records, and it was all James Brown, Isaac Hayes. Forty-fives from the late '6os, early '7os. As I'm playing them, I'm realizing, *Oh, these dudes are taking these records and putting them in these machines like I have here, and rhyming on them.*

Then, something on *Video Music Box*, they showed Prince Paul's DJ and production setup and he has a Casio SK-5 sitting there. So I'm looking at it like, *Oh snap. I have the same tools that they do, I can make the same kind of records.*

J-Live (artist, New York): *Video Music Box* superseded *Yo! MTV Raps*. It superseded *Rap City*. I'm pretty sure Dee Barnes's *Pump It Up* came way later as well. Those were our sources in terms of hip-hop videos. *Video Music Box* also gave you access to all these different party scenes.

It'd be videos and Ralph McDaniels's deep voice talking about what he's about to play next, and then they cut to a scene at a party. Some of these parties were around my way. Different mixtape DJs would be spinning, like Ron G, Double R, S&S, Chuck Black, Kid Capri, Chill Will, Doo Wop, Tony Touch. That was a huge part of the culture, just in terms of showing it to you live in your living room, whether you were there or not.

Sha Money XL (producer, New York): I used to watch *Video Music Box* all the time. Ralph was everything, because he gave you the interviews, he gave you the club scenes, he gave you the whole vision of hip-hop through the real eyes of what was going on in New York. There was other things that came along, but *Video Music Box* was the foundation for videos in hip-hop.

WHEN RALPH MCDANIELS pitched MTV on a hip-hop show, the cable channel, still slow to acknowledge the genre, declined. But as hip-hop's variety and popularity continued to expand throughout the golden age, MTV eventually relented by allowing two employees, Ted Demme and Peter Dougherty, to film a pilot built on a show first introduced in MTV Europe.

The pilot episode of *Yo! MTV Raps* aired in the summer of 1988. Run-DMC guest-hosted a show that featured DJ Jazzy Jeff & the Fresh Prince and kicked off with a video of Eric B. and Rakim's "Follow the Leader." The show was a ratings bonanza and was green-lit with Fab 5 Freddy—the original conduit between hip-hop and downtown New York City—as the host.

André "Doctor Dré" Brown (co-host, *Yo! MTV Raps*): Rap music was still so underground. The only thing that made rap music relevant was *Yo! MTV Raps,* because for the first time you could see the same video in New York that you'd see in Los Angeles, that you'd see in Houston, that you could see in Atlanta, that you could see in Oregon. Now, we have to pay homage, of course, to the great Ralph McDaniels and *Video Music Box*, who was there five years before we got there, but he was limited, because it was only in the Tri-State Area.

Michael Holman (journalist/filmmaker/creator, *Graffiti Rock*): After '84, everything changes. It gets so big. It's on the radio. It's on television. It's just massive and it travels around the world. It's so big that by the time MTV does *Yo! MTV Raps* with Fab 5 Freddy, it just makes perfect sense.

> **BASED ON THE** success of the weekly show, MTV executives decided to air *Yo! MTV Raps* daily on weekdays, and looked for hosts to complement Fab 5 Freddy. They landed on what would become a dynamic pairing: Doctor Dré and Ed Lover, a member of the hip-hop parody group No Face. T Money, a member of Original Concept with Doctor Dré, later joined the pair.

André "Doctor Dré" Brown (co-host, *Yo! MTV Raps*): Peter [Dougherty] came, saw me. I was DJing at this place called Payday in the city, and he walked over to me and said, "Hey, Dré. Man, you're killing it." He said, "You see this show called *Yo! MTV Raps?*"

I said, "Yeah, I saw it."

He said, "What do you think about it? You want to come to my office and talk to me?"

I said, "Why not?"

So I go around to his office and we're talking and he goes, "Yeah, so what do you think about *Yo! MTV Raps?*" And I told him, "Hey, it's pretty cool, but you need something in there to give a different balance. Fab is cool, but you need something that's going to entertain people, too."

He said, "Well, give me an idea."

We came up with this idea of doing this barbershop skit. So, I shoot the whole thing. He goes, "Great." Takes the tape. "See me on Monday."

I go in his office on Monday. "Everybody loves you. They thought it was great. We want to make *Yo! MTV Raps* a daily show. Are you interested?"

I said, "Are you crazy? Look, I'm a big, fat Black guy from Long Island. There's no way you want me on television."

"We want you on television. I want to introduce you to my production assistant, Ted Demme."

Ted comes down, shakes my hand. "Hey, man. I want to do an audition tape with you."

So, I do an audition tape with him. But when I look outside of Ted's office, I see this tall, skinny guy sitting across from the office. I'm like, "Aw, shoot. They've got another dude. This guy's gonna get the job. I watch MTV and I know I don't look like MTV."

He says, "I want to introduce you to my man, Ed Lover."

"Hey, what's going on, Ed? I'm Doctor Dré."

He says, "Oh, I know who you are. I listen to you at BAU and Original Concept."

I said, "You know who I am? Get out of here."

[Demme] said, "Would you mind you guys doing something together here?"

We're doing some really crazy stuff, improvisational stuff, and Ted is filming the whole thing. I leave, and Ted calls me later that day and he says, "Hey, man. Would you mind if I pair you and Ed together to do the show? It's up to you. You can do it by yourself, or you can do it with him. It's on you. You got the job."

I said, "Nah, there's too many times in our history we play crabs in a barrel. Why am I going to put this guy down? Let's do this. We'll get to know each other as we do it. I've done it before with what happened with Chuck [D]. Let's do this."

THE RATINGS FOR Yo! MTV Raps continued soaring as the show introduced a national audience to artists they would never have otherwise seen or heard. Fab 5 Freddy took the weekly show on the road—interviewing N.W.A in California and the Geto Boys in Texas—as Doctor Dré and Ed Lover honed their comedic talents on the daily version. Soon, hip-hop shows like Fox's Pump It Up and BET's Rap City followed, adding further to the variety of hip-hop shows on television.

André "Doctor Dré" Brown (co-host, *Yo! MTV Raps*): MTV wasn't every-where in New York. . . .

We didn't realize how popular we had become 'til we went outside of doing the studio show. Ted was always telling us, "You guys are blowing up. You're blowing up."

We went out [to Daytona Beach]. We had A Tribe Called Quest, Biz Markie, Leaders of the New School with Busta Rhymes. We walked onto that stage of fifty thousand screaming college kids of all colors, all creeds, and they went berserk as we walked through the door. It was surreal, and Ed turned back and looked at me and I said, "Yeah, I think we're winning."

MOST EARLY HIP-HOP music videos involved directors who had never worked with, and often never heard of, the artists beforehand. Ann Carli recognized the potential of DJ Jazzy Jeff & the Fresh Prince, and the importance of their first video. She sought a director who would work with them to bring their aesthetic to life. She landed on Scott Kalvert, who hit it off with the pair.

The result, 1988's "Parents Just Don't Understand," was hip-hop's first music video to gain considerable traction at MTV, and for many suburbanites it represented their first rap encounter. In Will Smith, mainstream audiences found a wholesome, presentable artist who rhymed about universal themes like the challenges of adolescence. The music video showcased walls tagged with graffiti. Smith's infectious charisma led NBC to eventually green-light the pilot for his show, *The Fresh Prince of Bel-Air.*

Ann Carli (senior VP, Jive Records): Rap videos were basically all kind of the same back then. When I first started at Jive, all of that stuff was done in the UK. And I saw it and just said, "Wow, this stuff's really horrible. It doesn't actually have anything to do with the cul-ture."

And my boss, which was Clive Calder, who I owe everything to really, he said, "Okay, well, you do it." And I said I didn't know how to do that. And he goes, "Well, you better learn."

We made the video for "Parents Just Don't Understand," and then we did a film-to-tape transfer to video the next day. And we're watching the footage and we're freaking out, because the camera just loved this gawky kid, the class-clown dude with the pimple on his face who was always making jokes, and who was so animated. And Scott [Kalvert] and I looked at each other and went, "Oh my God."

Barry Weiss (president, Jive Records): It was a watershed moment, and they were one of the first big pop crossovers. It was exciting as hell. That shit never gets old.

André "Doctor Dré" Brown (DJ, artist, Original Concept): DJ Jazzy Jeff & the Fresh Prince was one of those big groups that broke some of those walls down, to allow people to say, "This is alright."

Jeff Sledge (A&R, Jive Records): No one on Jive besides Will, at that time, really had crossed over. It was still looked down upon, like with Hammer. People could still kind of look down upon you if you had a commercial or pop success.

THE GOLDEN AGE also saw hip-hop's expansion past its party-centric origins and into the political and social arenas, an evolution initiated by Duke Bootee and Grandmaster Flash and the Furious Five, and galvanized by Public Enemy.

In 1987, Stetsasonic's "A.F.R.I.C.A." was one of the first hip-hop tracks concerned with Afrocentric issues. And 1988's Stop the Violence Movement marked a collaborative effort to foster positive change.

As hip-hop diversified and diverged, some groups began promoting Black pride and the Five Percent Nation—a movement group that took its name from the Nation of Islam teaching that five percent of humanity knows the truth of existence and strives to educate the oppressed majority. Groups like X Clan, Poor Righteous Teachers, and Brand Nubian formed in the late 1980s and promoted Afrocentrism.

Brand Nubian's *One for All* was generally praised for knowledge-filled songs like "Drop the Bomb" and "Wake Up," and for its overall lyrical creativity. X Clan's two albums, *To the East, Blackwards* (1990) and *Xodus* (1992), earned a loyal cult following. Poor Righteous Teachers broke through with "Rock Dis Funky Joint" in 1990.

Daddy-O (artist, producer, Stetsasonic): Everybody was party rap then, so it was like, "Okay, so how do we take this serious thing and make it?" It was a challenge, but it was a dope challenge.

The coolest thing about "A.F.R.I.C.A.," we have the longest-running rap record ever, because we had a record that not only translated into music, but part of the project was with a group called the Africa Fund, and we got to tour. We actually had a study guide for kids for that record.

BY 1988, HIP-HOP found itself at an early crossroads. The genre had started gaining national and international momentum. But following a Run-DMC performance in Long Beach, California, that erupted in gang violence in August 1986 and the stabbing death of a teenager at a Dope Jam concert in September 1988, mainstream media started documenting the supposed dangers inherent in the culture and music. Nassau Coliseum, the site of the Dope Jam concert, even instituted a rap ban in the fall of 1988.

In response, KRS-One, who had lost DJ Scott La Rock to murder a year prior, combined with Ann Carli and journalist Nelson George for an anti-violence movement. Their efforts resulted in Stop the Violence, commemorated by "Self Destruction," a track that united many of hip-hop's most prominent stars, including Public Enemy, Kool Moe Dee, Just-Ice, MC Lyte, and Stetsasonic. "Self Destruction" maintained the top spot on *Billboard*'s brand-new Hot Rap Songs chart for nearly three straight months in the spring of 1989. It earned over $100,000 for the National Urban League.

Ann Carli (senior VP, Jive Records): It was Dope Jam at the Nassau Coliseum. As soon as I got into the arena and I saw these groups of older guys kind of walking abreast and mowing people down in their path, I was like, *Oh, this is not going to be good.*

It was bedlam, people were stabbed. One of my friends, Oran

"Juice" Jones, his brother was stabbed. KRS-One was like, "Annie, you got to get out of here." I ended up with Doug E. Fresh's mom and grandmother, hiding behind some bleachers.

The next day, the *[New York] Post* for sure, and maybe the *Daily News* as well, was blaming rap music and the culture for inciting violence. Which, it wasn't that at all. During the earlier days where we had the Swatch Watch and the Fresh Fest, this was a big event for young kids, and people would come out with their best clothes on, their best jewelry. Kids would come with their parents, and certainly there was no air of danger.

Around that time, things were changing. There was a Michael Jackson concert where kids were getting robbed, chains ripped off. So it wasn't just hip-hop where this was happening. But the papers blamed the culture. We were all shaken up. And Nelson George, who's a dear friend, called me at the office and he said, "We've got to do something. This is horrible." And then I thought, *Well, let's make a record.* Boogie Down Productions had put out a record called "Stop the Violence." So, I thought, *Let's see if we can reach out and band together.*

It's probably one of the things that I'm most proud of in my career. Not just because of the record that we made or the money that we raised for the Urban League, but also the undertaking of getting people to work together where everybody said it couldn't happen in that way.

It happened.

Paradise Gray (manager of the Latin Quarter, X Clan): We used hip-hop to give young Black people a voice where we had no voice. So that led to us creating the Blackwatch Movement [a hip-hop collective that promoted community activism and social awareness] when the Latin Quarter closed, and that led to X Clan. That led to us mentoring and having meetings.

And also, we started representing a lot of the teachings of the Nation of Islam with groups like the Poor Righteous Teachers, and Big Daddy Kane, and KRS-One. Brand Nubian were espousing the science of the Five Percenters. So that was a big part of it, that knowledge became as respected in hip-hop as lyricism, as DJing, as rapping.

Sadat X (artist, Brand Nubian): A major criticism that we faced is that we didn't like white people.

It wasn't that we didn't like white people, it was just that so many of our brothers were in such a bad state that we had to save them first. And we would tell critics and people, "That's inherent in all races." When the Jews do something, they save the Jews first. Spanish people, they save the Spanish people first. We've seen it in the Korean communities and the Chinese community. They tend to help their own kind first.

And we were like, "We've got this crack epidemic going on that's taking a large percentage of our population. We've got this new law about drug selling that's a three-strike law that's sending a lot of our brothers to jail. We didn't make crack. Crack was put in the community, and now we're penalized for it and it's hurting a lot of our people. We've got to stop this."

DATING BACK TO Sugar Hill Records' role in raising hip-hop's visibility and viability, New Jersey had played a prominent role in hip-hop. Artists like Queen Latifah, Chill Rob G, and Lakim Shabazz emerged out of the Flavor Unit, orchestrated by DJ Mark the 45 King. Queen Latifah convinced a group from East Orange to change its name from the New Style to Naughty by Nature.

Soon a new generation of dynamic New Jersey artists surfaced, which included Redman, Lords of the Underground, the Fugees, Artifacts, and Rah Digga of the New Jersey collective Outsidaz.

Dupré "DoItAll" Kelly (artist, Lords of the Underground): Before I got with Lords of the Underground, Redman was my DJ and we had a crew with a bunch of other guys from New Jersey, and we used to call ourselves Revolutionary Party of Terrace, RPT. We was trying to break in the industry and it was hard. We were doing a lot of stuff ourselves—doing our own shows, renting limos, popping up at New York parties. Myself and Redman, we used to always wait in Def Jam's office for eight hours, nine hours, just sitting in the lobby. We were persistent.

DOITALL, DJ LORD Jazz, and Mr. Funke first met while at North Carolina's Shaw University, eventually attracting the attention of legendary producer Marley Marl. Marl produced the bulk of the Lords of the Underground's 1993 debut album, *Here Come the Lords,* which included hits like "Chief Rocka" and "Funky Child."

Dupré "DoItAll" Kelly (artist, Lords of the Underground): We came up to his house, just to be standing outside the garage door, hearing this vibration of music and for Marley to say, "Welcome to the House of Hits," to two Newark, New Jersey, guys and one Cleveland, Ohio, guy, it was just an amazing moment. And then walking through those doors to see this guy with a wifebeater on and a bell Kangol standing in between the speakers, listening to his music probably on a thousand, was LL Cool J, who was one of my idols. So, to see him was amazing. I think I even turned to Funke and [DJ Lord] Jazz and whispered "We made it" to them.

Just Blaze (producer): I went to Rutgers and spent a lot of time in Newark. And this is at the time where it's like that second wave of Jersey artists. First you had the Flavor Unit: Latifah, the 45 King. And then you have this next generation: Redman, Lords of the Underground, the Outsidaz. [Dray] from Das EFX is from Teaneck.

There was an open mic that used to happen in Newark at a club called the Pipeline. And this was really a major turning point for me because I'm probably at this point seventeen, eighteen. I got into college when I was sixteen. I skipped a couple of grades when I was in grammar school. They thought I was like some kind of rocket scientist genius.

I get the chance to DJ at this open mic night. Newark was the mecca of that area. So a lot of these local artists are blowing up. El Da and Tame from the Artifacts decides to jump up on stage during the open mic. Or Redman shows up or Young Zee from the Outsidaz shows up. Or DoItAll from Lords of the Underground shows up. And I'm the one DJing. And a lot of times I'm playing my own beats off of a tape.

Artists that I look up to are asking to freestyle on these tracks that

I'm playing at this event. As a kid, a lot of these artists, you only see them on TV, you only hear them on the radio. So they're kind of almost like superheroes in a sense. These mythical beings, they're all of a sudden right in front of you, rhyming on one of your tracks.

Dupré "DoItAll" Kelly (artist, Lords of the Underground): You had all of those Jersey crews in the '90s from Queen Latifah to Apache to Naughty by Nature to Redman, Lords of the Underground, Rah Digga, the Artifacts. Even though it was hard for us to break in, most of the New Jersey acts, we broke in by teaming up with New York crews. Lords of the Underground, Marley Marl. That's the House of Hits and everybody came to that house, from Heavy D to LL Cool J to TLC.

And then you had Redman, who teamed up with the Long Island crew. I introduced him to Erick Sermon, EPMD. Then you had the Outsidaz. They teamed up with New York crews. You had Rah Digga. She teamed up with a New York crew. You had the Fugees, and they teamed up with different crews that wasn't from Jersey.

THE FUGEES CONSISTED of Wyclef Jean, Lauryn Hill, and Pras. The group, which blended reggae, rap, and R&B, issued their debut album, *Blunted on Reality,* in 1994 through Ruffhouse Records before dropping 1996's *The Score,* paced by the lead single, "Fu-Gee-La." *The Score* showcased Hill, regarded as one of the most elite MCs of all time, easily switching between rapping and singing; and the group proving that instruments still had a place in hip-hop. *The Score* marked her ascension into superstardom through popular tracks like "Killing Me Softly" and "Ready or Not." *The Score,* which won the 1996 Grammy for Best Rap Album, is heralded as one of the defining albums of the 1990s.

Chris Schwartz (cofounder, Ruffhouse): When they first auditioned for us in [Steven] Soderbergh's office, it was a hot mess. But, for me, what was really important was that Wyclef was playing an acoustic guitar over a beatbox. That's what sold it. It was completely different from everything.

We weren't sure how it was going to turn out once we went to make a record, but our instincts were right. Hip-hop had gotten really boring. It was kind of like when bebop just became tattered until the whole fusion genre happened with Herbie Hancock and Miles Davis. I felt the Fugees were a total breath of fresh air, and their live show was unbelievable. Because it was all real musicians and I had always been pushing for live music in hip-hop.

Salaam Remi (producer, New York): The "Fu-Gee-La" beat actually was something I made for Fat Joe. Basically, Fat Joe saw me when I did "Nappy Heads" for the Fugees, [he was] like, "Yo, I need a beat like that."

So, Fat Joe and Chris Lighty came to my house. Chris Lighty's like, "Yo, can you give us a beat like that?" So I was like, "Cool, give me a week, I'll make up something."

But then Fat Joe heard it and didn't like it. But then Lauryn heard it and loved it. So, then it became, "Yo, play that Fat Joe beat," and then it became "Fu-Gee-La" ultimately.

> **PETE ROCK, A** cousin of legendary hip-hop artist Heavy D, earned his first DJing break under Marley Marl at WBLS in 1989. He emerged with CL Smooth to craft 1991's EP *All Souled Out* and the following year's classic *Mecca & the Soul Brother.*

DJ Marley Marl (producer, Juice Crew): I was doing a song for Heavy D called "Gyrlz, They Love Me." [Pete Rock] came up to the crib with Heavy D just to watch and see what we was doing. He saw the turntables and started scratching and I was like, "Oh, you kind of nice."

So I said, "Yo, why don't you do the scratches on 'Gyrlz, They Love Me'?" So, he actually did do the scratches on the record.

I was already doing *In Control* [the WBLS radio show] with Kevy Kev and Clark Kent. So Kevy Kev called me, "I had a car accident, I can't make it to the radio station." I was like, *Damn, who am I gonna get as a DJ?* I remember, *Heavy D's cousin was kind of nice.* So I called Heavy D. I said, "Yo, tell your cousin to meet me at the radio station. I want him to DJ on the radio tonight." And that's how I met Pete Rock.

Dante Ross (A&R, producer): He'd play his demos on air sometimes. They were crazy-sounding. That guy was massively talented. Nobody had cranked the snare that loud. No one was chopping things up quite like that. And obviously the horns. No one was using horns the way he was. It was some next-level shit.

Sadat X (artist, Brand Nubian): The first time when I didn't even know Pete yet, to go into the basement and just watch him create was incredible, because here was somebody that was my same age demographic that was making music and making fly beats. And just to watch him work was amazing.

Dante Ross (A&R, producer): Pete Rock, he was the DJ on [the] *In Control* show. He was amazing. He was seventeen years old and they're just making really great music.

CELEBRATED FOR HIS sampling of both classic and obscure soul songs and instrumental interludes, Pete Rock became an architect of New York's sound. He worked with everyone from Nas to basketball star Shaquille O'Neal.

Jeff Sledge (A&R, Jive Records): Pete was on fire. Shaq is originally from Newark, so he's a very East Coast guy, and he wanted to work with Pete, so he came to New York. Pete worked out of his aunt's basement, which was on the same block from where his family lived.

I meet Shaq and Shaq's cousins and we drive from the city up to Mount Vernon to Pete's crib. We knock on the door a couple times and no one's answering. But I see a light on and I'm like, *What the fuck, man? I got Shaq here, rookie of the year.* I'm knocking, knocking, knocking. Finally, the door opens and it's Pete's father. He sees this massive-ass dude behind me and his eyes kind of got big like, *What the fuck?* So he's like, "Pete's not home."

Shaq was maybe like twenty-one; he was a kid. He was so excited to meet Pete and Pete's not home. I get reamed out, of course, by them niggas all the way back to the city and it was terrible. Bottom line, the Pete/Shaq thing never happened. I go, "Pete, you're fucking killing me, dude."

He's like, "I'm sorry, bro, I'm sorry. Next time, I promise."

So, a little while later I was A&R on Will Smith's album and I was like, "Okay, we should get you to work with Pete." Again, Pete's pretty hot. Will's a super hip-hop guy too, so he was like, "Bet."

So, Will comes into town. We ride up to Mount Vernon. He was on *The Fresh Prince* at this time. Like, I got the nigga with the number one show in the country. He's a fucking superstar. We get to Pete's crib and his whole family—I mean aunts, uncles, everybody—is in the crib waiting on us. Mom is cooking. But who's not there? Fucking Pete. I'm like, *I cannot believe this nigga right here.* Me and Will are sitting in Pete Rock's family's living room watching television with them, waiting on Pete. Unbelievable.

So then Pete finally shows up like, "I'm here! I just went and got a haircut. I'm sorry. The barbershop line was long. I'm sorry. Y'all ready to go?"

And we was like, "Yeah, let's go, man."

We come out the house. It's a mob scene. The whole Mount Vernon heard that Will Smith's here. The cops literally had to escort us to Pete's aunt's crib three doors down 'cause it was that many people on the block. Heavy D pulled up in a motorcycle. All kinds of niggas is coming in and out 'cause they wanted to see Will Smith. It actually was not really that much of a productive session, but it was a fun day.

10 LIKE A BLUEBERRY

Philadelphia, Los Angeles, Compton, New York City 1985–1995

Groups like Run-DMC and Beastie Boys, through the vehicles of Def Jam Recordings, had demonstrated hip-hop's mainstream appeal. Through Public Enemy, the music had displayed its prowess for political and social commentary. But no hip-hop group provided as much of a lightning bolt to the genre, or shock to mainstream America, as Niggaz Wit Attitudes, or N.W.A, when they arrived in the late 1980s.

N.W.A formed in Compton toward the end of Ronald Reagan's second presidential term, as the crack cocaine epidemic rotted the vicinity and Los Angeles police chief Daryl Gates engaged in a draconian war against drugs and the city's gangs, leading to rampant allegations of corrupt law enforcement.

N.W.A labeled themselves "The World's Most Dangerous Group," jolting the West Coast from its electro hip-hop beginnings by presenting unflinching and first-person accounts of the harsh conditions facing young minorities in Southern California, far from Hollywood's glitz and glamour. They described their music as "reality rap," the unfiltered truth as they lived and survived it every day. Soon the media rebranded the subgenre as gangster, or "gangsta," rap. With 1989's *Straight Outta Compton,* N.W.A punctured the mainstream.

However, N.W.A was not the first practitioner of reality rap. Philadelphia's Schoolly D is widely credited as being the originator, with

1985's hugely influential "P.S.K. What Does It Mean?" Over a thunder-
ing drum pattern, Schoolly D offered a tribute to a Philadelphia gang
named Parkside Killers, which he released through his independent
label—with another heralded offering, "Gucci Time," on the B-side. On
"P.S.K.," Schoolly D—who signed Ruffhouse Records cofounder Chris
Schwartz as his manager—nasally crafted a tale that included guns,
sex, drugs, and one of the first uses of the word "nigga" in hip-hop
music.

The song proved critical to the rise of West Coast gangster rap.

Ice-T took Schoolly D's direction for his trailblazing song "6 'N the
Mornin'." Eazy-E and N.W.A's breakout "Boyz-n-the-Hood" followed
shortly after, as another Los Angeles label created a brand of hip-hop
more palatable for radio play.

Schoolly D (artist, Philadelphia): It happened fast. [DJ] Code [Money]
walked up to me. He was like, "Yo, I want to be your new DJ." He was
still in high school. He didn't have turntables yet. So, we took them to
his grandmother's house, and he started scratching. I was like, "Yeah,
man, I like that shit."

So, we just got the 909 [Roland drum machine], and it was like
all the stars were lining up. I programmed the beat, but I also played
it live, because all the James Brown specials that I saw, they always
showed those guys in the studio recording and singing live at the
same time. Those four albums, I did them live in the studio, played
the drum machine and rapped, and Code scratched on the back end.

We rehearsed, and two weeks later we recorded both "P.S.K." and
"Gucci Time" the same night.

We rolled up a bunch of big fat joints—and just smoking all night.
We woke up five o'clock in the morning and I remember listening to
it, and I was like, "What the fuck is this?" And the engineer saying,
"All you kept saying was more reverb. *More reverb. More reverb. More
reverb.*"

We went home and fell asleep, and Code was up already making
tapes, handing 'em out to everybody on Parkside. I came out and
motherfuckers was just like clapping. I was just like, "Man, this is
some space shit."

I think that was one of my first lessons. There were plenty of times when I wanted to make a radio hit, plenty of times when I wanted to be Marley Marl or Heavy D, just have something played on the radio. [But] I was gonna be myself no matter what. It was like, *Dude, this is your art. This is yourself. This is who you are.*

From then on, the music inspired the art, and the art inspired the music.

Chris Schwartz (cofounder, Ruffhouse Records): I was working for [Ted Wing, the former Graterford Prison guard who put out a Bill Cosby live album] doing marketing and promotion, and I was in his office one day and I saw all these yellow records stacked up against the wall: Schoolly D "Gangster Boogie" on a Place To Be Records. I knew Schoolly. I got his phone number and called him up, and I just ended up managing him and running his record label and we put out "P.S.K./Gucci Time."

Lady B (artist, radio DJ, Philadelphia): So, I'm already Lady B. I'm already the godmother you gotta go to to get your song played. And here comes this b-boy with his song.

I had just got on Power 99 and we've got to be on our best behavior, because one slipup and they'll say, "Hip-hop's got to go." And here comes this kid with mother-effer this and mother-effer that after every lyric. And I'm like, "What do you want me to do with this?"

I remember having a conversation with Schoolly like, "Can you say the same story without the mother-effer?" I just wanted him to reach the masses. I wasn't trying to change his swag, but I'm like, "Schoolly, in order for people to start playing this stuff, you're gonna have to tone it down a little. They have FCC rules that you can't break."

Schoolly D (artist, Philadelphia): My reaction was, you wouldn't tell Picasso to change his art. People are so afraid of art and what it can change. They want you to just fall in line. I was like, *Well, who the fuck is gonna tell our story then, if I'm not gonna do it?*

It was a hard pill to take, 'cause I didn't understand. Like, these are words. They were half fantasy and half real, but it was real. We're

talking about weed. What's the big fucking deal? Talking about somebody got shot. What's the big fucking deal? It was on the news every
fucking night. What's the difference?

Richard Pryor and Lenny Bruce said something that I remember
from a kid. "If it was music behind these words, I couldn't even make
a record, because once you put music behind it, people understand."
The powers that be understand the power of music. If you put a message behind music, it just sucks people in.

Lady B (artist, radio DJ, Philadelphia): Schoolly tells the story that when
he came to the radio station and I told him that I couldn't play it
because it had too many curse words, Schoolly sat on the curb and
started crying. He tells everybody that I made him cry, as if I did
something really bad to him, but all I did was say, "Listen, I can't play
this. I'll tell you what, me and my DJ, we're gonna try to do an edit."

Schoolly D (artist, Philadelphia): I was in the right place at the right
time, because then the station manager pulls up and he's like, "What
are you doing out here?" And he takes me in, and he listens to it and
he's like, "Dude, gimme two weeks and it'll be on the radio." And it
was. Two weeks.

Lady B (artist, radio DJ, Philadelphia): Back then, we didn't have the
technology. You literally had to put a song on reel-to-reel to do an edit,
but I just liked his tenacity and his swag. I actually did an edit on his
song. Mind you, it brought the song down from like seven minutes to
three minutes after I took the profanity out. But I did give him a spin.

Schoolly D (artist, Philadelphia): She played an amazing part. I remember
she called me up, saying she was tired of doing the fuckin' radio edits.
It wasn't like she didn't like the music. She was just like, "Look, we
just got on the radio."

Lady B (artist, radio DJ, Philadelphia): Philly, I will say this about us, we
had something to prove. Schoolly was so raw, and I think that's what
the audience loved most about him. Not only was he raw and told their
truth, but he lived around the way. You could see him and trust him.

It just felt like to me that the Philadelphia hip-hop community just felt proud of him and rocked with him, and what he's saying is really just how we talk every day on the corner, but he put it on the record. That's the first gangster rapper. Not N.W.A, not anybody on the West Coast. That is the original gangster rapper right there.

Schoolly D (artist, Philadelphia): A lot of people say it was an accident. "I just happened to be in one place, and I could talk some shit, and somebody gave me a microphone and some beats." Because before, if you're a Black man in this country and you're positive about yourself and about your journey, you were deemed an arrogant, uppity nigger.

Chris Schwartz (cofounder, Ruffhouse Records): "Gangster Boogie" did really well, but when "P.S.K./Gucci Time" happened, it was insane. I had sent out the "P.S.K./Gucci Time" to all these record pools and the response was unbelievable. Suddenly, I was getting all these white rock clubs who wanted to book Schoolly, and college gigs and everything. He had never played in front of all-white audiences before.

DJ Nu-Mark (Jurassic 5): Schoolly D really fucked me up because he was almost the opposite of Spoonie Gee. He was laid-back in the mix, but the drums were gigantic. That was the first time I heard a 909 properly. It was like you were really in a concert hall with high ceilings, because they flooded it with so much reverb. They made it sound like it was a live jam.

Peanut Butter Wolf (Stones Throw Records): I grew up in San Jose and I was that kid that was always trying to find the New York records that nobody in San Jose had. I would go to this record store, and they would basically get one promo copy sent to them from the labels and sell it for ninety-nine cents. I would always be the guy buying them all and making the mixtapes at my high school. That's how I found "Gucci Time" and "P.S.K." from Schoolly D. Schoolly D was the epitome of cool.

Schoolly D (artist, Philadelphia): Coming home as I was touring from England down to the whole Eastern Seaboard, getting a call from Ice-T. My mother, God rest her soul, if you had to get in contact with me, everybody knows you gotta call Schoolly's mom. She said, "This boy has been calling. Call this boy now." So, I called [Ice-T's manager] Jorge [Hinojosa] and he got Ice and he played "6 'N the Mornin'." It was kind of like, *Holy fucking shit.*

ALREADY ENTRENCHED IN the West Coast's electro hip-hop scene, Ice-T found inspiration in Schoolly D's offerings and turned his own music toward grittier lyrics.

In the summer of 1987, Ice-T released his seminal debut studio album, *Rhyme Pays,* through Sire Records. The album produced the single "6 N' the Mornin'" (the B-side to "Dog 'N the Wax (Ya Don't Quit—Part II)." Over a minimalist beat by DJ Unknown and Afrika Islam's pounding 808 drums, Ice-T expounded—like no hip-hop artist before him—on a lifestyle that had consumed Los Angeles inner-city youth. The action pulsated from the very start of the song, whose title refers to the early morning hour when Los Angeles police were known to bust through doors: "Six in the mornin', police at my door / Fresh Adidas squeak across my bathroom floor."

From there, Ice-T delivered a vivid, winding narrative involving crime, abuse, jail time, and catching a flight to New York. While the song contained extreme elements, it featured seeds of reality in its name-checking of places—like Crenshaw Boulevard—that helped provide the foundation for West Coast gangster rap. Ice-T was opening the door for others to describe their own lives and experiences with similar sharpness and frankness.

Ice-T (artist, Rhyme Syndicate): Everybody knows "P.S.K." was an inspiration for "6 'N the Mornin'." It was different, because at that time everybody was yelling on records. LL was yelling on records. I was yelling on records. Run-DMC was yelling. Schoolly was just laid-back talking, like he had a little drink or something. And the productions of the beats, it sounded like [an] angel dust sound. Lots of reverb. Lots of echo. And it felt like you were high. I just dug it. I tried to come in with more of a laid-back vocal delivery, and that's how "6 'N the Mornin'" was born.

Afrika Islam (DJ, producer): On a tour with Rock Steady [Crew] through Los Angeles, I played the Radio club, or Radiotron. The hip-hop community met there. Me and Ice hit it off—there were a couple of things that were instinctive to us. One was the Iceberg Slim stuff. I was versed in it; he was definitely versed in it. So I knew that because I had read the Donald Goines books.

Second was, I kind of had a military background; he was in the army. Me, being a Zulu King, and him coming out of gang affiliation, it was a basic honor system. I was also a person that believed in helping another brother out, that was just instilled in me in the Zulu Nation.

I had no idea I was introducing hip-hop in a true sense to the West Coast, but I was instrumental in it. At that time, "Planet Rock" was the dominant force, music-wise, in hip-hop. I guess I carried that torch. And then I brought Ice back to New York where he hooked up with [Melle] Mel and [Grandmaster] Caz, and that formed the Zulu King group in New York.

And then the lyrics in "6 'N the Mornin' " changed the way the West Coast saw itself.

Ice-T (artist, Rhyme Syndicate): "6 'N the Mornin' " was a B-side to a song called "Dog 'N the Wax," which was a Part II to a song called "Ya Don't Quit." We had made what we thought was the A-side, and we had an 808 drum machine and we just wanted to do something slow, casual—storytelling shit, the type of raps that I would do just to entertain my friends.

I made this little story about a guy that went through the normal shit that kids do in the hood, going to the county, coming out. The long version that's on the actual *Rhyme Pays* album takes you all the way into New York after somebody got shot. No special mindset, just bullshittin' it.

Afrika Islam (DJ, producer): If you look at the previous work of Ice in the movie *Breakin'*, he's doing "Reckless," or "Tibetan Jam" with Glove. They were poppers. They weren't really b-boys. Poppers preferred soul music and "Planet Rock" type music because of the kicks, "Planet Rock" or Kraftwerk. They could kick and hit and boogie to that, better than anything else—and, of course, funk.

But when "6 'N the Mornin' " came out, it dropped the BPMs down, then all of a sudden "6 'N the Mornin' " became like, "Oh wait up, that's a gangster rap, a hustler rap, reality rap." And at that particular time, there weren't a lot of records that were that slow. That's not a dance record; that was a listening record that you put in the car, especially with L.A. being a car town, and lowriders having huge sound systems. So, when you hit that lane, you got that sound system and you dropped that big 808 boom, and all of a sudden you're talking about "Six in the mornin', police at my door," real dudes understand that.

Because six in the morning is when the cops do roll. The number wasn't picked arbitrarily. That's when they roll to kick down your door. So that's what I meant by why it was such an influential drop in the beat, because you could actually hear what the brother's saying, and what he was saying, a lot of heads identify with it.

Jorge Hinojosa (manager, Ice-T): [Cofounder of Sire Records] Seymour [Stein] called us into Warner Bros. and told us he had reservations about some of the lyrical content. We went back and forth with him about it and then Ice said to him, "Maybe that feeling you're having is money."

I remembered thinking that was a wild thing to say, but Seymour looked up at Ice and me and said, "Okay, I'm going to release the record. I'm in no position to judge what you do." After that, he never questioned Ice about his albums or his music—not even "Cop Killer."

Ice-T (artist, Rhyme Syndicate): Like Chuck D says, "The B-side wins again." I had no idea it was going to have that kind of impact, really until I got two sold-out shows in the Fillmore West. That let me know people were really digging this particular song.

Jorge Hinojosa (manager, Ice-T): Even my New York friends, who were rap snobs and felt nothing from the West Coast could be good, went mental over that track. They were really impressed with his rhymes and his visual storytelling style. Back then there weren't a lot of rappers that were telling stories.

Greg Mack (KDAY): Him and Unknown DJ had told me about a song, "6 'N the Mornin'," and I started playing it. It got a real negative response. We had C. Delores Tucker on our ass and some other politicians and community leaders. My boss, Jack Patterson, made me take it off the air. I know that it really pissed off Unknown.

Killer Mike (artist, Dungeon Family): "6 'N the Mornin' " gave firm reality to what was going on in the world. He was really educating with his rap in a very sophisticated way in talking about drugs and politicians and things of that nature. Ice-T was the person who politicized my young mind more than anyone else. Because he was still a hustler.

Ice Cube (artist, N.W.A): We loved "6 'N the Mornin' " because it was a West Coast version of "P.S.K." He took that same pattern and style but made a West Coast version of it. Schoolly D, Just-Ice with "Latoya," KRS-One, Scott La Rock, *Criminal Minded*, these are the seeds that create gangster rap. These are the seeds that's creating Ice Cube, Dr. Dre, Eazy-E, Yella, MC Ren.

ALONZO WILLIAMS HAD already cautioned Andre Young (Dr. Dre) repeatedly about showing more consideration for his time and pockets. When Dr. Dre wound up in jail for unpaid parking tickets one time too many, Williams declined to bail him out. Dr. Dre, increasingly frustrated over not seeing more financial dividends from his work with World Class Wreckin' Cru and wanting to change the direction of his music, phoned Eazy-E (born Eric Wright).

Eazy-E was a neighborhood hustler, eager to earn a legitimate living. For weeks, he had frequented Steve Yano—who owned a record stand at Torrance's Roadium Swap Meet and sold popular mixtapes—requesting to be introduced to Dr. Dre. When Eazy-E received the call, he bailed Dr. Dre out of jail with the understanding that he would produce records for him. A loose collective formed around Eazy-E, Dr. Dre, DJ Yella, and Arabian Prince.

Originally, Eazy-E did not plan on being an artist himself for the new label, Ruthless Records. But when a New York duo named Home Boys Only failed to deliver on a track that Dr. Dre recruited Ice Cube to pen, Eazy-E stepped behind the microphone. Debuting his distinctive voice, 1987's "Boyz-n-the Hood" kicked off with the iconic line "Cruisin' down the street in my '64." Macola Records, the independent Hollywood label that distributed World Class Wreckin' Cru, pressed the record, and Yano sold the 12-inch at Roadium. The group settled on a name—Niggaz Wit Attitudes, or N.W.A—aimed at gaining attention. Ice Cube, the youngest member of the group, left C.I.A. (Cru' in Action!), the group that he had formed with Sir Jinx, Dr. Dre's cousin. MC Ren (Lorenzo Patterson) also joined, and Dr. Dre successfully recruited an artist from Dallas, the D.O.C. (Tracy Curry).

As "Boyz-n-the-Hood" gained underground traction, Eazy-E asked Williams to broker a meeting between himself and Jerry Heller. Heller, who had already spent decades in the music industry with the likes of Marvin Gaye and Otis Redding, agreed to manage the group. In 1987, Ruthless released the single "Panic Zone," and a few months later Macola's Don MacMillan released the group's first album, a compilation—*N.W.A and the Posse*—that went mostly ignored.

It would be the last time the group flew under the radar. Ruthless signed a partnership deal with Priority Records, whose previous success consisted of releasing a series of high-selling albums that featured the fictitious California Raisins delivering R&B covers; and, in early 1987, distributing *Straight Outta Compton*.

The album began with the line: "You are now about to witness the strength of street knowledge." The album forever changed hip-hop music. The group viscerally and forcefully documented poverty, violence, and disenfranchisement, enhancing the subgenre started by Schoolly D and pioneered by Los Angeles artists like Ice-T, Mixmaster Spade, and Toddy Tee, whose "Batterram" in 1985 also provided an early glimpse of West Coast gangster rap.

N.W.A propelled reality rap into the mainstream and even shifted the fashion of hip-hop artists. The group's misogynistic lyrics would also come under criticism. Multiple women accused Dr. Dre of physical violence, and in 1991 he pleaded no contest to assaulting the music journalist Dee Barnes.

Greg Mack (KDAY): I used to do a thing on my show called a "High Five," where I would invite kids from high schools, sometimes colleges, every now and then an elementary school. They would come in and we'd play their top five songs. There was a particular song that kept coming up called "Batterram." I started asking the kids, "How did you hear this? What's going on with 'Batterram'?"

"Oh, man, that's Toddy Tee. He sells them out his car. He comes by the school."

So, I went and got one from him. Sure enough, he was selling them out of the back of his car. I got it on the air, and it instantly became number one. Everybody could relate to it because that's what was going on in the community. The cops were using their "batterram" to break people's doors in. So it became an instant hit, and Toddy Tee just took off.

Cold 187um (artist, producer, Above the Law): Ice-T was a big influence for us because we were hustlers, so what he was talking about was what we actually was doing. My man Toddy Tee, he was in the streets, and Mixmaster Spade, rest in peace, was like the god at the time. When we were developing *Livin' Like Hustlers,* those were the only influence that we had, because we were out there hustling in the streets together.

Murs (artist, Los Angeles): Eazy-E, Mixmaster Spade, Toddy Tee, they were street dudes from L.A., but they were really involved in the shit, and they really sounded like they were from Compton and L.A. and South Central.

Ice-T and Ice Cube are rappers. They're artists. They're thespians. They're entertainers. So, I think that's why I gravitated more toward Toddy Tee.

The D.O.C. (artist, Dallas): [Los Angeles is] a beautiful place but you gotta be really careful because back in the late '80s it looked really cool outside, but right around the corner, that's when gangbangin' was super fresh and the drug scene was really at its height. It was bad news.

Arabian Prince (artist, producer, N.W.A): There was a record store at the Roadium Swap Meet and we all used to go there and that's where we first met with Eazy-E. At that time, they weren't even talking about a group. It was more me and Dre complaining about how we had records and hits on the radio doing production for other people and weren't really getting paid what we thought we should be getting paid. We didn't really know much about marketing and publishing and royalties and all of that stuff. He was like, "Well, dog, let's get together. I'm trying to get out of what I'm doing."

I joke to people. If you ask, "What was Eazy doing?" I'm like, "He was the neighborhood pharmaceutical technician at the time." He was trying to get out of being a pharmaceutical technician and we was trying to make some money.

Ice Cube (artist, N.W.A): At the time, we really looked up to Cli-N-Tel, the Wreckin' Cru, Dre, Yella, DJ Unknown, some of the people who were actually doing hip-hop on a professional level. Even though they were considered locals, they was making records and they was doing shit that we only dreamed of. We were doing it for fun. We battling people and shit on the street. And then, these pros kind of walked into our life. We met them at the perfect time.

Sir Jinx (producer): The things that I remember most is when Cli-N-Tel had came to the studio and Dre was still with Wreckin' Cru, it was like seeing the biggest star. We asked him to rap on our little cheesy mic and he turned us down.

Ice Cube (artist, N.W.A): At first, he didn't want to rhyme for us when we asked him. But when we went to Lonzo's house, Lonzo Williams, who was pretty much the leader of the Wreckin' Cru, and we caught Cli-N-Tel in his element, he was real generous. He's just a cool dude. Me and him always been cool like that.

Cli-N-Tel (artist, World Class Wreckin' Cru): They was two knuckleheads. They were still, like, in junior high school and Jinx was there first because Jinx is Dre's cousin. We had, like, thirty guys in our crew, so Jinx was a roadie for us. He would always be begging us, "Hey, man, I got a crew and we gonna do this. We gonna do that," and all this big talk and we're like, "Alright, little man. That's cool."

One day they were having a barbecue in Cube's backyard and somehow Jinx convinced us to go. Me and Dre went over there, and they had some turntables and microphones. And this one kid jumped on the mic and I said, "Damn, that dude sound like me." But he had fire. He was really digging deep on his stuff, and he was articulate.

And I was like, "Man, I like the way this kid raps." And I pulled Dre to the side and said, "Man, we should go ahead and work with him. Jinx is right. Let's do something with him." And Dre was like, "Nah, man, fuck that. We don't have time for that." I'm like, "No, man, I think this dude might have something."

Sir Jinx (producer): Dre just didn't let us come in. When Dre would listen to it, it wasn't even like, "Let Dre hear it. He'll put us on." It was like, "Hey, come through. I might got some beats." And we came together like that. I was the biggest cheerleader. I'm like, "Well, my cousin already got music out." So I was gassing it to the fullest.

Cli-N-Tel (artist, World Class Wreckin' Cru): We eventually got him into our little four-track pre–recording studio and just started working with him and helped him to hone the craft and I kind of took Cube under my wing. Actually, Cube jumped under my wing because he wouldn't let up. He was very, very aggressive and enthusiastic and curious about everything. He wanted to know everything about everything. Wanted to know microphones and speakers and just rap and how to rhyme and what was the best ways to write, tell stories. So I just started working with him more. I was like, "This dude's going to go somewhere, because he's really into this."

Ice Cube (artist, N.W.A): When I first started, the biggest records was like "Roxanne, Roxanne," Biz Markie, and all these dudes. Me as a writer, or a rapper, I was influenced by my favorites: KRS-One, Rakim, Chuck D. I was the craziest Run-DMC fan. I just thought they are an example of how to do it at a high level.

Sir Jinx (producer): When N.W.A happened, Dre and them said, "Let's make it a group." And then Cube came to me and K-Dee and asked us, "Do you think I should be in the group?" And me and K-Dee both said, "Yeah. Yeah. Go ahead. Do it." So, he went on. And he said, "When I get on, I'm going put you on." That's what Cube said to me and K-Dee. And he did that for both of us at one time or another.

Cli-N-Tel (artist, World Class Wreckin' Cru): I was actually joining N.W.A. But I had close friends of mine who had got involved with gang activity, or were victims of gang violence, and there was no way in hell I was going to promote that because that was just something that affected me personally, and I couldn't see myself talking that talk when I wasn't walking the walk.

Arabian Prince (artist, producer, N.W.A): We was at my mom's house. I remember we were trying to come up with the name of an album. I said, "We should call the album 'From Compton, with Love' and have a bunch of fools on the cover with guns." They said, "Aw man. That shit's corny." But we started getting mad about the state of what was going on and police. And somebody said, "Man, I feel like a nigga with an attitude." Boom. There it is.

Sir Jinx (producer): When Run said, "'Cause I just made the motherfuckers up last night [in 'Here We Go']," that changed the whole ballpark of rap. It started changing everybody's rap into parody rap, right? So, the first one we did was of course "My Rubber." And then "My Rubber" was "My Adidas." And then we did "VD Sermon," and that's when we did "Pee-wee Herman." Then we did "I'll Fuck Your Friend" off of "I'll Take Your Man" from Salt-N-Pepa.

So, at the time, while we doing these parodies, Cube ends up doing a parody off of "P.S.K." We really liked that song and he ended up doing a song called "Boyz-n-the-Hood."

Ice Cube (artist, N.W.A): I was able to help Dre write a Wreckin' Cru record that ended up getting big play on KDAY. I wrote a song with Dre called "Cabbage Patch Dance." It was after some fuckin' Cabbage Patch doll. They had created this dance off the shit, so we created a song using "Pied Piper," that sample that Run-DMC used. That shit became a hit. It was playing all the time. Dre was like, "Cube can write. He helped me write that song."

That's how Dre entrusted me to write the record for Eazy's crew, "Boyz-n-the-Hood," this group H.B.O. [Home Boys Only]. H.B.O. didn't want to do it. Eazy ended up doing it.

Arabian Prince (artist, producer, N.W.A): [Ice Cube] was a prolific writer. And I've got to give equal shout-outs to MC Ren. To me, they're equally great as far as writing. Me and Dre, we handled a lot of the music and production stuff. Those are the storytellers. They would just come in one day, talking about some shit that happened in the neighborhood, and turn it into something.

Alonzo Williams (DJ, World Class Wreckin' Cru): Eazy never ever wanted to be a rapper. Eazy wanted to be a behind-the-scenes man, put some money up, own a record label, and put out some stuff. He wanted to be Russell Simmons, and the guys came over here were some New York cats Dre had met. When he put them in the studio, Cube had wrote the song "Boyz-n-the-Hood," and these guys were like, "I can't do that shit. I don't know what the fuck you talkin' about."

When Eazy walked in the house with the cassette from "Boyz-n-the-Hood," they laughed at it. "He ain't got no bass in his voice. Turn your nuts up. Got his nuts in a vice or something." They clowned him.

I said, "You know what, man, don't laugh. That shit could possibly work." At the time in hip-hop, one of the big stars was Biz Markie and he had records called "Pickin' Boogers." So, if "Pickin' Boogers" can be a hit, you got action.

Arabian Prince (artist, producer, N.W.A): Out of everybody, [Eazy-E] was the real deal. He was that dude. He was living that life every day. Everything that you talked about in the records, pretty much he had done or was doing. That was the Eazy thing that was a really big influence on making it sound the way it did.

Murs (artist, Los Angeles): Hearing him rap about Compton, hearing him rap about Alpine stereos, '64 Impalas, having a Jheri curl, it blew my fucking mind. From that moment on, I believed that I could rap. That if he could do it, I could do it.

Greg Mack (KDAY): I had brought in this kid named Tony G, a Cuban kid out of El Monte who was probably the best DJ, I think, that ever existed. We were playing one night, me and Tony, at this place, the Casa Camino Real. Dr. Dre had called me earlier that day and he said, "Hey, man, I've got this kid I want to introduce you to." He walked into the Casa and he's got this little short kid with a Jheri curl. He said, "Greg, this is Eazy-E. We got this song we want you to hear. Can you come listen to it in the car?"

I said, "Yeah, okay." So, we walked outside and got in my car. He gave me a cassette of a song called "Boyz-n-the-Hood."

I listened to it, and I said, "Well, this is pretty good, but I can't play it. It's got too much cursing in it."

They went back in the studio that night. When I get to the station the next day, Dre is there with Eazy. He said, "Alright, we changed it." And they had changed the lyrics and everything. I played it and it was an immediate most-requested song.

Ice Cube (artist, N.W.A): The trust in a sixteen-year-old kid came from me writing that record that ended up on KDAY, so we ended up being real cool with Greg Mack. He would do parties at night and have us come down and perform, especially when we had "Boyz-n-the-Hood." We started doing hit records, he started having us—it just became a place where we knew we could get our records played if we keep 'em hot.

Alonzo Williams (DJ, World Class Wreckin' Cru): Jerry Heller had signed Egyptian Lover. He had signed Rudy [Pardee], and he was trying to get Wreckin' Cru. We got an offer from CBS on our own and I'm like, "Why do I want to give you twenty thousand dollars when I can do this myself?"

But shortly after we got signed to CBS, we got our check. I did the accounting and I realized we were about forty-eight hundred dollars short and I couldn't figure out where it went. I called Jerry and asked him about it, and he found where the money was, and, in the eyes of Dre and Yella, Jerry was a god. "Man, we gotta sign with him. We gotta sign."

Now that Jerry found this money and they in love with him, Dre is pumping Jerry Heller up to Eazy. So now Eazy wants to meet Jerry. Eazy owed me some money, and I wouldn't let him meet him until he paid me my money.

In the eyes of Jerry, Eazy paid me seven hundred and fifty dollars to meet him. When in actuality he only paid me what he owed me [five hundred dollars], and he gave me another two hundred and fifty to get my attention to meet with Jerry. I told Jerry, "Hey, man, I got this guy I want you to meet."

"I don't wanna meet anybody else. I'm good."

"No no no," I said. "He's a cool dude." I had to sell him on him.

This is the era of pre-gangster. Jerry is used to dealing with me, Egyptian Lover, Rudy from the [L.A.] Dream Team. We're all businessmen. Eazy's a street dude. He never wore a dress shirt. He never wore slacks. He wore jeans and a T-shirt every day. He kept his dope money in his sock. When he finally met Jerry, I didn't think this connection's going to work.

Arabian Prince (artist, producer, N.W.A): Before he became our manager, the company, Ruthless Records, and all of us were equal partners and everybody shared in the revenue. When Jerry got involved, that all stopped, and then money stopped too. Nobody was getting paid. There was a lot of records being sold, but it was hard for us to get our hands on it. That's when I started having a problem.

ARGUABLY, NO OTHER single song in hip-hop music history has generated as much backlash and controversy as N.W.A's protest against police harassment and brutality, "Fuck Tha Police." In a satire of a courtroom proceeding, Ice Cube, MC Ren, and Eazy-E narrate the strains between Black youth and law enforcement as Dr. Dre presides over the hearing.

While "Fuck Tha Police" provoked consternation among police supporters, the song was a cathartic expression of protest for many people whose lives had been touched by negative encounters with law enforcement.

Alonzo Williams (DJ, World Class Wreckin' Cru): I remember distinctly the day Dre and them got jammed by highway patrol, 'cause him and Eazy thought it was a good idea to ride down the Harbor Freeway in L.A. and shoot at people's cars with paintball guns. Highway patrol snatched them out of Eazy's Suzuki Samurai and they put guns to they heads, man. They would've been dead if they did the same shit today.

They came back to my house literally shaking and damn near crying. "Man, fuck the police. Man, them motherfuckers didn't have to do us like that. Fuck the police. Fuck the police."

The D.O.C. (artist, Dallas): Cube had that song in his folder and when he pulled it out, we all went nuts.

Ice Cube (artist, N.W.A): I threw [the lyrics] away [at first]. Dre said he didn't want to do the song. I had rapped it to him a year before we actually did it, and he was going through an issue where he had to go to jail every weekend, Friday night, get out Monday morning. He didn't want to do the record, 'cause he was like, "Dude. I don't want these sheriffs fuckin' me up when they find out I produced this record when I go in every weekend." He had just served like three months or something, so he was like, "Nah."

When he said that, I'm thinking, *Okay, this song is never going to get made.* I was in school in Phoenix, Arizona, and I was going through my lyrics in my rap books, and I was busting raps to my homeboy Phoenix Phil. And I came across "Fuck Tha Police" and I rapped it to him, and he freaked out. When he freaked out, I just tore it out the book, 'cause I was like, "I don't want to keep this shit if we ain't going to do it." I just balled it up and threw it in the trash and he was like, "Aw, hell no." He took it out of the trash, he opened it back up, spread it across the table and made it flat, and he put it in the folder part of my notebook.

So, when it was time to work on the N.W.A record, I had my notebook. When I got Eazy there and Ren there and Yella there, I said, "I had a song called 'Fuck Tha Police,' but Dre don't want to do it." And then Eazy was like, "Pull it out. I want to hear this shit."

When I pulled it out, I did my verse and he was like, "We doing this. We all going to write a verse and we're going to do this fuckin' song." Dre, by then, he had been off of that weekend program. He was just "Fuck it, let's do it. Let's start working on it."

Bryan Turner (cofounder, Priority Records): Sonically, [*Straight Outta Compton*] sounded amazing. But then when I heard the lyrics, really what blew my mind was "Fuck Tha Police." It was something that I had never experienced before. When you hear something like that, you just know it's something special.

If you wanted to hear the record, you had to either go to a swap meet or somewhere that somebody could dupe it on a cassette. You didn't hear them on the radio, because they weren't getting any airplay. But what really, really enforced it to me was, there was maybe three hundred kids in that roller rink and every kid knew every lyric to every song. I'm looking around, and literally, they're lip-syncing every fuckin' lyric. I was absolutely blown away.

Greg Mack (KDAY): [Eazy-E] listened. He was a good person. People would mess with him and threaten him, and he'd laugh. If somebody pulled a gun out, he'd start laughing. He just wasn't afraid of anything. I think that out of all the people in the business, he's really one of the good guys.

Bryan Turner (cofounder, Priority Records): Eazy was the mouthpiece. He was funny and he had a great sense of humor and he did a lot of the talking. Dre was polite. Ren and Cube were really not saying anything. They were like fuckin' nineteen or something. You could tell that Cube was the star, like, right away. I could tell Eazy and Cube were stars. Eazy was the guy that gave them their image, that made sure that they looked the way they wanted to look on the covers, all the images were the way they wanted to be. That certainly was his contribution.

We never would have predicted it would have been as big as it was, but I knew we would all make some money, and I knew we could continue to make records and have a good relationship. And as it started to get bigger and bigger, I had bigger problems: Cube leaving, and then [C.] Delores Tucker and then Tipper Gore, I mean there was all that backlash, so there was a lot going on.

Cheo Hodari Coker (journalist): I cannot tell you the visceral reaction of what it felt like to listen to "Straight Outta Compton" for the first time. The power of that record was like, *Holy shit.* It just blew my mind because it was so raw. N.W.A comes out and they just drop a bomb. If you really start digging deeply into what N.W.A is saying, they're like the cultural revolutionaries, which makes them the Black Panthers. They're saying if we can arm and educate the brother on the street who's fearless, and put a gun and ten-point program, put that in his arsenal, this is something you can't stop.

IN THE SUMMER of 1989, Priority Records received a surprising
letter from Milt Ahlerich, an assistant director of the Federal Bureau
of Investigation. In it, Ahlerich conveyed his dismay with N.W.A and,
specifically, "Fuck Tha Police": "I wanted you to be aware of the FBI's
position relative to this song and its message," he wrote. "I believe my
views reflect the opinion of the entire law enforcement community."

The letter drew sharp criticism from First Amendment advocates,
and N.W.A began to bill itself as the group that even the FBI sought to
suppress.

Bryan Turner (cofounder, Priority Records): We would all get together and
discuss how we were going to respond. There was no better spokes-
people who lived it and breathed it and were as close as you could
be to it than the band members. And that's where Cube really broke
out and he really shined, because it was so meaningful to him as the
chief lyricist of the group. He took it upon himself, really, to defend
the work that he'd done and the perspective that he had. Our job was
just to make sure that he had that platform.

Alonzo Williams (DJ, World Class Wreckin' Cru): It was only a letter, but
they spun it into a marketing frenzy 'cause it turned N.W.A into the
group that the government wanted to get. They were bigger than the
Black Panther shit. That letter changed their whole careers. It just
blew them up.

Bryan Turner (cofounder, Priority Records): As young guys who were having success and we were all making money, I think we were a little bit
arrogant and we weren't going to be intimidated, because we felt we
were on the right side. And we used that letter. We sent it to our local
congressman. We got all the controversy whipped up, and we really
took advantage of that in many ways to expand the group's profile
and increase sales.

Arabian Prince (artist, producer, N.W.A): Tipper Gore had the whole
PMRC [Parents Music Resource Center] thing, putting that [Parental
Advisory] label sticker on stuff. And then they got a bunch of N.W.A

records and bulldozed them or set them on fire, and the whole time I'm looking at it like, *So, they bought them from stores and burned them?* I'm like, *That's more sales,* and then people are going to want to buy it and hear it and see what's up. Once you get promotion and get your name out there, it don't matter if it's good or bad. People want to hear it.

Bryan Turner (cofounder, Priority Records): It was a great marketing tool. We were respected and appreciated by the industry that we cared about, which was our guys' independent hip-hop labels. And so we all took a stand, and we all stood together.

Ice Cube (artist, N.W.A): The press person at the time was Pat Charbonnet. She worked for Bryan Turner and Priority Records. Then [she] actually became my manager once I left.

Shit was getting heated with N.W.A, she would set up interviews and I'd be on time. Some dudes wouldn't come. Some dudes would be hella late. When I come on time, I'm standing there with Pat Charbonnet and we chopping it up. She giving me game on what this record means, and make sure you know what you're talking about because they're going to come at you for what you said on these records. I already knew what I was talking about, so it was just making sure that I was cocked and loaded. I thank her for putting me up on it.

Atron Gregory (tour manager, N.W.A): The guys were never, ever any problem. What was challenging was the stigma that N.W.A had. They had the songs, "Straight Outta Compton," "Fuck Tha Police," "Dope Man." They were super popular around the country from one coast to the other, but you go from the Midwest to the South, and no one wanted them in their town. Ice Cube and I literally had to go in and talk them into not canceling our show.

Cube wasn't some guy who had guns in his socks. We weren't out there perpetuating a certain type of lifestyle. These guys were doing records about stuff that was going on in everyone's neighborhood, and that's why it became so popular.

Cli-N-Tel (artist, World Class Wreckin' Cru): It was more like street reporting. Interpreting the sights and sounds of what we grew up in. We weren't gangbangers, but we had homies in the crew that were serious gangbangers and drug dealers. We could see their lifestyle and tell stories through those observations.

> **PROMOTERS WARNED N.W.A** against performing "Fuck Tha Police" while on their national tour over concern that the song's controversial lyrics could incite violence. The group stayed away from the track until the tour's final stop in Detroit, where they were joined by the likes of Slick Rick and LL Cool J at Joe Louis Arena in August of 1989. During the finale, the members started "Fuck Tha Police," and chaos ensued.

Atron Gregory (tour manager, N.W.A): It was the last show of the tour, and the two most trying parts of any tour are the beginning and the end—there's a lot of energy going into the beginning, so things happen; and at the end, everyone's tired, just ready to go home.

So, there were two songs they couldn't do. It was "Straight Outta Compton" and "Fuck Tha Police." There would be a huge fine if they did those songs. That was the prerequisite for the promoter taking us out on tour.

So, Dre goes up on the turntables. Ice Cube walks out, and he looks up at Dre and they had this strangest look that I've never seen. And all of a sudden, Dre scratched and dropped the record "Fuck Tha Police." The Joe Louis Arena explodes. Everyone just went crazy.

And I guess there were undercover cops in the audience. You hear *bam, bam, bam*—they had some cherry bombs to make way, so they could get to the front of the stage, and they started trying to jump up on the stage. Because they were undercover, our security started fighting them back. I call the guys off stage, and then we run back to the dressing room like, "We need to get out of here."

Everyone took their hats off, reversed their jackets. I called for cars. One car got down and I got the guys in the car. But before the other car could get there, police with horses started coming down. I had personal security with me at all times, and a couple of the other guys, we just walked back to the hotel about a mile and a half away.

Arabian Prince (artist, producer, N.W.A): All I remember is trying not to get killed by the police. That's what I remember.

Atron Gregory (tour manager, N.W.A): The police surrounding the hotel. It was a lot. I jumped in a cab and checked into another hotel, and I was communicating with Eazy the rest of the night.

The police finally caught them in an elevator, took them down to the basement, checked their IDs—of course there's no warrants or anything. But they couldn't arrest them. It wasn't illegal. They just didn't like it. So, they kept them for about an hour and a half. After a while, they were like, "Okay. See you guys later, but don't come back into our town doing that song."

Cold 187um (artist, producer, Above the Law): When *Straight Outta Compton* blew up, it started forming as a label. And it's funny, it became the build and the demise all at once, basically. No one knew what contracts meant. None of that shit. That's how fast it happened.

Arabian Prince (artist, producer, N.W.A): What I tell everybody when they say, "You were stupid for leaving during *Straight Outta Compton*," I'm like, "You've got to look at it like this: I was the only one in the group who had been a solo artist before, who had his own records."

I think what happens when you young and you become famous a little bit, you get kind of blinded by it, because you're having fun and people are all about you. You're not really worried about the business. You get a little money, and for some dudes in the hood, having a couple g's in your pocket, that was satisfactory in the short term.

Where me, I'm looking at: *Well, when I was solo, I sold X amount of records and I knew how much money I made. Here, we've done sold a million records and I can't even get two thousand dollars to pay my rent and car payment. There's something up.* And then I had [J.J. Fad's] "Supersonic," which had just blown up, and I produced that record by myself and brought it to Ruthless Records and put Dre and Yella's name on there, because we were a production team. And "Supersonic" is the thing that really funded everything else.

So, for me, I was really pissed. Because I've got something that's really a hit over here and I can't get paid? Oh, hell no. Got me an attorney. Sat down with Jerry. Got it straight and I'm like, "Y'all, I'm out. I can't be here. I don't trust him."

I remember the next day, I went and bought a Porsche. Jerry Heller had given everybody Suzuki Samurais. I rode up to one of their concerts in a Porsche. I was still friends with everybody; it wasn't no hard feelings between me and my people, it was Jerry I had a problem with. So, I rode up in a Porsche. They were like, "Man, where'd you get this from?" I was like, "I can't really talk about that. All I can tell you is you need to go holler at Jerry." Maybe a week or two later, Cube was gone. He figured it out.

I even spoke up on it like, "Man, y'all tripping. Y'all let the wrong person broke y'all up." I just couldn't understand why everybody couldn't stick together and get rid of Jerry.

Greg Mack (KDAY): Jerry Heller was not the evil person that he was portrayed to be. I think that what happened is when they got going, Jerry was Eazy's manager. I think that they anticipated Jerry being a manager for N.W.A as well. All along, Jerry was looking out for Eazy. If you'll notice, none of the guys ever sued Jerry, because they knew that he hadn't done anything wrong. He was just looking out for Eazy.

In order to sell records, they had to talk about his ass. I do know from my conversations with Eazy that he felt bad about that, because he probably could have handled it better. Jerry was basically running Eazy's company. At one time, we were in Eazy's office, he said, "Look at this." Nine out of the top ten stocks trading on the market, Eazy had bought in early and was just making tons of money off the stock market. But that was all Jerry. Jerry was taking his money; he was investing it properly. Eazy's company at one time was making way more money off his business dealings than record sales.

And so I think that there was just a lot of naïveté with these guys. And then when some of the stock market starting going down, and some of the business interests that he had invested in for Eazy were on the downside, Jerry was starting to have to come out of his pocket to pay the bills, and that's when I think a lot of the questions started popping up.

I would look at Eazy's accountant trying to rob Peter to pay Paul. He would lay out all of the bills and all of the credit card charges, and all of the cars, and all of the houses, and there just wasn't enough coming in to pay them. It wasn't, in my opinion, anything that was being done wrong. But I think people were getting in his ear.

It's complicated. They were all right about what they were saying, but they were all wrong because that was not the way it was originally set up. If they would have set it up that way in the beginning, they'd probably have stayed together.

Sir Jinx (producer): It took a long time for it to hit the fan, because I think Cube couldn't understand that a person would do that, to take that kind of money. He couldn't believe that he would write the songs and still get cheated out.

Ice Cube (artist, N.W.A): [Pat Charbonnet] is the one who told me, "We need to pay attention to Jerry Heller. He has a reputation from the past."

The D.O.C. (artist, Dallas): Cube was the spirit of that group. He brought the Public Enemy aspect to it, sort of a political kind of thing. For me, that was N.W.A's whole mystique. The energy that Public Enemy had, every young Black dude on the street had that.

Arabian Prince (artist, producer, N.W.A): Money does strange things. Money destroys countries, brings down kingdoms, right? It's no different than what happened there. Once people figured out that there was a whole lot of money that wasn't moving the way it was supposed to be moving, I left. Cube left.

Cube went somewhere and got successful. I was making so much more money in technology, I'm like, *I ain't got to get chased or shot at or watch my back no more, because I'm hanging out with tech people making big money.* Then Dre was looking at Cube like, *Wait a minute. Cube went over here and started his own empire. I'm over here, I'm still just a producer. I ain't making the big money.* So, that's when he figured it out, that he really was getting ripped off and not making that money that he should've been making in the beginning.

FOLLOWING HIS CONTENTIOUS split from N.W.A, Ice Cube set out to work on his solo debut album. At the time, Los Angeles and East Coast hip-hop constituted two distinct entities, with New Yorkers often looking down at the brand of hip-hop created by their West Coast counterparts.

In crafting *AmeriKKKa's Most Wanted,* Ice Cube opted to collaborate with the Bomb Squad, Public Enemy's heralded production team. Sir Jinx accompanied Ice Cube to help ensure that the final product remained true to the West Coast, while the Bomb Squad showed that their capabilities were not bounded by any region. In his lyrics throughout the album, Ice Cube aggressively challenged institutions for policies that negatively impacted minorities. Released in May 1990, *AmeriKKKa's Most Wanted* launched Ice Cube into stardom as a solo artist, and remains one of the defining hip-hop albums of the 1990s.

André "Doctor Dré" Brown (artist, Original Concept/co-host, *Yo! MTV Raps*): I got a call from Ice Cube and he said, "Yo, I'm leaving N.W.A. None of us are getting paid and Jerry Heller's making all the money."

And at that time, I used to talk to Jerry Heller every other day. Anything that we needed, he would make sure and send it for us. I said, "Man, you're going to mess the group up."

He said, "Man, I've got to go. Could you get me to Chuck [D] and the Bomb Squad?"

I put the meeting together. So, Keith [Shocklee] came and I drove him out to 510 South Franklin, and we had a big meeting and we talked about what was going on with N.W.A and how he wanted to break out, and how he wanted them to produce his first album.

Keith Shocklee (producer, Bomb Squad): [Producer] Sam Sever was supposed to do that project. Sam Sever never showed up to the appointment. Chuck [D] tripped over Ice Cube sitting in the lobby of Def Jam, waiting for Sam, and he told Chuck what he was doing. And Chuck said, "Well, I got a song that you can get on and start your career." And after he saw us work, he's like, "Why don't you all do my album?"

Took us about three seconds to feel like, "Okay, we'll do it."

We felt that everything in the stars lined up. He was from the West Coast. We're from the East Coast. Dre and them had a feel like we did, and we knew Cube understood our feel, and we just said, "Let's see what we can do." We kind of had the idea like East Coast meets West Coast or some crazy shit.

Bryan Turner (cofounder, Priority Records): [Jerry] Heller was very obstinate. He was a very tough guy to deal with. You never wanted to take his phone call, because rarely was it something that you wanted to talk to him about. There's always a problem. So, I understood it.

Cube decided, "I'm going to New York and I'm going to work with the Bomb Squad."

I thought, *Okay, well, that's sort of cutting-edge.* And I thought it would be great because it could unify the West and East Coast—for that moment, anyway.

Ice Cube (artist, formerly of N.W.A): I give credit to Ice-T. He, working with Afrika Islam and always paying homage to New York and what it did for hip-hop, was a big reason why I felt like, *This is okay and this is another step.* Not only was they my favorite producers, the Bomb Squad, even more than Dre at the time, to get a chance to work with them, I didn't even really think about the gap that we're bridging.

When we went to work on *AmeriKKKa's Most Wanted,* they took us to a place called 510 Franklin Avenue. It was like a warehouse full of records. I had never seen nothing like it. It was me and Jinx out there together—they gave us two crates and said, "When you fill up the crates with the samples you want, then we can go to the big studio at Greene Street and make the record," which blew our mind 'cause we just thought we was about to just get in the studio and start making music. It took us a few weeks to fill those crates up.

Eric "Vietnam" Sadler (producer, Bomb Squad): He had picked out the songs and we worked a little preproduction, and then we went straight into the city to start recording.

But at this time, it gets pretty complicated. People in the camp weren't really talking to each other because of the [Professor] Griff situation [in which he made anti-Semitic comments to a journalist]. Hank [Shocklee] wasn't really talking to Griff and Chuck, and it was just a mess because we were doing three things at the same time. We were doing Ice Cube, but we were also doing *Fear of a Black Planet* and Bell Biv DeVoe, so we were really, really stretched.

Ice Cube (artist, formerly of N.W.A): I always thought the more ideas I go to the studio with, the more I can just be in there executing. I don't like being cooped up in a room that long, even if I'm doing something that I love like making music. I'm a six-hour guy. I like to have a few things I know I want to do, and then from there, if new ideas roll out from there, then I'll stay and work on those. That's just been my mentality from day one.

Eric "Vietnam" Sadler (producer, Bomb Squad): The whole album was done probably in about twenty-eight days, and out of those twenty-eight days, I think Hank might have been there only seven to ten days, but was important with his contribution. He brought in a massive collection of special effects and sounds that we used throughout the album. Keith was there probably about seventy-five percent and I'm the only person who was there one hundred percent of the time, because I lived two blocks away.

Now, Chuck, when he got off the road, Chuck came and destroyed shit with Cube. Cube was exactly like Chuck to me. He didn't really drink. Had no women in the studio. He was straight business. He knew what he wanted.

The way we used to do stuff with PE and we were going to do with Cube is: We would have a whole bunch of songs, and once we had five or six really good songs, we got rid of the rest and we made those five or six songs our worst songs.

I remember this one song, he was like, "Yo, what's up with this song? We're not finishing?" I'm like, "Look, man. This is the best this song's going to be. Some songs can be a ten. Some songs can only be a seven at their best. This song, I can't do nothing to make a ten." He's like, "Fuck that shit. Throw that shit away. Let's do another one."

I was really, really impressed by that, because most people are like, "We're still going to keep it on the album." He wasn't like that.

Ice Cube (artist, formerly of N.W.A): To me, Eric was the workhorse when it comes to the Bomb Squad. Before Hank and Keith Shocklee, Chuck, and all those other members started to put their stamp on the record, it was Eric who had that bottom beat rolling. Being prepared was something I felt like I was obligated to do. I had always been prepared, but I was extra prepared working with Eric.

Eric "Vietnam" Sadler (producer, Bomb Squad): He was gung-ho. He was brilliant. The storytelling, the style. I was like, "This shit is good," as I listened to how we started to begin to sequence [*Nation of Millions*]. The most important thing in them days was the sequencing of the album, how things went from one song to another, because back then it was a side A and it was a side B, so your feeling from song number one going into song number two, everything was a microscope for us. We'd sit there maybe for two hours deciding how many seconds it was going to be until the next song started when you play it. It's got to be about feel.

Ice Cube (artist, formerly of N.W.A): I knew that Jinx was a bad motherfucker. A lot of that record, Jinx should get credit for orchestrating. We had ideas, and we was going to make sure that the record cared for our West Coast flavor and presence.

Eric "Vietnam" Sadler (producer, Bomb Squad): Jinx, he was trying to make sure that Cube's music didn't turn into something else, to keep the core beliefs that they had, and I understood that. And he was such a great guy, and very, very fun to work with.

Sir Jinx (producer): Being from L.A., we think all East Coast people hated L.A. I came out there wanting to bang and do what we do. But they was like, "Nah. That's the media, man. We come in here to work." And then Run-DMC was in another studio, so when they were working on their music, I was in the back kicking it with Jam Master Jay. So, I was just getting new trends from them.

Keith Shocklee (producer, Bomb Squad): We wasn't going to interrupt Ice Cube's vibe and where he came from. We adapted to a lot of the artists, and who they were, because we sat with them, we talked, we'd build. "What are you looking for? What do you need to do?"

Sir Jinx (producer): They left me in the studio and the first song I did was "Who's the Mack?" And when they came back with the Marvin Gaye and all that, then it was all love. But life before that I was like, *East Coast, West Coast.* But what I was doing with Keith and Hank Shocklee, they took me under their wing, and I met so many guys by them changing my attitude on how I came out there. That's why you see the Kool G Rap stuff [that I went on to produce].

Keith Shocklee (producer, Bomb Squad): Ice Cube was the most prepared. LL was prepared, too. LL, he would have shit in his head and knock that shit out. But Ice Cube had books and knew the shit he wanted to do, and he came like he was going for his PhD. His project, he had the concept. We just had to shape it and give it the right things.

Eric "Vietnam" Sadler (producer, Bomb Squad): He picked a song of mine that I thought was straight garbage: "A Gangsta's Fairytale." I'm like, *Why in the fuck did he pick this? This is whack. This is a piece of shit.* But he felt it and he knew where to get in and out of it and dance with it to make it something that people still remember to this day. And that's the true genius of a lot of people. They'll take something that you don't think can work, but they'll have a vision in it and be able to create something incredible.

Ice Cube (artist, formerly of N.W.A): Eric was chopping up beats. We would give him stuff. He would cut it up and do the bottom beat to it—records that they wasn't using with other groups.

I think there was a group called the Son of Bazerk. They had a beat that I loved, and he wasn't coming out before me, so they ended up giving me that beat, which ended up being "AmeriKKKa's Most Wanted," the bottom beat to that.

Eric "Vietnam" Sadler (producer, Bomb Squad): We had a lot of songs like that, that had gone to other people, and we used to call them stabbers, because you'd have a great track, but [the artists] were so horrible they were stabbing that shit to death. It was like murder. But then you'd take a brilliant artist like Chuck or Slick Rick or LL or Big Daddy or Doug E. [Fresh], they're so talented and so good, they can make it into gold, and it is a talent.

Ice Cube (artist, formerly of N.W.A): I was just thankful that they were so generous, and I learned so much from them about how to put a record together in the right order. When Chuck told me, "Man, I wrote *Nation of Millions* on the [Long Island Expressway]. Back and forth to the studio, I'm writing the songs," it made me feel like I should write anywhere.

The Bomb Squad liked working at night, so we didn't go to the studio 'til six P.M., which was new to me, but what it gave me was a chance to wake up in the morning, after being at a session all night, listen to what we did, and then use the day to figure out what I'm going to do when we go back in at night. I wanted to stay ahead of the curve.

Bryan Turner (cofounder, Priority Records): He had a tremendous amount of pressure. And there was no fucking around. There was no partying late at night. There was no drugs. In the studio especially, it was work. And they did it fast. To have that kind of masterpiece so quickly was another thing that confirmed his genius to me.

Everybody had something to prove, right? The Bomb Squad had to prove that they could make a record that wasn't a PE record and that could have that kind of impact. You know what Cube's motivation was: Dre wasn't there anymore. He didn't have those guys around him.

Eric "Vietnam" Sadler (producer, Bomb Squad): Cube didn't play. If anybody had any questions, they were going to have to answer to J-Dee and T-Bone, and those were some rough motherfuckers. When they first came into the studio—usually people will sleep on the couch— them motherfuckers were sleeping on the concrete in the corner with a little paper towel pulled over them, and they were talking about gaffling and ganking.

They might be nice until you get to the other side. When they get to the other side, they'll shoot you in the face, but if y'all all boys and y'all chilling, everybody's cool. No issues. A bunch of fun. Cube brought them out here just in case there were any issues with anything.

Ice Cube (artist, formerly of N.W.A): There was a show on TV called *America's Most Wanted,* and they would show criminals that were the most wanted ones. I was like, "Man, this the perfect title for my record. *AmeriKKKa's Most Wanted.* I'm one of those." I saw America spelled like that on a Last Poets record, or it was one of those kind of Black Power poetry records, and I was like, "I'm going to name my record *AmeriKKKa's Most Wanted,* but I want to spell America like that to let people know that this ain't no goddamn TV show. This has got another undertone going on. I'm making statements about our conditions here in America."

It worked and it just got everybody's attention.

Bryan Turner (cofounder, Priority Records): That was one of the greatest moments of my entire career, listening to that record for the first time. Sonically, beats-wise, production, lyrically, I think it was one of the first few times ever that I was so inundated that I couldn't distinguish between listening to the beats or the lyrics. And his rapping, I mean, God, you could just see the force of his vocals on that record. It blew me away.

Ice Cube (artist, formerly of N.W.A): I approached the record like a mixtape. Records, a lot of them had big pauses in between them. It was like three seconds and then the next record came on. I'm like, *Man, let's have enough shit where this just seems like one long-ass experience.*

We started cutting stuff tight. Making one song go right into the next, go into a skit, come back into the music, short song, long song. Stay creative, 'cause Slick Rick is one of the greatest storytellers ever. That's ultimately what we doing in a way is storytelling. I'm always going to go back to the essence of that, to tell a great story in the perfect way to a beat. That is, to me, the magic of being an MC.

Sir Jinx (producer): He cared less about the flow because he had more to say than how to say it. Some people do better at writing and some people do better at lyrical combat and Cube wasn't a lyrical combat guy.

Deadly Threat (artist, Los Angeles): Finally, for the West Coast, we had ammunition that was some foreign type of shit. And even the East Coast knew. They was like, "Aw, shit, these niggas got a new fucking weapon."

"What's the name of it?"

"It's called Ice Cube, nigga. *AmeriKKKa's Most Wanted*."

BORN TRACY CURRY, the D.O.C. started as a member of Dallas's Fila Fresh Crew before moving to Southern California, linking with Dr. Dre, and playing a pivotal role in penning N.W.A's lyrics. In the summer of 1989, the D.O.C. released his debut album, *No One Can Do It Better*. The milestone album proved the depth of Ruthless Records and reflected another leap in Dr. Dre's production ability. The D.O.C. seemed on the verge of becoming one of hip-hop music's best-known talents before a devastating car accident in the winter of 1989 left him with several serious injuries, including damage to his throat that robbed him of most of his voice.

The D.O.C. (artist, Dallas): It was just a moment we were all in and everybody came together, and everybody was pretty good at the same time, so we were able to make some really cool music. . . . It was always a little competitive. And when you're young and wild and free, that's just fucking fun. We had a blast. We talked a lot of shit, drank a lot of fucking beer. We were happy and just really calm.

Big Gipp (artist, Goodie Mob): If that guy didn't have that accident, he would've been bigger than life. He never even got to go and do that fucking album live. I really think that D.O.C. would've changed the whole history of the West Coast if people would have known back then that he was a Southern rapper from Dallas, Texas. If people had really known that the South helped build the West.

The D.O.C. (artist, Dallas): I just wrote what I was asked to write. But when I wrote songs for myself, I always put subliminal little lines that could tell people I was from Texas.

LONG-SIMMERING TENSION BOILED over in the spring of 1992 when a Southern California jury acquitted four police officers charged with using excessive force against Rodney King, a Black driver pulled over for a traffic violation. Long before the advent of social media and camera phones, King's beating was captured on video following a high-speed chase. The verdicts ignited waves of disbelief and outrage. For days, civil unrest erupted in South Central, including arson and looting. By the time it ended, more than fifty people were dead. Property damage totaled more than $1 billion, with Korean-owned businesses assuming an excessive amount of loss. For many involved in hip-hop music, the trial's outcome crystallized the message prophesied by N.W.A—that institutional forces routinely dehumanized people of color and left them with little recourse.

Alonzo Williams (DJ, World Class Wreckin' Cru): After the Rodney King verdict came out in '92, that record became the national anthem for the rioters and for the street, period. For the first time folks started saying, "Oh, okay. I see what you talking about from another perspective." That's what made it blow up.

Sir Jinx (producer): Until there's a difference between the relationship between the police and the community, it's always going to be happening. The community stayed the same, but the police have changed. You build relationships with certain people and then they leave, and a new squad comes in, and at some point it's an explosion if the inner core of the police are not encouraging relations between the Blacks and the Mexicans and stuff like that. It's always going to be happening out here.

Deadly Threat (artist, Los Angeles): I was in the riots. We were actually on the front lines of this thing, uniting the Crips with the Bloods. That gave me the knowledge to know that in a crisis, it's going to be possible that most people are going to stick together. And so, it really turned things in a different direction.

I remember we was getting ready to go in one of the supermarkets and the police was sitting outside. And people running in and out of the place just grabbing stuff, looting the place all the way to the ground. The police looked at us and said, "Man, go on, get what you all are going to get. You got like another twenty, thirty minutes, man; we fitting to shut this down." So, it was a different respect.

Alonzo Williams (DJ, World Class Wreckin' Cru): For the first time, especially after the Rodney King situation, people saw what we were talking about. Blacks have been mistreated in this country for decades, and the cops would get away with all kinds of shit, including murder. And for it to have a spokesperson, a spokes-group, the timing was fucking great for everybody, and it just changed history.

IN MARCH 1995, Eazy-E disclosed that he had been diagnosed with AIDS. He penned a final statement to his fans and died from complications of the disease less than ten days later. He was thirty years old.

Greg Mack (KDAY): Right before Eazy died, I decided, *You know what? I'm tired of making people rich. I'm going to go about my own radio station.* I had some partners that screwed me over pretty bad, [so] I called Eazy and told him what was going on. He's like, "Fuck them niggas. Come down here, man. We'll buy one. Man, I got you." He got me a place to stay. Got me a car. Started paying me on payroll. We had everything set up, and bam—Eazy died.

Deadly Threat (artist, Los Angeles): I just remember Eazy picking me up, and we'd go to one of his houses, he'd drop me off, be like, "Call me when you're ready. I'll come back and get you." Be a fucking room empty with just a trash bag of weed. And he'd say, "Man, the weed is in there, there's some blunts over there." And just sit there and listen to beats and fucking smoke weed and write rhymes and shit, and drink beer.

Kokane (artist, producer): He was the coolest of the cool. He gave everybody a chance. He opened up his heart and his checkbook. Eazy was one of a kind, period. And everybody, every human being got bads on this planet. I got bads, he had bads, you got bads. But as far as being a G, a real G, he was that to the core. Every fabric of his being was so solid. He was granite. Eazy was granite for real.

OVER GENERATIONS, LOS Angeles–area natives like Xzibit, The Game, Kendrick Lamar, and Nipsey Hussle picked up where N.W.A left off, and subgenres like trap and drill sprang from gangster rap. Variations have continued to evolve, as has the social environment that birthed them. But many of the original practitioners of what they originally termed "reality rap" are quick to point out that they never intended to glorify the climate that they illuminated. The protagonist in Schoolly D's "P.S.K. What Does It Mean?" decided against pulling the trigger, and the lyrics for Ice-T's "6 'N the Mornin'" include his going to jail.

Schoolly D (artist, Philadelphia): I said that shit 'til my face turned like a blueberry like that bitch in *Charlie and the Chocolate Factory.* Nobody wants to hear that shit. I'm like, *Fuck it.* I just gave up.

I understand it years later, why do young African Americans always got to explain they self to the man? Y'all don't explain yourself to us. Explain why y'all killed all the fucking Indians. Explain that shit. Explain why women only make seventy-nine cents to your fucking dollar. Explain that shit. We always got to explain ourselves and it was like, "You know what, dude? I'm tired of trying to explain myself. Go ask Kenny Rogers to explain his fucking lyrics."

Ice-T (artist, Rhyme Syndicate): I actually been through most of this shit I rapped about. I had a lot of friends that are in prison for this behavior. So, for me to act like whatever it is, gangbanging, hustling, pimping, it's some great thing that you're going to survive and you're gonna be victorious—that would've been a lie, and I felt like that would've been jinxing my life. I always felt like I could tell you the life of crime, but I had to tell you the consequences. That was just a way of me keeping my karma correct.

Schoolly D (artist, Philadelphia): There's gangster rap and gangsta rap. Gangster rap is a celebration of a personal choice. You can be a preacher and do something gangster. You can be a mother . . . Mom's gangster. That means Mom ain't taking no shit. That's gangst*er* rap, *e-r.*

Gangsta rap is a celebration of hood life, gangsta life, group life. It means a celebration of yourself. You stood up to the powers that be.

I don't think we're supposed to experience everything pleasant. Then there's not growth. Not saying that we should just stay in the same hard times for as long as we live on earth. I'm saying hard times make it interesting. All the good shit came out of hard times.

Ice-T (artist, Rhyme Syndicate): We didn't give it that name ["gangster rap"]. The press gave it that name, but we'll rock with it. Gangster rap. Me, myself, gangsters are people that basically make their own rules. They don't back up. They say what they're gonna say. So, if that makes you a gangster, I think everybody needs to have a little gangster in them. But I call it reality rap, because it was my reality, but it's not everybody's reality.

Alonzo Williams (DJ, World Class Wreckin' Cru): I never hated on gangster rap. I hated on the name. N.W.A, Niggaz Wit Attitudes. I'm a kid from the civil rights movement. I remember [Martin Luther] King marching. I remember Malcolm X. I remember the Black Panthers. And I remember calling somebody a *nigger* would get yo' ass whopped, and so for somebody to tell me they're going to name their group Niggaz Wit Attitudes, I'm like, "Dude, they gonna shut that shit down."

DURING THE HEIGHT of West Coast gangster rap, two Los Angeles nightclub DJs teamed up to form the record label Delicious Vinyl, and created a blend of mainstream hip-hop that found its way onto radio stations across the country.

Mike Ross and Matt Dike met in 1983. They discovered that they were members of the same record pool and shared an appreciation for the new music and culture that had emerged from the East Coast. Inspired by Def Jam, they built their own label with the in-house production team the Dust Brothers.

The pair struck pay dirt by unearthing Tone Lōc and pairing him with Young MC, a New York City transplant who was attending the University of Southern California. In 1988, Tone Lōc's "Wild Thing" climbed all the way to number two on the Billboard Hot 100, and his second single, "Funky Cold Medina," earned him a Grammy nomination. Young MC

helped pen both hit songs, and a few months later he followed with his
own eternal hit "Bust a Move."

Mike Ross (cofounder, Delicious Vinyl): Matt [Dike] was probably the biggest underground club DJ, playing funk and soul and hip-hop, which
wasn't something that a lot of people were doing at that time. We
gravitated towards each other because we were into the same music.

So, as we were playing in clubs more underground, labels were popping up and obviously Def Jam, Rick Rubin, he is doing it yourself,
and there's Profile and Tommy Boy and there's all these labels in New
York that aren't affiliated with big labels. It got to a point where we
just said, "Let's do it ourselves. Rubin did it." You see Hurby "Luv
Bug" is producing records, and he's a DJ, and he's doing all this cool
shit with Salt-N-Pepa and other people, like Marley Marl.

Me and Matt had gotten a couple of different drum machines, trying to make dope drumbeats and patterns. And then the SP-12 [drum
machine] came out and that changed the game. We were able to start
sampling records and putting tracks together and we figured, "Let's
work on making a rap record. We need a rapper." We were looking
for someone that sounded kind of cool, and I asked a friend of mine
at the record pool and he said his cousin rapped. His cousin happened
to be Tone Lōc.

So I basically cold-called him, and I remember getting him on the
phone and I heard this unbelievable voice. I went and picked him
up and smoked a bunch of weed and he got on the mic and his voice
sounded incredible. He had swag like a motherfucker.

Paul Stewart (producer, promoter): Delicious was just a really family-run
operation. Hip-hop was so new at that time, and they were doing it
in this fresh way that started really taking off, and their whole visual
aesthetic was different and on some California kind of shit.

Young MC (artist, New York City): Growing up on the East Coast made
you think, *If you're an MC, everybody's got to do the same thing the
same way*. Coming out to the West Coast, everybody's groundbreaking.
There's two different sounds from the jump.

Mike Ross (cofounder, Delicious Vinyl): I used to go record shopping in New York City at Rock and Soul Records. I got a lot of my early hip-hop records there. One of the 12-inch buyers there, this kid named Eric, and I became friends, and once he saw that I was making records, he told me to look up a friend of his who was going to USC that was a dope MC, and it happened to be Marvin Young [Young MC].

Young MC (artist, New York City): A friend who worked at Rock and Soul Records in New York City tells me he knows guys that own a label called Delicious Vinyl. So, literally before my junior year, I call up the guys from Delicious Vinyl and I spat about three verses over the phone.

Mike Ross (cofounder, Delicious Vinyl): He was at 'SC and he started hitting me with rhyme after rhyme on the phone. Just funny, clever, hysterical rhymes. I went down there, and I picked him up and brought him to our studio, and basically that's how I started working with Young MC.

Young MC (artist, New York City): Within a week they sent me a contract, and that's how I got signed.

Mike Ross (cofounder, Delicious Vinyl): Matt had come up with this kind of rock-rap concept using Van Halen's "Jamie's Cryin'," and we were vibing off it. It's kind of a little homage to "It's Tricky," because it started really taking that rap format that Rubin did.

[Fab 5] Freddy was a friend of Matt's and mine, and he'd been hanging out with us. I don't know why it popped into my head, but that line where he says, "Yo, baby let's go back to my place and do the wild thing," from the *She's Gotta Have It* movie? That was in my head, and I just thought, *Let's make this record about a guy trying to get laid.* Basically, a story about Tone trying to get laid.

I fed that concept to Tone when I played him the track and he wrote a couple of verses to it. We needed more verses, and so Young MC was a very prolific writer and he came up with a couple of verses for it as well.

Paul Stewart (producer, promoter): When I started working at Delicious, I spent time around Young MC a fair amount. It was drastically different. Tone Lōc is a Crip. He would have a house of twenty Hoover Crips smoking blunts in it, and Marvin Young, Young MC, who's a USC economics student—it was like night and day.

Mike Ross (cofounder, Delicious Vinyl): You couldn't have had two more diametrically opposed human beings. Tone was a local L.A. kid who was definitely in a gang, and Young MC was a more scholastic, kind of nerdy student at 'SC who came from Queens.

Young MC (artist, New York City): I had no connection to the gang culture out there, so I had no clue of what color to wear or anything like that. There'd be some rough people, too. All I had was my skill. All I had was my ability to get my records out and performing them at Skateland, performing them at World on Wheels, a lot of the little clubs downtown, and seeing how people reacted. That was really important for me.

Mike Ross (cofounder, Delicious Vinyl): Young wrote some verses for "Wild Thing" and "Funky Cold Medina," and his clever lyrical sensibility went well with Tone's cool, laid-back style.

Young MC (artist, New York City): When I co-wrote "Wild Thing" with Tone, I said, "I hope we make enough money so that I can pay off my student loans." He said he wanted to make enough money to buy a car. And the song sold four million records.

Mike Ross (cofounder, Delicious Vinyl): We both knew that this song definitely had the elements to be something. Tone's voice with that concept over that track, it was kind of hard to miss it. We were getting a lot of plays with a lot of our records on KDAY and some of the local stations. Greg Mack was our guy. He helped us a lot.

"Wild Thing" really popped off in this weird way, because KROQ jumped on it. One of their DJs was friends with Tone's manager, and they just put it on. And then KDAY started playing it, and it really jumped off. It crossed over; it wasn't some underground hip-hop record, and it really put Tone in this whole other lane right from the get-go, and put a lot of attention on us right away.

Young MC (artist, New York City): It was weird, because especially East Coast, there was a stigma about who wrote rhymes. But we're talking about massive records. Not something that's just going to be local or you're going to be lucky to get on the radio, but multiplatinum sellers. "Wild Thing" and "Funky Cold Medina" takes off and then I'm sitting here like, *Oh, wow. I helped write these things. Now what am I going to do as an artist?*

Then I get the track for "Bust a Move."

Mike Ross (cofounder, Delicious Vinyl): "Bust a Move," it started off as a beat that Matt had put together with this Ballin' Jack sample. Another record that we were influenced by, "It Takes Two" by Rob Base, had a similar vibe to it when it was just in the building-block stages.

Originally, [Young MC] wrote this song called "Make That Move" and Matt had the idea to change the title to "Bust a Move." Actually, Flavor Flav says "bust a move" on an early PE record. Couple of guys had used that phrase before and it just fit perfect with the vibe of that song, and then we started layering the track. We brought in Flea to play bass, and then we brought in a singer to sing a live hook over it, to give it the final gloss that just brought it all together.

Young MC (artist, New York City): It's a totally different sound. I wrote it in an hour and a half in the dorm. It was literally a flow of consciousness, because that's how I was writing back then.

Mike Ross (cofounder, Delicious Vinyl): We definitely knew when we were working on it, it was definitely a track that had potential, and we already were building momentum after dropping "Wild Thing" and "Funky Cold Medina." We had a lot of eyes and ears paying attention to us, so it just took off.

Young MC (artist, New York City): When I touched down in a city that I've never been to, thousands of miles away from where I live, and they know my record and they're singing my hook back to me, I'm like, *Wow. They know the record here.*

Mike Ross (cofounder, Delicious Vinyl): Dre and Eazy-E and Ruthless were doing their thing at the same time we were doing ours. They were cornering a certain culture that they were about and bringing it to the forefront, and we were representing where we were coming from more as DJs.

DJ Nu-Mark (Jurassic 5): Within the first ten gigs of doing house parties, we'd have a gangster leaning over our mixer like, "Yo, play Toddy Tee now."

"Oh shit, do we got it? We better have it. Shit, you got it?"

"Oh yeah, it's in my crate." Like, *Thank God. Shit.*

Then in the same party you would have Latin people going, "Yo, can you play some salsa?" Like, *Shit, salsa?* "Yeah, we've got like five records in the back of one of those crates."

So, I kind of laugh now when people say, "No requests." That's how I became good, is learning how to weave in different genres. So that era, the diversity even between Delicious Vinyl and Macola and Ruthless Records was very, very dynamic for young kids.

DELICIOUS VINYL CONTINUED signing innovative acts, including the Pharcyde, a group of Los Angeles natives who creatively fused hip-hop with jazz and soul while interjecting their lyrics with social commentary and wit. The group's original four members were Bootie Brown, Fatlip, Imani, and Slimkid3; J-Swift and later J Dilla served as their producers. The Pharcyde's 1992 debut album, *Bizarre Ride II the Pharcyde,* featured the classic "Passin' Me By," which topped *Billboard*'s Hot Rap Songs chart.

Mike Ross (cofounder, Delicious Vinyl): Paul Stewart brought me a demo tape [of the Pharcyde]. The first track was "Ya Mama," the second track was "Officer," and the third track was "Passin' Me By." After I heard "Ya Mama," I thought it was super dope; and "Officer," I thought was hilarious; and "Passin' Me By," as soon as I heard that, I was like, "Where are these guys? I need to meet them immediately." I was just obsessed with signing them as soon as I heard the demo.

They were kind of the anti–gangster rap. They were talking about not getting the girl and the opposite of a lot of the macho, street posturing that was going on at the time. They were kind of the children of De La Soul, in a way. They were definitely coming from that place of Tribe, De La, Jungle Brothers—they had that irreverent, jazzy, hip-hop influence. They were the baby Native Tongues, the West Coast version.

11 LIKE COACHELLA IN THE STUDIO

New York City
1988–1994

Nearly six months before N.W.A exploded out of the gate with their first album, a New York group named Jungle Brothers released their own meaningful debut, *Straight Out the Jungle*. Shortly after, the trio helped found the Native Tongues, a New York–centric collective that would impact hip-hop's sounds and styles throughout the genre's transformational golden age.

The Native Tongues consisted of influential groups like De La Soul and A Tribe Called Quest. Soon others, including Queen Latifah, Monie Love, Black Sheep, and Chi-Ali, joined their efforts.

They fed off one another's creativity, while inspiring groups like Black Star, Dilated Peoples, the Pharcyde, and legions of others. Their defining trait was joy. The songs, sound, and lyrics were Afrocentric, and their vibe arced toward the positive and good-natured. They introduced the genre to wide-ranging sampling. And if N.W.A was at home wearing black Starter jackets with Raiders logos, groups like Jungle Brothers were just as comfortable in their khaki safari gear.

De La Soul's *3 Feet High and Rising* and A Tribe Called Quest's *People's Instinctive Travels and the Paths of Rhythm* and *The Low End Theory* were not just landmark albums that defined the collective. They defined the very best of hip-hop.

It began with Jungle Brothers—Mike Gee, Afrika Baby Bam, and DJ

Sammy B—who grew up listening to jazz and helped introduce house music to hip-hop.

Afrika Baby Bam (artist, producer, Jungle Brothers): I heard a lot of [Melle Mel's] tapes [growing up], and I heard some of the socially conscious stuff and I heard the routines from Grandmaster Flash and the Furious Five. I could hear how they was dicing stuff up together, representing they crew in a battle, and then telling you how it is on the street and then telling everybody to throw their hands in the air and get the crowd going. I heard all three elements mixed together. To me, that was like a multivitamin right there.

And then I heard "Sucker M.C.'s" and probably "Planet Rock" around the same time. I heard the braggadocio thing and then I heard the socially conscious thing, and I was like, okay, between these three records right here—"The Message," "Sucker M.C.'s," "Planet Rock"—that gave me enough input to come at it, not just party rapping. It gave me more colors on the palette to work with. You've got three lanes you could draw from to make something new out of that, or pick one and just keep it about that, which was like, "Straight Out the Jungle" was like Melle Mel's "The Message."

Mike Gee (artist, Jungle Brothers): DJs looking for breaks, they look at everything, and then some of the strongest breaks will come from jazz, the biggest probably being Bob James. You cannot go wrong if you're looking for breaks or just parts to sample from jazz. It's another one of those commandments in hip-hop. Go back to the real jazz, blues, Afro beats.

Afrika Baby Bam (artist, producer, Jungle Brothers): That's when records started to get sampled. Drum machines were getting pushed out of the way, too. So it kind of got minimalized down to more groove, basslines.

So, the style was changing to keep it fresh. Jungle Brothers, a bit of EPMD, a bit of Rakim, and then De La Soul came, and Tribe came. Biz Markie came and Big Daddy [Kane] had his own style of dress, which was more swagger, more stylish. You could draw from other things besides the sweatsuits, and it became more about the haircuts and then the medallions, and then being more conscious, and then bringing those throwback grooves in, like bringing in "Keep Risin' to the Top," bringing in "Don't Look Any Further" by Dennis Edwards. The bassline for that was in "Paid in Full," the album track of Eric B. and Rakim's first album. Big Daddy Kane used Mary Jane Girls' "All Night Long." So it was leaning more towards throwback R&B grooves. Basslines over smoother breakbeats.

It was just the timing and the ideas. There was so much of a buzz. What's the next sound going to be? Who's the next crew going to be? Marley Marl went into that kind of production style where you could chop up beats and it was like, *Whoa, there is innovation still coming. Who's going to answer to that?*

That was us.

Mike Gee (artist, Jungle Brothers): I think people gravitated towards our sound because of the way that we use breakbeats and our laid-back style.

Afrika Baby Bam (artist, producer, Jungle Brothers): With Jungle Brothers [it was] a bit of EPMD, a bit of Rakim—I mean they still had the sweatsuits and gold chains, but it was the first step into another vibe. It wasn't loud yelling and being big and large, like how Run-DMC was, LL Cool J was. It was more laid-back, and more [in the] groove.

> **STRAIGHT OUT THE** *Jungle* also marked the debut of Jonathan Davis, or Q-Tip, who shouted out his newly formed group, A Tribe Called Quest, on "Black Is Black." Afrika Baby Bam coined Q-Tip's moniker while they were in high school.

Mike Gee (artist, Jungle Brothers): Tip was already in school with us. We knew him before he blew up. We used to be in talent shows. It was myself and Ali went to school with us, [DJ] Ali Shaheed [Muhammad]. We all went to school together [with] Afrika Baby.

Afrika Baby Bam (artist, producer, Jungle Brothers): Just back in the day, everybody would say, "Get off my tip," and Q-Tip's from Queens. So, I just took the "Q" from Queens and "tip" from the slang and made Q-Tip.

Mike Gee (artist, Jungle Brothers): One thing I will always remember about Tip. He used to be in this group called Four Horsemen, so he used to dress with the blazers and everything like that, like kind of fly guy, *GQ* kind of style. Sometimes, I laugh when I think about those days, but Tip was always sharp, a really intelligent dude.

> **KELVIN "POSDNUOS" MERCER,** Dave "Trugoy" Jolicoeur, and Vincent "Maseo" Mason formed De La Soul after bonding in summer school at Long Island's Amityville Memorial High School in 1985. They crafted a demo tape, "Plug Tunin'," which caught the ear of another Amityville native—Prince Paul, a member of Stetsasonic. The tape made its way to Tommy Boy Records.

Monica Lynch (president, Tommy Boy Records): We had Stetsasonic on the label and Daddy-O from Stetsasonic called me. This was late '88—he was shopping some groups. That's how a lot of labels would find acts. They'd find them through acts that they already had or producers they were already working with.

Daddy-O said, "I've got these three acts."

He mentioned that one of them was an act from Long Island that was being produced by Stetsasonic's DJ, Prince Paul—De La Soul. And I remember thinking, *Wow, that's a real interesting, cool name.* He had one cassette and it had three groups on it. In the middle of the tape was De La Soul and it was the demo tape for "Plug Tunin' " and "Freedom of Speak." It sounded radically different from anything I'd ever heard. I felt like we needed to move quickly, because Daddy-O was shopping it. So we did move quickly, and we signed De La Soul.

> **THE MEMBERS OF** De La Soul, Jungle Brothers, and A Tribe Called Quest met at a Boston concert in July 1988. Appreciating their similar interests and musical leanings, the groups developed a kinship.

Mike Gee (artist, Jungle Brothers): De La came out with "Plug Tunin'." The scene at that time, there was not really anybody stretching their imagination. I guess from the outside looking in, they saw we were in a different league. We met De La in Boston and we kicked it.

Afrika Baby Bam (artist, producer, Jungle Brothers): Up to that point, a lot of the artists I was meeting were either right before me or way before me. Like, I was either meeting Joeski Love, which is right before me, and Rob Base, right before me, or Grandmaster Flash and Melle Mel and Busy Bee, which is way before me. I was always in those circles from being around [DJ] Red [Alert].

In Boston, meeting De La, it was like the first time that we was like, "Okay, this is our peer group. So, what are we supposed to do?" 'Cause all those dudes that I mentioned that was right before me or way before me, they were all from the same neighborhood, the Bronx or Harlem. They knew each other from around the way. They knew Red.

But meeting De La, they didn't know Red, and they didn't know all those other cats. They was just coming out of Long Island. But they knew Jungle Brothers. And we knew one of their songs.

Mike Gee (artist, Jungle Brothers): When we got back around the city, we kicked it some more. It was more Bam and Pos[dnuos] kicking around the whole Native Tongues idea, and saying "Yo, let's form a collective."

DE LA SOUL'S single "Buddy" featured Jungle Brothers and Q-Tip. The remixed song resulted in a Native Tongues posse cut that included Queen Latifah and Monie Love.

Afrika Baby Bam (artist, producer, Jungle Brothers): I remember we was about to go on tour in England. I think Prince Paul or Maseo called us to come down to do that cut. It was like treading on new territory. Like, "Oh, wow. We in a room with our peers again."

Prince Paul was kind of like just before us too. Him and Maseo just had this strong musical relationship based on DJing and pulling the right records. So, they were standing at the turntables by the big console, playing the tune and going, "Yeah, we want you guys to do something on this."

I think Pos said, "This song's called 'Buddy' and it's another word for 'body.' "

They used this break called "Shifting Gears" that we used to rehearse to a lot in my house, so that was familiar. And after Pos gave us the concept, we just went away and started writing some stuff and it didn't take long to come together.

Monie Love (artist, London): Calliope Studios was a big hippie commune. And that was the existence of the Native Tongues. When I think about it now, I'm surprised we didn't have tents in the studio. There's always somebody at the console tinkering away at a beat or somebody at the sampling machine, sampling something.

Bob Power (engineer): Early on, in the late '80s and early '90s, all sorts of different people would come through the studio. Sometimes they'd lay down a rhyme, sometimes they wouldn't. But it was certainly a very friendly atmosphere.

Mike Gee (artist, Jungle Brothers): It was cool to have all of De La there, Monie, Latifah, us. That really felt good.

Monie Love (artist, London): You never know when you're going to get called upon. And you can't be complacent. The day I went to the studio when they happened to be doing "Buddy," I'm not really paying attention; I'm sitting in the back talking with Phife [Dawg] and joking around with Jarobi [White]. And then Pos turns around and he's like, "Monie, come up to the console. I need you to do sixteen bars."

I'm like, "Okay, tomorrow? Or the next day?"

"No, now."

That was it. It was pressure. I'm like, "Huh. Okay. Alright."

He's like, "What do you need? You need headphones? You need to just sit in the booth? You need me to just put the beat on loop and just run it?"

I was like, "Can I hear what everyone has done so far, so I can get an idea around what type of vibe?"

So he ran the lyrics. Mike's verses were already done. Afrika's verses were already done. Pos, his verse was already done. [Trugoy the] Dove's verse was already done.

Then I was like, "Alright, you could just loop the beat by itself."

And I sat in there for maybe an hour, hour and a half. And the pressure in my head was there. Like, I have to write something that is going to outshine everything that I've heard already. For the simple reason that I have to do better because I'm a woman. It can't be mediocre. I have to write something memorable that's going to stick out, that everybody's going to repeat.

Afrika Baby Bam (artist, producer, Jungle Brothers): It was uncharted territory, featuring on someone else's record, or just coming in like that. 'Cause we were used to sitting down and writing our stuff, then memorizing it and then rehearsing it and then going into the studio and recording it. So, you didn't know what was going to come of it.

> **DE LA SOUL** released their groundbreaking debut album, *3 Feet High and Rising,* in February 1989. The album showcased music as De La Soul's canvas, on which the group laid out their mission to celebrate boldness and diversity. The tracks included witty, colorful skits, and the lyrics were punctuated with inside jokes. Prince Paul, who produced the album, eschewed James Brown breakbeats in favor of dozens of far-flung samples, forming a dynamic sonic collage.
>
> In 2010, the Library of Congress added the album to the National Recording Registry.

Nashiem Myrick (producer, Hitmen): That turned my life around, literally. Like that one album, that one moment in hip-hop. I just was all-in with that record and that group.

I was around nineteen years old and that broadened my horizons, because it made me realize that there's no limits to what you can sample, what you could do concept-wise. It just took me by storm.

> **QUEEN LATIFAH RELEASED** her studio debut, *All Hail the Queen,* in November 1989. This pivotal album displayed the synergy that existed among the collective. De La Soul appeared on "Mama Gave

Birth to the Soul Children," and Monie Love joined Queen Latifah on "Ladies First," a rallying anthem for women.

Monie Love (artist, London): We were so excited to do the song that every four or so bars she kept running up to me, like, "Listen to this." And then I'd write four bars and be like, "Listen to this." The whole song went like that—this adrenaline rush just to get every four lines out.

We had such a good time in the studio doing that song, hanging out, and I guarantee you we had no idea the caliber of anthem that we were writing at that moment. We did not know that that song was going to become so synonymous with women on a generational level. We knew we wanted to do a song that was uplifting for women, but we didn't realize we were writing a song that other women would identify themselves.

IN ADDITION TO Q-Tip, A Tribe Called Quest came to consist of Phife Dawg, Ali Shaheed Muhammad, and Jarobi White. The group signed to Jive Records and released their visionary debut album, *People's Instinctive Travels and the Paths of Rhythm,* in April 1990. Q-Tip's conversational lyrics easily switched between joyful and jocular. The album featured classics like "Bonita Applebum" and "Can I Kick It?"

Ann Carli (senior VP, Jive Records): Sean Carasov brought them to the label. Sean was a pretty interesting guy, and he'd been the tour manager for the Beastie Boys, and he was working for us in A&R. We listened to the demos. I mean ridiculous, you know?

And then meeting the guys—I think Q-Tip was seventeen at the time—just having these sort of weird-ass existential conversations with this seventeen-year-old guy making these lyrics. The whole concept of the group, I mean what was not to like? I think that they got offers from everybody.

Dante Ross (A&R, producer): That was the one that broke my heart. I tried to sign Tribe to Tommy Boy and they wouldn't spend the money.

Ann Carli (senior VP, Jive Records): I just think that our company, Jive at that time, we had a real reputation for being very artist-centric. And I think that that was partly because I'd never worked for a record company before, really, so I didn't really know what you were supposed to do.

Barry Weiss (president, Jive Records): They were part of the whole Native Tongues movement. Jungle Brothers were buzzing like crazy. So, that was a really highly sought-after deal. I knew they were musically interesting and really cool. I didn't really know what the commercial potential was going to be there, but I kind of knew Q-Tip was a star.

Jeff Sledge (A&R, Jive Records): De La had come out, and then Latifah and them was kind of doing their thing, so it was kind of like that Native Tongues thing was catching a massive wave.

Q-TIP METICULOUSLY SAMPLED mellow jazz and rock through pause tapes, rewinding his father's jazz records hundreds of times to capture the desired snippet on a cassette deck, opening new sonic and conceptual horizons for hip-hop production.

Bob Power (engineer): Their thesis in the rhymes and the music was something that had never been done before. [It] was almost free association, but it had the structure of a rhyme. The music was a total mash-up of things that I had never heard anyone try to put together before, so it was fascinating to me.

I remember Tip coming to me and saying, "Have you heard these records [from N.W.A]? I really want my records to sound like this."

Tip, right away, heard [Dr.] Dre's kind of sonic vision and the straight-up-the-middle muscle behind it, and was attracted to that and told me that I should check it out.

Muhammad Islam (security manager, A Tribe Called Quest): Their whole style of music was different from everybody else. They had a way of doing things, the process, and the storytelling, and their delivery to convey their message.

AN OBSESSIVE PERFECTIONIST, Q-Tip toyed endlessly with his tracks, which created worry for the executives on his label.

Barry Weiss (president, Jive Records): He was a complete pain in the ass. Had it not been for Chris Lighty, I don't think the records would have ever been delivered. Chris Lighty literally had to pry the records out of Q-Tip's hands to deliver the album. He never stopped tinkering.

Bob Power (engineer): They were always reaching for something special. It was never quite done for them, because they were always trying to make it better and trying to make it cooler and trying to do something more interesting.

I think that's where a lot of that completion anxiety came from. I know Tip and Ali were very careful about what they put out there. They were very much into making sure that it was the absolute best thing that they could do. I think that's where that thing with Barry came in.

CHRIS LIGHTY STARTED in hip-hop by carrying crates of records for DJ Red Alert and the Zulu Nation DJs, before he started managing Jungle Brothers and A Tribe Called Quest. Lighty blended street smarts with business acumen. He remained largely behind the scenes as he rose to become one of hip-hop's most influential figures, helping to transform the genre into a commercial juggernaut. While at Def Jam, Lighty orchestrated the Warren G signing that helped resuscitate the label. With Mona Scott-Young, he cofounded Violator Management, where they steered the careers of 50 Cent, Missy Elliott, LL Cool J, Busta Rhymes, and many others. He also brokered 50 Cent's watershed deal with Vitamin Water.

In August 2012, Lighty was found dead from a gunshot wound. The

New York City medical examiner's office attributed his death to suicide; many expressed skepticism over the ruling.

Mike Gee (artist, Jungle Brothers): Chris was one of the fellas. He was the go-getter, so much that people really thought he was in the group because he had the looks. He was a handsome guy.

But he was not about that. He was about his business, and he was a scrapper. And he was the youngest of the Violators. He was a genuine, solid dude. You could count on him.

Chris was the one that took it serious—he took road managing us serious, taking care of us seriously, making sure we got to where we were going in one piece, and make sure we got home in one piece, and making sure we got our money. As you saw later in his career, he really saw a future from the music and the culture and the business of it.

Russell Simmons (cofounder, Def Jam): Chris Lighty was a guy from the street who loved his artists and was passionate about them. He worked hard to protect them. That's why he became the manager he became.

Chris Lighty wanted everybody to get their due. And he loved them all. A Tribe Called Quest and the whole group that he came out of. He was one of them. He could have been a rapper, except he couldn't rap. Like me. He had the courage to be in [the streets], but yet at the same time he was compassionate, sweet, and he loved hip-hop and he loved the artists.

THE LOW END THEORY, A Tribe Called Quest's second landmark album, from 1991, is revered as one of hip-hop's most influential of all time. Q-Tip and Ali Shaheed Muhammad did not just meld hip-hop with jazz; they made the sonic fusion complete by crafting multiple beats on top of one another. Engineer Bob Power helped the group achieve a level of crispness and clarity in the samples by painstakingly removing the static that commonly accompanied samples, and the tracks blended seamlessly into one another. Phife Dawg, often in the background of *People's Instinctive Travels and the Paths of*

> *Rhythm,* emerged as a dynamic rhyming partner to Q-Tip. The album
> also featured a notable appearance from Busta Rhymes, helping to
> launch his career.

Jeff Sledge (A&R, Jive Records): I remember Barry [Weiss] walking me
downstairs at Battery [Studios] and he introduced me to Q-Tip, and
they were in the studio making *The Low End Theory*. Everything
back then was sample-driven. He always had a ton of records in the
studio. I've seen him take the records and do all these kind of different
things with them that people weren't doing that much at the time, like
filtering and chopping the samples and flipping things. He was very
interesting, because he could swing back and forth.

At times, he would be just working by himself on some shit. Then
there'd be other times, he'd walk into the studio and it'd be a mini-
party. The De La guys would come by a lot. The Black Sheep guys
would come by a lot. The Naughty [by Nature] guys would come by
a lot, especially Treach. And obviously Leaders [of the New School]
would come by a lot, Busta [Rhymes]. Then, there'd be Rosie Perez, or
just his homeboys from Queens that would just come through.

And then Phife had homeboys, so it was like this cast of people that
would come by and hang out and kick it and talk shit. It wasn't no
drugs or nothing like that going on. It would be just these different
kind of energies, depending on what he was feeling at the time or the
inspiration that he was looking for.

From a technical standpoint, him, Pete Rock, Large Professor, and
Easy Mo Bee are the best guys I've ever seen on an SP-1200. They just
really had it down to a science, and a lot of times Pete would come
by or Large Professor. They'd come by and they'd be trading secrets
on how to work the machine. So, he's really a master of that drum
machine more than most people. He's a genius.

He's a master of drops. He knows how to make their music drop in
the right place; he knows how to make your records move so all the
Tribe records have these dynamics. It takes you on a journey.

Muhammad Islam (security manager, A Tribe Called Quest): Phife was
always heavily into sports. Sports and the women. Though Tip was

into sports and women also, Tip had an incredible well-rounded view of the world. He was [of] the political mindset. So he saw things differently and they played off each other's ability. It was just a wonderful combination.

Jeff Sledge (A&R, Jive Records): So then, when the record comes out, and then Phife was rapping way more in this one, and had really stepped it up lyrically, he became really a full part of the group. Tip, Ali, and Phife, they kind of gelled as a unit. Jarobi had left by that time, too, so now it's down to three.

Barry Weiss (president, Jive Records): I knew that they had great taste and tone. I did not know how big the commercial appeal would be. I'm not going to lie: I wouldn't have predicted that they would be as big commercially as they turned out to be.

Muhammad Islam (security manager, A Tribe Called Quest): You could tell that they were answering a need in hip-hop. They were authentic about where they were from, but they were also educated men. They had gone to school. They had come from good backgrounds of parents wanting their children to do better, and it came through in the music.

> **ON *THE LOW** End Theory*'s "Check the Rhime," Q-Tip declared: "Industry rule number four thousand and eighty, record company people are shady." The line became an iconic acknowledgment of often unscrupulous record label dealings, although Jive executives mostly laughed it off.

Jeff Sledge (A&R, Jive Records): I don't know how upset people really were. We made T-shirts for it.

Ann Carli (senior VP, Jive Records): I was like, "Oh my God, this is awesome. Let's put this on a T-shirt."

There were a lot of complicated things around everything that had to do with Tribe, including even the way they were structured. Their arrangement amongst themselves was that Tip and Ali were full members, and Jarobi and Phife were backup members. And we were like, "This doesn't make sense; it could lead to some issues. Are you sure?"

So I think that there were a lot of complications around all the things to do with their various people, and the record company got painted with things that actually had nothing to do with us. So I absolutely never took any of that serious. I didn't feel personally attacked. I laughed my head off.

Jeff Sledge (A&R, Jive Records): That album came out '91? And all these years later, people still say it, it's crazy to me. The slogan is almost thirty years old.

Muhammad Islam (security manager, A Tribe Called Quest): In hip-hop, that'll probably always be a great all-time quote.

DETROIT'S JAY DEE first met Q-Tip, one of his hip-hop inspirations, at 1994's Lollapalooza festival. Jay Dee—soon to be known as J Dilla—handed Q-Tip a demo of his group, Slum Village. Q-Tip, impressed, brought J Dilla into his fold. Immensely talented, J Dilla worked with A Tribe Called Quest, De La Soul, the Pharcyde, and many others, furthering the scope of neo-soul and influencing a litany of producers.

J Dilla, born James Yancey, died in 2006 at the age of thirty-two from complications of a rare blood disease.

Bob Power (engineer): Tip brought Jay Dee towards the end of [A Tribe Called Quest's third album, *Midnight Marauders*]. Amidst the hustle and bustle of the control room or the lounge, Jay Dee was not jumping out to me, because he was so quiet and so introverted in many ways. The first couple of times I heard Jay Dee's music, I was like, "Somebody doesn't really know what they're doing," because there was always a hitch in the beat, and it wasn't perfectly in time. It was kind of like listening to Louis Armstrong or Charlie Parker. You listen for years and years and you go, "I know these people are great. Everybody says they're great." Then one day you listen to something you've heard hundreds of times before and you go, "Holy shit."

So, my thing with Jay Dee was kind of the same way.

Mike Ross (cofounder, Delicious Vinyl): After the first Pharcyde album, they had a falling-out with the producer, J-Swift. They were working on the second record, and they went to New York to work with Large Professor and Diamond D and Q-Tip. They were going to work with New York producers to keep a consistency to their sound and experiment a little bit.

When they were in New York, they called me. They were working with Q-Tip and they were playing me some tracks of this kid, Jay Dee, that Q-Tip introduced them to. One of the tracks they played me over the phone was a track they were working on called "Runnin'." I heard the beat and the hook of that song, and it blew my mind. I was like, "This shit's crazy. Let's bring Jay Dee to L.A. and let's work on some tracks."

And that was how it started. Dilla was Jay Dee before he was J Dilla. Knowing that they needed someone to really fill J-Swift's footsteps, I felt Jay Dee was the guy, just based on some tracks that I had heard. He did four tracks on their album, *Labcabincalifornia*, and from there I kept working with him. He was a unique talent. You run across stuff like that, if you're lucky, a few times in your life.

If Marley Marl had a baby, it was J-Swift and maybe Jay Dee, Dilla, could have been more of that offspring, kind of that ilk. His shit was just on a deeper level, the way he could mix his drum programming with what he was cutting up, samples, and just making these sonic masterpieces.

Peanut Butter Wolf (Stones Throw Records): I started working with J Dilla right around the time of putting out my album *My Vinyl Weighs a Ton*. I met him because I put out a record called *Peanut Butter Breaks*, with my own beats. This guy, [DJ] House Shoes, worked at a record store and he called the number on the record, [because] he wanted copies for the store. He would always tell me about this guy, Jay Dee. He would play beats over the phone. "You hear my man Jay Dee? He's killing the game right now in Detroit."

It went from telling me about Jay Dee making great beats, to then one day: "Oh, Q-Tip is actually managing Jay Dee now and he's working with Pharcyde and he's working with Tribe. He's working with De La and Busta and everybody."

I was working at a record distributor at that point. One day, House Shoes told me, "Me and Jay Dee want to put out this record of all his remixes." He asked if I was down to press it up and sell the record for them and split the profits. That's what we did.

[Producer] Madlib and I went to a show and met him in person. It was cool seeing the two of them so excited about each other. Because Jay Dee was a big Lootpack fan. It was a mutual love, for sure.

I like to speak of Dilla and Madlib almost in the same sentence. Because they remind me so much of each other and they both took a lot of chances. With Jay Dee, he almost single-handedly created that neo-soul sound, and then he turned his back on it and he was like, "I don't want to be known as the neo-soul guy."

His stuff was just a feeling. Whether he was creating his own stuff with just drum machines and keyboard sounds, or if he was getting a full band together, or if he was just using raw samples, he was just a musical guy all around—he could do it all. He and Madlib, they both learned from Large Professor and Pete Rock and DJ Premier and put their own spin on it. Just like those three took from Marley Marl and put their own spin on what Marley Marl was doing.

THE NATIVE TONGUES collective revamped not just the sound of hip-hop, but also the feeling around it. Groups like Jungle Brothers, De La Soul, and A Tribe Called Quest dismissed assimilation and the notion that the Black experience was monolithic. In doing so, they sent hip-hop down different experimental paths, paving the way for the creativity of groups like Outkast, and artists and producers such as Kanye West and Pharrell Williams.

Afrika Baby Bam (artist, producer, Jungle Brothers): You're a fan and an artist at the same time. So you already know what the people want. 'Cause it's the same thing that you expect, to take a beat, flip it another way, and change the topic of the record. And that collective was all about that; it just added more power, more emphasis. Because De La had their angle of using these funk records and taking you to the far left with coded language and trippiness and flipping stuff. And Tribe had this groove thing going with the jazz records, and they were finding their way through that.

So, they was borrowing a bit of the Jungle Brothers' identity, just out of respect for the tradition and the culture, and then leaning the left of center with De La, when they did "Me Myself and I," and it just kept things organic and loose and open to interpretation.

Bob Power (engineer): The whole Native Tongues thing, which I consider sort of the second wave of hip-hop, was a fascinating social phenomenon to me. The Afrocentric way people were dressing was very interesting, and the subject matter of the rhymes on the first couple of records was sort of psychedelic. It was transcendent. It wasn't people just talking about how tough they were and how they were going to knock somebody else out. It was really far-reaching and very broad in vision.

Mike Gee (artist, Jungle Brothers): That is one of the golden rules, like the Ten Commandments of hip-hop. Number one: Be original.

Watching it from the beginning to now, I think it probably had one of the strongest influences on hip-hop. I am talking outside of De La, Jungle, Tribe—I am going even into your Brand Nubians, your Pharcydes, guys like that—they all go back to the number one commandment: Be original—and they always stretched it.

Monie Love (artist, London): Every day was like Coachella in the studio. Whenever we performed all together—Jungle, De La, Tribe, Latifah, throw in some Black Sheep—that was an official festival vibe on stage. The legacy of us is we allowed people to feel good about being themselves, and not having to conform to any specific type of role because you're in hip-hop. Our legacy really spells out freedom. Freedom in the music genre to do what you want.

12 PARENTAL ADVISORY

Riverside, California; Miami
1984–2003

The 2 Live Crew is synonymous with Miami bass, the popular booty-shaking subgenre that rose out of South Florida's mobile DJ empire and skating rinks in the 1980s. Luther Campbell, one of hip-hop's first business tycoons, headlined the group, and knew how to attract attention. 2 Live Crew courted controversy by producing the first album to be deemed legally obscene, before transforming into First Amendment advocates.

Before Campbell, the group began all the way across the country at March Air Force Base in California. David Hobbs (DJ Mr. Mixx) met Chris Wong Won (Fresh Kid Ice) at the base in the early 1980s, following an overseas deployment where Hobbs witnessed a hip-hop performance featuring DJing and b-boying. Soon, Yuri Vielot (Amazing Vee) joined, rounding out the group's initial lineup. In 1984, the group released its debut vinyl single, "The Revelation" (with "2 Live" on the B-side), for Fresh Beat Records, distributed by Macola Records.

Mr. Mixx (DJ, producer, 2 Live Crew): It's really funny because my roots for rap music, or just being involved in hip-hop period, is really me being overseas my first two years in the service. I was in London. "Planet Rock" came out and kind of changed the whole landscape of how records were being made between R&B and electronic music.

This thing that I went to [in London], Rock Steady Crew and Afrika

Islam was at the event. And before I had seen that, you would read on the back of records, people spinning on their heads and their shoulders and backs and I said, "Man, there's no way in the world people are doing that." It wasn't on TV or nothing. So, you just thought it was just fables, until I seen that exhibition.

Before I seen the exhibition, I had no idea or understanding how scratching was being done. When I seen Islam on turntables scratching, and how he was moving his hands, I said, "Oh, it's like he's playing an instrument." Once I seen him do it, then I went and got me some little off-brand turntables and started practicing. I just equated it to me playing the guitar or the bass, how one hand is doing one thing and the other hand's doing the other. Other guys would come to London, this guy [DJ] Whiz Kid would come over and do exhibitions too, and I was able to actually see him up close and see what he was doing.

When I got stationed from England to California, I was the only person in the barracks with turntables. That's basically how me and Chris [Fresh Kid Ice] met up. We met at the hospital, because I worked in the dining hall, and he worked outpatient records. He would come through to get lunch. I'm working the grill. He was from New York and basically just asked me about us hooking up. "Because we heard you got turntables. I'm from New York."

Everybody was finding out about me as far as having turntables. They didn't really know what I was doing with them, but at that time, that's when *Breakin'* and *Beat Street* was starting to bubble, and people was starting to find out about stuff.

MEANWHILE, FUTURE 2 Live Crew member Mark Ross (Brother Marquis) had released two 1983 singles—"Westside Storie," and "Rhythm Rock" with Rodney-O—as part of the Caution Crew in 1983. The 12-inch singles from the Rochester, New York–born Ross are some of the West Coast's earliest hip-hop records.

Brother Marquis (artist, 2 Live Crew): I was onto Spoonie Gee, King Tim III, Busy Bee [Starski], on a lot of the first pioneers, the first great ones. Some of that came from Rodney, and some of that came from being [from] New York. The culture just drew me in.

I take my hat off to Mr. Oliver [Rodney-O], because he actually was the first one to show me how to structure a rhyme, and he was the first one to take me to a studio. We had a breakdancing crew and we called ourselves the Caution Crew, and we just took it over to rap. We made our first record in the ninth grade, and we had our second record when we were juniors in high school.

THE EARLY MOBILE DJ groups that populated Miami in the late 1970s were unified in their belief that bass, above all else, electrified and moved a crowd. The better the sound system, the better the bass, and the larger the crowd that gathered. Rival crews operated in different neighborhoods, with the most popular finding regular work inside teen-magnet roller skating rinks. Luther Campbell and his Ghetto Style DJs started hosting an event named the Pac Jam at Sunshine Skateway North, where, once the teens put up their roller skates, dance parties closed the evening.

Campbell, who assumed the moniker Luke Skyywalker, and later Uncle Luke, developed into a pivotal figure in Southern hip-hop. He was a product of Liberty City, a once bustling Black community north of downtown Miami that had declined when the construction of Interstate 95 displaced thousands from their homes (similar to how the Cross Bronx Expressway decimated the Bronx). In 1980, the acquittal of the four police officers who beat to death Arthur McDuffie, a Black insurance broker, during a traffic stop, ignited civil unrest in the area, resulting in an estimated $100 million worth of damages.

Campbell carved his own path at a time when few business opportunities existed for Black entrepreneurs. In 1986, his Ghetto Style DJs opened the Pac Jam Teen Disco, where he often hosted out-of-town artists.

Mr. Mixx (DJ, producer, 2 Live Crew): Luke was a concert promoter that was doing hip-hop events in Miami. He was bringing down a lot of the underground rap groups in New York.

Schoolly D (artist, Philadelphia): He called me. I was distributing my records and I had my phone number on the record. "P.S.K." was part of starting the Miami bass. Just like with me, Mantronix, the Geto Boys, and 2 Live Crew.

There was a cat from Atlanta that said, "That's what they fucking love. I put this shit on, man, that shit be sneaking up on people."

So he has his own label, I had my own label. I would get my records pressed in Atlanta, and we would switch, so I helped promote some of his stuff in the Northeast, 'cause he wanted to get played in Philly and New York.

Mr. Mixx (DJ, producer, 2 Live Crew): He brought up Egyptian Lover from L.A. He brought out Ultimate 3 MC's, T La Rock, Mantronix, all of those guys used to come to Miami to do shows at this teen club that he had in a skating rink.

DJ EFN (Crazy Hood Productions, Miami): At the skating rinks, they would come and do events. Luke had Pac Jam. It was a teenage club that was like a rite of passage. It was the infamous dangerous spot. It's like a badge of honor to go to the Pac Jam and come out of it alive.

> **LUTHER CAMPBELL'S POPULARITY** in Miami soared, and he harnessed his influence as a DJ and promoter to spread the word about new records. He promoted the work of little-known artists, inviting them to perform at Pac Jam and increase his bottom line. Upon discovering the name "Skyywalker" referenced in "2 Live," Campbell asked the 2 Live Crew to do some shows in Miami.

Mr. Mixx (DJ, producer, 2 Live Crew): We didn't realize that the little record that we had put out in Los Angeles was making any kind of noise anywhere. We were getting invoices saying that we was selling records in different places, but it was never no money. But then he reached out to us to say, "Hey, man, I want you guys to come out and do some shows for me."

We had never had anybody reach out to us before. I said, "Yeah, man, we can come out there and do a show." But we was green as hell.

I didn't know nothing about no contracts for no show. And he could tell that we was genuinely green. He said, "Well, I'm gonna send you guys some money to get the flights to come out."

AFTER AMAZING VEE left the group due to creative differences, Mr. Mixx made good on a promise and invited Brother Marquis to Miami.

Brother Marquis (artist, 2 Live Crew): I saw Mr. Mixx DJing at a park in Riverside [a city in California]. Mr. Mixx was cutting and everything, and I guess I started talking to him and found out that he was from Corona [a city near Riverside], and one thing led to another. I think me and Rodney probably met him at the same time. We were all into the same thing, so we were drawn to one another by the culture.

Mr. Mixx was loyal when he told me that [we would collaborate in the future]. He was like, "Man, if I ever have an opportunity, I'm going to put you in the group."

I had went back to Rochester [New York] in the dead of winter. I was working at a nursing home and Mr. Mixx called me and it's snow outside, twenty below, and he calls me talking about "I have an opportunity to go to sunny Miami, would you like to join the group?"

I'm like, "Hell, yeah."

And bam, he kept his word. And that's why I always tried to show loyalty to Mr. Mixx, because he really showed me the ins and outs of hip-hop, and I'm forever grateful to that young man for that.

AFRIKA BAMBAATAA'S 1982 "Planet Rock" had not just inspired the electro scene in Los Angeles. The song's reliance on the Roland TR-808 drum machine—and its ability to produce a thudding bass— also jump-started Miami bass, which provided the soundtrack for Miami's renaissance as a party destination.

Early South Floridian pioneers included Maggotron, Mantronix, Pretty Tony, and Amos Larkins II. In 1985, Larkins produced MC A.D.E.'s "Bass Rock Express," based off Kraftwerk's "Trans-Europe Express."

The song is widely viewed as the first Miami bass song to gain national popularity, and was in rotation when Mr. Mixx landed in Florida.

Mr. Mixx (DJ, producer, 2 Live Crew): You process the ghettoness of the city, all of the different variations of Caribbean people that's in the area. The thought process of how people would talk about sex and how they would deal with issues. A lot of the early phrasing of hip-hop came out of Miami, too. "Pussy-ass nigga" was a phrase I had never heard before. "Fuck boi." All of that stuff is Miami lingo. "Baby mama, baby daddy." Never heard that until I got to Miami. But that was in '85.

Brother Marquis (artist, 2 Live Crew): Having somewhat of a childhood in the South, in Alabama, in Birmingham, I'm like, *These guys are like Alabama guys. Alright, I can fit in.*

So, I jumped right off the porch. But it was kind of a culture shock to me. I didn't like it at first. It was different, and back in those days it was kind of wild. You had to really, really be careful, and there was a lot of gangster shit going on. We were right in Liberty City and it was rough over there and it was kind of frightening. That's where I seen my first dead body.

Mr. Mixx (DJ, producer, 2 Live Crew): England kind of got me accustomed to [large sound systems] because of the reggae sound systems that they would have over there.

Brother Marquis (artist, 2 Live Crew): I was very impressed as far as the equipment, because I'd never seen a DJ playing off that many speakers. It had an amazing sound.

As far as the DJing, it took me a while to get into that, because it seemed like they were yelling over the records, and I was used to cutting and scratching and less talk. So I'm like, *That's kind of whack.*

But as I got into it and stayed around and became part of the Miami culture, I'm like, *Okay, it's cool. It's working.* But first, when I was hearing those guys DJ, I'm like, *Man, I don't know. They need to let the record play.*

Mr. Mixx (DJ, producer, 2 Live Crew): There was no rappers in Miami when we got there, except for this one guy, Shy D. He was from

Atlanta, but he had a record that was out with this company called 4 Sight. So, when we came up there, we heard that record and we had never heard it before, being in California, 'cause certain records just wasn't going outside of their regions at that time.

LUTHER CAMPBELL ADVANCED from serving as 2 Live Crew's manager to being the hype man and then a leading member of the group, the person who best knew how to make the crowd move. Under his direction, 2 Live Crew switched toward more sexually explicit lyrics. The single "Throw the D" developed from one of the dances at the Pac Jam.

After no New York labels showed interest in the group, Campbell, in one of the first acts of Southern hip-hop entrepreneurship, founded his own label, Luke Skyywalker Records (later changed to Luke Records after Campbell faced a lawsuit from George Lucas over appropriating the Skywalker name). The 2 Live Crew released *The 2 Live Crew Is What We Are* in July 1986.

"Throw the D"—with scratches, 808 booms, and sampling from Herman Kelly & Life's "Dance to the Drummer's Beat"—provided a blueprint for the future of Miami bass, and established Mr. Mixx as one of the subgenre's architects.

Brother Marquis (artist, 2 Live Crew): My whole journey with 2 Live Crew was off of Mr. Mixx. I'm loyal to Mr. Mixx, because he was loyal to me. He really thought Luke was his brother. He's like, "Luke is like my brother. I trust him with my life."

We were young, full of energy, no knowledge of the business. One thing led to another, and Mr. Mixx appointed Luke as the manager.

Mr. Mixx (DJ, producer, 2 Live Crew): Luke was the one that was handling all the business. He was the point man. He had the influence. He had the market. Miami was the only place that we had any records popping off—at least, that's what we believed. There was records being sold in other places, but we had never gotten no shows from anywhere else before we connected with him.

We knew how to make records and come up with stuff. We didn't know nothing about the business at all. Period.

As long as I could make the music, I wasn't really tripping off of the business aspect of it, because it hadn't got real to me yet that real money was being made. I just wasn't thinking about it the way he was thinking about it.

Brother Marquis (artist, 2 Live Crew): I was there on the word of Mr. Mixx, and I was on his coattail. We both were in a new place together. He's doing the beats. I'm doing most of the writing.

Mr. Mixx (DJ, producer, 2 Live Crew): You had the guy MC A.D.E., he had "Bass Rock Express," which is off of "Trans-Europe Express." The atmosphere of it was party music. Then we start understanding Kid Ice's song "2 Live," which is mainly known as "Beat Box" now. It was sitting in the zone of tempo of the "Bass Rock Express" and a couple of other things. And then the Florida dude, Amos Larkins, actually did an offshoot of our record "2 Live/Beat Box," so our record had been doing very well there. We didn't have no idea what was going on with it all.

So when I seen that, I said, "Okay, well, the people are paying attention to what it is that we did." They would play the breakdown of "Dance to the Drummer's Beat" at the heat of the party and everybody was going crazy. They was doing this dance that they called the Throw the D dance. When we went back to California, we said, "We gonna make an appreciation record with these guys down here."

Luke talked to Chris [Fresh Kid Ice] about doing the lyrics for the Throw the D dance and I just came up with the track. But the track was based off of "Dance to the Drummer's Beat." Just the combination of how they partied to that song and having that coming out of the speakers booming changed the whole landscape of how records ended up being made, because nobody was doing it.

I just knew with the way that the bass came through the sound systems that if I took the records to where it was mainly just bass all the way through, it would be a big deal down there. 'Cause some of the offshoot records, they were already being loosely done like that, but MC A.D.E. wasn't no vocalist and Amos Larkins just did a beat and just had instrumentals. There was no vocal presence really on the records outside of voices being sampled. But there was no rappers. There was no actual group presence.

"THROW THE D" also featured an audio sample from Rudy Ray Moore's *Dolemite,* marrying the group's song with comedic insight.

Mr. Mixx (DJ, producer, 2 Live Crew): The thought process of how it got put together was how wild and crazy the guys and girls would be freak-dancing each other, and just that thought process about sex in general in Miami, and so I just said, "A lot of this shit that they're talking about and the phrasing that they be saying, be like these comedy albums."

I had a gang of comedy albums, and I was actually scratching in *Dolemite* parts and Richard Pryor pieces on little mixtapes. So, I took the *Dolemite* parts and started using certain parts of the records that I felt like expressed the average Miami attitude. And those parts got scratched into the record.

Brother Marquis (artist, 2 Live Crew): Hats off to Mr. Mixx for adding that element of entertainment to what we were doing. You got some *Dolemite* scratches and bits in it, and I'm coming with some rhymes that I thought were super dope, and it just went together really well. It was new and it was right on time for that current time.

IN 1985, TIPPER Gore, wife of then-senator Al Gore, founded the Parents Music Resource Center (PMRC) after hearing lyrics she deemed offensive on an album she had given her daughter. The future Second Lady's cofounder was Susan Baker, wife of Secretary of State James Baker. The committee launched a congressional hearing on song lyrics in an effort to institute ethical boundaries.

They compiled a list of fifteen popular songs they found objectionable—soon dubbed the "Filthy Fifteen"—including offerings from Prince, Twisted Sister, and Black Sabbath. Hip-hop music, still entering the mainstream, had no songs on the list. However, the PMRC and 2 Live Crew soon became adversaries.

The inclusion of a "Parental Advisory" label on albums with explicit content, introduced by the Recording Industry Association of America, was one of the PMRC's lasting effects.

Mr. Mixx (DJ, producer, 2 Live Crew): First album that we did, a woman bought the album for a fourteen-year-old kid and then when they found out what was on the damn album, Tipper Gore got involved where you had to start stickering the product and letting it be known what's on the projects.

A lot of the distributors wouldn't take the explicit version. So, we made a cleaned-up album. The ones that would only take the clean got that one; the other distributors that was getting their hustle on, they took the explicit. The explicit was outselling the clean nine to one. It didn't make sense to lose out on any money.

We were hot in the market, but everything was doubled. Double pressing, double mastering.

DJ EFN (Crazy Hood Productions, Miami): 2 Live Crew, I remember going to the store and the whole Parental Advisory thing started happening with them. I had to get my mom to buy the tape for me, and it was mad funny: the guy's face, this Cuban lady can barely speak English, getting the 2 Live Crew tape. She had to get the *Straight Outta Compton* tape for me as well. And then when I got a little older, I was just stealing all the music I could get my hands on.

2 LIVE CREW quickly transitioned to releasing its second album, *Move Somethin',* in 1988. The album was laden with more explicit humor and crassness.

That same year, Tommy Hammond, owner of a record store in Alexander City, Alabama, was arrested for violating local obscenity laws and fined $500 for selling *Move Somethin'* to an undercover law enforcement officer—the first case in which a record-store owner was held liable for recorded music. An Alabama circuit court later overturned his conviction.

The album expanded 2 Live Crew's popularity and landed on the Billboard 200. But the group still could not gain the respect of New York hip-hop artists, who had often visited Miami to perform at Luther Campbell's invitation.

DJ EFN (Crazy Hood Productions, Miami): In the mid to late '80s, in that scene you got 2 Live Crew, the Gucci Crew [II], and all this stuff coming out of the South and coming out of Miami. But there was a weird thing that happened a few years later where it seemed like New York kind of shunned everybody else across the country, and was like they called the South "the 'Bamas," and they kind of didn't respect what was going on musically in the rest of the country.

Brother Marquis (artist, 2 Live Crew): Rush Management at that time, that guy Lyor Cohen—oh my God, that guy was a hell of a manager—he didn't want to give us a break.

"2 Live Crew, you guys get five minutes to perform, no riser, no backdrop, no dancers."

It's like, *Really?* Yeah, they really was trying to shit on us. But thanks to Brother Luke, he did step up in a major way with that. He was like, "Nah, y'all ain't doing that to us."

He did actually fight for us to get respect amongst the New York guys when it came to that aspect of performing, and I kind of thought that was odd, because when it came to doing shows, Luke was a promoter. So, shit, Luke would be promoting Run-DMC. He would be promoting LL Cool J. He would be promoting Eric B. and Rakim. So, when they came to Miami, everybody was cool, but when we get on something with them, we're whack.

Everybody has something to say. You know how it is in the culture. Everybody got something to say.

DJ EFN (Crazy Hood Productions, Miami): What happens is, at least on a local level here, those cats like 2 Live Crew, the bass movement kind of picks up, and it's known as Miami bass. It kind of became this parallel genre of music to hip-hop, which at the time was viewed as this New York thing, like the traditional boom bap coming out of the Northeast. It became almost like rivals, and I'm kind of stuck in the middle as a fan.

Miami bass started to evolve into a different thing in terms of BPMs and the style. It became kind of like a dance music, where hip-hop started going more on the side of beats for lyricism or for the sake of the flow, and I'm loving both. But then I'm kind of gravitating more towards lyrical hip-hop coming out of the Northeast, but I'm looking at how New York kind of made itself, where it's like each borough battled, and they each had their own pride, and then collectively, that competition made them better, and then they had pride for their city as a whole.

I wanted that pride for Miami. I felt like I wanted to have the same lyricism and the same production value, but just very representative of Miami.

THE ONLY THING more explicit than 2 Live Crew's lyrics, at the time, was some of their shows.

Brother Marquis (artist, 2 Live Crew): I seen a guy in the crowd [at one performance] and I remember we had this dancer Deaf Jam. We would call her Deaf Jam because she was obviously deaf, but she was fine. She had a nice body, and she was a great human being, that girl.

Anyway, so I'm like, "That guy over there, he's looking like Biggie Smalls. He has the fake chains on, he has the fake Versace on with the hat. Put the water up in your vaginda and go over there and squirt him."

He came to the stage, and she squirted him. The next thing I knew, they had him on stage penetrating him. He's in the crowd looking like a playa, just looking all pimped-out, like he's a gangster and got forty gang members with him, and he's on the stage getting penetrated. I'm like, "Oh my God, this shit's crazy. 2 Live Crew's just turning out pimps."

That was the wildest crew of dancers I ever had.

THE 2 LIVE Crew reached new levels of popularity—and scrutiny—with the release of "Me So Horny," a single from 1989's *As Nasty as They Wanna Be* that revolved around a voracious appetite for sex. The track featured audio samples from Stanley Kubrick's *Full Metal Jacket* and Richard Pryor in *Which Way Is Up?,* and contained music samples from Mass Production's "Firecracker." It topped the U.S. Billboard Hot Rap Songs chart.

Mr. Mixx (DJ, producer, 2 Live Crew): We was in D.C. We were doing some music with Trouble Funk. We had used one of their records on the *Move Somethin'* album, so the third single we redid the song with them actually being involved in it.

Brother Marquis (artist, 2 Live Crew): Every hotel room that we'd check in to, we would turn on HBO and there would be the movie *Full Metal Jacket.* And at that time, I'm horny and I'm a young man, and I'm watching the movie and that part just stuck with me: "Me love you long time." That just stuck with me.

Mr. Mixx (DJ, producer, 2 Live Crew): Marquis, he's watching *Full Metal Jacket* and he seen the scene and I said, "Man, we got to do something with that. We got to do something with her saying that shit."

I recorded the movie on a VHS tape, and I sampled all of the stuff off into the SP-1200 and chopped up the words to where it could rhythmically go to the beat. And that's how it went down.

Brother Marquis (artist, 2 Live Crew): I told Dave [Mr. Mixx], "Go get the movie *Full Metal Jacket,* 'Me so horny,' sample that and put it to the song 'Firecracker.'" Dave came back with a cassette and said, "Here's your song."

Mr. Mixx (DJ, producer, 2 Live Crew): We knew it was a hit as soon as we got finished with it. But Luke didn't necessarily like it because it was the first time that Marquis and Chris [Fresh Kid Ice] was actually rapping slow. Most of the records that were hits for us, they was rapping at the same pace as the beat was going. He didn't really like the lyrical delivery on it. But he knew that what it is that we hooked up was great.

The construction of the Cross Bronx Expressway began in 1948, displacing nearby African American and Puerto Rican communities. The borough's bifurcation cemented the economic disparity between the North and South Bronx.

(UPI/BETTMANN ARCHIVE VIA GETTY IMAGES)

1520 Sedgwick Avenue in the Bronx, where DJ Kool Herc threw parties in the apartment complex's community room in the 1970s. The site is recognized as hip-hop's birthplace.

(AL PEREIRA/GETTY IMAGES)

Early MCs found inspiration amid the desolation and decay of the South Bronx, seen here in 1977. "We were creating something that took up our time and made us feel good and brought us together," said Easy A.D. of the Cold Crush Brothers. "You have to imagine walking out your house every day and seeing abandoned cars burnt up, empty buildings, and you're going to elementary school."

(JEROME LIEBLING/GETTY IMAGES)

 B-boys and b-girls sought out parties featuring pioneering hip-hop DJs, where they would perform acrobatic dance moves during the music's breakbeats.

Grandmaster Flash helped shape DJing into artistry. His "quick mix" theory served as a backbone for hip-hop music.

Kurtis Blow (left) attended some of hip-hop's earliest jams in the Bronx, which often were presided over by DJ Kool Herc (right), widely credited with originating the genre by isolating and prolonging breakbeats.

 The Cold Crush Brothers (left to right: DJ Charlie Chase, Grandmaster Caz, Almighty Kay Gee, Easy A.D.) had the foresight to record and photograph their performances, providing some of hip-hop's earliest documentation. Before the group formed, DJ Charlie Chase was a pioneering turntablist and Grandmaster Caz served as a trailblazing lyricist, whose words were used in "Rapper's Delight."

(AL PEREIRA/GETTY IMAGES/MICHAEL OCHS ARCHIVES)

 "I said a hip-hop, the hippie, the hippie / To the hip, hip-hop and you don't stop the rockin'." The Sugarhill Gang (left to right: Wonder Mike, Master G, Big Bank Hank) introduced hip-hop's first commercial hit song with 1979's "Rapper's Delight."

(MICHAEL OCHS ARCHIVES/GETTY IMAGES)

The Funky 4 + 1 included pioneering female MC Sha-Rock (center) and broke ground by appearing on *Saturday Night Live* in 1981.

(LAURA LEVINE/CORBIS VIA GETTY IMAGES)

Rick Rubin (back, left) and the Beastie Boys (back: MCA and Ad-Rock; front: Mike D) were New York punk rockers turned hip-hoppers. Rubin produced the Beasties' 1986 debut, *Licensed to Ill,* the first hip-hop album to top the Billboard album chart.

(JANETTE BECKMAN/ GETTY IMAGES)

Run-DMC established hip-hop's crossover appeal in the 1980s. The group's groundbreaking deal with Adidas was the first sponsorship between a hip-hop group and a sports apparel company, and an early hint of the genre's mass potential for commercialization.

(MICHAEL OCHS ARCHIVES/GETTY IMAGES)

DJ Marley Marl transformed hip-hop in the 1980s by discovering how to sample pieces of songs into a drum machine using a sampling keyboard, and served as a leading figure in the Juice Crew collective.

(AL PEREIRA/GETTY IMAGES/MICHAEL OCHS ARCHIVES)

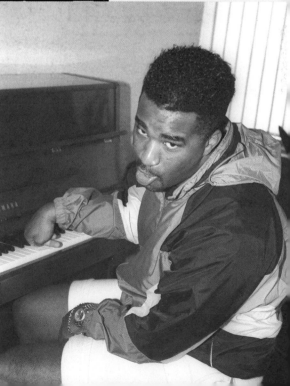

In Los Angeles, DJ Greg Mack transitioned the radio station KDAY 1580-AM into an early outlet for hip-hop, helping to break out nearly every major West Coast artist who emerged in the 1980s.

(ALLEN BEREZOVSKY/WIREIMAGE)

Philadelphia's Pop Art Records released Roxanne Shanté's "Roxanne's Revenge" in 1984. The song spawned countless response records and established Shanté as one of hip-hop's first female breakout stars.

(DAVID CORIO/MICHAEL OCHS ARCHIVES/ GETTY IMAGES)

MC Shan was one of the earliest hip-hop artists hailing from Queensbridge, the public housing development that also produced Roxanne Shanté, Cormega, Nas, Mobb Deep's Havoc, and many others.

(DAVID CORIO/REDFERNS)

For many, Rakim, with his effortless flow and intricate rhyme patterns, sits atop the list of best rappers, followed by every other artist to touch a microphone.

(RAYMOND BOYD/GETTY IMAGES)

The debut of *Yo! MTV Raps* in the late 1980s brought the genre to TV screens beyond America's major markets. Ed Lover (left) and Doctor Dré (right), shown with producer Ted Demme, hosted the show's weekday version.

(FRANK MICELOTTA/GETTY IMAGES)

Philadelphia's Schoolly D released "P.S.K. What Does It Mean?" in 1985. The classic track laid a blueprint for gangster rap that Ice-T and N.W.A soon followed.

(JANETTE BECKMAN/ GETTY IMAGES)

Monie Love (left) and Queen Latifah (right) performing "Ladies First" at Newark Symphony Hall in April 1990. "We knew we wanted to do a song that was uplifting for women, but we didn't realize we were writing a song that other women would identify themselves," Love recalled.

(AL PEREIRA/GETTY IMAGES/MICHAEL OCHS ARCHIVES)

Ice-T (left) and Kool Moe Dee (right) secured their reputations as influential MCs during hip-hop's transformational golden age. Both also dealt with controversy. Kool Moe Dee did not follow other hip-hop acts in boycotting the 1989 Grammy Awards, while Ice-T's heavy metal band dropped "Cop Killer," a song that provoked negative reactions from law enforcement advocates and politicians.

(RAYMOND BOYD/GETTY IMAGES)

Salt-N-Pepa changed the prototypical image of an MC in the 1980s through sex-positive tracks and brash personalities, while becoming the first female hip-hop act to go platinum.

(DAVID REDFERN/REDFERNS)

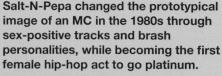

Long Island's Public Enemy redefined hip-hop as a vessel for stirring consciousness and awakening minds. The group was marked by the impactful voice of Chuck D, Flavor Flav's energetic delivery as a hype man, and the powerful sonic backing of the Bomb Squad.

(JACK MITCHELL/GETTY IMAGES)

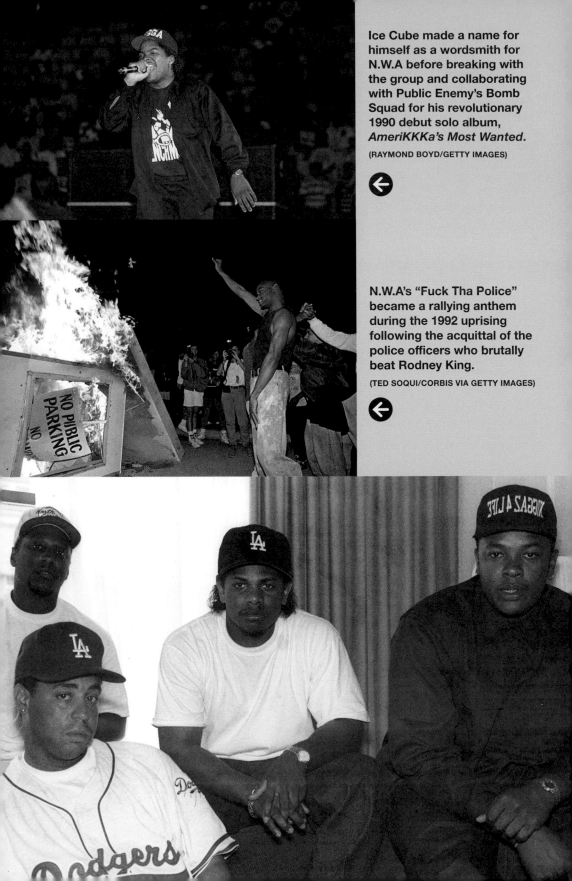

Ice Cube made a name for himself as a wordsmith for N.W.A before breaking with the group and collaborating with Public Enemy's Bomb Squad for his revolutionary 1990 debut solo album, *AmeriKKKa's Most Wanted*.

(RAYMOND BOYD/GETTY IMAGES)

←

N.W.A's "Fuck Tha Police" became a rallying anthem during the 1992 uprising following the acquittal of the police officers who brutally beat Rodney King.

(TED SOQUI/CORBIS VIA GETTY IMAGES)

←

 Luke Skyywalker (with mic) and his pioneering Southern hip-hop group, 2 Live Crew, pushed boundaries with their lyrics and performances. The Florida artists fought off far-reaching obscenity charges in federal appeals court.

(RAYMOND BOYD/GETTY IMAGES)

N.W.A (left to right: MC Ren, DJ Yella, Eazy-E, Dr. Dre) stirred outrage with law enforcement and shocked Middle America, while amplifying overlooked and marginalized voices across the country. The group's 1991 album, *Efil4zaggin,* showed how deeply hip-hop penetrated communities when it topped the Billboard 200 after the advent of Nielsen SoundScan.

(AL PEREIRA/MICHAEL OCHS ARCHIVES/GETTY IMAGES)

The Geto Boys' Bushwick Bill performs at St. Louis Arena in 1991. The Houston group's classic lineup consisted of Scarface, Willie D, and Bushwick Bill. The trio helped put Southern artists on the map through hits like "Mind Playing Tricks on Me."

(RAYMOND BOYD/GETTY IMAGES)

↑ **Death Row's Suge Knight (right) recruited Tupac Shakur (left) to the record label while Shakur was incarcerated at Clinton Correctional Facility. The partnership aligned Shakur with Dr. Dre, one of hip-hop's top producers, and deepened a feud with New York's Bad Boy Records.**
(JEFF KRAVITZ/FILMMAGIC)

↑ **Puff Daddy and the Notorious B.I.G. watch Dr. Dre's performance at the 1995 Source Awards on a consequential evening that solidified hip-hop's coastal rivalry.**
(AL PEREIRA/MICHAEL OCHS ARCHIVES/ GETTY IMAGES)

Faith Newman (right), one of Def Jam's earliest employees, had recently landed at Columbia Records when she scrambled to sign a young Queensbridge artist, Nasir Jones (left). The debut album, 1994's *Illmatic*, is lauded as one of the greatest of all time.
↓ (JOHNNY NUNEZ/WIREIMAGE)

Jay-Z, shown here performing at New Jersey's Continental Airlines Arena, released his debut, *Reasonable Doubt*, in 1996. The album kickstarted the career of hip-hop's first billionaire.
↓ (MITCHELL GERBER/CORBIS/VCG VIA GETTY IMAGES)

Goodie Mob's *Soul Food* arrived mere months after the divisive 1995 Source Awards. Backed by Organized Noize's stellar production, CeeLo, Big Gipp, Khujo, and T-Mo simultaneously defined and broadened Southern hip-hop music throughout their debut.

(TAYLOR HILL/GETTY IMAGES)

Al Kapone (left) had established himself as an underground Memphis hip-hop legend before writing tracks that the actor Terrence Howard (right) performed in the 2005 film *Hustle & Flow*.

(JOHN SHEARER/WIREIMAGE)

Three 6 Mafia's Juicy J, DJ Paul, and Frayser Boy became the first hip-hop group to win an Oscar for Best Original Song, in 2006 for *Hustle & Flow*'s "It's Hard Out Here for a Pimp."

(JEFF KRAVITZ/FILMMAGIC)

Compton's Kendrick Lamar lifted hip-hop into new territory when his fourth studio album, *DAMN*, won the 2018 Pulitzer Prize for Music, an honor that historically had gone to classical compositions.

(SANTIAGO BLUGUERMANN/GETTY IMAGES)

I guess once people started hearing the actual song and the *Full Metal Jacket* movie had only been out maybe like a year, it was a no-brainer.

Brother Marquis (artist, 2 Live Crew): I wrote the biggest record 2 Live Crew ever had, which was "Me So Horny." That was totally me and Mr. Mixx. I gave the Chinaman [Fresh Kid Ice] that verse, and after [Mr. Mixx] appointed Luke to be the manager and I went along with him, we blew up and then we blew out. That's basically how it goes.

THE SUCCESS OF *As Nasty as They Wanna Be,* whose album cover showcased the group's members with bikini-clad women standing over them, infiltrated the suburbs and introduced 2 Live Crew to an audience who would have never otherwise heard their music. That new crowd included a conservative lawyer named Jack Thompson. Thompson had just lost a contested race for Dade County prosecutor to Janet Reno, the incumbent, whom Luther Campbell had publicly supported.

Thompson solicited Bob Martinez, then the governor of Florida, to investigate the group over Florida's obscenity statutes. Thompson also delivered some of 2 Live Crew's explicit lyrics to local sheriff's departments. Nick Navarro, the Broward County sheriff, obtained a county circuit ruling that they were "probably obscene." Navarro warned record-store owners against selling the album, which prompted Campbell to file a preemptive lawsuit, hiring Bruce Rogow as his legal representation.

Bruce Rogow (attorney for 2 Live Crew): I taught at the University of Miami Law School. One of my former students, Allen Jacobi, called me and said, "I want to bring 2 Live Crew up to see you."

And then Luther came up to my house and I liked him right away. We got along very well. And he brought a tape and I listened to it. And then the American Family Association, some conservative Mississippi group, had printed out the language, [which] had some rough words in it. And he said, "Well, do you think we can win?"

And I said, "I think we can win, but even if we lose, you'll win."

I explained to him that if the government tried to keep people from hearing something, everybody would want to see it or hear it, and then it would just sell more records. And so he got it right away.

My immediate reaction was to seek a declaratory judgment to declare that the record was not obscene. And that shifted the balance of everything, because then Luther became the plaintiff, and we were suing the state, and it puts you on a whole different plane.

There was no question that this is political. And this was the fortunate part, that it happened here in Broward County, because our sheriff, Nick Navarro, who happened to be a friend of mine, I knew loved publicity. He had already become very outspoken: "We're going to get him. We can't have this kind of talk, this kind of language."

And so, when I gave him the lawsuit with the tape attached to it, he had it jumping up and down in his hand like it was a hot potato.

BRUCE ROGOW FILED a lawsuit in federal district court that sought a judgment for the album to be deemed comedic art and not obscene, along with an order that would ban Nick Navarro from taking further action to limit sales of *As Nasty as They Wanna Be*. In June 1990, U.S. District Judge Jose Gonzalez Jr. ruled the album obscene, making it illegal to sell in Broward, Dade, and Palm Beach counties.

Shortly after, authorities arrested record-store owner Charles Freeman for selling a copy of the album to an undercover police officer.

Bruce Rogow (attorney for 2 Live Crew): Now there's a lot of publicity because the lawsuit's filed, everybody's going crazy—nobody ever filed a lawsuit to declare a record not to be obscene. And then the following Saturday, Charles [Freeman] gets arrested in Fort Lauderdale. And Nick Navarro had tipped off the press and so they had cameras, the TV trucks there.

So, Charles gets arrested. I get him, as I recall, acquitted. But we end up going to trial in federal court with Judge Gonzalez. He declares it to be obscene. But if he had found it not to be obscene, it would have kind of died out. It would have been gone.

> **UNDER THE COMMAND** of Nick Navarro, Broward County sheriff's
> deputies in plainclothes watched members of 2 Live Crew perform
> songs from the now legally-deemed obscene album at Club Futura in
> Hollywood, Florida, in June 1990. Shortly after the appearance, the
> deputies pulled over the Jaguar transporting Luther Campbell and
> Fresh Kid Ice, arresting them with charges of violating a prohibition
> against obscene and lewd performances.

Mr. Mixx (DJ, producer, 2 Live Crew): It was Luke and Chris [Fresh Kid Ice] that got arrested. They were just paying attention to Luke; they weren't really tripping over the band members. Me and Marquis was in the van with the dancers and a couple of other people. They didn't pull the van over. They pulled Luke's car over and Chris happened to be riding with Luke.

Brother Marquis (artist, 2 Live Crew): When it got to that point, I knew it was bigger than me. I knew that we were on that journey for all of the culture. But when "Me So Horny" came and all that publicity came, it started to shift.

I knew that it was big, especially when we got to the Supreme Court, but I'm like, "It's a lot of money being made, and everything is shifting to [Campbell]. You're forgetting about us." And all of the fuss started over the record that I wrote, and I used to complain to Dave [Mr. Mixx], and Dave was like, "Luke got us. Luke is my brother. I love Luke."

I was like, "Man, I don't think Luke has your back."

It didn't really bother me, because we've got the First Amendment, so you can't really do anything to me to take away my freedom, so I was cool with that—to the point where I would be late for court and Nick Navarro would send Broward County sheriffs all the way into Dade County, and they would wait until I'd take a shower and they would escort me to court.

So I'm like, "I think this is pretty cool, you fuckers coming to get me." I'm like, "Fuck it, Mom. I'm not going to court this morning. Fuck that shit." They came and got my Black ass.

Bruce Rogow (attorney for 2 Live Crew): [Nick Navarro] was the perfect foil. I mean, how many prosecutors were there in the country?

This was available all over the country and the only one who made noise about trying to bring them down—other than, I think, Tipper Gore was complaining about it, but she couldn't file anything—it was Navarro.

Brother Marquis (artist, 2 Live Crew): My mom was like, "I don't know where you got those cuss words from, son—you didn't hear me saying all of that profanity when I was raising you."

I'm like, "Yeah, you're right."

But then sometimes I thought it was pretty cool. I'm the first rapper that can get on a record and grab my nuts and talk about it. So I'm like, *This part of it is cool.* Then I'm like, *Okay, I'm pissing off a lot of people, I got the government mad at me.* That was cool for a period of time.

But I didn't expect it to go all the way to the Supreme Court. When the local authorities in Florida start getting wind of us, and all that controversy came about, I was getting stopped by the police left and right. Sometimes to get an autograph, but most of the time I was getting shook down.

Bruce Rogow (attorney for 2 Live Crew): One of the songs has a word, *splak*. So I said to [Brother Marquis], "So, what is this word *splak*?"

He said, "Man, you know when you're going at it and you're wet and she's wet, and you're slapping together like that? That's what you hear."

So then he's on the witness stand. And I don't ask him the question, but the prosecutor asked him the question. And he goes into this explanation of *splak* in more detail.

Brother Marquis (artist, 2 Live Crew): Now, that was funny. *Splak* was meaning like stealing something. Like, "I'm going to *splak* that car. I'm going to *splak* that pocketbook." *Splak* means like, "I'm going to go get it." Like the guys say in sports, "Okay, we want a W. Let's go get it."

Bruce Rogow (attorney for 2 Live Crew): It just broke me up. I just thought I'd fall out of my seat. It was so perfect. And of course, the prosecutor was left there with his mouth hanging open. "You got a big hard-on, and she's all wet, and you're ready to put it in. You got to put it in her, and then you're pumping at it, boom, boom. *Splak, splak, splak.*"

THE OBSCENITY CASE featured Henry Louis "Skip" Gates, then a professor of literature at Duke University, as an expert witness who defended 2 Live Crew. Gates described that hip-hop followed in the African American tradition of signifying, or "the Dozens," where contestants use spoken words to insult one another. He testified that 2 Live Crew was a parody group playing on the stereotypes of young Black men as hypersexualized.

Bruce Rogow (attorney for 2 Live Crew): It had everything. It had race. It had sex. It had rock and roll. It had hip-hop. It had this whole new music that was coming out. It had a plaintiff, Luther, who had the personality. And it had Nick Navarro. It had the guy on the other side, who was his own colorful character.

But it did introduce a lot of people, including me, to hip-hop. I didn't know about Grandmaster Flash, and then I had Henry Louis Gates as an expert. He was a great witness. He talked about the call-and-response and sampling. And he put it in a larger African American historical perspective.

SOME MEMBERS OF the jury laughed when law enforcement played segments of the largely unintelligible lyrics from the concert.

In October 1990, jurors took roughly two hours to find the members of 2 Live Crew not guilty of violating obscenity laws. The media circus catapulted the group's sales. *As Nasty as They Wanna Be* became the only Southern hip-hop album released in the 1980s to go platinum.

Mr. Mixx (DJ, producer, 2 Live Crew): The only reason why we won the case, to keep it one hundred, the undercovers' recording that they made by the cops was so muffled that the jury couldn't understand it.

Hip-hop wasn't being thought about at that time when it happened.

But Luke puts the spin on it now, making it seem like "I had to do it for hip-hop." Nobody was thinking about no hip-hop. Everybody was just thinking about get they ass out of jail.

Bruce Rogow (attorney for 2 Live Crew): I think, as any artist was, [Luther Campbell] was in it for himself. They were trying to sell records. I don't think his goal was to make any kind of political point. It was to create something, and he created something and then he was fortunate that it was done here. Had it been in some other place, probably people would have not paid much attention to it, and it would have just faded away.

But once it started, there's no question that he was into it. He was into the First Amendment angle. He was into becoming a proponent of the music. I think he learned stuff, too. I think he learned from Skip Gates. All of a sudden, this is now ratcheted up. It really raised the level of the whole thing. Here's a kid that lives in Liberty City, and ultimately we ended up in the Supreme Court, not on the obscenity case, but on the parody case.

IN MAY 1992, the Eleventh U.S. Circuit Court of Appeals in Atlanta overturned Gonzalez's obscenity ruling, declaring that Broward County had not successfully countered arguments that 2 Live Crew's music contained artistic value. The Supreme Court declined to hear the county's appeal.

But 2 Live Crew eventually ended up in the highest court anyway. On *As Clean as They Wanna Be,* the more sanitized version of the album, the group sampled from Roy Orbison's "Oh, Pretty Woman" without permission from Acuff-Rose Music. The publishing firm sued in a case that was decided by the Supreme Court, which ruled in 1994 that the work was parody and not copyright infringement.

Bruce Rogow (attorney for 2 Live Crew): [Luther Campbell] was smart from the very beginning, but his goal was not to create a whole new genre of music. His goal was to do something that was fun, and hopefully successful, and would make him some money. And then it morphed into something bigger.

But he morphed alongside of it into having a deeper understanding of what was going on, to where now he's an icon, because he basically started it and then the litigation was so effective. And the parody case was a big thing. I can't think of another musical artist who ends up in the Supreme Court in a huge case that we won nine to nothing.

It had an effect, because now, everybody wanted to hear it. So I think it opened the door to a lot of white listeners, and therefore opened the door to more hip-hop and to understanding rap.

2 LIVE CREW mostly went their own ways in subsequent years, re-convening only on occasion. MC Shy D filed suit for unpaid royalties from Luther Campbell, forcing him into bankruptcy. Joe Weinberger, one of Campbell's former attorneys, also claimed that Campbell owed him money, from an unpaid loan, and purchased 2 Live Crew's cata-logue.

The group was unable to replicate their success and controversy of the late 1980s and early '90s. But Campbell had provided a successful roadmap for subsequent Southern hip-hop entrepreneurs to follow, and shown that a deal from a New York or Los Angeles record label was not the only path to success.

In the early 2000s, Brother Marquis and Fresh Kid Ice pursued solo projects. Chris Wong Won—Fresh Kid Ice—died in 2017 at the age of fifty-three. He is regarded as one of hip-hop's pioneering Asian artists.

Brother Marquis resurfaced in the aftermath of one of Jay-Z's more recognizable songs, the Rick Rubin–produced "99 Problems." Brother Marquis had used the phrase for the original song, released by Ice-T in 1993, and in 2005 submitted a lawsuit against Jay-Z and Ice-T for unpaid royalties from the remake. The suit did not advance past the filing stage.

Brother Marquis (artist, 2 Live Crew): I hate that all of that situation ended the way that it did. I tried to reach out to Ice a couple of times, but I get no response. I probably hurt him, and I tried to apologize and make amends, but it seems like it's not working. I don't want to have any bones with Ice. I definitely don't want to have any bones with Jay-Z.

I always kid around and say Jay-Z has a device, has something on his phone that will blow out my back from where he's at. He stabs and Ice shoots, so I've got a problem with gangsters and a billionaire.

Besides the money, I hate that I lost the relationship with Ice. I learned a lot from Ice. I learned a lot from just his conversations and his stories and shit. I still love him.

Jay-Z, on the other hand, I'm scared to even say anything about Jay-Z. He's so fucking powerful, and I like to ride my bike around Miami and Biscayne and shit, I don't need no entourage of black Escalades pulling up on me, fucking with me about "99 Problems," so I'm leaving it alone.

13 CERTAIN POCKETS

Atlanta, Houston, Memphis, New Orleans
1982–1995

Outside the media epicenters of cities like New York and Los Angeles, vibrant hip-hop landscapes sprouted in Southern states like Georgia, Texas, Tennessee, and Louisiana. For years, the Southern hip-hop scene remained mostly regionalized, with its own ecosystem of labels, artists, and listeners, until many of the subgenres it birthed became dominant hip-hop music sounds.

In Georgia, Miami's electro-fueled bass music became Atlanta's preferred early sound. In 1982, the artist Mojo released "Let Mojo Handle It," considered Atlanta's first hip-hop single. MC Shy D, who relocated from the Bronx to Georgia, was among the first to introduce many in Atlanta to New York–centric hip-hop, straight from the teachings of Afrika Bambaataa. He worked with the influential Atlanta producer DJ Toomp, and signed with Luke Skyywalker Records. Raheem the Dream, Kilo Ali, and Hitman Sammy Sam are among the other pioneering artists who laid the framework for the city.

Meanwhile, Edward J. Landrum, known as King Edward J, birthed the city's rich mixtape tradition through the release of his popular "J-Tapes." Landrum and his coalition of DJs, the J-Team, advanced many of the area's early artists and acts, like Success-n-Effect and DJ Smurf (later known as Mr. Collipark).

Big Gipp (artist, Goodie Mob): The first artist that I saw that was representing Atlanta was a guy named Mojo. "Let Mojo Handle It." He was the first Atlanta artist to get his record played on the radio in 1982. But the first artists that really, really started being on the radio was Success-n-Effect, Kilo, the Hard Boyz, and of course, Raheem the Dream and Shy D.

MC Shy D (artist, producer): I was DJing at a young age. When I threw parties, I'd play a New York record, everybody go sit down; but then when I played Egyptian Lover—'cause he was hot back then—everybody go running to the dance floor. I said to myself, *If I ever get a chance to make a record, I'm gonna make an up-tempo record.* And then, 2 Live Crew, when they made "Throw the D," I was like, *Damn, that bass sounds dope.*

So, when I got a chance to make a record, I asked the engineer down there in Florida, "What kind of drum machine did the 2 Live Crew use?" He said they used an 808. I told him, "That's what I wanna make my song out of." I started beating the beat that I wanted, and he programmed it with the 808.

DJ Jaycee (the Aphilliates): I was on the ground floor, pretty much, when the Atlanta hip-hop scene really started taking off. There was DJ Len and Lazy Rock with the "Roll It Up My Nigga" record. Then there was Kilo, Hard Boyz, 9 Milli. Before Outkast, there was Parental Advisory—they were the first out of Organized Noize.

Killer Mike (artist, Dungeon Family): [Hitman Sammy] Sam and Kilo, in particular, that was the prototype for Atlanta street rap, what you would call "trap rap" today. All those elements were first in those two artists.

IN THE EARLY 1990s, Atlanta exported a brand of hip-hop music that found national popularity. Dallas Austin, who advanced to work with TLC and Boyz II Men, opened his DARP Studios, which became a home base for many who lived in Atlanta, as well as for out-of-towners, including Erick Sermon following EPMD's fracture. Arrested Development's 1992 debut album, *3 Years, 5 Months and 2 Days in the*

Life Of . . . , captured two Grammy Awards, and in 1993 Tag Team's "Whoomp! (There It Is)" climbed the national charts.

But few matched the popularity of a boy group put together by Jermaine Dupri (JD), who was not too far removed from his childhood days of dancing for Whodini when he discovered Chris Smith and Chris Kelly at Atlanta's Greenbriar Mall. Dupri, who received his producing start with the hip-hop group Silk Tymes Leather, molded Smith and Kelly into Daddy Mac and Mac Daddy of Kris Kross. He turned their clothes backward—starting the "Kiddie Rap Wars" of the early '90s with fellow Atlanta group Another Bad Creation, who wore their clothes backward in Bell Biv DeVoe's "Mental" style—and penned the songs for their debut album, 1992's *Totally Krossed Out,* released by Ruffhouse Records and Columbia Records.

Totally Krossed Out, boosted by the record-breaking singles "Jump" and "Warm It Up," topped the Billboard album chart, and Smith and Kelly became pop culture icons in the 1990s. The group's breakthrough success allowed Dupri to launch So So Def Recordings in 1993. The label became a trendsetter in both hip-hop (Da Brat's groundbreaking debut, *Funkdafied,* shattered sales records for a solo female rapper in 1994) and R&B (through groups like Xscape and Jagged Edge).

DJ Nabs (So So Def): I knew Jermaine because of Silk Tymes Leather, his first group. So when I saw him and Chris ["Mac Daddy" Kelly] and Chris ["Daddy Mac" Smith], I just said, "Well, these kids must be a group." And that was that.

Jermaine helped give the city an identity, no doubt about it. And it's the own individual stamp that represents JD's thoughts and ideas.

Chris Schwartz (cofounder, Ruffhouse): The record "Jump" wasn't really my cup of tea, but I could not deny its appeal. Rosie Perez, who was the talent coordinator for *In Living Color,* had put the group on the show for a performance. I was in a diner the next day and I heard all these people talking about seeing Kris Kross on *In Living Color*—like older, middle-age people—and how phenomenal these little kids were. I'll never forget, I looked at my wife and said, "Oh my God, this record's going to be huge."

Khujo (artist, Goodie Mob): They blew that thing clean out the water. The youth was wearing they clothes backwards.

> **IN HOUSTON, TEXAS,** the Rhinestone Wrangler offered a platform to battle rappers like K-Rino, Ganksta N-I-P, and Willie D, artists who went on to play pivotal roles in the emergence of the city's vibrant independent hip-hop.

Matt Sonzala (journalist, Houston): Run-DMC was a huge influence on UGK, and on all of the Geto Boys. But when it comes to rap happening in Houston, there were times where there were local people like K-Rino. Ganksta N-I-P was early. Willie D was early on. Johnny C and DJ Ready Red—who was a really pivotal member of that community, who really doesn't ever get the credit he deserves for producing that early music, forming the early sound of Houston, and being a DJ at clubs where things really were birthed in Houston.

But in the beginning, Houston was like anywhere, and what they really gravitated to, besides breakdancing, what really got Houston's spark lit, was the battling.

K-Rino (artist, South Park Coalition): We were accepted as far as "Okay, this dude can rap. This dude can battle." They stopped taking you seriously once you made any mention of putting an actual record out, because that's not something that people out here do. *That's something LL Cool J does. That's something that Run-DMC does. You're not on that level. You're good for the neighborhood.* That was the mindset in Houston, because no one had actually done it.

Matt Sonzala (journalist, Houston): K-Rino was born to rap. Ganksta N-I-P was born to be Ganksta N-I-P. Those two guys were two of the rawest. They were both Southside, and they had a rivalry. And when that rivalry came to a head and those two finally got down to battle— that was a big deal.

K-Rino (artist, South Park Coalition): We had been rivals for years. For some reason, me and N-I-P, we decided we had this tension between us, and I think it was because I knew that he was real good and he knew that I was real good. The two standouts were just gravitating towards each other.

One day in '87, we were on the phone one night, just talking a lot of crap to each other. "Man, let's go ahead and settle this, and get it out of the way. We're going to prove once and for all [who is better]."

We set up a neutral area to meet. His people came with him. My people came with me. We went to war from the evening 'til it got dark outside. Then we became the best of friends after that.

THROUGH HIS EMPLOYMENT of graphic, gory imagery in 1992's *The South Park Psycho,* Houston's Ganksta N-I-P, who later changed his moniker to Ganxsta Nip, became an originator of horrorcore. This subgenre, utilized by those like the Geto Boys, Three 6 Mafia, and Esham, typically involves over-the-top descriptions of psychosis, the occult, and other horror elements aimed to shock the listener.

K-Rino (artist, South Park Coalition): When he first released on Rap-A-Lot, he got a lot of notoriety. His first album [*The South Park Psycho*] was classic. After that, guys started capitalizing on the genre. N-I-P was never caught up in actually branding hardcore. We called it psycho rap because that's what it was.

To me, there's a difference between his way of doing it, in comparison to other people. He's more intricate with it. He's more clever with it. It's not just slashing, killing, cutting, bloody. It's not direct like that. You have to really listen to it to discover all of the intricacies of the way he does it in comparison to everybody else.

Matt Sonzala (journalist, Houston): If you listen to the early Houston rap, it was hard as shit. If you listen to the first K-Rino album—or especially *Grip It! On That Other Level* with Willie D and Scarface, that's the one that broke through—they were pushing boundaries everywhere. There was not hardcore rap before Ganksta N-I-P. People weren't talking about the crazy shit that he was before him.

JAMES PRINCE, WHO often shortened his name to J. Prince, was a one-time car salesman who recognized that coastal executives were ignoring the developing Houston hip-hop scene. Spotting a lane for himself, he founded Rap-A-Lot Records in 1987 with Cliff Blodget, who had recently moved to Texas from Washington State. Prince possessed a keen eye for talent and sharp business acumen. His label would at some point work with nearly every influential artist who came out of Houston.

He started with the Ghetto Boys. The original version of the group included Raheem, Sire Jukebox, Prince Johnny C, and, soon after, DJ Ready Red. In 1986, the Ghetto Boys released "Car Freak," one of the first Houston hip-hop songs to circulate on local radio.

K-Rino (artist, South Park Coalition): When J. Prince started Rap-A-Lot, and he started putting artists out like the original Ghetto Boys, and Raheem the Vigilante, and those guys started doing it on a bigger scale, it gave a lot of us confidence to try to do it as well.

What he decided to do is, "Okay, well, if they're not going to give us an opportunity, then we'll create a platform and opportunity for ourselves." When we saw that it could actually be done, then that was the birth of Houston with all the independent labels.

THE ITERATION OF the Geto Boys (the spelling of the group's name was also changed) that gained fame fused when J. Prince joined together Willie D, a former boxer who had made a name in the city's battle circuit; Bushwick Bill, a native of Brooklyn who was born with dwarfism; and Brad Jordan, a lyricist of cutting depth who started his career as DJ Akshen before assuming the moniker of Scarface.

K-Rino (artist, South Park Coalition): When Scarface and Willie D joined the Geto Boys, the second inception of the Geto Boys, they did a skit. They were talking to this big-time record executive, and at the end of the skit he tells the dude, "F you," and he hangs the phone up in his face.

Just by us hearing that skit, we got motivated. To see him, as a Black man, start from that level, and elevate all the way up to what he became, and what Rap-A-Lot became, and what those who followed behind him became, it was very inspirational and motivational for us.

THE ALBUM COVER of 1991's *We Can't Be Stopped* featured Scar-face and Willie D flanking Bushwick Bill on a hospital gurney, after he had shot himself in the eye during a dispute with a girlfriend. Scarface conceived and wrote the bulk of the album's gargantuan single, "Mind Playing Tricks on Me."

The song used a sample from Isaac Hayes's "Hung Up on My Baby" and was introspective to a degree rarely seen in hardcore hip-hop at the time, detailing the mental anguish and toll of trying to endure in the midst of despair. "Mind Playing Tricks on Me" became one of the first Southern hip-hop tracks to receive airplay outside of the region.

K-Rino (artist, South Park Coalition): It wasn't a typical type of sample that people were using at the time, particularly down here in Houston. We would always try to find some old gangster sound and '70s funk sound. Something that's hard. For them to come with that Isaac Hayes sample, you got the Geto Boys making this dance tempo that can be played in the clubs—people can dance to it, DJs can mix to it, a radio version was made, so it could be played on the radio. It was just the perfect storm. The planets lined up perfectly for them.

Bun B (artist, UGK): It was its own very unique-sounding song. It didn't sound like anything from the Geto Boys' lineage in music, much less in hip-hop, period.

Matt Sonzala (journalist, Houston): "Mind Playing Tricks" was a hit. The radio ran with it. The video was hard. It was the first time a Houston artist or Houston group got real shine.

Bun B (artist, UGK): It actually dealt with mental health—nobody really pays attention to that part of it. But it also goes as far as any other song from any other region goes, so it perpetuates the notion that if we execute this right, our songs in Texas can go just as far as someone from L.A. or New York or anywhere else in America.

And from an artist's perspective, just being able to see guys that are making music in the same way that you are, the same region that you are, go and have the number one hip-hop record of the year—arguably one of the biggest records of the year, period—it's absolutely inspiring. So, we just wanted to see how far they could go, so that we could see just how far we could possibly go.

Matt Sonzala (journalist, Houston): They went from playing clubs to arenas, and went from getting booed in New York to headlining Madison Square Garden. It was just a huge level-up for Houston, to let everybody know that it was actually possible.

K-Rino (artist, South Park Coalition): In the beginning, when I first started, there was battle rap and there were talent shows. That's all it was in Houston. Once people started putting out records, when people started focusing on the business side of it, and trying to make some money, then the battle rap kind of subsided. People were trying to get their break, because we had seen the Geto Boys go platinum at this point. It's like, "Man, you know you're wasting time doing that battling."

Matt Sonzala (journalist, Houston): Back then, Houston was dank and fucking dark. At night there was a group of people called the Urban Animals, and they literally would dress up like *Mad Max*–looking people and just roller-skate through dark-ass downtown. Our center of our city was desolate, and surrounding downtown was just decay. It wasn't until early, mid-'90s that downtown started revitalizing a bit. You can call it gentrification, but when a crucial part of your city falls down that far, something had to be done.

K-Rino (artist, South Park Coalition): A lot of us didn't graduate from high school. A lot of us came out of prison. A lot of us were selling dope. To look up and see a lot of these same individuals now making hundreds of thousands to millions of dollars, legally, just doing music, we've already accomplished something that nobody saw us accomplishing.

The last thing we need to do is to be out here going to war with each other over a side of town. Nobody wins from that, and just like the East Coast/West Coast beef, we make the mistake of perpetuating it through our music. It trickles down to the fans, who start to actually be the real ones who are carrying out the acts of violence on each other. It's not the rappers.

Luckily you had people like [Lil'] Keke—and Slim Thug and E.S.G., who did projects together, one being from the North, one being from the South. To me that defused a lot. When the giants from different sides of town worked together, that should be our example. If they can let it go, then we should let it go.

FEW HIP-HOP ARTISTS have authored a career comparable to that of Scarface, who gained success outside of the Geto Boys and is widely regarded as the favorite rapper of many rappers. Scarface, a gifted narrator, battled depression throughout his early life. He used his pen, poise, and prose to provide voice and depth to the angst and rage felt by many Black youth.

The Diary, Scarface's third album, from 1994, included "I Seen a Man Die," a haunting tale of failed redemption. *The Untouchable* (1997) topped the Billboard charts and contained the unforgettable "Smile," featuring Tupac Shakur.

Young Buck (artist, G-Unit, Nashville): As far as being in the South, I can never forget Scarface. He was more or less that real essence for me as an individual. I'm just soaking up the music because it compared to the life I was living. Any of the artists that were speaking what I seen, directly from where I was at, was the kind of artist I was drawn to.

Matt Sonzala (journalist, Houston): Scarface doesn't play the game. He's just pure talent and pure vibe and pure consistency. He's been in and out of the business portion of the hip-hop game for most of his career. He's just that rapper, he's living it.

IN THE EARLY 1990s, Houston's DJ Screw pitched down his turntables to mix and scratch hip-hop songs, taking elements that he inherited from one of the city's mixtape legends, Darryl Scott. The process resulted in songs produced at a lethargic tempo, with each word delivered through a decipherable and hallucinatory haze that fit the city's laid-back and mellow vibe. In 1993, DJ Screw began recording free-styles of friends and local Southside rappers, known as the Screwed Up Click (S.U.C.). Many of the early group members and affiliates— including Big Moe, Fat Pat, E.S.G., Lil' Keke, K-Rino, Trae tha Truth, and Devin the Dude—broke out as some of the region's largest names.

Lil' Keke (artist, Screwed Up Click): Screw, he wasn't giant DJ Screw before I got there; he was just Screw, somebody that was doing tapes. But the flows that me and [Fat] Pat had put on some of these pages had a lot to do with how big this thing grew, just as big as Screw did. We all became real big and famous together. I was just so happy to be able to survive each turning point of the game.

DJ SCREW MOVED to a house in the eastern section of South Park, where fans arrived from all over the state and waited hours to obtain one of his tapes. When the demand continued surging, DJ Screw opened a shop, Screwed Up Records & Tapes, on Houston's Cullen Boulevard.

Lil' Keke (artist, Screwed Up Click): We have a lot of significant artists who make up the Screwed Up Click: Big Hawk, Big Moe, Fat Pat, Lil' Keke, Big Pokey, AI-D. These are the real cofounders of it, and then we have all kinds of members that added and went on.

K-Rino (artist, South Park Coalition): I went to school with Screw, so I knew Screw before he was the Screw that everybody else knows. Years passed, and then you would hear people riding down the street, playing this music that sounded like back in the days when you'd slow down your record player on purpose.

Everybody said, "That is Screw. Screwed and chopped. DJ Screw."

Then I ran into him. Then it all made sense. He was like, "That's what I'm doing, man."

I was just proud of him, because he's another one who innovated a sound, who innovated a style, and basically created another genre within a genre.

Bun B (artist, UGK): It was very interesting seeing this whole subculture of Houston come together. When he actually started making the Screw tapes, the music switched from where he was just making a regular mix-tape to something that was his own personal creation. That's when things really started to take off. It became this phenomenon—something that culturally was very new for everyone, but distinctly Houston.

Matt Sonzala (journalist, Houston): Most people, the first time they heard Screw, didn't like it. But if you lived in Texas at that time, Screw became an undeniable force. There were people who literally grew up not hearing albums regular-speed. They grew up with slowed-down DJ Screw mixes being the norm.

Paul Wall (artist, Houston): When DJ Screw, Lil' Keke, Fat Pat was first doing it, I was the generation that that was my hip-hop. It was something that I took a lot of pride in. Just the way they were talking, the slang and stuff they were saying. You'd hear this with the Geto Boys too, but they spoke to the ghettos of the world, where the Screwed Up Click was more just a local Houston thing. The Screwed Up Click is what I aspired to be: a rapper that's speaking for my tribe, for my section, for my area.

A lot of times we'd make music just for the car, just because, "Shit, I got to have my playlist to ride around the parking lot tonight for about forty-five minutes. I've got to have a good little mixtape." So that's how we would hear the music, is on the Screw tape. That's how we would hear our local artists.

And to me, local is always better. Snoop Dogg to me is as local as it gets; he's as Long Beach, West Coast, as it gets. Lil Wayne is New Orleans. Jay-Z is Brooklyn. The top artists, they're local as fuck, for the most part.

DJ SCREW, BORN Robert Earle Davis Jr., died in November 2000 at the age of twenty-nine. A coroner's report attributed his death to an overdose of codeine (the active ingredient in drank, a mixture of cough syrup and a soft drink) and alcohol intoxication. He did not live to see the oversized impact he had on hip-hop.

Matt Sonzala (journalist, Houston): There's better DJs than DJ Screw. There's bigger DJs than DJ Screw. But worldwide, there's never been a DJ that had a bigger impact on his own community than DJ Screw. No one.

> **IN RESPONSE TO** being overlooked, Houston artists, producers, and executives constructed and supported their own economic ecosystem. Independent labels—like North Houston's Swishahouse, founded by Michael "5000" Watts and OG Ron C—flourished. Most utilized Southwest Wholesale Records & Tapes, which grew into one of the country's largest one-stop distributors.

Matt Sonzala (journalist, Houston): Houston had literally zero media attention. The Geto Boys got *Source* covers because they were working with Rick Rubin. But when that record [1989's *The Geto Boys*] was about to come out, it was so controversial that David Geffen said he wasn't even going to distribute it. Then that became big news and catapulted the Geto Boys into the spotlight.

But people weren't coming down interviewing K-Rino. People weren't coming down interviewing the Screwed Up Click. There was no chance of these guys being heard outside of the region.

So, what the Houston artists did was made themselves very visible in Houston, and if you could get on a Screw tape, or a Swishahouse tape, if you were [with founder of Dope House Records] South Park Mexican, you were even more visible. That was a big part of how that music spread organically.

K-Rino (artist, South Park Coalition): When we didn't have major labels that would deal with us, our next option was to go through one-stops and distribution companies that would put our music out regionally. Southwest [Wholesale] was the avenue that all of us used to accomplish that. They were the ones who, in a lot of ways, taught us the business.

Matt Sonzala (journalist, Houston): Back in the day, the record stores were the center of the community, and these guys would go directly in there, sell their music, put it on consignment, go to a club that night, jump on a microphone.

K-Rino (artist, South Park Coalition): We're the king of that as far as just having all these independent labels sprout up, and going through regional distribution companies, and selling thirty, forty, fifty, a hundred thousand units in some cases, and making a better living than people that were going platinum on majors, because they were only getting pennies on a dollar per sale, compared to us getting eight, nine bucks per unit. That template was laid by Rap-A-Lot, and we followed it. A lot of labels, from Bigtyme Recordz to Jam Down to Wreckshop, followed that template and made a lot of money off of it.

Paul Wall (artist, Houston): Houston was always the land of entrepreneur hip-hop hustlers. One thing that we were so blessed by was that all of the people that we saw as being the movers and shakers, like J. Prince, D-Reck, Tony Draper, they all were very open to sharing how they did it. They would just tell us, "Man, you don't need nobody. Do that shit yourself. You do that with somebody else, they taking all the money." They showed us from the jump.

> **IN MEMPHIS, DJ** Spanish Fly helped to transition the city from the disco and electric funk eras by spreading hip-hop during his stint at Club No Name in the late 1980s. His early mixtapes were marked by booming 808s, and he played a key role in introducing the Gangsta Walk and the Triggerman beat. Memphis emerged as a mostly underground scene; however, its pioneers laid the framework for popular hip-hop music subgenres like trap music and crunk.

DJ Spanish Fly (Memphis): I already was in this little crew from the streets and they hipped me to "Fly, you need to get in the DJ contest." This is [at] one of the biggest clubs in Memphis back in '85, '86—Club No Name. I was like, "Sure, man. I'm down for it."

They had the DJ contest first and then second was the MC contest. The DJ contest, I won it hands-down. I was doing turntables, spinning around. All kinds of little stuff.

Next up was a rap contest. And I just kind of took a shot at it and they was going crazy. So I won the rap contest, too.

That was the biggest club in Memphis and they was right on the state line. We'd get Mississippians, Arkansas right across the bridge, and you get all of Tennessee. Memphis is the distribution center. Even now. I guess that's why FedEx moved here.

Anyway, I won both of those. I just had so many things on my side to promote the movement and me. I started doing the *No Name Hot-mix* [on the radio]. And that's where the name started building. And then I just started doing my mixtapes. Before you know it, I started giving them away by the thousand.

Reginald Boyland (owner, OTS Records): Shit, [Club No Name was] buck wild. The game was there, far as with the dancing—Spanish Fly, Soni D, Ray the Jay. They had all kinds of DJs that was up in there. They was rapping. It'd be packed.

Then they started that Gangsta Walk, they'd be like Indians goin' in circles. And then they'd start fighting. Then they stopped. Start back again. It was buck. That's where all that Jookin' and that walking and all that shit come from.

GANGSTA WALKING, OR Buck Jumping, emerged from the youth who attended the performances of popular DJs like Spanish Fly, Soni D, Squeeky, and Zirk at skating rinks and dance halls. The music whipped the crowd into a frenzy, and they partied by moving in a frenetic circle. The dance gained in popularity in the 1990s, as more of the music in the city's fledgling hip-hop scene reflected the energy of the dance.

DJ Spanish Fly (Memphis): When I DJ'd, they would get up and Buck Jump, which is moving your feet like you're marching along with a little head gesture to the right. I was playing music that the disco people was not used to. So when I come up, they have to stop dancing. Those guys jump in and do the Buck Jump. They would get buck. "We buckin'." Like, "We fixin' to buck when you go up."

The Buck Jump was awesome. That line started with three or four dudes. Over time, that line got as long as twenty, thirty, forty people. No lie. Everybody doing the same kind of dance, and it look like a snake.

Al Kapone (artist, Memphis): Gangsta Walking was the first dance that was cool for hood dudes to do. Because you wasn't really fully dancing, you basically was just walking in a circle. It was a little tribal thing. But you could only do it to certain beats, like a Triggerman, which was the Showboys' "Drag Rap."

DJ Spanish Fly (Memphis): Being a DJ back in the day, I had to play songs that the radio did not play. That was my number one rule. So, I went out to scout records.

Now, a lot of promoters used to bring me records to break. Numerous LL Cool Js, Whodinis, Mantronix, Rodney-O. It was just a lot of songs I broke back in the day.

When I go purchase records, I started buying labels—meaning, if I seen a Profile label, get it. We don't care if they're just saying "Uh" all the way through. Just buy it. I would buy Profile. I would buy Def Jam. I would buy Sunnyview, Jive.

I grabbed this one, and it said "Trigger Man." So that caught my eye, and it was Profile. When I took it home, I bust it open, and I listen to it. And I liked the way it started off with the *Dragnet* theme. And when he started rapping, I was like, *Damn. They found some dope boys, some little gangsters.* Then the 808 came in. And I was like, *Whoa. Okay, hold on. That's what we're looking for.*

So, I started playing it. And then, put it on my mixtape. And I kept on repeating it so many times on mixtapes, it was like I was trying to shove it down their throats.

Al Kapone (artist, Memphis): I first heard "Drag Rap" on a Mr. Magic *Rap Attack* album years before it became popular in Memphis, because I was one of those hip-hop nerds that was really into it. Years later, it became that song that became the Gangsta Walk staple song whenever they played it.

John "J-Dogg" Shaw (promotions, urban A&R, Select-O-Hits Distribution): [In] New Orleans, they use the term "Buck Jump" to refer to what people do at a second line. But in Memphis, Buck Jumping was an early name for the Gangsta Walk. The two cities had a shared rap beginning, in a way. But then they diverged.

Part of it was that the gangster scene from California just did not have a big impact on New Orleans. There were groups that tried to be more gangster. But most of New Orleans rap didn't follow those trails. It stayed on its own course that was largely influenced by brass-band music.

In Memphis, gangster rap had a profound impact once Memphis rappers understood what N.W.A was, what Too $hort was, what the Geto Boys were.

REGINALD BOYLAND'S INDEPENDENT label, On the Strength Records, became a launchpad for several early-breakthrough Memphis artists, including Gangsta Pat, Al Kapone, 8Ball & MJG, and Juicy J and DJ Paul.

Reginald Boyland (owner, OTS Records): A friend of mine [Fat Tony] was trying to set up a label down here. He was in contact with Eazy-E. So, I kind of felt like some things were fittin' to happen. So if he needed money or whatever, I was just supporting what he was doing.

Unfortunately, something had happened to him. He got murdered.

I just pretty much kept it going. Set the label up. Got an artist, Gangsta Pat. Went through little independent labels with the record and ended up getting a deal.

Al Kapone (artist, Memphis): Gangsta Pat was the first rapper that really represented that Memphis sound, and he was young and real aggressive. He was the first person we actually heard a song getting consistent radio play with "I'm Tha Gangsta," and then he actually came out with a real album that was on a national label.

At that time, we was making a name for ourself at the clubs, but when [Gangsta Pat] came out and did what he did, we knew then we could actually put records out. This could be something more than what we ever thought, just by his success.

Reginald Boyland (owner, OTS Records): Phone started ringing off the hook. People started coming from everywhere. I started signing a lot of groups.

Al Kapone (artist, Memphis): Once Gangsta Pat blew up, we gravitated to OTS, because it's like, *That's the place where you can actually get a record out in real life.* For myself, a group I was in called Men of the Hour—producer Psycho, 8Ball, MJG, Squeeky—was in on it now. SMK was there. DJ Zirk was there.

Reginald Boyland (owner, OTS Records): I signed 8Ball. I liked the way he rapped. He was a lyricist. He was kind of a poet, so he was good with words.

At that time, his name wasn't 8Ball. When I got him, we had them eight-ball jackets. I just said, "I'm going to name you 8Ball, man. You hard. You round. You a big old cat."

We worked on a record, and we put MJG on that record. We named him MJG—his name is Marlon Jermaine Goodwin, so we just used his initials. We just went from there. We did "Listen to the Lyrics." That shit took off.

Al Kapone (artist, Memphis): We were fans and in competition at the same time, but it was friendly competition. It wasn't like beef. It was more like, *I'll go and record a song and 8Ball and them probably hear the song I recorded and be like, "Oh, shit. That's dope."*

They were loving it, but at the same time they were thinking, *I gotta come harder than what Al just did.* So they'll make a record, and I'll hear it, be like, "Oh, shit, that's dope, I love it." Now I gotta try to come better than that.

Reginald Boyland (owner, OTS Records): The only battles they have will be rap battles going on in the studio. We'll put a beat on and got 8Ball right here. Got Al Kapone right there. You got Tela over there. A lot of them could have been in the streets—shooting, killing, whatever. But all of them was there creating, man. Pretty much most of them got careers.

Al Kapone (artist, Memphis): It was an era that I never really experienced, far as Memphis hip-hop, ever again, because at some point it became all about beef. But that was a time where it was more friendly competition.

> **8BALL & MJG,** who would come to represent the city's grinding mentality, left Memphis to release their 1993 studio debut, *Comin' Out Hard,* through Houston's Suave House Records. A teenage Tony Draper founded the independent company that he transformed into a regional powerhouse by signing those like Tela, Big Mike, and Jazze Pha.
>
> *Comin' Out Hard* proved influential as a template for Southern artists. Over the course of the decade, the duo refined their conception and sound, punctuated by the single "Space Age Pimpin'" from 1995's *On Top of the World*.

John "J-Dogg" Shaw (promotions, urban A&R, Select-O-Hits Distribution): ["Mr. Big"] was their first big hit beyond Memphis. Now, they had had a hit locally with *Lyrics of a Pimp*, and that was when they were still with Reggie.

Reginald Boyland (owner, OTS Records): I'm flamboyant like that. I had the bad chicks around. All that shit. I had a little money. Benzes. I always be talking that tough shit. That was just my thing. You say "space age pimping" back in the day. That's how 8Ball and them picked it up, though, and they ran with that. I knew that's something that will work for them. Because Memphis got that image, that pimping shit.

John "J-Dogg" Shaw (promotions, urban A&R, Select-O-Hits Distribution): They got a lot of radio play out of that and it was really, really popular locally. But it didn't get distributed beyond a certain Mid-South region; it wasn't big like "Mr. Big"—"Mr. Big" got played on the radio all over the South. It was their first big hit, and it was so simple in one sense and so repetitive, but that was why it worked. It was catchy.

Reginald Boyland (owner, OTS Records): They went to Texas. It wasn't going to work in Memphis. But they took off with what they was doing. I was happy about that, though. Because they legends now.

BY THE EARLY 1990s, Memphis hip-hop largely revolved around the city's thriving mixtape scene, headed by DJ Squeeky and DJ Zirk and DJ Paul and Juicy J. The various camps typically produced bass-heavy tracks that sampled soul and funk songs, and incorporated the hardcore mentality from West Coast acts and Houston's Rap-A-Lot Records. Artists like South Memphis King (SMK), Al Kapone, Tommy Wright III, and Project Pat developed reputations as regional stand-outs.

DJ Paul and Juicy J eventually formed Three 6 (originally Triple 6) Mafia. Over the years, the group cycled through lineups that included Paul's half brother, Lord Infamous; La Chat; Koopsta Knicca; Gangsta Boo; and Crunchy Black. In 1995, the group released its studio debut, *Mystic Stylez.* Laden with occult and gory references, the album laid the groundwork for the group to be trendsetters in the horrorcore and crunk subgenres.

John "J-Dogg" Shaw (promotions, urban A&R, Select-O-Hits Distribution): We later have a studio downtown called the Warehouse with Eli Ball. Eli was doing a lot of production work with Polygram. He had SMK. Back then, he said it stood for Scratch Machine King, but now it stands for South Memphis King. He was recording him, and then Al Kapone was recording there. Lil' Pat was one of the engineers at that studio.

The hottest thing in the underground, you had DJ BK doing mixtapes. You had [DJ] Squeeky doing mixtapes. Paul was making mixtapes. Juicy had his. DJ Sound and Frayser [Boy] were putting out mixtapes. These mixtapes were interesting because they weren't blend tapes. But they were a collection of hits of the day, along with local arts that were unique to those tapes.

Al Kapone (artist, Memphis): If you wanna hear the raw shit, you gotta get the mixtapes.

Carlos "Six July" Broady (producer, Hitmen): I produced on Al Kapone's first record. We were all working on the record—SMK, myself, Lil' Pat. So, we were right there from the beginning of it all, and then Juicy and Paul jumped off with doing what they were doing, and you got DJ Squeeky, DJ Zirk, and DJ DVD, which was Al Kapone's DJ.

Can't forget Gangsta Pat. He produced on Al's first album, too. So, we were all at Warehouse Studios together.

Al Kapone (artist, Memphis): When I was first told that ["Lyrical Drive-By"] became popular and it was influential, was from a DJ and burgeoning producer by the name of DJ Squeeky. He was DJing at this club called Studio G. I remember him calling me one day and [he] was telling me, "Man, you gotta come down here. Whenever I play your song, man, they go crazy."

I'm like, "Nah." I just didn't believe it. I never had nothing like this, so I'm like, "Whatever."

Then one day I went down there, and he played it, and it blew my mind. That was my first time really realizing, *Oh, this song is influencing the Memphis hip-hop style.* I don't wanna take full credit as if I influenced the whole sound, but I am one of the contributors.

John "J-Dogg" Shaw (promotions, urban A&R, Select-O-Hits Distribution): Paul and Juicy would not have an aboveground release until they signed a distribution deal with Select-O-Hits, which I guess occurred with the release of *Mystic Stylez.* But because they had done sixteen volumes of mixtapes prior to that, it's almost as if their debut CD was their seventeenth album.

Carlos "Six July" Broady (producer, Hitmen): We had North Memphis, South Memphis, and different parts that didn't rock with each other. There was a time when DJ Squeeky and Paul and them didn't get along. I'm used to rivals, but that shit was on some otherworld shit.

John "J-Dogg" Shaw (promotions, urban A&R, Select-O-Hits Distribution): It originally all fell into two main camps. Paul and Juicy and their adherents, and Squeeky and his adherents, with Al Kapone being sort of a neutralist, who wouldn't line up with either side, and 8Ball & MJG largely outside that system because they left the city. Criminal Manne was up under Squeek. Zirk was up under Squeek. You can almost line everybody up under one of those camps.

Reginald Boyland (owner, OTS Records): Then Three 6 and them started forming from there. Paul put it together. He was determined. That dude might come in there with a little tape with like a motherfuckin' million songs.

Juicy was quiet. He was a DJ. He wasn't even rapping. But he was cold on the wheels. He cut on 8Ball and them shit. He used to bag up with them. All of them worked together.

John "J-Dogg" Shaw (promotions, urban A&R, Select-O-Hits Distribution): There were fall-outs, disputes, and disagreements. All the sales of these tapes was going to the DJ. So of course there was no reason for an artist to feel loyalty to anybody, because the business model was fatally flawed. The rappers weren't making any money.

From the DJ's standpoint, they were being exposed. And that was in one sense true. Squeeky could be a kingmaker, DJ BK could, Paul and Juicy, they could make you or break you. But at the same time, you can't eat on fame, and at some point the artists began to feel like, *The DJ is making a lot of money and I don't see any of it and my song is on it.*

THE ROOTS OF African American music in Memphis are deeply planted, ranging from soul and gospel to blues and rock and roll. Long-established recording sites like Sun Studio and Stax Records provided fertile influences for the city's generation of hip-hop producers.

Drumma Boy (producer, Memphis, Atlanta): Music came from the influence of my mom. Since I was in her womb, she was putting her stomach up to the speaker playing Earth, Wind & Fire, Michael Jackson, the Temptations. And my dad is in the Memphis Symphony Orchestra. My mama was in the opera, then she was in the choir with the Baptist church. So there's just so many different worlds of music that I'm in.

Sampling was the beginning of hip-hop to me. Before the keyboards and synthesizers, you had the SP-1200s, the MPCs [MIDI production centers]. It was kind of the beginning of not using bands as much but using these little electronic instruments and these fuckin' radio beatboxes. From Memphis, we was always inspired to sample other people.

We come from blues, country, orchestra, bluegrass, funk, rhythm, soul. It's just a collective collage of music that we come from in Memphis.

Al Kapone (artist, Memphis): Certain pockets had scenes. New Orleans had the bounce. Miami had more of the up-tempo, booty-shaking scene. Texas had more of the slower, Screw scene. And Memphis, it all connected with the dance, Gangsta Walk. The beats had to have that feel so we can Gangsta Walk off of it, so it always had that mid-tempo to sometimes slower tempo with the triplets.

One thing I can say about Memphis, the vibe of the beats always stayed the same, but you could hear old-school soulful songs sampled, which made those beats more pimpin', and those are more of what 8Ball & MJG rapped off of. You would take that same drum pattern, put eerie and scary sounds on it, and that would get you that wicked vibe. You'd take the exact same drum pattern and just put chants on it to make people get crunk or get buck. It was always that underlying beat that had that feel, no matter what style of music you put on it, and that beat is what we feel like is where trap originated from.

NO SOUTHERN CITY'S musical footprint was as deep as that of New Orleans. Still, the offerings from other Southern regions initially influenced the early Crescent City hip-hop scene. Gregory D, who started his career as part of the Ninja Crew with Sporty D, became one of the first artists to earn distinction, through 1989's "Buck Jump Time." For the single, Gregory D collaborated with Mannie Fresh, who had learned music production under his father, DJ Sabu, a heralded New Orleans DJ and producer.

"Buck Jump Time" utilized drums and horns in the tradition of the city's famous "second lines," which trailed bands at Mardi Gras, while Gregory D called out the names of the city's various housing projects. The combination propelled the song to become a regional hit, and provided a template for the subgenre of bounce to develop.

Mr. Serv-On (artist, No Limit): Gregory D was one of the pioneers that first got a deal, and I idolized him. The South had all types of things going on, so Luke Skyywalker's music hit right on time. MC Shy D's music hit for the guys that were hustling hard. Now you've got the Geto Boys speaking to the life I live and where I come from. Mr. Scarface, he was my idol. He spoke about death. New Orleans was such a murder capital so many years in a row, it was just blood, it was death, and Scarface brought something I can relate to—losing so many different friends.

> **"DRAG RAP," THE** once forgotten offering from the Showboys, played a large role in early hip-hop music in New Orleans, just like in Memphis.
>
> Popular New Orleans DJs isolated the one-bar drum loop from the song, known as the Triggerman beat. The loop, coupled with pioneering San Francisco DJ Cameron Paul's instrumental "Brown Beats," became a foundational component of bounce, typically punctuated by energetic and repetitive music and call-and-response routines.

DJ Spanish Fly (Memphis): I was giving away a lot of those tapes from the club. I remember guys asking me, "Fly, we got to go to Freaknik. We need some music now." So, I would make sure I do a good volume for their weekend to Atlanta. And they would come back and tell me, "Man, they buy the tapes off us, Fly, when they hear us bumping them."

That's back in the day when they was riding Astro vans, bumping the Alpine system with the doors open in the van, so you can hear all of this shit wherever you at loud and clear. And guys used to come up while they was out of town: "Can we buy that from you?" Because they couldn't get it.

The same thing happened with the New Orleans thing. So yeah, man, that's how those tapes got out. Them motherfuckers started playing that shit. Boom. It's the New Orleans bounce.

> **IN 1991, DJ** Irv sampled the Triggerman beat for MC T. Tucker's "Where Dey At." The song inspired DJ Jimi to record a remix of the

song that included call-and-responses that became bounce standards. Others, like DJ Jubilee, Partners-N-Crime, and Big Freedia,
poured significant contributions into New Orleans's early bounce
scene.

The regional appeal of 1986's "Drag Rap" left Cory Robbins, the
cofounder of the record label that had originally produced the track,
stunned over the popularity that had manifested organically.

Cory Robbins (cofounder, Profile Records): Cliff Hall was the producer
and the older brother of Orville. Orville and Phil [Price] were the
Showboys. Cliff Hall started to tell us they were getting booked in New
Orleans because the beat from "Drag Rap" became a really big beat
there. I don't know who the first one was to use it, but then it was on
every record out of New Orleans. I think hundreds of other records
were made with that beat.

14 OUT HUSTLING

The Bay Area
1983–2006

Long an epicenter of political activism and cultural diversity, the Bay Area came to own hip-hop crossover success during the early 1990s, when artists like MC Hammer and groups like Digital Underground found their videos played regularly on MTV. Like the South, the Bay Area lay outside the large media markets and was marked by a do-it-yourself mindset, developing a flourishing independent scene.

Perhaps no artist was more influential in the area's journey to prominence than Too $hort. Born Todd Shaw, Too $hort relocated to Oakland from Los Angeles and hawked his own music, which soon wafted through the Bay Area streets. Along with his early partner, Freddy B, Too $hort gained early popularity by honoring special requests through custom-made cassettes. He spawned a generation of Bay Area go-getters who stayed true to themselves and sold their music out of the trunks of their cars.

The Bay Area birthed an eclectic and dynamic range of artists. Beyond MC Hammer and the funk-influenced Digital Underground, there was E-40 and his colorful slang, the legend Mac Dre, the impactful collective Hieroglyphics, the duo Luniz, and the birth of the hyphy movement.

The area also served as launchpads for the careers of Tupac Shakur, who linked with Digital Underground early on; and Master P, who later flourished in Louisiana.

Money-B (artist, Digital Underground): A friend of mine in junior high school was actually related to somebody that was getting the first- or second-generation Too $hort tapes, which was really rare. He would bring them to school, and listening to him using the slang that we use and talking about the streets that we're on and the buses that we ride, I can visualize it and see it. And then, every once in a while, you'd be riding on the bus and you'd see a guy with a hat that said Too $HORT and you're like, "Oh shit, that's Too $hort."

Ant Diddley Dog (artist, Bad-N-Fluenz): I remember vividly in early junior high, standing outside in East Oakland in the hood and a big Bronco-looking truck came up with the top off and they had these big, huge speakers. I was like, "What's this noise?"

So, I was exposed to Too $hort right at that moment and when I heard it, not only was I exposed to music in the car like that, loud like that, I was exposed to a rapper coming from Oakland, and then I was also exposed to crazy usage of curse words.

Mac Mall (artist, Bay Area): A lot of hip-hop got passed around from dope dealers. Too $hort tapes and Magic Mike tapes, a lot of those were passed from baller to baller. I used to get Too $hort tapes from a baller in our neighborhood. And that's just how music got passed. If you from somewhere you connected to that spot, and you connected to your hood no matter how big you get.

> **GROWING UP IN** the heart of Oakland, Ant Banks gravitated to musical instruments. He participated in his school's band, playing the saxophone and trumpet. But classical music came to bore Banks. He taught himself how to play Parliament-Funkadelic on his Casio keyboard. The dawning of hip-hop captivated Banks, and he began crafting his own beats.

Ant Banks (producer, Dangerous Crew): Everybody growing up in Oakland has some type of hustler's mentality.

In elementary school, I used to actually go to the corner store, and I would steal a box of Now & Laters. I would go to school, and I would sell it for ten cents a pack. It was a hustle. That was our thing, we was calling it "grinding." My other homie had the Blow Pops. Other homie had Mike and Ikes. So, we was slinging candy.

Once we got to high school, everybody always has some kind of hustle going on to make some money. We actually got into music. Once again, it was a grind. Oakland scene was really, at that time, nobody. We're talking about before the Too $hort era. The only thing you knew about Too $hort was his tapes on the streets.

So of course everybody else was doing the same thing. We was all out there making our own little music. But what we was really doing was rapping the instrumentals on the other side of them 12-inches that was put out—"The Message," and Dr. Jeckyll & Mr. Hyde. It was a whole bunch of little records that had instrumentals on the back of them that we would all rap over and sell our tapes.

STILL A TEENAGER, Too $hort established the blueprint for Bay Area artists when he self-released his debut album, 1983's *Don't Stop Rappin',* on his label, 75 Girls Records and Tapes. Too $hort became one of the first artists to use the word "bitch," which would become a trademark of sorts.

Money-B (artist, Digital Underground): I never thought that Too $hort would make a real record because it was just so original and it was so nasty, and it was so street and dirty that I hadn't heard it on a record like that before. Because remember, this is like 1982, 1983. There was no N.W.A or Ice-T at this time. But he's talking that raw shit. And he's talking about cocaine and pimping and flat-booty bitches and "slap that bitch" and smoking dope.

But then they put out "Shortrapp." And the B-side was "Girl (Cocaine)." That just blew my mind that he was actually on a record. It just kind of put a battery in my pack and I was juiced, probably like every other aspiring rapper in Oakland.

Ant Diddley Dog (artist, Bad-N-Fluenz): East Coast rap didn't have all of that. Run-DMC wasn't cussing. They wasn't doing like $hort was doing. I was in complete and utter shock.

And then I start seeing these posters on telephone poles with Too $hort on 'em and the record label was called 75 Girls and that was our East Oakland rap right there. Hear his music bumping out of the truck, which was the start of an era and then, not only that, he's using every cuss word in the cuss-word arsenal.

East Oakland was where the drug dealing was happening. You heard people talk like that on the basketball court and pickup games. My parents used that language, so it wasn't like I wasn't used to that language. I just never heard it in music like that, which was kind of a reflection of my environment in the inner city. So I think we gravitated toward that because it felt comfortable.

IN 1988, JIVE Records re-released Too $hort's *Born to Mack,* marking his major label debut after he had sold thousands of the album himself. *Born to Mack,* which established Too $hort outside of the Bay Area, included "Freaky Tales," a detailed description of Too $hort's sexual escapades and one of the first explicit hip-hop songs to receive a major release. The album sparked a run of gold and platinum albums for Too $hort.

Jive, hoping to replicate Too $hort's success, later signed Bay Area native Spice 1 and Vallejo's E-40, who had started his own independent label, Sick Wid' It Records.

Barry Weiss (president, Jive Records): Arista was always a really hot company. RCA was not a hot company. When we went from Arista to RCA, it completely opened up the playing field for us, and that's when we went out there and signed Steady B, Schoolly D, Jazzy Jeff & the Fresh Prince, Too $hort, UGK, E-40. We were able to really spread our entrepreneurial wings, and really, really go for it, because it was like shooting fish in a barrel at that point. The competition was nowhere near what it became five years later.

The minute I heard "Freaky Tales" I was like, *I'm fucking sold.* It's almost like Jon Landau said he saw the future of rock and roll: His name was Bruce Springsteen. I felt like I saw the future of rap and his name was Too $hort. And it was nasty, dirty, and everybody at RCA

Records rebelled. There were pressing plants that rebelled. I was like, "Fuck it, go find another pressing plant because this shit's coming out." And we went with it, and it was just explosive, and it did exactly what I thought and hoped that it would'do. It started to break in the South—Louisiana, Mississippi—with heavy 808, heavy bassline. No radio play and a platinum album.

Killer Mike (artist, Dungeon Family): My friend Raheem Beyah, he lived like three doors up from me. We circled around the fucking record listening to the first Too $hort, *Born to Mack*. That was some cold shit. That was shit I had only heard running errands for players and shit, sneaking out of church and sneaking downtown. In the literal sense, I grew up with [hip-hop], not with an artist; with the culture.

AS TOO $HORT developed his national reputation, Ant Banks started recording tapes in the 1980s with his friend, MC Ant. The pair sold hundreds of thousands of their tapes out of the trunk of their car, and rose in popularity throughout the Bay Area.

Ant Banks (producer, Dangerous Crew): We were fourteen, fifteen years old making rap records. We go to Radio Shack, buy a thirty-pack of TDK old-school cassettes. I think it may have been fourteen dollars. We would go out, sell those for five dollars a tape. It was a little independent grind. You're just out hustling trying to get your name out there, trying to get your music out there, and trying to make some money at the same time.

So, lo and behold, Big Trav, one of the homies from the hood, was out hustling in a little major way. We really need[ed] to just go cut some records. So we ended up going to the studio. He paid for the studio session. We went in there and recorded the whole *MC Ant the Great* album [in 1989].

We got some albums pressed. We took the albums to one of the record stores in Oakland. They always would take everybody's records on consignment, and they would pay you at the end of the month what you sold. K-Cloud was another guy who was basically doing the same thing we were doing. K-Cloud would let us come perform with him at Kesha's Inn, and it was a cool little crowd in there damn near every Friday. We kind of start making a little name for ourselves around Oakland with that. After so long, the buzz got so big, KSOL, the main radio station out there, they start playing it. And it just took off.

> **TOO $HORT AND** Ant Banks combined to produce music that came to define the Bay Area. Their collective, the Dangerous Crew, was a mix of talented artists and live musicians steeped in funk. Banks produced, programmed, and mixed. Shorty B, Sean G, and Pee Wee handled an assortment of instruments, while Too $hort rapped with a group that included Dangerous Dame, Spice 1, Rappin' Ron, and Ant Diddley Dog. The Dangerous Crew released a self-titled six-song album in 1988. The group's "Only the Strong Survive" appeared on *Menace II Society*'s soundtrack along with the film's lead single, Spice 1's "Trigga Gots No Heart."

Ant Banks (producer, Dangerous Crew): With all the rappers that I was producing independently from Oakland, I was really more focused on making Oakland look like a little mini-Motown myself, because I used to read the little Berry Gordy books, and all the shit about how he put the whole Motown thing together, and I was like, *Man, we got what it takes here,* with all the independent artists that we had out.

Everybody was on the independent grind back then. [Pooh-Man] didn't blow up to everybody knowing who he was until we did the whole "Fuckin' wit' Dank" thing. But you had [the group] 415. You had MC Ant. It was K-Cloud. It was Kimmie Fresh. Dangerous Dame was another one. Everybody was young, fresh. MC Hammer was out.

Oakland was this little melting pot of a whole lot of talent with no major label behind nobody. It was like, *How can I find a way to bring everybody together? Let's all blow up somehow independently to where we don't need [a label].* We can sell one hundred thousand, two hundred thousand units, and basically our favorite rappers is selling a million records and they broke as hell, and we out here riding around in a Benz and doing our own thing. What the hell do we actually really need the labels for?

I think it got to the point where everybody wanted to be famous, and you couldn't be famous unless you had that label behind you. But being independent we was more or less having money, because we was selling these records. It's like a dope dealer's mentality. Just the hustle, the grind, the being out there trying to find a way to get to the next stop.

Mac Mall (artist, Bay Area): Strictly Business Records was the label of The Mac and Mac Dre. They were independent. [E-40's] Sick Wid' It, independent company. JT the Bigga Figga, Get Low [Recordz]. 75 Girls from Too $hort was an independent company before he signed to Jive. Because we didn't have the actual labels here in the Bay Area, we made the industry.

> **TOO $HORT AND** Ant Banks collaborated on the platinum-selling *Shorty the Pimp,* released in July 1992. The album utilized funk samples in displaying Too $hort's evolution as an artist, and introduced the Dangerous Crew to the masses. "So You Want to Be a Gangster" earned placement on the soundtrack for the movie *Juice.*
>
> Years later, the album's second track, "In the Trunk," was featured in the opening scenes of Marvel's 2018 blockbuster film *Black Panther*.

Ant Banks (producer, Dangerous Crew): Working with Too $hort, he was the only hands-on artist as far as what he wanted in the production of his music. He was very instrumental in how he wanted it to sound. He would say, "I only want this instrument right here playing while I'm rapping. I don't give a shit what y'all do during the chorus, but while I'm rapping, this is all I want to hear." Whether it just be the bass, whether it just be the beat, he never wanted a whole lot of other shit going on while he was rapping.

Ant Diddley Dog (artist, Bad-N-Fluenz): When you hear about '90s music, it ain't no way that you'll be able to leave Ant Banks out at all, because he was a part of developing the sound of Oakland, especially as it relates to what the pioneer was doing at the time. $hort was kind of dabbling in his own beats at first. He still had those deep basslines and those hard 808s, and then when Ant Banks came on the scene with him, he took those sounds to the next level.

Ant Banks (producer, Dangerous Crew): [Dr.] Dre ran the whole L.A. situation at that time I was running the Bay Area situation. L.A., they had more resources, so they were always doing things on a bigger scale than us. All the record companies was right there in Hollywood. We had nothing in the Bay Area. It was more or less a battle for us to try to really compete on their level, because by the time N.W.A hit the scene and did their thing, they already had a deal, where we were still out there independently trying to just get there.

What people don't understand about Oakland is we are a slow-moving little city. You can't really do nothing too fast there but drive. So, regardless what kind of music was out, or however it sound, only thing that matters is what does it sound like in the car?

When we ride, it's always a slower- to mid-tempo type groove. We like the bass to be low. It was just a more mentality where you ain't trying to do nothing too fast, just from people moving slow from being loaded all the time, from being high, just not really on that fast shit. I can't say that nobody is more so responsible for that sound than Too $hort.

IN 1987, SHOCK G, born Gregory Jacobs, formed Digital Underground with Chopmaster J and Kenny K. During a time when the militancy of Public Enemy and the gangster rap popularized by N.W.A battled for hip-hop's consciousness, Digital Underground ushered in an eccentric brand of hip-hop, backed by their love and respect for Parliament-Funkadelic. The group came to feature a rotation of members, including the group Raw Fusion.

Money-B (artist, Digital Underground): Raw Fusion, we were shopping our demo and doing talent shows and just going up to college radio and trying to be heard. So we kind of got a name for ourselves in the Bay Area.

At the same time, around '88, there was this group Digital Underground that had a single called "Underwater Rimes," and we were kind of on the same circuit of local hip-hop shows. They needed a DJ, and word was going around that [Raw Fusion's DJ Fuze] was one of the best DJs in the Bay.

Fuze and Chopmaster J, who was in the group with Shock G, as Digital Underground, they had a mutual friend from Berkeley and it just so happened at the time, Fuze was renting out a room in our apartment, from my mom, which worked out because we were doing so much music together. They wanted Fuze and Fuze was like, "We'll do it. I'll rock with you, but you got to rock with us." And it kind of worked out like that.

AS DIGITAL UNDERGROUND and other local hip-hop artists and groups started making noise, their work became amplified through the innovative format introduced by KMEL, a Bay Area pop radio station. Keith Naftaly became the station's program director in the mid-1980s. He embraced hip-hop culture and rap in order to connect with the area's young and diverse population, and increase the station's ratings. The station bypassed the Top 40 rotation in favor of hip-hop, R&B, reggae, and house selections. It was among the first to play Vanilla Ice's "Ice Ice Baby" and MC Hammer's "U Can't Touch This," while also introducing local talent.

KMEL debuted Summer Jam, a popular annual concert with hip-hop and R&B acts serving as headliners. The format would be replicated in urban areas around the country.

Paris (artist, producer, San Francisco): Keith Naftaly and Hosh Gureli were two of the leading programmers in the nation, and a lot of other stations followed what KMEL did. My first single, which was "Break the Grip of Shame," broke out on that station, and a lot of other stations followed suit. KMEL is always going to have a special place for me, because they were instrumental in breaking me out the gate. Not only me, but a lot of other people. They got on Hammer and Digital. They got on DJ Quik.

"UNDERWATER RIMES" CAME to the attention of Tommy Boy Records, which had experience with innovative hip-hop music groups such as De La Soul. Digital Underground signed with the New York label and released their debut album, *Sex Packets,* in March 1990. "The Humpty Dance" featured Shock G's playful alter ego, Humpty Hump, and vaulted the group into pop success. The album is also noted for the tracks "Doowutchyalike," a party jam, and "Freaks of the Industry," an ode to the group's free-love mindset.

Money-B (artist, Digital Underground): The whole "Freaks of the Industry" experience, if you listened to the song, Shock's verse is much longer, because originally it was just supposed to be him. And then we get in the studio and he, at the last minute, asked me if I wanted to be on it, and I get on the song.

Then the original sample can't be cleared. We have to remake the song a day before we're supposed to leave to go to Europe for this two-month tour. So we were hectic trying to figure out what we're going to do with it. And then re-recording it and me not being confident in it, because it sounded so different from the original version, just because the tempo had sped up and me thinking, *Oh, nobody's going to like it.*

And then the album comes out and that's the song that people began to recognize my voice nationally. Because remember, "Humpty Dance" was a hit. The first time that I experienced celebrity outside of the Bay was because of that song.

DIGITAL UNDERGROUND WAS a forerunner to hip-hop's synchronicity with popular music, and advanced the legacy of George Clinton before Dr. Dre popularized G-funk. The group continued touring for decades with Shock G and Money-B as the two constants, before Gregory Jacobs died in 2021 at the age of fifty-seven.

Money-B (artist, Digital Underground): We didn't have anybody to ask what works, so we just kind of did what we felt and hoped that people liked it. And it just worked out. Maybe because we didn't have any guidelines or anybody to tell us "This is the way that it has to be done," from it just came authenticity of who we were and where we were. Because the Bay Area is very diverse, and you're allowed to be a freethinker and do you, for the most part. I think it kind of came through in the music.

ANDRE HICKS WAS born in Oakland before moving to the Vallejo area and assuming the stage name Mac Dre. In high school, he first gained attention for a cassette tape that featured the single "Too Hard for the Fuckin' Radio."

In the early 1990s, law enforcement began focusing on the Vallejo area. Mac Dre, who was vocal about the police department infringing on the rights of citizens, came under scrutiny by law enforcement officials, who attempted to use his lyrics as evidence against him.

In 1992, Mac Dre was sentenced to five years in federal prison after accepting a plea deal for conspiracy charges over a bank robbery in Fresno, which many argued he had little to do with. He refused to testify against others. While incarcerated, he recorded an entire album, *Back n da Hood,* over the phone.

Released after four years, he eventually moved to Sacramento and founded an independent label, Thizz Entertainment. Mac Dre offered aspiring local rappers a platform. He was influential in the birth of the hyphy movement, the subgenre named by Keak Da Sneak, known for its pounding basslines, frenetic dancing, and "ghost riding" (exiting a moving vehicle and dancing around it).

Mac Mall (artist, Bay Area): He did four years for a crime that he didn't commit. Most people would be very, very sad, very mad, very angry. Dude didn't come home like that. He came home, hit the ground running. He came home with a smile on his face; he wanted to party. He spread that party throughout Vallejo, throughout the whole Bay. Mac Dre made all of us party.

FOLLOWING A CONCERT in Kansas City in November 2004, a vehicle pulled alongside the van that Mac Dre was traveling in. An assailant fired into the car, killing him. His death remains officially unsolved.

Mac Mall (artist, Bay Area): His legacy has grew to [be] iconic. Dude is the King of the Bay and he's dead. He will never be challenged for his crown. No matter who come after. He is synonymous with the Bay Area. He went from being a rapper to a god. Now the biggest rappers in the world—from Drake to Lil Wayne—everybody has either said something or aligned themself with Mac Dre, because that is the way you become loved in the Bay Area.

MUCH OF THE Bay Area's hip-hop was popular inside the region but had not crossed over into the mainstream. Following Mac Dre's death, the hyphy movement did. In 2006, E-40's *My Ghetto Report Card* peaked at number three on the Billboard 200. E-40 and artists like Mistah F.A.B., Too $hort, and Keak Da Sneak helped to popularize the sound and personify the movement.

Mac Mall (artist, Bay Area): For me, "the hyphy movement" is a label that people put on the way that we act and the things that we do. We was just making music and people called it hyphy. For us, that was just a beat to go with the dances, the drugs, the drink, the cars, the fashion. It wasn't like we said, "Hey, we're gonna chop and screw." We was just doing what we do.

To me, it was like a gift and curse because in some sense, within that hyphyness and that label, and because cats put a name on it, motherfuckers start trying to run with it. We kind of lost our areas being individual. The sound started to bleed together. From Sacramento to San Jose, everybody is sounding the same. When before, it wasn't like that. That was a bad thing. But it has evolved. Slowly but surely, cats is getting they own swagger back.

15 PULL QUOTE

Beverly Hills
1992

As hip-hop continued gaining in national prominence, the genre constantly navigated pockets of controversy and charges that popular groups—like N.W.A, 2 Live Crew, and the Geto Boys—glorified and promoted misogyny, homophobia, and violence. It seemed like only a matter of time before the renegades of hip-hop music collided with opportunistic politicians and the corporate interests of their recording labels' parent companies.

The tension boiled over in 1992 on the heels of the Los Angeles riots. By then, 2 Live Crew had already challenged obscenity laws and run afoul of Tipper Gore's Parents Music Resource Center. Her husband, Al Gore, was the running mate of the Democratic presidential nominee, Bill Clinton, in the 1992 election. Seeking to connect with conservative voters, Clinton, who had served as the governor of Arkansas, repudiated an out-of-context quote from a frustrated Sister Souljah, a Public Enemy–affiliated political activist who had told *The Washington Post,* "If Black people kill Black people every day, why not have a week and kill white people?" (Clinton's criticism entered political lore; whenever a politician attempted to grandstand in showing that they could stand up to extremist members of their own party, it became known as a "Sister Souljah moment.") The critique of Sister Souljah was bipartisan, as Republicans such as Dan Quayle, the Republican vice president, piled on as well.

Meanwhile, "Cop Killer," a song released by Ice-T's heavy metal band, Body Count, gained the ire of police groups that summer. The ensuing controversy included a call for consumers to boycott Warner Bros. Records and its parent company, Time Warner Inc. Families of slain officers protested outside a July 1992 annual shareholders' meeting at the Regent Beverly Wilshire Hotel, adding to the pressure faced by executives like Gerald Levin, Mo Ostin, and Lenny Waronker.

Inside the hotel, the National Rifle Association's representative, Charlton Heston, a well-known actor who had played Moses in 1956's *The Ten Commandments,* addressed those gathered. Heston recited some lyrics from "Cop Killer" and another song from Body Count's self-titled debut album, "KKK Bitch," which name-checked Tipper Gore.

All along, Ice-T had cited "Cop Killer" as a work of fiction and a protest against police brutality, a plague that has continued mostly unabated in subsequent decades. And even though "Cop Killer" was not a hip-hop song, the hip-hop genre received constant criticism.

Ice-T decided to remove the song from the album of his own volition, citing the death threats received by record company employees. Warner Bros. Records and other major labels started screening lyrics and album artwork—particularly of hip-hop music releases—in order to head off potential controversy. Warner Bros. Records declined to distribute Kool G Rap and DJ Polo's *Live and Let Die* through Cold Chillin' Records. It also prevented the release of Paris's *Sleeping with the Enemy* by Tommy Boy Records. Paris, an artist and producer heavily influenced by Public Enemy, had included tracks like "Bush Killa," about President George H. W. Bush, and a police-killing scenario titled "Coffee, Donuts & Death." An employee of Tommy Boy Records had leaked the album's provocative artwork, which depicted a would-be assassin lurking behind a tree with a gun while Bush waved to a crowd.

Ice-T left Sire/Warner Bros. Records after executives sought changes to the cover of 1993's *Home Invasion*. Time Warner released Paris from his contract. He eventually started his own lucrative imprint, Scarface Records, releasing his next three albums on the label.

Ice-T (artist, Body Count): That whole "Cop Killer" shit was a bunch of bullshit. It was just meant to be a record. It wasn't meant to be some political platform to say anything.

Jorge Hinojosa (manager, Ice-T): I was invited to the Warner Bros. shareholders' meeting by Jenette Kahn, who was the editor-in-chief of DC Comics, a division of Warner Bros. We had a deal with her to do a comic book called *Players*. She told me that the board was concerned about the meeting, and didn't know what was going to happen.

Before the meeting, where they announced a two-for-one stock split and a fantastic quarter, I went to the bathroom. As I'm washing my hands, Charlton Heston walks in the restroom trailed by two NRA guys peppering him with what he needs to say when he speaks. He spins arounds and snarls at these guys, "I know what to say!"

Ten minutes later in the ballroom, Heston stands up and interrupts [Time Warner CEO] Gerald Levin's presentation and demands to speak. Levin acquiesced, a huge mistake. Heston gave his dramatic speech that basically lambasted Warner Bros. for putting out "filth."

Monica Lynch (president, Tommy Boy Records): There's nothing like hearing Charlton Heston get up in the back of the Beverly Wilshire and start reciting "KKK Bitch." That was one for the ages.

There was a huge presence of law enforcement and friends of the law enforcement at the shareholders' meeting. This is happening at a time when Gerald Levin was actually making a lot of efforts within the Time Warner ranks to be engaged and create interest. He's doing these in-house panel discussions about what hip-hop was for the higher-ups. The whole idea was to sort of educate the ranks of Time Warner executive elites about the emerging hip-hop culture.

Jorge Hinojosa (manager, Ice-T): Levin and the board stayed tight-lipped until the end, at which point they said they supported the First Amendment. That First Amendment defense sucked. They should've said that the lyrics talked about a fictional character and didn't endorse killing cops, no matter how you read it.

Levin was a nice guy, but a pussy. He was a newly installed CEO who had no backbone when he needed it most. Shortly thereafter he merged Warner Bros. with AOL and we know how that turned out. Amongst other costly missteps, he also screwed up the music division, which led to Interscope leaving and going to Universal.

Paris (artist, producer, San Francisco): There was a lot of false starts with [my debut album] *The Devil Made Me Do It*. Any artist's debut project is something that has been honed over time. I would listen to things and record and go back and re-record, do new things and throw things out. By the time *The Devil Made Me Do It* was done, it was the cohesive project that I originally envisioned because I did all of the production myself.

Monica Lynch (president, Tommy Boy Records): We get the artwork for his [*Sleeping with the Enemy*] album cover, and I was like, "Oh boy. This is going to be a challenge."

It was the artwork of pointing a gun at the White House. We hadn't made a decision at this point about how to proceed. We knew, whatever it was, it was probably going to be difficult. But the artwork was stolen by this young woman who was my assistant at the time. After she retired, she told me, "Oh yeah, my husband's a cop. My brother's a cop. My cousin's a cop. My uncle's a cop." Everyone in her family was Irish Catholic, a New York cop family. It was like *Blue Bloods* or something.

She took the artwork and leaked it to someone in her family who then in turn leaked it to, I think it was the New York State Sheriffs' Association in Albany. We started hearing the news reports and I'm like, *What the fuck? How did this happen?*

When she didn't show up for work, then I was like, *I think I know what happened here.* But it was a fucking mess. That's your pull quote. It was a fucking mess.

Paris (artist, producer, San Francisco): It was a blessing in disguise, honestly. It forced me to realize the importance of being independent, and the importance of control. It was trial by fire, basically. I delivered the project, then I delivered the artwork. There was a lot of publicity that had been put in place when the outcry from Ice-T's "Cop Killer" boiled over and forced everybody who had anything incendiary to say to be released from their respective contracts.

It wasn't just me. It was me, it was Ice-T, it was Kool G Rap. We had a big roundtable meeting with [Warner Bros. executives] Lenny Waronker and Mo Ostin, and we all got let go on the same day. I ended up threatening suit, and they ended up paying me out one hundred grand and giving me control of my masters, which in turn allowed me to start Scarface Records.

By then, the industry buzz was that this album was red-hot. My preorders were half a million. I knew it was going to be a money-making enterprise out the gate, and everybody wanted a piece of it. I controlled the masters and I was able to do what I wanted to do, and I started to realize that fifty cents an album is a lot less than six dollars and fifty cents an album, which is what labels were making for the three formats that were available, which were vinyl, cassettes, and CDs.

So I said, "Let me go ahead and put this out on my own." And I did a distribution deal and put the record out and it was gangbusters out the gate.

Ice-T (artist, Body Count): Years later now, people are still being abused by police and shot by police, so this record was valid. The key words to "Cop Killer" is: "Cop Killer, better you than me / Cop Killer, fuck police brutality."

That's what the song was about. Now, I'll go out and say it: Killing a cop isn't the answer to police brutality, but in art, you're just saying how angry you are about it, that if you want to kill me, I feel like I want to kill you. Now, that's still artistic license. All the politics that go along with these records, you can take it or leave it.

Jorge Hinojosa (manager, Ice-T): The groups that hated "Cop Killer" focused most of their attention on Warner Bros. I think they realized that Ice probably had a right to hate cops and knew there was little to no recourse they had against him, so they went after Warner Bros. to punish them.

Ice-T (artist, Body Count): The first inroad is just acknowledging the situation. I think with the input of technology with the camera phones and visual media, people are actually for the first time, really in the last three to five years, seeing it firsthand. I can't even watch it anymore.

So, I think now people realize cops do dirty shit. So do people. But cops are supposed to be holier-than-thou and they aren't—not all of them. That's all we're trying to say.

Jorge Hinojosa (manager, Ice-T): Ultimately, it hurt Ice's recording career. When his next album came out, retailers were skittish about giving it proper placement on endcaps, and that impacted sales. Fast-forward to today and Body Count and Ice were nominated for a Grammy Award, so he still has something that people want to hear. That's a victory.

16 A HIGHER LEVEL OF EXECUTION

Los Angeles
1992–1993

Some moments in music history are measured by comparing what arrived before and after. Breakbeats served as the foundation for much of hip-hop production prior to Dr. Dre's release of *The Chronic* in December 1992. Most of *The Chronic*'s tracks featured Parliament-Funkadelic samples. The slowed, thickly compressed basslines, created with the Moog synthesizer, became the basis of G-funk, a hip-hop subgenre whose sound was simultaneously lackadaisical and ominous.

The album featured an ensemble cast that included Dr. Dre's star-powered apprentice, Snoop Doggy Dogg (later Snoop Dogg), along with the likes of Nate Dogg, Daz Dillinger, Warren G, Kurupt, the Lady of Rage, and RBX. Named after a potent weed strain, the album landed like a haymaker, providing a soundtrack for West Coast hip-hop and influencing generations of producers. "Nuthin' but a 'G' Thang" became a perennial summer anthem. Dr. Dre and Snoop went scorched-earth against N.W.A and other adversaries in "Fuck wit Dre Day (and Everybody's Celebratin')." "Let Me Ride" offered an ideal soundtrack for driving slow with the windows down as the California sun set.

The Chronic was released by Death Row Records, a label that became synonymous with gangster rap, and which never departed from its street roots while dominating the charts in the early to mid-1990s. Dr. Dre, the D.O.C., Dick Griffey (a longtime record producer and music promoter), and Marion "Suge" Knight served as the label's founders.

Before becoming a record executive, Knight, a former college foot-
ball player, was a full-time bodyguard who worked his connections to
start an artist management company. A menacing and polarizing figure,
Knight engineered the escapes of Dr. Dre, the D.O.C., and Michel'le
from their contractual obligations to Ruthless Records following the
fracture of N.W.A.

Knight launched Future Shock Records, eventually named Death
Row, following a cash infusion from Michael "Harry-O" Harris, a businessman who at the time was in the beginning stages of a lengthy
imprisonment for attempted murder and his role as a major cocaine
distributor. In 2021, President Donald Trump pardoned Harris after he
had served more than thirty years in a California jail.

The D.O.C. (cofounder, Death Row): I met Suge through one of the musicians at the studio and we just started hanging out. We went everywhere. We got in all kinds of trouble, and he was a good guy. It just
went bad later on.

Chris "The Glove" Taylor (DJ, producer): When Death Row started, Dre
and D.O.C. took their money from a publishing deal, got a million
bucks, and started this record company. And then D.O.C. had a bodyguard named Suge Knight who said, "I know Dick Griffey. He's down,
blah blah blah." And so, it was all good, right? We'll roll with this dude
because we needed protection because we was leaving Ruthless, which
was no easy thing to do.

The D.O.C. (cofounder, Death Row): Suge knew a guy that could put us in
the game, and he did. . . . It just started coming together once Snoop
came. Once we had that nucleus, we really had everything.

Colin Wolfe (musician, songwriter): Warren G brought [Snoop Dogg]
down to the studio. Dre had him just freestyle on some random beat,
and he came out and killed it.

SNOOP DOGGY DOGG and Warren G, Dr. Dre's stepbrother, evolved
into West Coast hip-hop titans. Born Calvin Broadus in Long Beach,

> California, Snoop earned his nickname from his likeness to the *Peanuts* comic-strip character. He made his first demo tape with Sir Jinx at around the age of fifteen and, along with Warren G, Nate Dogg, and Lil' ½ Dead, formed the group 213.

Sir Jinx (producer): [Snoop Dogg] and Warren used to catch the bus all the way down from Long Beach to where Dre used to live with me and my mom. I had the equipment. And so we ended up doing demos—me, Warren, and Snoop.

I've got a deep connection with Long Beach, with Kelvin Anderson—that's the dude that ran VIP [Records]. Kelvin was one of the first people to help me get into the music industry. Kelvin bought me my second drum machine, paid twenty-three hundred dollars. He made a little studio, we're working, and one of the dudes there, DJ Slice, he started working on it and I started teaching him how to work on it.

Now, Warren ends up coming up there, because this is the only area that has this drum machine, and starts working with DJ Slice. And then one guy comes and he's looking over the shoulder, and he's sampling "Computer Love." That guy turned into DJ Quik. This one drum machine gave birth to a whole bunch of people.

> **WHILE THE OFFERINGS** of Death Row Records came to dominate the charts, other artists and groups also made lasting imprints on West Coast hip-hop throughout the 1990s. They include Compton's DJ Quik and MC Eiht and South Gate's Cypress Hill.
>
> Although often rivals, DJ Quik and MC Eiht both offered vivid portrayals of life in Compton. DJ Quik served as a landmark G-funk artist and producer, crafting distinctly West Coast sounds.

Rodney-O (artist, Compton): The impact that [DJ Quik] had, it was just so musical, way beyond rap.

Murs (artist, Los Angeles): We keep Quik in the same regard as Rakim. As a producer, he sounded very West Coast. "Born & Raised in Compton" and definitely "Quik Is the Name" was definitely West Coast records. So we have the funk, [but] *Straight Outta Compton*, it's not super funky, and to me that's the West Coast sound.

Zaytoven (producer, San Francisco, Atlanta): MC Eiht and DJ Quik, I was raised off of they music, and their music have more of a influence on my music than any other producers or any other rappers. This is where I got all my music from.

CYPRESS HILL CONSISTED of Sen Dog, DJ Muggs, and B-Real. The group released their self-titled debut album in 1991 through Ruffhouse Records. Cypress Hill introduced a new brand of West Coast hip-hop, merging English and Spanish lyrics, connecting Compton and East Los Angeles via their craft, and showcasing an unabashed embrace of marijuana long before states ever thought of legalizing cannabis. The album's double A-side single "The Phuncky Feel One"/"How I Could Just Kill a Man" became a nationwide hit.

Chris Schwartz (cofounder, Ruffhouse): It was West Coast subject matter and vernacular, but the beats were East Coast. Back then, you could hear a West Coast record and East Coast record and know the difference immediately. But that's what made it really cool.

You really had two elements. You had B-Real and Sen Dog, who had like this whole cornucopia of different voices. It was really weird, because a lot of people thought there was like five or six guys rapping in Cypress Hill when their first album came out. But then you had Muggs, who had this really amazing ability to find these great hooks to give it these really cool, very funky loops.

And then, the production. To me, that's what made it unique. It was completely different than what anybody else was doing.

SNOOP DOGGY DOGG exploded out of the gates with his debut feature for the Dr. Dre title track of the 1992 film *Deep Cover*. The song marked Dr. Dre's solo debut following his departure from N.W.A. Just as important, it introduced Snoop as his protégé and partner. Originally, Snoop Dogg was slated to come up through Ruthless and the group Above the Law.

Cold 187um (artist, producer, Above the Law): [Meeting Snoop] was through Warren G. He used to always talk about his homie. So, he brought him through, and he was an incredible artist. I was like, "Man, I'd love to work with you."

So, Snoop vibed out with the whole original G-funk family, and we started that. Because Warren used to live with me. I met Nate Dogg and Snoop Dogg, and at the time they were trying to develop [their group] 213 and I was going to help them. But they wanted to develop Snoop first.

I had worked with him for maybe a month, and he was coming through at the time when the labels were breaking apart. Dre was going to form Death Row, and Eazy wanted to keep Ruthless. So, when Dre ended up leaving totally, he's like, "I hear you're developing this kid, Snoop. I want to sign him."

I'm like, "Yeah, man, he's incredible." I just gave him my blessings and the rest is history. But Warren is the guy that plugged everything in.

Kokane (artist, producer): Above the Law and Kokane first met Nate Dogg through Warren G, and we met Snoop through Warren G as well. Because actually, Above the Law was going to put out Nate Dogg and Snoop, and that's facts. So a lot of the influence, coming from where we came from, really had an impact on the game, indirectly and directly.

Cold 187um (artist, producer, Above the Law): Suge wanted me and Dre to be like the [production team of] Jimmy Jam and Terry Lewis of hip-hop. That was his dream. Which was fine. Me and Dre thick as thieves, so I had no problem with it except for one thing: my loyalty to Eazy-E—and I was only two years into my contract at that time, so I couldn't leave Ruthless.

It was a great idea. Because creatively, I worked with all of them all the time. So, for me, it was like splitting hairs.

Kokane (artist, producer): Suge, at one time, became my manager. He was there when my twin boys was born, too. I've never had no problem with Suge.

Above the Law and Kokane actually was going to be the first that was going to leave because it was discrepancies at Ruthless Records, and Eazy-E wanted to make sure Above the Law and Kokane was cool. Because he was just getting wind that Dre, no matter what, was going to leave. So we backed out of the deal and Snoop, they the ones that took our place for the original Death Row thing.

Next thing, we look up, people are dissing us. And I'm like, "Man, we didn't say one thing about y'all." A lot of real shit people don't know behind closed doors was going on. But we stuck with Eazy-E. That was our homeboy, and none of this would be possible if Eazy-E didn't put up his hustle money.

Of course you can't leave Dr. Dre out, because he orchestrated something that was incredible. But Eazy do not get the credit he deserve. So we felt like, "Nah, man, we're going to ride this shit out with Eazy." But unfortunately, life had a different plan.

Chris "The Glove" Taylor (DJ, producer): We get with Suge, and next thing I know, Suge's the owner. And then he ran out of money, so this investor, Harry-O, he puts up all this money and we get off the ground and he starts getting into all kinds of dope shit.

I was the first one to sign on Death Row.

IN 1990, JIMMY Iovine, a veteran music producer, and Ted Field, an heir to the Marshall Field estate, founded Interscope Records. The pair became enamored with Dr. Dre's production after listening to *The Chronic*. They negotiated a deal to finance and distribute Death Row Records, which required a leap of faith due to Dr. Dre's contractual issues following his separation from Ruthless Records.

The Chronic established Dr. Dre outside of N.W.A's hemisphere, solidified Snoop Doggy Dogg as a full-fledged star (even though he had yet to drop his own album), lured kids from the suburbs to hip-hop in droves, and yanked attention from New York, the birthplace of the art. The D.O.C. was featured as a writer on most of the album's hits and served as a mentor to Snoop. "Let Me Ride" captured a Grammy for Best Rap Solo Performance, and the album rose to number three on the Billboard 200, and spent more than half a year in the top ten.

Colin Wolfe (musician, songwriter): I think [D.O.C.] was the first one that said Dre should do [an album]. I know Ice Cube left at that time, so I know that definitely had an impact on the lyrics. But then D.O.C. stepped up as he always has, writing lyrics.

G-funk is heavily influenced by Parliament-Funkadelic, and that's really all it comes down to. We always like to do things that just sounded out there and just kind of crazy. So that's exactly what we were going for—the Moog, 808 drums, and then live musicianship on top of that.

Fabian "Fade" Duvernay (rap promotion, Interscope): When I started at Interscope, we hadn't completed the Death Row deal yet, but I started a week before it closed. They just wanted to make sure they had somebody in-house that could deal with that shit.

Dre was supposed to deliver *The Chronic*. Dre delivered that *Chronic* about nine, ten, maybe twelve months after that thing was due. You can't rush Dr. Dre. So, meanwhile, I put out my Tupac album [his debut, *2Pacalypse Now*, in November 1991]. Pissed them off. That was my first conflict with them. I put that fucking record on the schedule before we came with the *Chronic* album, and a little bit of shit hit the fan right there, but the only reason it came out [first] was Dre hadn't delivered his.

Colin Wolfe (musician, songwriter): We had to record that record ["Nuthin' but a 'G' Thang"] three different times. I think the first time the tape melted by being left in the car. It had to have been Dre's [car], because we wouldn't have let anybody else take the tape. The second time, I think the tape got lost somehow. So, we literally had to re-record that song three different times.

Chris "The Glove" Taylor (DJ, producer): When Dre and I finished *The Chronic,* we looked at each other and Dre said, "Have you ever smoked weed?"

And I said, "Hell, no."

I said, "Have you?"

He said, "No."

We didn't tell nobody this shit, right? We said, "Man, we got to smoke a joint before we finish mixing that shit or it won't be authentic, bro."

Snoop and them smoked, but we didn't. We was always in the studio. We was just nerds. But we got together at the homies' house, and me and Dre smoked the fucking joint, and it was like *Wayne's World.* It was funny as fuck. We were laying on the ground looking up at the fucking sky laughing like a motherfucker for no apparent reason at all.

Colin Wolfe (musician, songwriter): We was just doing what we loved, and it just came out the way it did by us putting all our heart into it. We all had fun together. I think that had a lot to do it with it, too.

Zaytoven (producer, San Francisco, Atlanta): *The Chronic,* it was like getting addicted to a drug almost. It's not really the content, but just the sound, the musical sound of it. It made me just want to hear it over and over again.

Fredwreck (producer, Aftermath): It was sonically better than anything that had came before it. Before that, I was really into sampling and making beats, but once I heard that, my whole perspective of how to make music completely changed.

I had cliqued up with people that were into freestyle music. Mantronix had a couple of freestyle records, and I was a fan of Mantronix. And that freestyle is no samples, it's all just keyboards and drums and drum machines. So, when I heard *The Chronic,* I was like, *Oh, you can do live instruments in hip-hop?* He opened the door for that.

So that completely changed how I looked at producing and hip-hop. Musically and sonically, that shit was incredible, and it really made me want to learn more than just making beats. It made me want to learn engineering. It made me want to learn everything in the studio.

Bud'da (producer, Aftermath): Something that Dre told me years ago, he said, "The hardest thing to do is to get an idea from your head to tape." Because we have these elaborate ideas in our head that are amazing. But the hardest thing for a lot of people is to get the ideas out so other people can hear exactly what you're hearing in your head.

Chris "The Glove" Taylor (DJ, producer): We're DJs, right? We're programmers, so all our shit got to be like a party. Like a house party starts off cool, it gets faster, and then it kind of eases out at the end, right? Put on *The Chronic* and play it all the way through at a party. You don't even got to change it. It's like a movie.

Bun B (artist, UGK): It's about not really trying to re-create the sound, but re-create the work ethic, right? Re-create the idea of how far-reaching music can be, and to not take any shortcuts when it came to the presentation of your music. Like if there's a new technological advancement that's being used in pop music, or rock music, or jazz music, or any kind of different art form, then we need to find a way that hip-hop can benefit from that kind of thing and incorporate it into what we're doing. It's just constantly about achieving a higher level of execution. That was definitely something that we still look at a person like Dr. Dre for inspiration for.

Colin Wolfe (musician, songwriter): I was in Atlanta at a stoplight, waiting to cross the street. Probably three out of five cars that was making the turn was bumping the *Chronic* album, and that's when I noticed the impact of it. I was like, *Damn, that shit is blowing up.*

Neal H. Pogue (engineer, producer): *The Chronic* had came out and it made a huge impact on us, because during that time, New York was first, then L.A., and then it was the South, but the South didn't get that much respect. When we heard *The Chronic*, we knew that we had to come harder, and so [Outkast's *Southernplayalisticadillacmuzik*] came out of hearing that *Chronic* album and knowing, *Okay, now we have to compete. I have to go hard.* That album really pushed us to whole new heights.

Murs (artist, Los Angeles): As a kid in L.A. that was smoking weed before that, it was dope because I was in love with Snoop Dogg from the

Deep Cover soundtrack. I was a huge N.W.A fan and hearing Kurupt for the first time, and then documenting the vibe and the feeling on the street, it was amazing. It was very, very, very in tune with the city. Whether it's Dre, Daz [Dillinger], or Warren G, whoever's supposed to get the credit, all three of them created a sound for the West Coast finally. We had a sound and that felt super good.

Paris (artist, producer, San Francisco): The G-funk era kind of ushered in the polar opposite of that [Public Enemy urgency], where everything is laid-back and cool and breezy and causes the listener to stand down from red alert. I think we always need to be on red alert, given the social conditions of things, especially now. Hip-hop is definitely an influential art form. It, to me, molds the culture in many ways that educators and parents seem to be incapable of when it comes to reaching young people. I always want to infuse some type of a message that's good for us in some type of way in my content.

Fabian "Fade" Duvernay (rap promotion, Interscope): There were no records getting mainstream radio play as far as gangster rap records out of California, across the nation. I credit [promotion director] Mark Benesch and [head of urban music] Step Johnson for making that happen. They go hard at radio. Jimmy Iovine throws money around like it's a softball. We spent like crazy on the first *Chronic* album.

" 'G' Thang" set a lot of trends, because it's the first record to receive national airplay. I think we sold eight million records. We broke with Black kids, but the other seven and a half million, that's white kids. So you can't really just say that this is niche, urban, ghetto, whatever. That was kind of the first record, I think, that truly mainstreamed rap music and was history-setting in that respect.

FOR GENERATIONS, THE music industry utilized the Billboard charts to measure the popularity and profitability of genres, groups, and artists. The system relied on surveying retailers, which left it ripe for abuse by record companies looking to grease their rankings through manipulation. Hip-hop music remained on the fringes of the Billboard charts until the introduction of Nielsen SoundScan in 1991, which

> counted sales through scanners and computers. SoundScan's imple-
> mentation proved hip-hop music's popularity. N.W.A's second album,
> *Efil4zaggin* (a.k.a. *Niggaz4Life*) debuted at number one in 1991, and
> *The Chronic* climbed the Billboard charts shortly after.

Cheo Hodari Coker (journalist): Once the record companies in the mid-
'80s, early '90s really began to understand that this hip-hop thing was
real, they began to give it real distribution. SoundScan, to a certain
extent, changed everything.

If you want to get deep into the Ponzi scheme that was the music
industry, there are all these different ways to manipulate the sales
charts in terms of how many records were shipped, what record stores
were reporting. In a weird way, the parallel is the electoral college and
precincts and redlining. All that kind of shit that's happening politically, in terms of who gets to vote, the labels used to do all the time
with certain record stores. You could say that Donna Summer went
platinum because you shipped a million records. But did a million
records actually sell? That's between you, the owner of the store, and
the Gambinos.

But now, once SoundScan hit and there was an independent electronic process that could verify what actually sold, what it revealed
is that basically America loved entertainers with hats, either wearing cowboy hats or wearing baseball caps to the side, because all of a
sudden hip-hop and country music became real forces. This kind of
Top 40 sheen that has always been able to keep all the regions in their
place was thrown out the window, because you began to understand
that there was a huge audience for hardcore hip-hop that had nothing
to do with the radio.

Now, there was a bunch of suburban kids that couldn't necessarily
scare their parents with rock and roll—but then once you actually
started playing records with niggas calling themselves niggas, and
everybody freaks out. So outside of the audience that it was meant for,
it leads to these huge record sales. And while everybody else is waking
up, all of a sudden, the East Coast is in this place where, "Okay, how
do we compete with this?"

The first thing that happens, [MC] Hammer blows up. And then,

Vanilla Ice from Florida with his thing blows up. Meanwhile, every-one's kicking themselves because "Under Pressure" was one of those records that was just too obvious to sample. Like, "Who would sample that?" And then somebody does, and everyone's pissed off for three reasons: First, "Fuck, why didn't I sample that?" Because that's a perfect record to sample. Two, this white boy, he's doing his thing. So it's one of those records that when you first heard it, you liked it. But then it was like, "What the fuck? It's a novelty. It's cool. It's not supposed to be this." And then he's selling fourteen million records and getting all this respect, and people are like, "Oh my God. Get the fuck out of here."

And then once white kids discovered N.W.A, it was as if they basi-cally graduated from marijuana to heroin. All of a sudden it was like, "Whoa, we want the real shit." And then the genius of what Dre and all those guys figured out is, if we could basically take the spirit of a hardcore record, but remove the profanity, so that you still get that vibe but there's no cursing, that's how you get "One, two, three, and to the four, Snoop Doggy Dogg. . . ."

And *The Chronic* drops and *The Chronic* was the record that just changed everything, because you had radio edits and that was no lon-ger seen as a sellout, because the record itself was so goddamn hard, it played everywhere.

Fabian "Fade" Duvernay (rap promotion, Interscope): I don't know how well Dre treats his artists. I used to see him in the studio all the time putting his name on Sam Sneed's beats and Emanuel Dean's beats and fuckin' L. T. Hutton's beats where I'm in the studio, hearing L.T. make the whole fucking record and then reading the *Chronic* credits and seeing it produced by Dr. Dre. So it depends on who you talk to. I'm sure if you talk to Emanuel, L.T., Sam Sneed, and a few of the dudes that were in the studio, they might argue that.

WHILE DR. DRE'S *The Chronic* popularized G-funk, the sound likely originated through the production and work of Above the Law, the Ruthless Records group that hailed from Pomona, an Inland Empire suburb of Los Angeles. The group and its affiliates included Cold 187um, KMG the Illustrator, Go Mack, DJ Total K-Oss, and Kokane.

Cold 187um, also known as Big Hutch, is the son of Richard Hutch, a writer for Motown Records, and the nephew of R&B singer Willie Hutch. Kokane's parents are Motown composer Jerry B. Long Sr. and singer Debra Long. Such lineage proved influential as they cultivated their own sounds.

Cold 187um (artist, producer, Above the Law): When I was young, my dad and my uncle, they were doing shit like *The Mack* and *Foxy Brown* and all that shit. So, major influence on me as far as actually wanting to be motivated to get up and do music. So as I got older, with me being a musician and a writer, I started getting more into hip-hop as hip-hop evolved.

Kokane (artist, producer): It was the best of both worlds. All kinds of genres of music that we were exposed to, because that's what helped us through those struggles, especially people being born in the ghetto. All we had is our music. And growing up in the '70s, where funk music was alive, even old rock and roll, like Led Zeppelin. And at the same time hip-hop, it was like a big pot of gumbo.

Now, I happened to come from a musical background, which my dad was one of the greatest writers, composers at Motown. He worked with everybody from the Temptations, Smokey Robinson. The list is big. So music has always been in my DNA.

I can remember traveling with Moms and Pops—my moms is a singer as well—and they would hit different recording studio sessions. I was always not just fascinated with the music, but also fascinated with the imagery and the technical part. How you put this together and put that together. That was acquired as a young shorty.

So, it just stuck with me. And of course my cousin, he was definitely an inspiration, Cold 187. And we just couldn't help it, man, we got it naturally.

Cold 187um (artist, producer, Above the Law): When me, DJ K-Oss, and KMG developed the idea of Above the Law, we wanted a yin and yang, and I was more of yin and [KMG] was more of a yang. He was the focus, the anchored person as far as the topics were concerned. That's why he was named KMG the Illustrator, because he would break down what I was saying, because I was more like a gun, the AK going off. So that's how me, him, and DJ K-Oss developed Above the Law's theory.

A lot of people tell us it mirrors Public Enemy and Run-DMC because we used to tag-team like Run-DMC used to, but we used to break it down. I was the off-the-hook like a Chuck D, and he was like a Flavor Flav that broke down what Chuck says. But he broke it down in more of a cool-player, cool-cat theory. And then when I show up, I just go off.

That's what we wanted to convey in music, and it worked for us, because our theory in music wasn't ever to be political. It wasn't never to be gangster. It was more to be like, "This is the way we see the world in its entirety."

Signs of a conscious mind, but on a gangster level. Our whole thing with Above the Law, which was always cool, we never wanted to take people to school, we just wanted to school you. We wanted you to have a good time. But we always want to put things in there and say, "Okay, I got to think about that."

Kokane (artist, producer): Hutch would always put me on hooks, which is a blessing because that was an intricate part of how I'm doing hooks today. Because Hutch exposed me on a lot of those incredible records that we all masterpieced together. And Eazy gave me an opportunity to get my first platinum record in 1991, being a co-writer of "Appetite for Destruction." And going back to what Hutch did, that was the starting point.

WHEN COLD 187UM started work on the group's second album, *Black Mafia Life,* he decided to try melding the group's hard lyrics with the melodic Parliament-Funkadelic songs he had grown up on.

Ruthless Records soon began to unravel amid financial disputes and departures from the label, which held up the album. Cold 187um recalled Dr. Dre, who had produced two songs on Above the Law's debut, *Livin' Like Hustlers,* listening to some of the music as he finished

N.W.A's *Efil4zaggin*. Soon after, Dre left Ruthless, began Death Row, and released *The Chronic* less than two months before the debut of *Black Mafia Life*.

Cold 187um (artist, producer, Above the Law): Everything's a theory. A producer is a visionary, right? So, everything is his ideas. It's like, *Okay, I want to fuse jazz, soul, R&B, funk music with hardcore lyrics.* Everything comes with a theory when it comes from a producer's perspective. It comes with you want to fuse different things together that you haven't seen.

So, for me, really it was to be different than what N.W.A was doing, basically, which was more hardcore metal sounding—like big beats, big drums. I wanted to slow it down and put grooves to it, but still keep the same lyrical content that, say, we had on *Like Hustlers*.

The brilliant writers dictated what those melodies were going to be saying with words. No one was fusing it the way we were fusing it at that time.

Kokane (artist, producer): The dopeness got to be in you, and we had well enough years to prepare different styles. Music is very powerful. Music is a vibration. It's a frequency. So those vibrations and frequencies, we were locked into the universe. We didn't try to explain it. We didn't try to figure it out. It was just the universe and where we were locked in, and the times we were locked in, everything clicked.

Cold 187um (artist, producer, Above the Law): When I studied jazz, we would always have to listen to a bunch of stuff before we started playing in the jazz ensemble. But my theory would be like, *Okay, I want to make a record like Parliament-Funkadelic, but I just don't want to loop. I want to actually re-create what the sound of that would be, if we done it if we were Parliament.* So, when we did it, we're actually emulating the way they did it, but in our era, with the same type layers of things that's going on with making the funky record.

I remember when I was at the "Appetite for Destruction" video and Dre was listening to the records that I was doing on *Black Mafia Life*, he was like, "Damn, man, you on some other shit, fusing that funky shit with hardcore hip-hop. What is that?"

"I call it a G-funk, man."

So, by the time they finished *Niggaz4Life,* I was finished with *Black Mafia Life.* I was already fusing this shit. I was trying to take a dark groove and then created our own sound with it, from a Parliament perspective or from a Willie Hutch perspective or a Miles Davis perspective. We fused a lot of different music into that and then we slowed it down, but still keeping the same hardcore hip-hop shit.

Black Mafia Life was just a funky record and transitioning out of locally pimping. That's why it was such a drastic change, because I wanted to come out of just breakbeat shit. Everything was about the break, the breakbeat and you rapping on top of it, and then I would come in and I will put nothing but live music on top of everything.

Kokane (artist, producer): We put the G in funk, and everybody rocked with it. And people around us soaked up our game. They knew who the creators is. Cold 187 constructed everything. He would go in there and do some beats and have some ideas, shoot it to KMG, rest in peace, shoot it to K-Oss, Laylaw, whatever. Or we'd be all in the same room and I'll come up with something and Hutch would build around my vocals.

It was all of us on that G-funk mothership. So, Hutch exposed it to Dre, who exposed it to Warren G and, of course, Nate Dogg. And years later, it's a trip to see the impact that that particular genre of music—which derived from P-Funk and the funk in general—it's a trip to see where that particular genre of music took off.

SNOOP DOGGY DOGG'S debut album, *Doggystyle,* landed in 1993 on the heels of *The Chronic,* cementing the influence of G-funk. Snoop's smooth, seamless delivery paired perfectly with Dr. Dre's sonic leanings. The first single, "Who Am I (What's My Name)?" sampled George Clinton's "Atomic Dog" and rose to number eight on the Billboard Hot 100.

The album topped the Billboard 200 and sold more than 800,000 copies its first week, a record for a first-time artist.

Chris "The Glove" Taylor (DJ, producer): All the time we was working on Dre's album, we would talk about how many record sales Snoop's album would have. Snoop was like, "Shoot, man, Michael Jackson could sell this many, I'm going to sell this many." We would throw out these big-ass numbers, right?

He would ask, "Am I being arrogant or what?"

I was like, "Hell nah, bro. You got to think big."

Whatever the number was, it was a big number, and we did it. He sold the most records of any new artist on one single day—even more than 50 Cent. Three hundred thousand albums in the first day.

> **DIRECTOR JOHN SINGLETON'S** *Poetic Justice* starred Tupac Shakur and Janet Jackson both in the romantic drama and on the soundtrack. The soundtrack also featured the debut of Usher Raymond IV, the notable R&B singer, and Warren G's breakthrough in Mista Grimm's "Indo Smoke."

Paul Stewart (producer, promoter): John Singleton told me, "I need someone to music-supervise my new film, *Poetic Justice,* and run my record label."

So he ended up hiring me. I was in the Death Row studios a lot as the music supervisor. That's where I got to know Snoop real well, and Dre, and all these people. And there was a young guy named Warren [G], and he came up to me and was like, "Yo, cuz, I got my own shit."

I was like, "Okay, cool." So, we went out to my truck, and he put this cassette in, and it was "Indo Smoke." The song started to play, and it was funny because I only heard the first verse into the hook and I was sold. I loved the song so much. I just ejected it, and Warren's looking at me kind of crazy and I'm like, "Oh, it's done. We're putting this on the soundtrack."

The next day, I played it for John. John loved it. I said, "Look, I'd love to do this, but I'm managing these artists, Pharcyde and Coolio."

He's like, "Oh, great. I want to start a management company." So I brought my management clients over and we started a joint management company as well. So Warren was going to be under that banner. That was the plan.

We started managing and we ended up taking a Tupac song ["Definition of a Thug Nigga"] that he had produced to put on the *Poetic Justice* soundtrack, as well as the Mista Grimm song that he had produced.

To be honest, me and John, and I really believe Warren too, were looking at him as a producer who could rap. We weren't really looking at him as an artist. All praises to [Def Jam executive and Violator cofounder] Chris Lighty. When I got promo copies on VHS for the Mista Grimm "Indo Smoke" video, I sent twenty of them out to my A-list industry. Chris Lighty was on it, and he called me back and said, "Hey, who's the guy in the third verse rapping?"

I was like, "Oh, that's Warren G, Dr. Dre's brother, Snoop's DJ."

Def Jam, who had missed out on the whole Death Row thing, that's all they needed to hear. Next thing I know, Russell Simmons is calling me, who I had known, but he never gave me the time of day.

When he called the office, it was really funny. He's got that heavy-ass lisp and I thought it was one of my homeboys playing a joke on me, and I cussed him out twice.

"Paul, this is Russell Simmons."

I was like, "Shut the fuck up."

And it was Russell. That's how the deal went down, and then obviously there was some controversy about the song, if it was a Death Row song or a Def Jam song. The "Regulate" song was recorded very shortly after that. I remember being in the studio and just hearing the song and being like, "Whoa. This is a smash."

More than anything, I remember the drama that quickly ensued because the song got leaked, then there was a whole drama going on who gets it. Obviously, Suge being a big bully was like, "I'm not going to clear Nate [Dogg] unless I get to use it for my shit, too." They kind of had to work together because if they're not going to work together, then nobody gets this hit song, right? And that ain't gonna happen, right?

It ended up being shared by two companies that did not get along at all. Suge had a chip on his shoulder about Def Jam, and Def Jam was scared to death of Suge, just to keep it one hundred. And there I was with my little white ass in the middle like, *What am I supposed to do?*

> **WARREN G'S DEF** Jam signing, despite his West Coast roots, helped revitalize the once powerful label. "Regulate" featured a harmonizing Nate Dogg and sampled from Michael McDonald's "I Keep Forgettin' (Every Time You're Near)." The hit led Warren G's 1994 studio debut album, *Regulate . . . G Funk Era,* which quickly became a G-funk staple.

Cold 187um (artist, producer, Above the Law): It's the vibe of our cities, Southern California itself. It's the sunshine, palm trees, slow riding, beautiful women, the sun is out, the air is cool, the smoke is good, the beach. To me, the way we wanted to do it was definitely the definition of California. *Chronic* took it and put it on a big stage and that's the lesser of two evils. But I think it defined sonically who we were.

When Warren's record came, it was another record that was tapered, locked up, and right in that zone, but it was a pop record. He's from our camp, so it's the same elements. So, when the G-funk–era record took flight, that was a record that took it pop.

Like I said, we always go back to theory because a producer has a theory. The guys who created trap music had a theory. DJ Screw had a theory. Pimp C, rest in peace, had a theory. We used to talk about it all night. Me, KMG, DJ K-Oss go back as writers and producers, we highly influenced groups like UGK. From a Southern perspective, they mirrored what we were doing, to be where they're funky, soul, bluesy—all those elements are G-funk.

> **DEATH ROW HELPED** popularize G-funk, but it maintains a divisive legacy. Suge Knight drove Death Row Records to dominance through a combination of menace, intimidation, and foresight. The label starred for a short time in the 1990s when Dr. Dre, Snoop Dogg, and Tupac Shakur all released multiplatinum albums.
>
> Just as quickly, the label imploded following Shakur's 1996 murder. Death Row Records filed for bankruptcy nearly a decade later. Knight

continued courting controversy. In 2015, he was involved in a hit-and-run incident—over an argument involving the film *Straight Outta Compton*—that killed Terry Carter and injured actor Cle Sloan. In September 2018, Knight was sentenced to twenty-eight years in prison.

Fabian "Fade" Duvernay (rap promotion, Interscope): After the great Tupac success, after great success with the Death Row records, things are well on their way there, but it started getting really gangster. They moved Death Row into 10900 Wilshire, which is where we were [in the Interscope offices], which was cool for all of them. They had a whole lot of security, but it wasn't cool for me. It wasn't cool for Step [Johnson]. They put one door between us and them.

It was hard. . . . Whereas mistakes that I made before, we laugh off, we keep it moving. Now mistakes I make get my ass kicked and/or murdered.

The thing with Interscope, I was really in the streets. I was at the clubs. I was touchable by all these guys. Nobody else in the building was.

It was just all too gangster for me up in there after a while, and my own mistakes almost got me busted up a couple of times. Again, I don't blame none of those guys. Given the opportunity to do it again, I would do everything completely different. I wouldn't insult them no matter how fucking ignorant I think they are. I would also make sure that they knew that I am not managing [West Coast hip-hop group] Tha Alkaholiks. I am devoting myself to Interscope Records, Death Row, Tupac, and all of your artists, Suge Knight.

But of course, some asshole DJ is DJing at a club and he tells Suge Knight, "I need that record, man. Fade's holding out on me. I'm playing all his Alkaholiks shit and he's holding out on me."

Suge walked into my office the next day like, "What the fuck is you doing, nigga? You're all about Tha Alkaholiks now."

I said, "No, dude. I left Tha Alkaholiks when I came over here."

"That's not what the fuck I'm hearing. You and me need to talk, nigga."

That situation led to a confrontation with myself, Suge, and all his homies, where they didn't hurt me by any means whatsoever, but I also won't say that they didn't put their hands on me, and that was kind of the environment there. I knew I couldn't stay there long.

Suge was super cool with me when I left. I did not leave with any hard feelings toward him, nor does he have any hard feelings toward me. It was just some shit that we were going through, but my mistake could have really led to something worse, because somebody from his neighborhood told me, "He's trying to get somebody to get you."

I'm like, "What?"

He's like, "Suge's trying to get somebody to get you. I told him no."

I'm like, "He asked you?"

He's like, "Who else he going to ask? I told him you need to leave Fade the fuck alone and stop bullying these little record niggas and get back in these streets if you want to try and bully somebody."

That came back to me months after it happened. I didn't even know how close I was to catching it.

Greg Mack (music director, KDAY): I will say this, though, that Suge was very good for the rap business. He started making sure a lot of people got their money that they were due. For that, I'll give him credit. For the record execs that were fucking over these kids, Suge stopped that.

17 RAISING THE BAR

New York City
1993–2003

In the early 1990s, as the harmonic G-funk offerings from West Coast artists like Dr. Dre and Snoop Dogg dominated radio stations, Staten Island's Wu-Tang Clan offered a bold and brash debut that revitalized New York hip-hop music. Subsequent breakthroughs from a new generation of artists like Nas, the Notorious B.I.G., and eventually Jay-Z enlivened and emboldened the East Coast, moving the spotlight back to the region that created the genre. The artists benefited from dedicated outlets that championed their music, like *The Source* magazine and *The Stretch Armstrong and Bobbito Show* on Columbia University's WKCR.

The seeds of the Wu-Tang Clan date to the late 1980s when Robert Diggs (RZA) formed the group Force of the Imperial Master with his cousins Gary Grice (GZA/The Genius) and Russell Jones (Ol' Dirty Bastard). The cousins, after a short stint pursuing solo opportunities, expanded the group to include Dennis Coles (Ghostface Killah), Jason Hunter (Inspectah Deck), Lamont Hawkins (U-God), Clifford Smith (Method Man), Elgin Turner (Masta Killa), and Corey Woods (Raekwon), and called themselves the Wu-Tang Clan (Darryl Hill, a.k.a. Cappadonna, joined later).

The group independently released "Protect Ya Neck," a track featuring eight of the members trading razor-sharp bars with no hook over

RZA's gritty production. The single established an industry buzz and came to the attention of Steve Rifkind, who had recently founded Loud Records with Rich Isaacson. In a groundbreaking negotiation, RZA arranged for the group to sign with Loud, but for the members to maintain the ability to pursue individual deals.

RZA produced the group's 1993 influential debut, *Enter the Wu-Tang (36 Chambers)*. The album was marked by its use of sped-up soul samples in a fashion that would be emulated by many, including Kanye West, and soundbites from martial arts movies. Meanwhile, nearly enough rappers to fill a basketball court competed competently and ruggedly bar after bar, yanking listeners into their tumultuous environment and introducing them to a new vocabulary. The Wu-Tang Clan surrounded, cornered, and conquered the music industry. Among the deals that spawned from the group: Method Man signed with Def Jam, Ol' Dirty Bastard joined Elektra, and GZA went to Geffen. Over the years, the group embodied a culture within a culture, pioneering hip-hop entrepreneurial projects—including a fashion line, Wu Wear—and starting several labels of their own.

Cheo Hodari Coker (journalist): Once Snoop dropped his record, it was all radio hits. So the East Coast was like, "Okay, we're doing really interesting records, but how do we break through? How do we ever get to a point where we're leading things?" And then that's when with the emergence of Wu-Tang, with Biggie basically coming together with *Illmatic*, which was such an incredible record that pulled together almost the Avengers of East Coast–based producers. Those records began to start staking a claim, and New York began to have a relevance because it leaned into an attitude and to a sound.

Easy Mo Bee (producer): Melquan [Smith] and Shabazz [Fuller] were the ones that first brought Genius [GZA] to my house [to produce GZA's 1991 studio debut album, *Words from the Genius*]. Melquan approached me with Shabazz and he was like, "I see you just did the [Big Daddy] Kane stuff. I want you to do some work with my artist. This is just one of them. There's nine of them, and they got an idea where they're going to fuse the hip-hop with the martial arts." This is 1990. It's a little too early to be talking snazzy concepts like that. So I wasn't really getting it. And he was serious about it.

And then when I met Genius, RZA used to come to the house too. Every time they came around, they would bring somebody different. They had this young brother, Shallah, talking about Raekwon. Next time they brought a dude around, he called himself Ason Unique. He was the Ol' Dirty Bastard. And then Melquan kept telling me, "See, I told you, G. Yo, they ill. And there's nine of them."

Matty C (journalist, A&R): The reason I knew about the whole Wu-Tang was Schott "Free" [Jacobs]. He's from Staten Island and knew RZA, and was the one who first told me about Wu-Tang, before they had really even formed the group. And so, one by one, a couple of them would come up to *The Source,* kick it with me, play some music.

It was like it was a different approach with Wu-Tang. They had some money—Ghost[face] Killah has some money, [RZA's business partner] Divine had some money—and they pressed up a 12-inch. Wu-Tang was unsigned, but we just helped them mail it out and featured it where we featured four singles a month that were usually major labels' singles. And so that was a major look for them.

Fabian "Fade" Duvernay (former executive, Loud Records): My street guy in Lansing, Michigan, he's the one who discovered Wu-Tang, Jason Staten. Jason Staten did a radio show in Detroit. I was on the phone with Jason one day and Jason was like, "Dude, I'm rocking the flip side of this fucking 12-inch out of New York. I'm playing this shit called 'Protect Ya Neck' and it's crazy. Niggas is requesting it left and right."

I'm like, "Really?"

He's like, "Yeah, dude. This 'Protect Ya Neck' is hot."

He sends it to me, and he sends it to my A&R guy, Trevor Williams, at Loud. I had just left Loud. I was just starting at Interscope.

Wu-Tang maybe had three songs I liked. That's about it. But in that same breath, I'm an L.A. gangster rap–minded kind of dude. I wasn't digging a lot of the shit that they were doing out there, but what they was doing was hot. Jason knew it. He's getting requests. Steve [Rifkind] finally takes the meeting and he signs the Wu-Tang Clan.

Steve Rifkind (founder, Loud Records): RZA didn't have an answering machine. So, on my thirty-first birthday, he just showed up at the RCA Building.

It was like a closet and all nine guys were in there. I had E-Swift from Tha Alkaholiks behind me. We're all standing up and the office is as big as a mosh pit. A mosh pit might even be bigger.

We had vinyl then in those days. So it was on a ten, the sound. We're in this two-by-two office, where nobody can move. Everybody's just bobbin' their head and this guy opens up the door and says, "That's that shit." And when we look, he stormed out and I never saw him again. Up until this past weekend, I really thought RZA set me up. Like he had somebody come in [and] say that, because the office was so small.

There was something in my gut, like that room was magical. I always felt the group would be bigger than solo artists. Mick Jagger had a solo record. [The] Rolling Stones always sold more records. I think the only time it didn't work was with Michael Jackson.

Matty C (journalist, A&R): To be honest, when [RZA] told me he wanted to sign to Steve Rifkind, I was like, "Are you crazy?" He was [previously] promoting Tone Lōc, Young MC. I was like, "Why are you going to go with this guy?"

Then he explained that part of it to me and I understood because I had actually turned Dante Ross on to Ol' Dirty already, and he wanted to sign him [to Elektra Records]. Then I knew Method Man had interest from Def Jam. When RZA explained that, it totally made sense. RZA had these visions, in a lot of ways, that were incredible, looking back.

Easy Mo Bee (producer): You got these artists from the same group with solo deals on different labels and the songs end up being on the charts. They actually end up competing with each other.

Steve Rifkind (founder, Loud Records): They were rebels. I mean, all hip-hop artists [are], but it was just nine guys and the energy, it's just hard, energized, raw music that's not going to go away.

Matty C (journalist, A&R): It was just really cool that it got its legs like that on its own from an independent angle. It was one of the first rap groups that was giving fans this impression that they just busted in the door, put their own shit out instead of signed to label, and molded and shaped into what they became.

DJ Nu-Mark (Jurassic 5): I got the album, and I was like, *This is some of the craziest shit ever.* And I started digesting more of the lyrics, and I was like, *What the fuck, nine of these dudes are spittin' like this? This squad is fuckin' deep.*

You don't hear this many dudes spittin' back-to-back. There's always one dude that's lackluster, and it was like everybody was picking up the baton and just running with it, and I was like, *These dudes are nasty.* Like I was really, really impressed.

Easy Mo Bee (producer): I'm just so proud of watching their journey, from nothing to making solo albums to their clothing line and merch. You see this big merch thing with artists, they were like one of the first doing that. Wu-Tang is not just a group. It ended up being an enterprise.

IN APRIL 1994, Queensbridge's Nasir Jones released his studio debut, *Illmatic,* a landmark album that single-handedly advanced and enhanced hip-hop music through its pinpoint lyricism and caliber of production. Nas, who broke through with his appearance on Main Source's "Live at the Barbeque," linked with MC Serch (a former member of 3rd Bass); his management company, Serchlite; and Columbia Records. Nas recorded *Illmatic* while coping with the murder of his close friend Willie "Ill Will" Graham, who was killed in the summer of 1992.

His efforts resulted in a tight ten-track album that featured a young Nas as an eloquent orator alternating between optimism and pragmatism as he works through the lingering, harrowing effects of New York City's crack epidemic.

Hip-hop albums typically relied on one producer throughout an entire album. On *Illmatic,* however, Nas employed a diverse roster of New York City producers—including DJ Premier, Q-Tip, Large Professor, Pete Rock, and L.E.S.—to create a dynamic soundscape. Lyrically, Nas utilized multisyllabic internal rhymes, elevating the art of MCing more than any single artist had since Rakim. A faded photograph of Nas as a child served as the album's cover art, a concept that would be replicated for many future album covers.

Cheo Hodari Coker (journalist): Nas went viral with his verse on "Live at the Barbecue." It was one of those things as a real hip-hop fan, when you heard that verse—and really, the lines that took him over the top were "I went to hell for snuffin' Jesus" and "Kidnap the president's wife without a plan / And hangin' niggas like the Ku Klux Klan." It was like, *Who the fuck is this?* And then you find out that it's a seventeen-year-old kid. In the back of your mind, you're like, *Okay, I'm going to hear from this guy again.*

Faith Newman (A&R, Columbia): I heard it on the Main Source album [*Breaking Atoms*], and Nas's verse came on. And I was just like, *What the fuck did I just hear?* [At the] "I went to hell for snuffin' Jesus" moment, it was just, who was this fucking kid?

I went to Large Professor to ask him about this kid, Nasty Nas. And he felt at the time that he was trying to push [Queens artist] Akinyele out there first and wait on Nas, and that's not really where my head was at.

Cormega (artist, Queensbridge): Large Professor is one of the most important people in rap. I've seen Large Professor make beats and give them to people, that they turned around and flipped and got praise for it. That's for one.

For two, he's one of the best coaches you could have in rap. You just got to put your ego in your back pocket. I've been in a booth before with him and he'd be like, "Nah, man, you got to do that over." Like, "Basically, that ain't shit." You got to be willing to take that. And I was.

Large Professor is one of the greatest producers. He is the embodiment of hip-hop. He is just so consistent and he loves this shit. He's very humble. He definitely deserves more credit than he gets.

But the thing that makes him so dope, he doesn't even want the credit. He just wants to do what he do. Some of us, like Styles P, me, few of us, we use the term Jedi, because the Jedi was the illest dudes, but they was low-key clandestine. Large Professor is like Obi-Wan Kenobi. He is like one of the greatest Jedi and just wants to be left alone to do what he do.

Faith Newman (A&R, Columbia): I was getting ready to leave Def Jam—I had a job lined up with Columbia—and so, apparently Nas and Large came up to Def Jam looking for me and didn't realize that I wasn't there anymore. And Russell [Simmons] took the meeting and heard the tape and turned them down. Said that Nas sounded too much like [Kool] G Rap. So he wasn't really interested.

So, when I get to Columbia, two weeks into being there they know that I'm still trying to get to Nas. And that was when Serch came to me with Nas's demo. I flipped out and took it down the hall to my boss. And I said, "I know I just got here a couple of weeks ago, and you don't have to let me sign anyone else if you just let me sign this kid."

He was like, "Okay." And so that's how I ended up signing him.

THE SOURCE, **FOUNDED** as a newsletter in August 1988 by then–Harvard undergraduate Dave Mays, advanced to succeed magazines like *Word Up!, Hip Hop Hit List,* and *Hip-Hop Connection,* becoming the entryway into hip-hop for many, and establishing buzz for the early careers of the Wu-Tang Clan, Nas, DMX, and a litany of others.

Mays and his Harvard roommate, Jonathan Shecter, brought in James Bernard and Ed Young to round out the masthead. They were soon joined by staff members that included Matty C and Cheo Hodari Coker. By the early 1990s, the magazine's rare five-mic rating became the gold standard for every hip-hop artist, and placement in Matty C's Unsigned Hype column served as the launching pad for many successful careers. Soon *Vibe,* a magazine founded by the producers Quincy Jones and David Salzman in 1993, came to rival *The Source* as a definitive chronicle of hip-hop.

The Source was eventually consumed by infighting, controversy, and the decline of print magazines. But, for a while, the magazine filled a vacuum by providing dedicated journalism for a young, urgent art form and culture, and living up to its billing as hip-hop's bible.

Matty C (journalist, A&R): I started there pretty early, before it was this national sensation. I knew Dave [Mays] from D.C., from when I was a kid. A mutual friend reconnected us when I got back to New York in college. The issue that was going on was the first KRS-One cover, which was '89. That's when I became aware of *The Source*. You instantly saw the power and influence that they had just based on the fact that all the record labels were sending advance music in.

J-Live (artist, New York): [*The Source*] was the magazine that you would cop every month religiously, just to see what was new and what hip-hop deemed newsworthy. Those were probably the two biggest things [in New York City to launch a career], *Stretch and Bob* [on the radio] and the Unsigned Hype [column].

Matty C (journalist, A&R): The idea wasn't mine. I got to give credit to Jon Shecter. He just thought it'd fit me well. In the early days of *The Source*, it was these two guys that started a magazine, and they were trying to figure out more roles for more people as they were growing. I had the most enthusiasm out of the group to find new stuff and turn people on to new stuff.

The process was pretty simple. It was just having the patience to sit in front of a box of mailed-in demos and listen. It had to grab me within ten seconds, twenty seconds, or it turned into a blank. I wasn't really making any money yet. And so, even just to have a blank to dub a new album was an opportunity that I would gladly listen to a demo to get in return.

Thirstin Howl III (Lo Life, Brooklyn): That was probably the equivalent to getting a record deal back then—being acknowledged from that level. I remember when I made my first demo, I probably made about fifty packages and I went to every label in the city. *The Source* was also on my list, to try to get the Unsigned Hype column. So, I went up to the receptionist and I asked her, "Who does the Unsigned Hype column?" And she told me the guy's name and she said, "Do you want me to call him out for you?"

I was like, "Sure."

And she called him out, and as soon as he came from behind the door, I started rapping immediately. I didn't even introduce myself or nothing. I just started rapping and he told me, "You got it." I just showered him with punch lines all day long.

A funny thing is when the column actually came out, I was back on Rikers Island. So now, I'm on Rikers Island with the Unsigned Hype column out, and now I got to battle everybody in the bathrooms every day. That was crazy.

Bun B (artist, UGK): *Source* magazine had a very strong association with hip-hop culture, and it was primarily where everyone went for their hip-hop information. Now, obviously they had *XXL* and *Blaze* and even *Vibe* magazines that spoke to the culture, *Murder Dog* and *Ozone* and whatnot, but *The Source* was the first and always held in very [high] regard in the culture.

Cheo Hodari Coker (journalist): *The Source* basically was the CNN of hip-hop publications, and it was kind of the go-to place that you could very easily track who was doing what where—also because you had somebody like Matty C, who ran the column Unsigned Hype.

Matty C would go on to become one of the legendary hip-hop A&R people. I would put Matty C, Faith Newman, Dante Ross—there are certain A&R executives that had an ear that were able to translate into major moves. And Matty really was one of them just in terms of writing about certain people—people that Matty wrote about ended up blowing up.

Matty's the one who discovered Common. It was a combination of, if Matty or Dante liked them, and then also if they ended up freestyling on *Stretch and Bobbito*, they were probably getting a record deal. Those ears were so discerning that you weren't even getting on if you weren't relevant. It was kind of like this filter.

And Nas was always one of those people that you started reading and hearing about. I think it was a combination of Faith—and you can't forget MC Serch, because Serch was also a part of that—and all these different people that liked the potential of this kid.

Faith Newman (A&R, Columbia): We wanted to get the best of the New York producers together and it hadn't been done before. So many people wanted to work with him: Q-Tip and Pete Rock and Preemo

[DJ Premier]. We wanted that to happen. And I think Large [Professor] wanted it to happen too. They would just play records for him until he found something that he clicked into. That's why it took us two and a half years to make an album.

Erik Parker (journalist): It did something that nothing else had really done at that point, in calling together the leading producers to work on one album with one of the greatest up-and-coming rappers. The top producers minus L.E.S., which is Nas's Queensbridge boy.

Before that, everybody had a sound. Run-DMC had Larry Smith. Then later it was Rick Rubin. That sound was their sound. And then you had Marley Marl would produce for Rakim and Eric B., and they had a sound. KRS-One had Ced-Gee and Scott La Rock and those guys, and that was a sound. At that time, Kool G Rap, again was Marley Marl.

So, this is a guy we introduce the first time lyrically, and then with each song, he had formed their dream of producers come together. It's kind of like what LeBron James did when he went to Miami to win a championship. He kind of changed the whole landscape, and that's what *Illmatic* was.

Faith Newman (A&R, Columbia): There were many nights when we had sessions where he just didn't show up, or he would show up and leave. I think Nas is very much about, if he's feeling it, he's feeling it. If he's not, he's not. And I was very frustrated because the process was dragging on and the studio fees were escalating.

I was feeling very upset [one] night, but he had left his rhyme book behind, so I picked it up and started reading it, and I said, "Fuck, this guy is a fucking genius and if it takes two years to make an album, then that's what it's going to take because it'll be worth it."

ILLMATIC'S OPENING TRACK, "The Genesis," sampled from *Wild Style,* the foundational 1983 hip-hop movie that represented the genre during its formative years. At a moment when commercialized hip-hop offerings from the likes of MC Hammer and Vanilla Ice were dominating the charts, the *Wild Style* sample linked *Illmatic* to the New York culture that had given rise to the art form.

Faith Newman (A&R, Columbia): I couldn't stand the commercialization of [hip-hop]. I was definitely a purist. Could not stand Vanilla Ice, could not stand Hammer. Thought it was sacrilege, but they were making a lot of money doing what they did.

But that's why I'm glad that New York had that moment that it had in the early '90s. That to me epitomizes the best of hip-hop: to have Nas and Biggie and Wu-Tang and Pete Rock and CL Smooth and Black Moon, it was such a great time to be here. So many great artists. That made up for the commercial shit that was coming out and rapping McDonald's commercials.

When I heard [Nas's] "N.Y. State of Mind," that just blew my mind. It crystallized everything that was amazing about him. Every song on there is brilliant to me, but there's something about that song that just crystallizes things.

Ras Kass (artist, Los Angeles): ["N.Y. State of Mind"], that was the first thing that I heard that I couldn't fix. I would try to fix other rap songs—grammatically, or just setting things up so it could be coherent—and that was just the one I couldn't find [something to fix].

I think it's one of the greatest produced. It's scored correct—the intonation, the feeling, the vibe, everything. It's basically the first perfect rhyme.

Erik Parker (journalist): Big Daddy Kane, Kool G Rap, KRS-One, and Rakim came and they kind of elevated the poetry of it. And then in the '90s, you had the next wave of evolution, and Nas was really the pinnacle. I think everything in hip-hop led to him and *Illmatic*, the greatness that it could come to as an art form, as written poetry. And then Nas, being the son of Kool G Rap and Rakim and even a little of KRS-One, he really elevated that form to the heights of what Shakespeare was.

Cormega (artist, Queensbridge): It was two, like, eras of Queensbridge greatness. It was the Juice Crew era, and then there was the Nas and Mobb Deep era. After *Illmatic* and *[The] Infamous*, that opened up the door for other [Queensbridge] people to be heard and to get on.

They set standards so high. Like, you're talking about two of the best rap albums that ever came out in history came out within a year's time. These dudes took it to a whole other level. I had to reinvent myself after they came out.

BROOKLYN'S JAY-Z, BORN Shawn Carter in 1969, grew up in the Marcy Houses in Brooklyn's Bedford-Stuyvesant. He learned under the wing of the artist Jaz-O before being mentored by Big Daddy Kane circa 1990. With Damon "Dame" Dash and Kareem "Biggs" Burke, Jay-Z founded Roc-A-Fella Records in 1995.

The following year, Jay-Z released his seminal debut album, *Reasonable Doubt,* through Roc-A-Fella and Priority Records. On this mafioso-rap album, Jay-Z depicted a hustler's life and mentality with depth and clarity. On "Brooklyn's Finest," Jay-Z matched bars with the Notorious B.I.G. On "Dead Presidents II," producer Ski Beatz sampled from Lonnie Liston Smith's "A Garden of Peace" and a Nas line from "The World Is Yours."

The album's deep production roster included DJ Premier, Clark Kent, and Irv Gotti, along with appearances by Mary J. Blige, Foxy Brown, Memphis Bleek, and Jaz-O. While *Reasonable Doubt* went gold in under four months in 1996, it was quickly overshadowed by several other projects. Critics and fans have retroactively praised its inventiveness and insightfulness in laying the foundation for Jay-Z and Roc-A-Fella Records.

DJ Mister Cee (producer): I didn't really get wind of Jay-Z until Kane brought him on the road with us. Some of Jay-Z's early demos would circulate the street, but that *Taste of Chocolate* tour album, that's when I got to really get to understand who Jay-Z is.

Greg Mack (DJ, KDAY): I got to know Kane, and Kane, he's very quiet and shy. Later, in Miami, I'm talking to Jay-Z. I said, "Hey, man, nice to meet you." He said, "Man, you've done met me before." He used to hang out with us, and I didn't know it.

He said, "I've studied your entire history." He knew where I'd worked. He knew a lot about my formula. I was just blown away. He's a very intelligent guy. He understands the history of hip-hop and he's accurate with it.

DJ Clark Kent (producer, Atlantic Records): I used to tell people he's the best. And the thing is, like, I really, really, really knew. I knew to the point where when the label I was working for wouldn't let me sign him, I quit.

And then I went to another label, and I definitely had a much better position. I was senior vice president and still got told, "Yeah, we're gonna chill on that." The funny thing is, both label heads, I told them both, "This is gonna kick your ass when this goes down." And then it went down, and they were all like, "Damn, you warned us, huh?"

I tried to sign Missy Elliott the same way. I tried to sign the Lox the same way. I tried to sign Mase. I tried to sign my cousin, Foxy [Brown]. I know rap and I know music at the same time, and then everybody else is getting these artists—it feels kind of crazy.

But you know what? It wasn't supposed to be. Jay wasn't supposed to sign to those two labels. He was supposed to be independent. He was supposed to control his own destiny. He was supposed to become a billionaire. If he would've been at these places, who knows? It might not have happened the same way.

Kyambo "Hip-Hop" Joshua (A&R, Roc-A-Fella): I met Dame through [Harlem artist Cam'ron]. He was managing Cam and Big L. So I would end up at Dame's house, and I would always have new music. So he kind of took a liking to me 'cause I knew what was going on about hip-hop. And he was like, "Oh, you always got some new shit. What you got now?" So, that's where my name Hip-Hop came from. It came from him.

So I'm still in high school at the time, and I know Dame managed Jay-Z, because he's playing the music when we go to his house. But my brother [Kareem "Biggs" Burke] told me him and Jay was gonna start a record label.

DJ Clark Kent (producer, Atlantic Records): I introduced Damon to Jay-Z. After I had signed two of Damon's groups to Atlantic Records, I kept telling him, "There's this guy I'm working with, his name's Jay-Z, he's the best MC in the world. Trust me when I tell you I got the best MC."

He didn't believe. He was like, "No, my guys from Harlem are the best. Big L, he's the best."

And I'm like, "Big L is dope. Big L is not Jay-Z." And I loved Big L, and so did Jay, but he wasn't Jay-Z.

Ski Beatz (producer): Big L was just dope, just bars and just charisma. He was super quiet. When he dropped them bars, it's punch lines. He was amazing.

You can definitely hear that Big L was influenced by Lord Finesse, but he just took Finesse's style to another level. Not to take nothing from Finesse, 'cause Finesse was obviously incredible. But Big L, you could tell he studied Finesse, his punch lines and everything was just good money. He had Harlem on lock. Dame knew that, so Dame had to bring Jay around. They had to have that friendly little rap-off.

DJ Clark Kent (producer, Atlantic Records): I had to find [Jay-Z to get him to record]. He was out of town tending to his business. I was like, "Yo, come to New York. I need you and Jaz to let us do these records." And then they introduced me to [Sauce Money], and I was like, "Okay, Jay, Jaz, and Sauce, we're gonna do these records."

And we started, and then Jaz would go off somewhere—life would happen, he'd be with his family down in Atlanta—and we would get records done between Jay and Sauce. And then Jay was doing more records alone and Sauce was doing records alone, but then Jay was just doing the records. But to get him to that point was crazy. I had to build a studio in my house to get him to record his record.

Kyambo "Hip-Hop" Joshua (A&R, Roc-A-Fella): It started real fast. Dame was like, "Yo, you want to work on this? You can start here as an intern. Come here every day after school." I was like, "Alright."

By the time my last semester came, I needed only two credits. So I was like, *Shit, I can take those with night school and go to Roc-A-Fella in the daytime.* So I started showing up before everybody.

They was like, "You ain't in school?" I was like, "Nah, I got night school." I just kind of was like, *This is an opportunity. This looks like it's gonna happen. Jay is great. I got something to do.* I never really had that in my life up to that point.

Ski Beatz (producer): I knew he could rap, but when he rhymed for me in person and he was just doing his thing, it was undeniable. The guy was incredible. I saw it as soon as he opened his mouth. I had never heard nobody as good as him.

I'm like, "Yo, this dude is super nice. It's not fair. I don't want to rap no more. He's too much better than everybody. Let me just make beats." I knew it, and Clark was dead-on. He was definitely pumping that up, like, "Yo, can't nobody fuck with my man Jay. He's the best ever."

Skillz (artist, Virginia): When I first started going to New York, Clark Kent was a very big influence on me. So, to try to impress Clark Kent, I'm like, "Yeah, I'll battle whoever. I don't care. I got to get my stripes. Man, you get any of these motherfuckers." And he would play me Jay-Z songs. And I was like, "Yeah, he cool, but I'll dust his ass." And he's like, "Yeah, okay, alright. Whatever."

And then, it got to a point, I would say, like day three, and he's like, "Skillz, listen. I like you. I think you're dope. You don't have to keep shooting down my friends or trying to challenge my friends. It's cool. We going to make some songs. I'm going to try to get you a deal. We good. You don't got to keep talking about my friends, especially this guy, because this guy's the Jesus Christ of rap."

I'm like, "Get the fuck out of here. The Jesus Christ?"

He's like, "He's that nice. He's the nicest person I've ever heard."

I'm like, "I ain't buying that shit."

Ski Beatz (producer): I was introduced to Jay, Sauce Money, and Jaz-O at the same time. They was all incredible. Listening to Jay and listening to Sauce, I'm like, "Yeah, these dudes is crazy nice." I remember being at a club, Jay-Z battle LL, ripped his ass out. I remember running up on Phife Dawg. Phife was scared. He didn't even want to battle. Sauce Money was ready to pit-bull him. They would just run up on any rapper that was popular. They would go around the city, find you, and battle you right there at the spot. Jay was an animal.

Peanut Butter Wolf (DJ, producer): I opened for Jay-Z once. It was a small place. I was at sound check with him, and I remember thinking to myself, *This guy is never going to make it. He's way too boring.*

I'm not always right.

Kyambo "Hip-Hop" Joshua (A&R, Roc-A-Fella): Dame always was trying to convince me that Jay is better than Nas. I was a tough customer. Nas did so much at the time. He had a classic album, but then I remember hearing a few songs and I was like, *Oh shit. This might be right.*

Ski Beatz (producer): I was at one of those conventions; I think it's How Can I Be Down? Nas has just dropped *Illmatic*. I heard this song, "The World Is Yours." I'm like, "This beat is incredible. I got to make something like this."

When I went home, I started digging for a sample, anything that vaguely gave me that feeling of "The World Is Yours." I found a Lonnie Liston sample with the pianos. I was like, *This is it.* I got that same emotional feeling. I made the beat, then I threw Nas's vocals on it just to hear what it was going to sound like. Then I played it for Jay and the Nas sample came in.

I'm like, "Don't worry about that. I'm going to take that part out."

He was like, "Nah, this is dope. Keep that shit in there. Trust me."

Kyambo "Hip-Hop" Joshua (A&R, Roc-A-Fella): After "Dead Presidents" was already out, Jay and them was like, "Hey, let's put 'Ain't No Nigga' on the B-side." And then that shit just blew up way past the A-side. We should've known that record was gonna be bigger than "Dead Presidents," but we decided to put it on the B-side, I guess, because "Dead Presidents" already had a little traction. We didn't want to cut it at the legs and move on.

DJ Clark Kent (producer, Atlantic Records): There was this beat, the "Brooklyn's Finest" beat. It was made for Jay, and I was in a session with Junior M.A.F.I.A. and the beat was on a DAT tape with a whole bunch of other beats for Big to decide whether he wanted to use them or not. And then the beat came on and he was like, "Yo, what the fuck is that?"

And I was like, "Oh, nah, that's to Jay." And he was like, "Man you gave this to Jay? I need that." And I was like, "Dog, it's Jay's beat. You're not gonna get it. It was made for him." He was like, "Clark, I need to be on that beat."

The crazy part is that later on that evening, I had a session with Jay. So I said, "I can't promise you anything, but come to the studio, wait downstairs, let me talk to him." I go upstairs. I track the beat. Jay lays his verse. When he comes out, I go, "Yo, you should let Biggie on the record."

He was like, "Well, if you can make it happen, then it's all good." And everybody was: "But we're not paying Puff no money. Fuck that."

So, I just ran back downstairs, and I was like, "Yo, come up." And we went up and everybody in the room was looking at me like, *You're a real funny motherfucker.* Instantly, he appears. Like, it was real funny.

And they met each other and it was like lightning in a bottle. They were instantly friends. I believe it was based clearly off of respect. And then I played the song, and he was like, "Yo, you fuck with it?" And Big was like, "Hell, yeah."

And then, after twenty minutes, Jay went back inside the booth and redid his verses and left spaces for Biggie to rap. So, that means he went in, in twenty minutes restructured and rewrote in his mind how the record was going to be, went back to the booth, laid it, came back out, and was like, "Are you ready?"

And Big was like, "Nah, I'm going to have to take that with me."

Now, prior to this, I had told Big, "Yeah, Jay don't write lines down." And he was like, "Impossible." And I was like, "Nah, he don't. He thinks them and he remembers them." And he was like, "Nah, can't nobody do that shit."

And then he saw it happen in front of him and he was like, "I'm gonna have to take it with me and I'm gonna figure it out." And then I think it was about two months later, he came back and did the verses right before we were mastering. But it was perfect.

Kyambo "Hip-Hop" Joshua (A&R, Roc-A-Fella): I got the album in the form of maybe fifteen different DATs—different songs, different versions—and then I had to kind of formulate them in the structure of Jay. We went back and forth over it, just moving stuff around.

And I remember Jay came to meet me after I finished so we could hear it, and it definitely was a moment where I was emotional, if not crying, like, *Wow, I seen this happen and this is about to come out. You're gonna hear this and you're gonna really think Jay is probably the greatest rapper.*

I knew the story was real. I knew the wordplay, the beats, the songs, the emotion, the story line—there was a lot going on there, and I just thought it was more than a lot of people was doing on a lot of levels as far as the depth of it. It wasn't as commercial as Biggie and it wasn't as hip-hop as Nas. One album I used to compare it to a lot was the Tupac album *Me Against the World*. That was a big influence, I should say on Jay's side, but also song-wise on my side.

So, it was a lot of the Biggie, Nas, and Tupac, I think all of them guys being around at the time, and then you got *Me Against the World*, *Ready to Die*, and *Illmatic*. I think those three were cool, but I felt like Jay had something that was definitely compatible, but also a little more authentic.

Skillz (artist, Virginia): Now, I'm listening to *Reasonable Doubt* from the MC standpoint, because I don't really know much about drug dealing. So the lines that are hitting me aren't the same lines that are hitting the hustlers. I don't know nothing about all that shit. All I know is this nigga can rap. I was like, *This motherfucker's dope.*

DJ Clark Kent (producer, Atlantic Records): What he was saying was real life. He was speaking exactly what he knew, exactly what he did, and he was speaking it in a way that was way more witty than the average guy.

Just Blaze (producer): It's very rare during that phase of hip-hop where we had albums of that production standard being released. In terms of the actual rhymes and the subject matter, you had plenty of records that either you could classify as a glorification or an observer's point of view on street life. I think this was the first time that you had somebody who was coming from the standpoint of having lived that life, and expressing their thoughts about how they felt about it afterwards.

When you have records like "D'Evils" or "Regrets," you got the braggadocio element of it, which is always going to be present in hip-hop. And there was also a reflective side. And that's something that, aside from his natural talent and his unique flow, I think that was ultimately what separated Jay from the others, is he's showing you both sides of the coin of that life.

Kyambo "Hip-Hop" Joshua (A&R, Roc-A-Fella): We still was doing videos for *Reasonable Doubt* and we started the next album. So we went to the studio, and Biggie was in the studio the same day doing Tracey Lee's record, "Keep Your Hands High." So, Biggie played that for Jay and he was all crazy. And Jay is like, "Yo, you need to hear this new record I just did. You've got to see what I'm fucking with."

Biggie's leg was messed up because he was in the accident. So his leg was propped on a chair. He had a cane, and I remember him telling Jay, "You the only rapper that I'll walk on one leg to go listen to." So he went to the other room to hear it and I just remember him making faces like, *Oh shit*. It was like he was raising the bar for niggas.

DJ Clark Kent (producer, Atlantic Records): I'm on the road with all these little guys [Junior M.A.F.I.A.] and Big and I'm telling him, "My man's nicer than you." It wasn't a shot. It was more of how much I believe in this guy. Like, he's *it*.

And he would be like, "Clark, I mean, he nice, but it's like you forgetting that I'm nice. You don't think I'm one of the nicest around?"

One time we were on the road, and I think the conversation just got to be too much, [so] he went to the studio and he records "Who Shot Ya." So he plays it, and I'm like, "Jesus Christ, that shit was fire."

He goes, "I ain't the nicest around?"

And I go, "You're definitely probably the hottest MC around." I said, "My man's nicer than you still."

Nashiem Myrick (producer, Hitmen): I'll say Big was pushing Jay to be better. Me and Big used to always recite to each other Jay's verses from his first album. We loved his first album. He'd be like, "That's the dude, huh? That's the only dude I got to compete with."

DJ Clark Kent (producer, Atlantic Records): He really only gave props to one dude. He only really gave props to Jay. He likes a lot of rappers, but he ain't speak about them the way he spoke about Jay. Jay's "that nigga," those words. Dude was that guy. He's still that guy.

Nashiem Myrick (producer, Hitmen): Jay-Z and Big was the same. They didn't write anything down. They just went in the booth and spit it. And they would walk around the studio, sit down, and come up with the verses in they head. And you could see them mumbling to themselves and putting together this structure.

> **JAY-Z TOLD HIS** associates that he intended to craft only one album, but that notion quickly dissolved. He followed *Reasonable Doubt* with one top-selling album after another. In 2017, Jay-Z's *4:44* became his fourteenth album to reach number one on the Billboard 200, the most of any single artist.
>
> As he famously stated on the remix of "Diamonds from Sierra Leone": "I'm not a businessman, I'm a business, man." Jay-Z, who served as the CEO of Def Jam Recordings for three years, maximized his brand through the clothing line Rocawear; his cognac, D'Ussé; the 40/40 Club sports bar chain; and the music-streaming service Tidal, in the process becoming hip-hop's first billionaire.

Skillz (artist, Virginia): And then, of course, Jay-Z becomes Jay-Z. Fast-forward. I know he's Hov at this point, and a super-successful rapper. And we're in the Manhattan Center one day, and him and [Timbaland] had done a couple things. And he comes in, and Tim's not there. It's me and [engineer] Jimmy Douglass. And he's like, "Tim? He here?"

Jimmy's like, "Yeah, he just ran out. He said he'd be back in, like, twenty minutes."

He's like, "Oh, alright, pull the joint up."

Jimmy played it, and he said, "This the one he want?"

And he was like, "Yeah. This is number one of three."

So Jay was like, "Alright, play me the second one." Played the second one. He's like, "Alright, play the first one again." He didn't even get to the third beat. Played the first one again.

He has this tennis ball in his hand, and he's standing there, and he's fucking just bouncing the tennis ball. He's bouncing this ball on the floor. It hits the wall. It comes back to his hand. Repeat. Wall, floor, hand. Wall, floor, hand. And he's mumbling to himself. He does this for, like, ten minutes. He tells Jimmy, "Alright, I'm ready."

He goes in the booth, and it just came out. Me and Jimmy were looking at each other, and I was just like, *No. This is the stuff of legends.* It was an amazing thing to see.

Sadat X (artist, Brand Nubian): I got a call from Roc-A-Fella that Jay wanted to do a record with me. I thought it was one of my friends playing around. I was like, "Yeah, right." I hung up. When they called back, he was on the phone. He was like, "No, it's for real. We're going to do it tomorrow."

When I got down to the studio, to Virginia Beach—that was Pharrell's spot—they had the whole studio rented out with Jay simultaneously working on four or five songs at the same time. He was going from studio to studio, laying it down like that. And that was a key thing for me, because then I was like, *Man, this guy's work ethic is incredible.*

PROPELLED BY JAY-Z'S success and the business acumen of Damon Dash and Kareem Burke, Roc-A-Fella, founded in 1995, became one of New York's premier hip-hop labels. Roc-A-Fella's founders—in partnership with young, talented producers like Just Blaze and Kanye West, and MCs like Beanie Sigel and Cam'ron—presented a dynamic, well-rounded roster that brought independent stewardship to life.

In 2004, Jay-Z, Dash, and Burke sold the trio's remaining 50 percent stake of Roc-A-Fella Records to Island Def Jam.

Russell Simmons (cofounder, Def Jam): Damon [Dash], from a creative standpoint, was brilliant and compassionate, even though he appeared to be a bully. He was a bully because he loved what he did. Damon brought me Kanye [West] the first time. He was belligerent to get him on the stage at *Def Poetry.* Damon bullied us into doing some of the good stuff we did for Jay-Z.

I was interested in both Foxy [Brown] and Jay. I heard Foxy and I'd never heard nothing like her. Jay sounded like one of these slick-ass clean Brooklyn niggas and he sounded great. He was one of the best I heard, right? But I had never heard a woman like Foxy.

Foxy did what everybody does. They get excited, they get to a period and are difficult to manage. It's just difficult coming out of the hood and getting all that success.

Jay, one of his greatest talents is honing his talent, rather than destroying it. DMX was arguably as talented at one time as Jay. Jay was so thrilled not to be a drug dealer, so thrilled not to be in the hood, that he took his time and guided himself to this status he has today. DMX continued. It's reckless, being hot when you're a kid. Jay was just old enough and smart enough not to.

Damon did all the dirty work, the pushing and the building his career early. I watched Damon build Roc-A-Fella and sign all the artists, including Kanye, and really do a lot of good work. Certainly not to take away from Jay, who was smart enough to get some of the most brilliant people to work with him, to do all the things he's done. But Damon was his first masterpiece. The first thing that Jay did that was smart was be next to Damon.

Just Blaze (producer): We had our schedules. [Memphis] Bleek was the early bird. He would be in the studio by ten o'clock 'cause he would like to be out in the afternoon and still have the day. Jay would show up around two. You had the Dipset guys showing up around six. State Property guys would kind of filter in between that, and then Beanie Sigel would show up at like four in the morning because he was a late owl. The real reason for that success was that you had all those creative minds under one roof. And, as the old saying goes, steel sharpens steel.

And then the same thing with the artists, where Free is in one room writing. Young Gunz are in another room writing. Cam is in Studio B recording. Juelz [Santana] walks in and hears something and it's like, "Oh, shit." Then Hov comes in and everything stops, and he's the one floating in and out of the room. There's that creative energy that you get from everybody being under one roof that you don't get in this modern era from just sending files back and forth. Nobody's in the same room, so that train of synergy isn't happening in the same way.

THE EAST COAST'S resurgence expanded beyond the boroughs of New York City and its street-centric lyrics. Philadelphia's the Roots (originally known as the Square Roots) was formed in the late 1980s when drummer Ahmir "Questlove" Thompson and lyricist Tariq "Black Thought" Trotter attended the Philadelphia High School for the Creative and Performing Arts; they later teamed with Malik B., an MC; and Leonard "Hub" Hubbard, a bass player. The group forged a following in Europe before breaking through with 1996's *Illadelph Halflife* and 1999's seminal album, *Things Fall Apart*. Members floated in and out of the band over the years as the Roots paced the neo-soul movement by injecting hip-hop with jazz and using live instrumentation.

Bob Power (engineer): Everything about the Roots and the way they went about making their music was different. The fact that they so effectively integrated live playing with sequence stuff and loops and samples, that was notable. Stets[asonic] had been doing it, but the Roots turned it into a common language. They were such good musicians, and it was so baked into the core of the band, yet so was hip-hop and so was sampling.

The Roots are a great example of creative anarchy at its highest, making great art. So there were always a lot of surprises in those sessions. Getting used to rolling with the creative ebb and flow and sharp turns of the Roots was challenging and interesting. And Tariq, Black Thought, is one of the most brilliant MCs ever to walk the face of the earth.

FROM THE JUICE Crew to LL Cool J to Nas and Mobb Deep, the borough of Queens birthed a litany of artists and producers who infiltrated and influenced hip-hop. None bullied their way to prominence quite like 50 Cent did near the turn of the new millennium.

Since almost the very beginning of hip-hop, mixtapes had circulated through the recordings of Kool Herc, Grandmaster Flash, and, shortly after, the Cold Crush Brothers. New York DJs like Kid Capri, Ron G, DJ Clue, and Tony Touch became synonymous with the city's mix-

tape scene, building buzz and engineering exclusives. 50 Cent, born
Curtis Jackson, innovatively deployed mixtapes to generate a following
and fast-track his rise, forever altering how artists deliver their product
to fans. He started under the auspices of Run-DMC's Jam Master Jay
and debuted on Onyx's "React." 50 Cent signed with Columbia through
Poke and Tone of the Trackmasters, and soon crossed paths with Sha
Money XL (then known as Sha Self), a young producer.

Sha Money XL (producer, New York): I was in the studio with Jam Master Jay. He let me ride around with him [and] he started being really my mentor. I was with him and [Jam Master Jay's business partner] Randy Allen and we were listening to a whole bunch of records: Suga, formerly Sweet Tee, Onyx, Joe Sinistr, Lost Boyz.

He was playing this little kid and I'm like, "Yo, who is this?"

He's like, "Yo, it's this new kid that live right up the street."

I was like, "Yo, I want to work with him."

He said, "Wait right here. I'll be right back."

He left me and Randy in the studio. Probably twenty minutes later, told us to come outside and he introduced me to 50 Cent.

50 CENT UTILIZED gritty, graphic street lyrics and seemingly never
met a beef he would not entertain. He accumulated an underground
following through "How to Rob" from his 1999 LP, *Power of the Dollar*. The single detailed how 50 Cent planned to stick up a number of
high-profile hip-hop artists. In May 2000, an assailant shot 50 Cent
nine times outside his grandmother's home following the release of
another polarizing song, "Ghetto Qu'ran." Columbia Records dropped
50 Cent while he was recovering from the wounds. With Sha Money
XL, 50 Cent started recording furiously, infusing the streets with mixtapes, jacking popular beats from popular artists and transforming
them into his own, which culminated in 2002's *Guess Who's Back?*

Sha Money XL (producer, New York): When we started the mixtape process after he's been shot and after he's went through that whole process, there became a demand, because guess what? He survived and he became the story, and then his lyrics and the shit he was saying was so powerful.

GUESS WHO'S BACK? impressed Eminem, who signed 50 Cent in a joint deal to Shady Records and Dr. Dre's Aftermath Entertainment. In subsequent years, artists emulated 50 Cent's mixtape model. In 2007, authorities attempted to crack down on the copyright violations of mixtapes by arresting DJ Drama, the orchestrator of the popular "Gangsta Grillz" compilations that enhanced the careers of artists like T.I., Young Jeezy, and Lil Wayne.

50 Cent's debut album, 2003's *Get Rich or Die Tryin'*, landed as a colossal commercial success, propelled by guest appearances from Eminem, Nate Dogg, Snoop Dogg, and 50 Cent's group, G-Unit, comprised of Lloyd Banks, Young Buck, and Tony Yayo. "In da Club," the Dr. Dre–produced lead single, was a constant radio presence, topping the Billboard Hot 100.

Through 50 Cent, G-Unit raised gangster rap's mainstream popularity for the first time since the Death Row era. But G-Unit Records missed out on one substantial signing that would have extended and broadened the group's appeal: North Carolina's J. Cole, who advanced to become one of the genre's great technical lyricists.

Sha Money XL (producer, New York): We're at 50's house in Connecticut and one of the guys that's with the crew brings in my boy, [the artist manager] Mike Rooney, and Mike Rooney brings J. Cole over.

Mike is like, "Yo, this kid is dope."

There's me, Banks, Yayo, everybody's in the house. When he starts playing shit, I literally start losing my mind. I told 50 in the morning, "Yo, that kid is fire, bro. We need to sign him. That shit was hot."

This kid, he wasn't no street dude. But the songs was so fucking amazing. Since Fif didn't want to do it, I started calling him direct and I was like, "Yo, can I join the management team?" I was trying to get involved in any way.

Shortly after him meeting us, he met [prominent manager] Mark

Pitts, and Mark Pitts took him to Jay-Z. They both locked him down the same week.

Young Buck (artist, G-Unit, Nashville): I never understand it to this very day. J. Cole come around, and I'm like, "This is probably one of the hardest lyricists I've heard in a long time." He was a genuine soul, a real brother, a real individual. And I just didn't understand why we wasn't making that move to actually sign this guy.

Sha Money XL (producer, New York): If I had the power, I would have did the same shit Jay did. I wouldn't have let him out the room. When I had that chance with Bobby Shmurda, I didn't let him out the room. When you're ready to do deals, you've got to do them, and I knew that J. Cole was a superstar. He would have been a great thing for G-Unit, but 50 didn't see it.

Young Buck (artist, G-Unit, Nashville): To watch these guys become successful, it shows me the willpower, but it also shows me the eye and the ear for the music that I have. Shout out to J. Cole, because it's dope watching him rise and seeing it in his message.

18 THE SOUTH GOT SOMETHING TO SAY

Atlanta, Houston, Memphis, New Orleans, Virginia
1995–Present

The Southern states have been fertile birthing ground for much of America's greatest music—from the blues and jazz to gospel and soul, in lounges, juke joints, and studios.

By the mid-1990s, hip-hop had established itself as a popular and significant genre. But the Southern region's impact on mainstream hip-hop lagged behind its potential. Southern hip-hop had been mostly discarded and dismissed by their coastal counterparts. Some exceptions existed: Miami bass broke through, the Geto Boys showed that a group from Texas could earn national radio play, and Jermaine Dupri's So So Def Recordings, while popular, produced music that could not be easily distinguished as originating from Georgia.

A seismic shift occurred as the South began incubating and supporting its own talent. Southern states like Georgia, Texas, Tennessee, Louisiana, and Virginia would come to dominate national charts and radio airplay. The region produced catchy tunes, heavy on sing-alongs and dances, but also skilled lyricists like Outkast's André 3000 and the Underground Kingz' Bun B, who could more than hold their own against any MC. The South served as home to some of hip-hop's top entrepreneurial titans, like Master P and Bryan "Birdman" Williams and Ronald "Slim" Williams, and for a while in the 2000s it seemed as though every major radio hit had been produced by a talented Virginia producer.

The makings of the Southern revolution started in earnest when Antonio "L.A." Reid and Kenneth "Babyface" Edmonds relocated from Los Angeles to Atlanta in 1989 and founded LaFace Records in partnership with Arista Records. The executives had been previously successful as a songwriting and production pair, working with the likes of Bobby Brown and Whitney Houston. They pictured Atlanta as a site for a reimagined Motown.

In Atlanta, Reid and Edmonds linked with Rico Wade, a young producer from East Point, Georgia, who helped them uncover local talent. Wade partnered with Ray Murray and Sleepy Brown to form Organized Noize, a production team that worked from the basement of Wade's mother's house. They called the space the Dungeon. An impactful collective coalesced that included Parental Advisory, Outkast, and Goodie Mob. They named themselves the Dungeon Family and creatively lifted hip-hop to new heights.

Neal H. Pogue (engineer, producer): I moved to Atlanta because I was working for Bobby Brown. I went there for a few months to work with him and then I woke up and it was twelve years later. I kind of felt something was happening there, so I stayed. And something did happen, because I felt that L.A. [Reid] and [Baby]Face were onto something.

Big Gipp (artist, Goodie Mob): We started forming really everything around '93. I think that's when I left [the group] Chain Gang and I was supposed to be just with Organized Noize. That's when Rico moved from East Point to Lakewood, and that's where the original Dungeon was born.

Neal H. Pogue (engineer, producer): I met Organized Noize through L.A.'s wife at the time, her name is Pebbles [Perri Reid]. She thought that me and them would be a perfect fit, and it ended up working out. My brain was an encyclopedia and then all the stuff that they listened to, we got together [and] it was just synergy. And being that they were in love with old soul music, and I was in love with old soul music too, I could apply that to the mixes. So I thought that it was the perfect marriage.

Khujo (artist, Goodie Mob): Me and Gipp and Ray [Murray] were in a group called Six Sense [in high school] and we were like the Southern Public Enemy. I was writing, but I wasn't able to really spit on a microphone, because my voice sounded like a little-bitty kid.

Big Gipp (artist, Goodie Mob): CeeLo [Green] was always connected to me. . . . I remember one day I went to go over on the Westside, and he was battling this little kid that always was around from that side of town. And I remember [CeeLo] just busting out and starting singing. It was the most gangster shit I ever seen in my life. I went back and I told Organized Noize. I said, "There's this kid on the Westside. I never seen anybody do nothing like this."

They said, "Bring him to the Dungeon."

Khujo (artist, Goodie Mob): Being in the Dungeon in the beginning, I almost felt like [it was] going to camp. Like when you go to camp for two or three weeks with some people you don't even know. And all of a sudden, you get to know everybody, and they become your best friend and then you all eating and drinking and playing and swimming and everything. So that reminded me of going camping, being in the Dungeon.

Big Gipp (artist, Goodie Mob): The original Dungeon was a two-bedroom house, and the bottom level was where the Dungeon was. And it was like a boys' club that had music attached to it.

Khujo (artist, Goodie Mob): It was a great feeling because everybody had the same destination. That destination was to put Atlanta, Georgia, on the map.

ANDRÉ BENJAMIN AND Antwan Patton met in the early 1990s as teenagers attending Tri-Cities High, an Atlanta magnet school. The MCs balanced each other out, becoming André 3000 and Big Boi and finding their way to Organized Noize and the Dungeon Family.

Over time, Outkast evolved into arguably the South's most influential hip-hop group, displaying intricate, conscious lyrics and pushing musical boundaries.

Big Gipp (artist, Goodie Mob): That was like the summer of '93, going into '94—'Twan [Big Boi] and Dre's [André 3000] last year of high school. I remember them coming up to where Rico worked. I played the instrumental in my truck, and they rapped until the instrumental went off, and Outkast was born.

At their age, 'Twan was very, very, very vicious with the microphone, didn't have no fear. Dre was the same, but you didn't know he had that fire 'til he started rapping, because he was just a laid-back person.

Neal H. Pogue (engineer, producer): They were right out of high school, and they would always come by the studio and just hang out with Organized Noize. They would be there rapping, not really putting anything down on tape but just coming in, showing Organized Noize that they wrote some lyrics. I noticed that André had such a unique style. It was something that I've never heard, as far as his cadence was so different. It was robotic. Big Boi had his own thing, too. He didn't sound like anybody else as well.

DJ Mars (World Famous Super Friends Crew): You know how some people are hip-hop? Like, you just know it. That's how they were from day one, before any record was ever even sold.

Big Gipp (artist, Goodie Mob): Once [CeeLo Green] came to the Dungeon, he seen 'Twan and Dre, they went to elementary school together. They been knowing each other since they were kids. Once CeeLo joined, the Dungeon was born. CeeLo was the special piece that was missing.

DJ Jaycee (the Aphilliates): This is what makes Organized Noize so key to Atlanta: They didn't sound like what you were used to hearing coming out of Atlanta, they weren't really sampling. There was a lot of live instrumentation going through Parental Advisory's album. And then Outkast's story, with "Player's Ball," it was originally on *A LaFace Family Christmas*.

Neal H. Pogue (engineer, producer): "Player's Ball" was actually a Christmas song first. I remember the long sessions that we had trying to match the vocals up, because Sleepy Brown had to change his hook from "Christmas Day" to "all day ery'day." I remember painstakingly trying to match the new vocals with the old vocals, so it was a process, but it was definitely worth it, because it became a huge, huge hit. It went number one.

DJ Jaycee (the Aphilliates): That shit took off way, way bigger than anybody fucking imagined. And then four, five months later, fucking *Southernplayalisticadillacmuzik*, the album [by Outkast], came out.

Big Gipp (artist, Goodie Mob): It was amazing because "Player's Ball" had caught. And then we came back to shoot "Southernplayalisticadil-lacmuzik" and we get downtown and two hundred and fifty thousand people showed up in Atlanta in the middle of our video. It was the most awesome shit eyes could see. That was the first time I met Too $hort, Above the Law. Tupac had came.

Neal H. Pogue (engineer, producer): "Player's Ball" set it off. Actually, that song made L.A. [Reid] a believer. Plus, he had the cosign of—during that time his name wasn't Diddy, it was Puff Daddy—he directed the video and his cosign on it was huge, too.

MC Shy D (artist, producer): I was just getting out of prison when Out-kast came. I knew they was gonna blow because Atlanta was always looking for original people from Atlanta. I'm from New York, so they never really gave me that one hundred percent Atlanta credit. When Outkast came, they was real country. They sound like they was from Atlanta, so when I heard them and I heard their accents, I said, "They outta here."

DJ EFN (Crazy Hood Productions, Miami): It was what it was at the time, which was lyricism and creativity, and not sounding like the next per-son. That was key. And to me, everything I'm describing is Outkast, and that's why they're so important to the South and our movement.

THE 1995 SOURCE Awards provided a combustible atmosphere, and the ramifications of the evening reverberated across the genre for decades. Hosted at Madison Square Garden's Paramount Theater, the awards convened artists, producers, and executives from the East Coast, West Coast, and points in between—many of whom had never previously been in one another's presence. The evening represented the moment that the East Coast/West Coast rivalry rose to the forefront of hip-hop. Puff Daddy and the Notorious B.I.G. had by now established Bad Boy Records as a New York counterweight to the West Coast's Death Row, where Suge Knight, Dr. Dre, and Snoop Dogg looked to continue the West's takeover of hip-hop. Knight, accepting the award for Soundtrack of the Year for his work on *Above the Rim,* took the microphone and made a recruiting pitch to an incarcerated Tupac Shakur, while taking a direct crack at Puff Daddy.

"First of all, I'd like to thank God," he began. "Second of all, I'd like to thank my whole entire Death Row family on both sides. I'd like to tell Tupac keep his guard up, we riding with him." He added: "Any artist out there that wanna be an artist, stay a star, and won't have to worry about the executive producer trying to be all in the videos, all on the records, dancing—come to Death Row."

As the event continued, Dr. Dre won the award for Producer of the Year, further aggravating the mostly New York audience. As boos rained down, Snoop Dogg addressed the crowd: "The East Coast don't love Dr. Dre and Snoop Dogg? Y'all don't love us? Well, let it be known then—we don't give a fuck. We know y'all East Coast! We know where the fuck we at. East Coast in the motherfuckin' house."

The awards show also had a colossal impact on Southern hip-hop. Outkast's Big Boi and André 3000 were still newcomers to the game, riding the wave of their scintillating debut album. *Southernplayalistica-dillacmuzik* hit shelves in April 1994. Organized Noize's funky production melded with the group's sharp lyrics in introducing hip-hop to the New South. Outkast won the award for Best New Group at the 1995 Source Awards; however, they too were hailed with boos on stage.

"I'm tired of folks, you know what I'm saying?" André 3000 said. "Close-minded folks. It's like we got a demo tape and nobody want to hear it. But it's like this—the South got something to say. That's all I got to say."

The words became a rallying cry that resounded throughout the South.

Cheo Hodari Coker (journalist): New York had a thing. If you weren't from the five boroughs, you were a 'Bama, basically. And even within New York, it was fractionalized. Harlem niggas didn't necessarily fuck with Brooklyn. Brooklyn niggas didn't fuck with the Bronx. Queens was kind of considered its own wasteland. Basically, look at New York as [*Black Panther*'s] Wakanda. Manhattan is T'Challa's crew because they've always worn the crown in some ways, but then "Wakanda Forever" is "New York Forever," because in a time of crisis they all come together to hate on everybody. . . .

[The 1995 Source Awards is] really when shit began to fall apart. Internally, at *The Source*, the original mind squad had fallen away from the magazine because of a lot of internal politics and some hip-hop gangster shit were all of a sudden affecting the ability to objectively cover the music. And then at the same time, you have the emergence of the Death Row Records and Bad Boy beef, but also Suge's overwhelming ambition and his issues already with baiting Puff. . . . And it just kind of came to a head because there was a certain vibe of the audience—East Coast insecurity.

Yes, they accepted *The Chronic,* and yes, they accepted the West Coast, because one of the reasons Death Row was such a huge economic force was because everybody around the country was buying their records, and they couldn't stop playing their shit on MTV. West Coast hip-hop became the dominant sound. And then Suge does his famous "Anybody doesn't like the executive producer of their records all up in the videos, dancing, come to Death Row." That was kind of the first thing that happens.

Then all of a sudden Snoop is up there. "You ain't got no love for the West? You ain't got love for Snoop Dogg? Let it be known." That whole rant. And at the same time, when Suge's doing this, it's to a certain extent a play at Biggie. It's basically Suge telling everybody in the room, "I'm coming for everybody."

Also, some crazy shit was happening behind the scenes once [Suge] began to manage Jodeci and Mary J. Blige. There was this infamous incident where he basically invaded Uptown Records and was doing some gangster shit up there. He came through as Terry Tate, Office Linebacker. He was basically just smacking people around.

The Source Awards and the fallout, with all those hurt feelings, that was kind of the first public acknowledgment that there was a fracture between East and West Coast that went beyond the normal. And then once Jermaine Dupri has his birthday party at Platinum House, and once one of Puffy's guys, Anthony "Wolf" Jones, gets into an altercation and ends up shooting Jake Robles, who was Suge's best friend, that was really the true beginning of the East Coast/West Coast war. And all that stemmed from all the shit that was talked at that Source Awards.

Big Gipp (artist, Goodie Mob): All of us adjourned in the Garden that night. That shit was like gladiator school. Because we was all young. We was all full of testosterone. I remember us stepping in the room and just looking around, just like, *Damn. Look at the Wu. Look at Death Row. Look at Capone-N-Noreaga.* It was the first time we got to see these people that we'd been watching at the Dungeon on TV.

Jay E (producer, St. Louis): There was so much tension at that show. It really cracked open the whole East Coast/West Coast thing. It was so intense in that room. It was almost like a WWF cage fight. Everybody thought that they were better than everybody.

DJ Jaycee (the Aphilliates): Seeing Dre make that statement, it was like, "Yeah, y'all got to fuck with us now." Because before that, Atlanta wasn't really getting no play. Especially not in New York. They got love in Cali, the Bay and L.A., but New York radio? Hell no, they wasn't fucking with Outkast.

This was the summer when New York had Biggie, *Ready to Die.* They had *Illmatic.* They had motherfucking Mobb Deep. They had the streets on fire with the fucking *Infamous* album. Black Moon, Smif & Wessun, all that shit. And then fucking Outkast won that fucking award. Hell yeah, they was mad as fuck. But it was from that moment where it was just like, "Okay, yeah, y'all have to start fucking with us."

Khujo (artist, Goodie Mob): The 1995 Source Awards, it was fun as hell until we got into the place where New York was booing us and shit. New York was a hard crowd. But we came back through there and they had to respect it. But to the credit of who was in there—Snoop Dogg and Q-Tip—they showed us love that day. But everybody else, they wasn't ready to see some boys from Atlanta, Georgia, up in there, winning.

DJ Nabs (So So Def): I knew [André 3000] was dead serious. I had no idea what that was going to mean at the time. But I felt the tension immediately. So, when André 3000 said, "The South got something to say," you know it's real.

Killer Mike (artist, Dungeon Family): When I saw it, I went fucking crazy. Shit, everybody did. Dre was like the king in that moment. And notice he didn't say, "Atlanta had something to say." He said, "The South." I think Dre saying, "The South's got something to say," it provided a roadway for a whole region.

Big Gipp (artist, Goodie Mob): To watch Kurupt and Daz walk outside of that Source Awards that night and feel like the West Coast was disrespected too, and just get to battling everybody that was out there, oh, that was the most awesome shit I had seen in a long time.

And it was so dope that that same week, that was Outkast's release party for the album. So, just imagine us performing, and we look up, and we see Biggie in the audience. And then after we finish, we go out and we just kicking it in this bodega. And we look up and we see Method Man and Raekwon and Ghostface. And we're like, "Yo, what's up? We the Goodie Mob," and they're like, "We're the Wu-Tang Clan." I got pictures of us sitting in front of that bodega drinking Boone's Farm.

And I remember them feeling the same way we felt, and they was from New York. They was like, "Yo, the game don't fuck with us because we from Staten Island."

Mr. Serv-On (artist, No Limit): It was so powerful. That was such a proud moment. And it became like, *New York, I respect you. I love you, but the South is going to conquer you, period.*

When André took that stand in that hostile environment, it put us in a together mode. If you notice, the South artists always work with each other. But when they disrespect Outkast, that was it. It became Southern pride.

GOODIE MOB'S *SOUL* Food arrived just a little more than three months after the divisive Source Awards. Throughout the album, Big Gipp, Khujo, T-Mo, and CeeLo—a soulful singer, rapper, and the youngest member of the group—crafted an album that simultaneously defined and broadened Southern hip-hop music through the organic production of Organized Noize and guidance of the Dungeon Family.

The lyricists displayed uniqueness yet were uniformly Southern to their core in discussing topics like police brutality and racial inequity, as well as the cultural wealth that sprang even out of hardship. On the album, Dungeon Family member Cool Breeze coined the phrase "Dirty South," which became canon in descriptions of Southern hip-hop. *Soul Food* climbed to number eight on *Billboard*'s U.S. Top R&B/Hip Hop Albums, but its impact far outpaced the sales. Goodie Mob delivered sermons to the people and region they hailed from, offering a precursor to Atlanta's eventual hip-hop dominance.

Big Gipp (artist, Goodie Mob): We walked away from that understanding that: "We gonna make it our business to beat y'all with music, with lyrics. You ain't gonna be able to touch us on the stage." And I think that they don't understand that when we left that room, we was at war with the industry.

We was fighting up against three things at the same time: We was fighting up against us being from a certain region, we was fighting that we talked a certain way, and then our music was different. It wasn't what New York and what L.A. was doing. And every record that we dropped sold more and more and more.

We recorded Goodie Mob's first album in Curtis Mayfield's house. So, we had the elder before he left us. We had him tell us, "Hey, man, never sell your publishing, until you ready to leave the game."

Khujo (artist, Goodie Mob): When we started going to Curtis Mayfield's studio in Southwest Atlanta, Ray was in there playing around with some music and we started doing the song "Thought Process." That was the first time I had ever freestyled before—without even thinking about it, just coming straight off the top of the dome.

Big Gipp (artist, Goodie Mob): In Atlanta, we bridged the older folks to the younger folks. Having somebody like CeeLo in your group that sung the way he did, there's some gospel for real. For him to sing hooks like "Soul Food" and the intro, all the people could listen to "Free" and really understand that that was something that the slaves would've probably sung. That's a record that came from the gods.

Khujo (artist, Goodie Mob): I would say that's a big deal [when Cool Breeze coined "Dirty South"]. That Dirty South, I got to say that definitely helped put us on the map, as far as being an identity. You also got trap, so that gave us another identity, too. You got mumble, too. So, you got all types of stuff going on down here in the South. It just keeps evolving.

Big Gipp (artist, Goodie Mob): We wanted to make sure that people understood who Atlanta was. And we made it obvious we was gonna educate the world on what it was like living in Atlanta in the Dirty South. And I think we did a hell of a job.

Khujo (artist, Goodie Mob): Kris Kross, they had gained commercial success from the music that they was doing with JD. And you got to give your props to Dallas Austin, too. Because what he did was important also.

L.A. Reid gave us a chance. I mean he didn't know what the hell "Cell Therapy" was. He was just relying on Organized Noize giving him the notice, saying, "This is the shit right here." Double hand salute.

Neal H. Pogue (engineer, producer): I think L.A. Reid wanted to be the next Berry Gordy, so that label was kind of modeled after the Motown thing and it felt like a machine, because we were putting out a whole lot of records in such a short span. We did a lot of work with Usher and Toni Braxton and TLC and Outkast, and so it was a lot of success within that twelve years.

Killer Mike (artist, Dungeon Family): Those guys [Organized Noize] were able to learn directly under Curtis Mayfield. Their sampling was not one of literally samplings of instruments, but sampling of a spirit almost. They were able to re-create soul music and funk in a cool way.

That stuff was dramatically different from Memphis, which had more of a hyper sound. It was radically different from Texas, which had a laziness or a swang with the sample, and it was something more Super Fly–ish in its orientation.

Big Gipp (artist, Goodie Mob): The old hip-hop rules and regulations that was set up North and set out West, they all dead. Ain't no sampling no more, baby. You gonna have to jump in these motherfuckin' studios and really learn how to play the instruments, like these Zaytovens and Organized Noize and all that.

You can't mess with that Dungeon family. All our shit original. From Outkast to Goodie Mob to Witchdoctor, original compositions.

Capital D (artist, Chicago): When Goodie Mob dropped, you could start to feel Atlanta feeling like, *It's our time to shine.*

LIL JON, WHO had advanced to work A&R for Jermaine Dupri's So So Def Recordings, dropped a run of regional hits. In 1997, Lil Jon & the East Side Boyz delivered *Get Crunk, Who U Wit: Da Album,* becoming the faces of the popular subgenre full of pounding beats and aggressive chants.

By 1999, Def Jam could no longer ignore the South. The iconic label started Def Jam South with the goal of tapping into the region's popularity, hiring Scarface, the legendary Houston artist, to head the imprint. Scarface quickly signed Chris Lova Lova, a former DJ for Hot 97.5, who had independently released his debut album, *Incognegro*, under the name of Ludacris, selling thousands of units from the trunk of his car.

The following year, Ludacris released his studio debut, *Back for the First Time.* Showcasing a comedic and energetic flow, Ludacris packed the album with radio-friendly hit singles like "Southern Hospitality" and "What's Your Fantasy." The album rose to number four on the U.S. Billboard 200.

DJ Jaycee (the Aphilliates): I first became familiar with Luda when he was Chris Lova Lova. I was doing college radio, [Georgia State University's] 88.5. His manager, Chaka Zulu, was one of the personalities on 89.3. He had a show called *The Panther Power Hour*. His family has a deep history of activism that goes back to the early days of the Black Panthers.

Chaka would be like, "Yo, we got tons of records up here." Every fucking label is sending all kinds of wax to the radio station, and they just had so many copies of things, and he would be like, "Yo, if there's some records that you need, just come through and you can grab some extras."

So, my first time going up there to grab records, Chris is an intern, and when Chaka introduced us, Chris was like, "Yeah, dude, I hear you on 88.5." And he quoted a very specific mix that I did. So I could tell that he was really fucking listening.

So he went from intern to then, all of a sudden, he turned into Chris Lova Lova, and he had his show with Poon Daddy. So now I'm seeing him in different little clubs. I'm seeing him at spots like [Club] Kaya, because I was also DJing with Nabs at this party called "Old School Sundays."

DJ Nabs (So So Def): Kaya was a creation that came out of frustration of promoters and really, honestly, radio stations also putting the culture in a box. I would be at a club, spinning for the radio station, to a degree, because the music needed to reflect what we played on the station.

So, I took my off day and found a spot where really, I could be free and create something. That's when *In the Lab with DJ Nabs* was created. So Kaya just came from my soul, and it was birthing, possibly, a '90s version of a Studio 54–type legacy.

I had already toured the world several times with Kris Kross, the Michael Jackson tour, all of that. But ultimately, I did not make millions of dollars. I had to get a job. So, I got a job full-time at Hot 97.5, and that's where I met Ludacris. And he started working on my show as Chris Lova Lova. So, that is young Luda.

DJ Jaycee (the Aphilliates): If you look up *In the Lab with DJ Nabs*, Chris had a song on there with Jagged Edge called "Is It You." Nabs put him on the album, then Timbaland put him on the "Phat Rabbit" record that was on Timbaland's first solo album. Then he just kind of started popping up on remixes from people like Tamia. Then the nigga was on the Madden 2000 game.

DJ Mars (World Famous Super Friends Crew): Chris released "What's Your Fantasy" independently, and then let's say a week or two before, he had gotten signed to Def Jam. So, Def Jam was having a listening party for DJs in L.A., and me and Chris were going as guests.

We walked in the room and [president of Def Jam Recordings] Kevin Liles is like, "Yo, everybody, I want to introduce you to our new signee, Chris Lova Lova, a.k.a. Ludacris, from Hot 97 in Atlanta."

After Kevin Liles introduced him, I ain't seen Chris no more the rest of the weekend. From that moment on, he went from Chris Lova Lova to Ludacris. He turned into an artist at that moment.

TRAP MUSIC, THE subgenre dedicated to street life, whose production typically showcases powerful synthesized drums and busty hi-hats, gained national popularity out of Atlanta and is a product of roots from all across the South—from the Dungeon Family to Houston's UGK and Memphis's Three 6 Mafia and 8Ball & MJG.

Following the disappointing sales of his debut album with Arista, 2001's *I'm Serious,* Atlanta's T.I. gained steam through a run of mixtapes fueled by a collaboration with DJ Drama.

In 2003, T.I. founded Grand Hustle Records with his business partner, Jason Geter. Through a joint venture deal with Atlantic Records, T.I. ushered trap into the mainstream, showcasing a Southern drawl, clever wit, and sharp production with 2003's *Trap Muzik,* a platinum album that included the singles "24's," "Rubber Band Man," and "Let's Get Away."

James Lopez (vice president of marketing, Atlantic Records): When I first met him, he had released one album on Arista and still was not a success and he was in between deals, and we were trying to sign him at Atlantic. He had just a rare quality of both charisma and confidence, authenticity, good looks, talent. He walks in the room, he commands attention.

TRAP BECAME ONE of hip-hop's dominant sounds through the output of proficient producers like Drumma Boy, Zaytoven, DJ Toomp, Shawty Redd, and Lex Luger, and artists like T.I., Jeezy, Gucci Mane, 2 Chainz, Rick Ross, Waka Flocka Flame, and Yo Gotti.

Some of the top Southern artists and producers often worked together—Zaytoven's elaborate piano runs and his use of synths, for example, helped Gucci Mane shine—creating competition and rivalries.

Drumma Boy (producer, Memphis, Atlanta): At the time of trap, Three 6 Mafia was going on, so we were talking about getting buck and getting drunk. Then right after that, Lil Jon took crunk to a whole other world, so nobody was really talking about trap outside of drug dealers. Trap was a location first and foremost.

Zaytoven (producer, San Francisco, Atlanta): [Gucci Mane] has a gift. I have a gift. And we just let our gift flow.

I think transparency is what made me and Gucci sound so attractive to people. It got a rawness to it where it has a different authenticity to it.

Drumma Boy (producer, Memphis, Atlanta): I think Tip [T.I.] gets the credit of popularizing trap music as well as Gucci and Jeezy. That helped put the forefront of trap into a genre. Then the producers painted the picture, like DJ Toomp, myself, Shawty Redd. I even credit producers like Midnight Black [and] Zaytoven. It was guys like us who was really delivering the beats. Zaytoven was with Gucci how I was with [Yo] Gotti, and then we just started fusing all that shit.

Zaytoven (producer, San Francisco, Atlanta): [I] always looked at it as competition. I always felt like, *They going hard, we got to come harder than them.* But it was friendly competition because I knew DJ Toomp. I knew Shawty Redd. They was cool people and I rock with them. But you know how it is. When you hear what somebody else has done, it makes you got to get on your game like, *We got to go harder than that. We got to do more than what they doing.* So, I think just us being competitive is what set the foundation of why Atlanta has been the hottest spot for so long.

ZAYTOVEN ELEVATED HIS pedigree as the go-to trap producer through a single fruitful session in 2009. On that day, artists like Gucci Mane, OJ da Juiceman, Yo Gotti, and Rocko created tracks—like "Make Tha Trap Say Aye"—that served as subgenre-defining anthems.

Zaytoven (producer, San Francisco, Atlanta): I remember Gucci calling me around seven A.M. like, "Okay, I'm fitting to come through." And "Bricks" was the first song we made that day. He was like, "Dang, Zay, we need some people over here."

So I started calling guys like Yung Ralph, Rocko. I called Yo Gotti just to come over. And the whole day until about four o'clock in the morning, the house was just packed with different artists. OJ [da Juiceman] came later on that day and we did "Make Tha Trap Say Aye." We did "Lots of Cash" with Rocko. We did "Ridiculous" with Yo Gotti. That was probably the most special day I had when it come to music, because it was so much heat was created that one day.

ATLANTA-AREA ARTISTS LIKE Soulja Boy, Future, Lil Baby, 21 Savage, Lil Yachty, Migos, and others picked up where Outkast, Goodie Mob, and Lil Jon left off in maintaining Atlanta's place as hip-hop's new epicenter.

Big Gipp (artist, Goodie Mob): Future has always been there, because Future is cousins with Rico [Wade]. You go back and listen to that album that Rico put out, Future was on there as Meathead, his street name.

The reason why Future has been so good and so successful, you ain't never seen him high. You ain't ever seen him make too many mistakes. He was able to see success and know what he wanted for himself.

Killer Mike (artist, Dungeon Family): Atlanta is truly a place for African Americans where they can come set their roots up and become a contributor to a culture where Black people—artistically, education-wise, financially—have such a diverse mix, that there's a niche for you somewhere here. These artists have made huge contributions, not only to the Atlanta scene, but to the South and nationally.

Zaytoven (producer, San Francisco, Atlanta): When I seen [Migos'] Quavo, I'm like, *Oh, he a star*. I knew they were going to be somebody and Gucci was the guy that agreed. As soon as I showed Gucci a video of them, he was like, "Oh, they too hard. You got to go find them."

Killer Mike (artist, Dungeon Family): Atlanta is what you make it and that's the beautiful part about this city. There's no hard rules to it. That's a great environment for an artist to pop up and create.

It's fitting that our symbol is a phoenix, a bird that burns itself and then rises out of the ashes, because every two or three years, Atlanta destroys its own sound and creates something new. You look at the rock star sound. You look at snap. You look at crunk music. You look at who was influenced by other regions and took it and tweaked it and made it ours a little bit. That's part of what keeps Atlanta around.

Big Gipp (artist, Goodie Mob): We brought up somebody every time they dropped. We never hated on those that came before us or those that came after us. In other places, I've seen them shun their heroes, soon as they got some money and got on the radio. They talked down on them because they were making more money and making better deals. We never did that.

Even today, if I come across Shy D, if I come across Raheem, I give the same respect I would've gave them as a child, looking up to them. I never turn my back on Atlanta.

Khujo (artist, Goodie Mob): The Hard Boyz and Success-n-Effect, Shy D and Mojo and Ghetto Mafia—each generation adds something to the culture. Those people was an influence on me coming up in Atlanta. So, in turn, I use some of those influences in my rhymes, and then the next generation that comes after me will kind of be intrigued. And they'll formulate their own style from that, and it's like we're building a wall together, a big Southern hip-hop wall.

Zaytoven (producer, San Francisco, Atlanta): Atlanta is everything. Atlanta has been snap music. It's been artsy music. It's been crunk music. There's been gangster music, then trap music. That's why they been winning for so long. I think we just ahead of the curve.

Killer Mike (artist, Dungeon Family): I hope that the region doesn't succumb to the tribalism of which region in the South I'm from and we throw away our legacy. Because the beautiful thing about the South was that 8Ball & MJG were as loved in Atlanta as they were in Memphis as they were in Houston as they were in Tallahassee as they were in Gainesville, and I think that we're tempting ourselves to lose that solidarity. And if we do that, we're worse for it.

IN HOUSTON, THE Geto Boys shined during an era when few Southern acts did, and DJ Screw presided over a vibrant regional scene. They established a stage for the region to achieve mainstream success in the early 2000s, launched by the success of the Underground Kingz.

Hailing from Port Arthur, Texas, UGK members Bun B (Bernard Freeman) and Pimp C (Chad Butler) labeled themselves the Underground Kingz because they thought their music would not land with those outside the Gulf Coast. The pair made a mark independently before signing to Jive Records in 1992.

In playing off one another's strengths, UGK proved that artistic lyricism existed in the South through a combination of brains, heart, and talent. Pimp C, colorful and charismatic, was the son of a blues singer and trumpet player. He helped pioneer Southern hip-hop through his creative production and sampling. The group helped lay the framework for a generation of Southern artists and producers.

Bun B and Pimp C produced their major label debut, *Too Hard to Swallow,* in 1991 and 1992, using some material from their EP "The Southern Way." "Pocket Full of Stones," a standout track that sampled from LL Cool J's "Going Back to Cali" and Mellow Man Ace's "Gettin' Funky in the Joint," was featured on the soundtrack for the hood drama *Menace II Society.*

Bun B (artist, UGK): I had been hanging with [an] MC down here by the name of Rick Royal, Royal Flush from Rap-A-Lot Records, and he was just excelling at lyricism, and I truly wanted to refine my craft. So, we spent a lot of time just freestyling and writing and talking about structure and how to phrase things.

When I realized that some of the best rappers were people who had great command of the English language, that's when I really started applying that to the music I was writing, and I started to see a distinct difference and capability about what I was actually able to do. And Pimp was also of the mind frame of like, "I think you're a great rapper. Keep pushing yourself as a writer, keep pushing yourself in your craft." . . . Being a part of the soundtrack was a big thing for us. To be from such a small town and have our record company be like, "Hey, we're gonna do this movie soundtrack and we want you guys on it." It was an acknowledgment of how far we had come, not just in the culture but within the company.

UGK BROKE THROUGH nationally with their third album, 1996's *Ridin' Dirty*. Pimp C, influenced by the production coming out of the West, sampled from the Isley Brothers, Bootsy Collins, and Curtis Mayfield in creating a smooth and funk-filled soundscape that would be emulated again and again.

Paul Wall (artist, Houston): *Ridin' Dirty*, that's the first time I think we might have heard the word "Screw tape," or "Screw," on a national level. But of course, from a fan's perspective, they never got their just due. You'd see the other artists on the label they were signed to get crazy amounts of promotion, and you would never see UGK nowhere.

Big Gipp (artist, Goodie Mob): When they recorded *Ridin' Dirty*, I was at Pimp's house and he was like, "Yo, Gippy, you want to hear the album?"

I said, "Yeah."

And he went over and he picked up a VHS tape. And he went and put it in the VCR and I'm like, "Pimp, what you doing?"

He said, "Gipp, I record the album on VHS tapes, so people won't steal it, one. And then I can hear the sounds, because of it being taped, it's damn near like listening to it if it was analog in the studio."

He also, in that same moment of showing me this, he took the back off the stereo. And I was like, "What you doing?" And that was the first time that he showed me how they "Screw" records.

Chinara Butler (executive producer, Pimp C's wife): I think he was a master of stealing other productions. I've never seen anybody do so much combining. I've seen him mix zydeco and different genres. I think that's what it is, him mixing so many genres of music—not just rap, but all music in general—made his sounds special. Some people get stuck just listening to certain things. He was everywhere.

Bun B (artist, UGK): [Me and Pimp C] were two absolutely polar opposite people, so we would never have the same construct of rhymes or the same connection with a topic content-wise. So, there would never be any lyrical toe-stepping. And that was the beauty of UGK, Pimp C and I were going from point A to point B, but we had drastically different views of how to get there. Even though our views were not the same, they were never opposing. So there was never any butting of the heads.

PIMP C AND Bun B developed a close relationship with Jive executive Jeff Sledge, a New Yorker who closely watched the upward trajectory of Roc-A-Fella Records. In 1999, Sledge was excited for UGK to extend the group's fan base by collaborating with Jay-Z on a track produced by Virginia hitmaker Timbaland that included an iconic Egyptian-inspired hook. (Osama Ahmed Fahmy, who owned the copyright for the 1957 song "Khosara Khosara," later unsuccessfully sued Timbaland, Jay-Z, and others for infringement.)

Pimp C at first balked at working with Jay-Z, and contributed to "Big Pimpin'" only after coaxing from Sledge and Roc-A-Fella's Kyambo "Hip-Hop" Joshua. Their efforts resulted in a summer party anthem that propelled UGK into new echelons and increased Jay-Z's national reach. But getting Pimp C to appear in the Hype Williams–directed video for the song required a new round of negotiations.

Jeff Sledge (A&R, Jive Records): Bun and Chad are as big of hip-hop fans that I've ever met. Chad listened to everything. He brought up all kinds of shit I'd never even heard of. He'd be like, "Yo, you never heard of this one, man? This shit jammin'." They would tell me about this Screw stuff and the culture of sipping lean [purple drank], how it was so big down there.

Kyambo "Hip-Hop" Joshua (A&R, Roc-A-Fella): I remember being blown away [by the track produced by Timbaland] and I remember Jay not being blown away. It made me move, and I used to go for a beat that's gonna literally make me get out my seat and be like, *Oh shit, what's that?* But then Jay didn't see it. It was too different, I guess, and when that happens, he basically always gave me the challenge of like, "Come up with a hook for it." And I'm like, "Alright, bet."

Before I did the hook, I said, "We gotta call Mama." That was Pimp C's mom [Weslyn Monroe]. I basically was saying, "We need to put UGK on this." So, I hit Mama up. She's like, "Okay cool, I have no problems. Send the song."

Jeff Sledge (A&R, Jive Records): Roc-A-Fella was on an upward trajectory like a rocket ship. It was exciting because Jay, to this day, he's a huge UGK fan. He was extremely excited to do a record with them.

Bun flew to New York and did his verse. He came in, pinned his shit up, and knocked his shit out. Bun's a master of the studio, so he don't take no time to do a verse.

Kyambo "Hip-Hop" Joshua (A&R, Roc-A-Fella): Did that shit so fast— boom—and he go back.

Bun B (artist, UGK): Musically, that song was not anything close to what we were doing. Content-wise, obviously, we fit right in.

Kyambo "Hip-Hop" Joshua (A&R, Roc-A-Fella): So, we sent it to Pimp C, and when he first gets the record, he called me like, "Yo, I can't be on a record with another man talking about playing with himself."

I was like, "What you talking about, man?"

He said, "This man is talking, playing with himself in the truck."

I'm like, "Nah, he says, 'Let her play with it in the truck.'"

He says, "Oh, okay, now that's understandable. I understand that right there. So shit, I'ma check the record again and see what I can do."

And then he come back again, he's like, "Man, this is like a funny record, man. This is a funny beat. You ain't got nothing else?"

Jeff Sledge (A&R, Jive Records): For us, New York was still on fire at that time. It was Roc-A-Fella. It was all the Bad Boy stuff, the Lox, and Puffy was killing it as well, and Ruff Ryders. New York was a hotbed. We were excited to have UGK get on this record, because we knew the exposure that it would give the group. We felt like it was gonna take them from a regional group to a national group.

So, when it came time to do it and Chad started bucking back, it was kind of like, "Oh my God, dude. What are you doing? This is a great look for everybody."

He felt like, "I don't want people in the South, who I ride for, who I'm so protective of, to feel like, *Oh, now you done did a record with the hottest artist in New York. So now you on some New York shit.*"

Bun B (artist, UGK): That was a big thing for Pimp, not wanting to do the song because he didn't want people who had never heard of UGK to have a distorted view of who we were and what we represented.

Kyambo "Hip-Hop" Joshua (A&R, Roc-A-Fella): I'm like, "Man, I'm telling you this is the one." So I'm calling up all the time to convince him to do it, and I'm like, "Man, trust me."

I remember him telling me straight-up, he said, "You know what? I'ma do it for you, Young Hop. You been one hundred with me for the whole time. I'ma figure out what to do with this record, man."

Later, he told me, "Man, that shit was so tricky, I had to call Big Gipp and say, 'Man, let me borrow your flow.'" He said, "Man, I took that from Gipp. That's the only one I know who could bounce around like that. Once Gipp gave me the blessing, that's when I called you and told you I got you."

Big Gipp (artist, Goodie Mob): Pimp didn't want to do the record. He was like, "I'm going to use your style."

"It's all good."

Me and Pimp was that close. Pimp's from the old school. He was a great, great friend of mine. I miss that man so much. Pimp and Bun will always be a part of me.

Kyambo "Hip-Hop" Joshua (A&R, Roc-A-Fella): The video part was tough because they did the video in Trinidad and [Pimp] couldn't leave the country. So, then we had to do another video shoot in Miami just so he could be in it.

Jeff Sledge (A&R, Jive Records): Chad was very, just, anti. I remember having a conversation with him and him finally doing the verse. And then he told me, "Yeah, you seen I only gave that nigga twelve bars, though." In his own way, he was rebellious about it until the end, and then he wouldn't go to Trinidad to do the video.

He was a car enthusiast. So, when he decided to do pickup days [for the video] in Miami, he called me. We were talking about this car, and he was telling about how he wanted to get it, and "I've got to figure out a way to get the label to pay for it," blah, blah, blah.

I had reached out to business affairs, and they made me aware that there was some money in the pipeline. Bun and Chad obviously both got their money. Chad used some of that money to purchase the car. He was all excited about his shit, and I was like, "Cool, man. Are you going to drive down to Miami?" He was living in Atlanta at the time.

He was like, "Drive? Nigga, we ain't driving shit. You're gonna ship this shit."

He didn't want any dust or any dirt; he didn't want it to get dinged-up on the way.

I was like, "What are you talking about? Nigga, I just got you money for the car, now you got me going back to ask them to ship it? Are you crazy? The fuck?"

Bananas.

But we knew the record was big, so they paid for him to ship the car down, and that's the car you see in the video.

Bun B (artist, UGK): Making the video on MTV, it was a whole other introduction to people, but it came through a Jay-Z lens. Not that we had a problem being associated with Jay-Z, but we didn't want people to get confused that "Big Pimpin'" was the aesthetic of UGK.

Chinara Butler (executive producer, Pimp C's wife): Chad just respected his fans so much, he didn't want to seem like he would do anything just to win, to just work with anybody.

Bun B (artist, UGK): With "Big Pimpin'," I think everything changes—the radio play changes, the calls for shows at different places changes, the price goes up, there becomes a level of awareness that goes from domestic to international. . . . Now we're playing in countries we'd never been to.

Matt Sonzala (journalist, Houston): UGK gained more fans by being on a big song with Jay-Z than Jay-Z did by being on a song with UGK. But shit, there were plenty of people in the South who didn't know who Jay-Z was. It worked both ways on both sides, and to hear that song blow up, and especially Bun coming out super fucking lyrical and just spitting in everyone's face, and then Pimp coming out just straight Houston, it was an incredible moment.

> **PIMP C WENT** to prison for a probation violation in 2002, shortly after the release of *Dirty Money,* UGK's fourth studio album. His incarceration sparked a movement for his release. Pimp C was freed in 2005, and two years later, the group dropped *Underground Kingz,* which landed on top of the Billboard 200. Pimp C died in December 2007 in a West Hollywood hotel room, at the age of thirty-three.

Barry Weiss (president, Jive Records): Pimp C came [into the Jive offices] and his managers were trying to basically renegotiate both the record contract and the publishing contract. The managers had a difference of opinion and the whole meeting imploded. It was almost like a *Spinal Tap* moment, like the managers started fighting with each other and stormed out, really pissed off at each other. And then Pimp C said, "Let's go into your office. I want to talk."

So, it's me and Pimp C and Bun B, and he said, "Listen, fuck my managers. I don't need no motherfucking money from you guys. I'll tell you what I need from Jive Records. I want a Blue Cross/Blue

Shield card, motherfucker. I want to be on the healthcare plan. That's all I want. Give me that bitch and I'm good."

It was so endearing in its own way that he was basically saying, *Listen, you took care of me, you put me on, you took the shot on me. I appreciate that. I don't need your money. I'm doing just fine. Just get me a Blue Cross/Blue Shield card so I can really feel like I'm part of the company.*

Chinara Butler (executive producer, Pimp C's wife): Chad is the underdog. . . . Where we're from, we don't even have a hundred thousand people in our city. Most of the big artists and names and people you think of from Snoop to Master P to any artist that you think of, usually they're in a big city. Even Houston, look at how many people Houston have.

We don't have that. It's a different struggle. He definitely represents the underdog: *If you put your mind to it, you can do it. Don't be a clone. Fuck the clones. There's no sense of being a clone. Be yourself.* That's what he was basically saying. Be yourself. There's only one you. Keeping it trill. That's a lifestyle. If people don't understand what it is, it's too real. I think keeping it trill is definitely one of his legacies. Being proud of who you are and going for yours.

IN THE MID-2000S, Houston commanded widespread attention with breakouts like Slim Thug, Paul Wall, Chamillionaire, Lil' Flip, Trae, Mike Jones, and DJ Michael Watts's Swishahouse. The culmination arrived through a revamped version of "Still Tippin'" that featured Jones, Wall, and Slim Thug, and the accompanying video stood as a primer to Houston rap, consisting of laid-back syrupy flows and candy-painted slabs.

Paul Wall (artist, Houston): I never thought I really had a chance at being a rapper, because it just wasn't a viable career option. But being a DJ, that was my dream job. OG Ron C started teaching me different cutting and scratching techniques, and I'd just sit there, literally five hours a day, just doing the same thing, just to master whatever the technique was.

Then other people wanted me to Screw and chop their projects. So I'd do that for them too. But being a DJ was something I really did up until "Still Tippin'."

Bun B (artist, UGK): Southern hospitality is a trait for many of us here. There's a very easygoingness about our lifestyle, our character, and our demeanor that people relate to. It's very personable.

So, for me, it just kind of confirmed what we had been trying to tell our record company for years: that people will like Southern rap if you present it as it is, not trying to present it through an East Coast or a West Coast lens, and major record companies didn't understand that. So when the young guys came through independently because it's their money, it's their labels, they're able to present their image.

BUN B'S EARLY endorsement of Drake, without having first met him, played a pivotal role in the Canadian rapper's leap toward hip-hop stardom. In 2009, Bun B agreed to make a guest appearance on Drake's mixtape *So Far Gone*. The song, "Uptown," also featured Lil Wayne.

Bun B (artist, UGK): I'm going to be very, very honest about this. It wasn't necessarily that I saw something special in Drake. It was the fact that Jas Prince [the son of Rap-A-Lot's J. Prince, who introduced Drake to Lil Wayne] saw something special in Drake, and I believed in his vision.

I was in the studio. I had been recording all day and I was ready to leave and he had been calling me, telling me that he had this artist that he was working with and he wanted me to do a song with him. And I was like, "Cool, I'm recording right now, but I'm going to try to get to it as soon as I can."

And he hit me: "This is the last day I got to turn this project in. I really, really want you to be on this project."

So I was like, "Okay, send me the song, and I'll go from there." And I listened to it, and I was like, *I've been knowing Jas since he was a child,* and he was so adamant about this kid and me being on this song, and I was just like, *You know what? I'm going to trust in your vision, and I'm going to help you make this happen.* And maybe a week later this thing drops and everything changes in music.

AFTER YEARS OF effort, writer and director Craig Brewer imported Memphis hip-hop to Hollywood by bringing 2005's *Hustle & Flow* to movie theaters. Brewer finally received backing for the project once John Singleton, who wrote and directed *Boyz n the Hood,* agreed to finance the film.

Hustle & Flow starred Terrence Howard as DJay, a Memphis pimp with dreams of becoming a rapper. Taraji P. Henson played Shug, a pregnant prostitute. (The duo later reconvened for Fox's *Empire,* a television drama revolving around a fictional hip-hop dynasty.) Howard was initially reluctant to play DJay but earned a Best Actor Oscar nomination for his performance.

Importantly, the movie provided a sizable stage for the Southern and Memphis hip-hop artists who worked on the film's score and soundtrack, produced by Grand Hustle and Atlantic Records. Three 6 Mafia became the first rap group to win an Oscar for "It's Hard Out Here for a Pimp." Meanwhile, Al Kapone's "Whoop That Trick," performed by Howard as DJay on the soundtrack, reached the U.S. Billboard Hot 100.

Al Kapone (artist, Memphis): I was doing independent distribution through a distribution company we had in Memphis called Select-O-Hits. Most rappers did they distribution through them. Craig was doing his independent film distribution through them.

We end up meeting each other through that distribution company, and that's when he told me about *Hustle & Flow.* Three years later, he told me that they had John Singleton that was gonna be funding the production of the film, and he was gonna give me a chance to do one song to see if John liked it.

Carlos "Six July" Broady (producer, Hitmen): I actually introduced DJ Paul to Craig Brewer. I was working with Craig, bouncing ideas. I was already working with Paul and Juicy on records, and one day Paul called me. He was like, "Bro, do you know that movie you was telling me about? That shit about to happen. We was just with John Singleton. He say he about to get involved with it. Yo, I want to meet your guy."

I was like, "Okay, bet."

So, we met on the lot. They chopped it up and then we went to Paul's house, and that was really the start of it.

Al Kapone (artist, Memphis): John had his mind set to work only with Three 6 Mafia, because he had did some work with them on the *Baby Boy* film. Craig said he was gonna let him know about me, but I needed to create this song, and I had to have it ready the next day while John Singleton was in town. I came up with the *Hustle & Flow* theme song with a friend of mine, and he actually came in, loved it.

While they was discussing using the song in the film, I ended up playing my own CD in the background, and that's when they heard "Get Crunk, Get Buck," which they was like, "Hey, we could put this somewhere in the film." And then "Whoop That Trick" came on, and they really was like, "Oh, shit, what the hell, what's that?"

John's eyes got a little bigger, and you could just tell he was salivating over there like, *Man, we need that one.* It was crazy how the whole thing came about. But the key thing was that I delivered on the first song at the time that they needed to have it, because if I wouldn't've, none of this stuff would've happened.

Paul Stewart (music supervisor): Al's a real good dude and a legend in the culture, so more than anything, I just feel really great that I was able to be involved in helping him to get that opportunity. Then he delivered with it like he did and that helped give the whole project this authenticity, because the guy's doing music that was created by Memphis legends. It was a big deal obviously for Memphis, and the South in general too, to have that treatment given to their art form.

Al Kapone (artist, Memphis): *Hustle & Flow* did wonders. Because at the time when that movie came out, Atlanta, they were the top dogs, because the whole Atlanta crunk thing had completely overshadowed Memphis. The Memphis hip-hop scene, we had got buried. By the time *Hustle & Flow* came out, it was like, finally, people were talking about Memphis again because of songs like "Whoop That Trick," because of songs like "It's Hard Out Here for a Pimp." It put a spotlight back on us.

WITH *HUSTLE & FLOW* on the verge of release in theaters nationwide, Three 6 Mafia rode on the success of the group's most successful commercial album to that point, 2005's *Most Known Unknown*. The album featured the widely successful singles "Poppin My Collar" and "Stay Fly," a triumphant Tennessee banger that lassoed in 8Ball & MJG and Young Buck.

Carlos "Six July" Broady (producer, Hitmen): Three 6 Mafia and 8Ball & MJG never did a record together. For them to come together to do that, that was crazy. Then they threw Buck on it. He from Tennessee, from Cashville. They was already respected and showing love, but they kind of put a stamp on it when you got them three titans together.

Young Buck (artist, G-Unit, Nashville): Triple 6 was the world in the sense to Tennessee. As well as 8Ball & MJG. Those are our ground-diggers and our bricklayers. Even though we are two cities within the state, we still have a separation, and it was almost like it was a beef between Cashville and Memphis. That record pulled everything together. And that bond has stayed in place to this very day through that record.

Carlos "Six July" Broady (producer, Hitmen): "Stay Fly" was a mixture, to me, of a hip-hop type of sample chop, but it had the Southern drums and the Southern beat pattern. Wasn't nobody chopping no samples like that on top of a crunk beat. It just wasn't being done then. So "Stay Fly" changed the paradigm.

Dino Delvaille (A&R, Universal, Sony): It made Memphis worldwide. It made Three 6 Mafia worldwide. It was the first time that their record was really played in New York. It was in heavy rotation. It was one of those records that crossed all the barriers.

> **HUSTLE & FLOW** shined a Hollywood light on Memphis hip-hop. In subsequent years, trap artists like Yo Gotti, Moneybagg Yo, and the late Young Dolph continued to showcase the city's individuality.

Carlos "Six July" Broady (producer, Hitmen): People really don't know how dope of a rapper Gotti is, but Gotti is a guy that I would give a lot of my beats to because I know that he can fucking rap his ass off.

Drumma Boy (producer, Memphis, Atlanta): When I met [Atlanta artist] Jeezy, Jeezy was like, "Boy, that shit you and Yo Gotti did."

Jeezy was a fan of Gotti because Gotti talked that trap talk. Like Gucci Mane fuck with Gotti. Gotti talk that shit and you know it's authentic.

You look at what he did done. You look at what we did done, just for the city of Memphis and then doing it again for the next generation— the Moneybagg Yo, the Young Dolph, whoever popping. I've always been loyal to that and trying to unify my brothers and not be so much concerned about the beefs.

Carlos "Six July" Broady (producer, Hitmen): Everybody is scattered all over the place. We got to bring the forces together and say, "Okay, this the hot new artist. All of the hot new producers from the town need to be involved in this project." And everybody get behind it and say, "Okay, this who we pushing for the next two or three months." Then from there, you building up an industry, you networking. That's what we got to do. It ain't hard, we just got to do it.

> **IN LOUISIANA, NEW** Orleans housing projects birthed two of the most dominant hip-hop forces in No Limit Records and Cash Money Records.
>
> Percy "Master P" Miller grew up in the Calliope Projects. Before music, Master P was a high school basketball standout who earned a

scholarship to the University of Houston. He later attended Merritt College in Oakland, remaining in Northern California. More businessman than artist, he used the $10,000 he received as part of a settlement for his grandfather's work-related death to open the No Limit Record Shop in Richmond, California.

Master P studied and learned the intricacies of the music business before embarking on his own career with his debut album, 1991's *Get Away Clean*. He promoted the album by opening for Bay Area artists like Tupac Shakur and Too $hort. Along the way, P connected with as many promoters and DJs as he could find. His business evolved into a family affair; Master P collaborated with his brothers, C-Murder and Silkk the Shocker, to form the group TRU. He moved enough units— mostly through sheer acumen and tenacity—to gain the attention of Priority Records.

Bryan Turner (cofounder, Priority Records): We were distributed through Capitol Records, though we also had our own sales staff and our own independent distributors. I think one of them tipped [Priority cofounder] Mark [Cerami] off about a little label up in Richmond, California, that was making some noise, and it was No Limit Records.

We had Master P come down to L.A., and we talked about what he was doing and listened to the records, and I said, "Let's do a distribution deal." And that just evolved.

FOR GENERATIONS, RECORD companies across all musical genres had shortchanged creatives on deals. Bryan Turner agreed to a distribution deal that proved groundbreaking. In the pact, No Limit retained complete ownership of their master recordings and 85 percent of their record sales, paying Priority Records 15 percent for pressing and distributing records.

In the meantime, Master P signed additional Louisiana talent to No Limit—artists like Mia X, Kane & Abel, Fiend, Tre-8, and Mr. Serv-On— and released music at a frenetic pace through the rip-roaring producorial talent of Beats by the Pound, No Limit's in-house production team, consisting of KLC, Mo B. Dick, Craig B, and O'Dell.

Mr. Serv-On (artist, No Limit): KLC was my producer, along with Craig B. Mia brought O'Dell. I think it was a mixture of all of them, and Mo B. was [Master P's] cousin, but the two main people with the biggest hits were my producers, Craig B and KLC. We had formed our little thing to try to step into the industry.

MASTER P GAINED in popularity as an artist through singles like "Mr. Ice Cream Man." The 1996 album of the same name sounded equal parts Southern and West Coast, and brought Master P his first mainstream recognition.

Mr. Serv-On (artist, No Limit): We're shipping off CDs to mom-and-pop stores in different cities, then picking up [promo CDs] that's been sent to him from other parties. We're dropping off, picking up, dropping off more stuff on consignment.

By lunchtime, [Master P] is going over to the graphics place, Phunky Phat Graph-X, and he's getting graphics done, but at the same time he's able to see their covers and he'd come back like, "Okay, I want to do this. I want to do that. Change this. Change that. I want to make mine better." And then he's conversating with these rappers, picking E-40's brain.

We go back and check on P.O. boxes and pick up money and then we pick up Mia and KL and we go to the studio 'til about eleven, twelve o'clock at night. He'll leave to do other things, and [then] we're back in the studio 'til four in the morning, and I drop him off at five. And he'll tell me, "Be here at eight o'clock."

Bryan Turner (cofounder, Priority Records): The guy was an absolute workaholic maniac.

I would have messages on my answering machine at four in the morning, any hour you could imagine, playing a track on the phone or telling me something that had to be done the next day. The guy was just fuckin' relentless. I've never ever, ever met anybody that worked as hard as Percy Miller. Ever. Never take no for an answer.

If he had to fly somewhere, three, four places in one day, no problem, he would do it. He was incredible. To the point where we actually got into battles sometimes because he was so prolific that he actually stepped on some records that still had a lot of life in them. He didn't care. He wanted the next one out. And they were successful.

Mr. Serv-On (artist, No Limit): Having fifteen albums in the top fifty was crazy. Once P saw that formula to smother the game, he would have us, "Go to that mom-and-pop's and see where our stuff at." And you would walk in there and you got twenty No Limit CDs and they were always selling out.

That's how it used to be at Priority. "Which one of you guys are on that verse? P?"

He used to be like, "That's C-Murder." "That's Serv." "That's Fiend."

It was crazy to see these great historic executives confused, trying to figure out, "Okay, it's twenty of them, so who's the next best thing? Damn. They're all good. What's the deal?"

Bryan Turner (cofounder, Priority Records): The guy was putting out so many records, he would take his bodyguard and throw him in the studio and have him rap, because he had this production company, Beats by the Pound, and if you couldn't keep up with his work ethic, you were out. And not necessarily he would get rid of you, you just couldn't keep up. And there were so many beats and so much product, that he would just pull people and have them rap. And No Limit at the time had so much momentum. They were the talk of the industry. And he recognized it and he capitalized on it.

And for sure, I missed it. I missed the overriding concept of what he was doing. He was just putting stuff out. He knew he had an audience, and he knew he had people that wanted a No Limit record. It didn't matter who was on it.

NEAR THE HEIGHT of No Limit's success, Master P relocated back to Louisiana, setting up shop in the state capital of Baton Rouge, about seventy miles from his hometown of New Orleans. He announced his retirement as a solo artist with plans to devote himself to his business ventures.

No Limit Films had launched with 1997's *I'm Bout It,* a popular straight-to-consumer movie centered around life in a New Orleans housing project, featuring a number of No Limit artists. Master P also started a sports management company, clothing line, travel agency, and phone-sex service.

Mr. Serv-On (artist, No Limit): P is easy, but complex. Meaning, if people know what Master P means, "I master what you do and do it better." He basically steals your shit, but he will outwork you.

And then he studied. His thing was always to overcome you. The No Limit army thing stretched from not just personnel, men, but to objectives and situations. He was smart enough to look at rap and say, "I can't spend a bunch of money, but I'm going to do it this way."

THE NO LIMIT roster continued expanding, as did the label's popularity. No Limit joined with Jive in 1997 to release Mystikal's second studio album, *Unpredictable*. An aggressive lyricist, Mystikal was among the first Louisiana hip-hop artists to break nationally.

The album climbed to number three on the Billboard 200 and featured a guest appearance from Snoop Dogg, then in the process of leaving Death Row for No Limit.

Mr. Serv-On (artist, No Limit): We were killing it, but when we went and got [Mystikal], that was like bringing [in Michael] Jordan.

The greatest feeling in the world that I would love for everyone to experience it, is to walk on stage in front of forty thousand people and all of them make noise. To look at their faces and some crying, some reciting your lyrics harder than you, it's no feeling like it.

> **JAMES TAPP STARTED** rapping as a teenager using the name Mag-
> nolia Slim. He would evolve into one of New Orleans's most authen-
> tic and raw voices, rebranding himself as Soulja Slim. In 1998, he re-
> leased *Give It 2 'Em Raw* through No Limit. Slim was on the verge of
> a breakthrough when he was killed on the front lawn of his mother's
> home in late November 2003. "Slow Motion," his posthumous song
> with Juvenile, topped the Billboard Hot 100.

Mr. Serv-On (artist, No Limit): This dude would just do songs that became
such cult hits, and it was real. Everything he was talking about. It
could've just happened an hour before. And he was a funny guy, but
he was a hardworking guy. He would go into that booth kidding and
joking, and he would just rip that shit.

He'd give you the shirt off his back. Your problem was his problem.
If your family wasn't eating, he wasn't eating until you get the money
to make sure your family ate. He wasn't like people think, this ruthless
thug. Nah. He was the coolest person.

> **IN THE LATE** 1990s, No Limit released more than fifty albums, sell-
> ing more than seventy-five million records worldwide. From this high
> point, the label began a slow decline. Master P attempted to catch on
> in the NBA, earning preseason contracts with the Charlotte Hornets
> and Toronto Raptors, and also devoted attention to the career of his
> son, Romeo. Meanwhile, Beats by the Pound departed over a contrac-
> tual dispute and No Limit filed for bankruptcy in 2003.
>
> But by then, Master P had sealed his legacy by becoming a self-
> made music and business mogul, leavng a blueprint for others to copy.

Khujo (artist, Goodie Mob): Even though P wasn't bragging about how
he was the best rapper, he gave an opportunity to the people in his
neighborhood and in the neighboring cities and New Orleans. He gave
all them a chance: Mia X, Fiend, Mr. Serv-On, Kane & Abel. He even
gave Snoop Dogg a chance to reinvent himself after Death Row. So,
Master P was more than just a record label exec. He was an entrepre-

neur. He actually showed people how you can come from nothing and be something, and he's still going to this day.

Mr. Serv-On (artist, No Limit): I think what No Limit gave to the world and the industry, we gave a work ethic. We made rappers decide to branch out. "I'm going to do what P did."

No Limit showed togetherness. Rap is the most egotistical sport in the world. Everybody thinks they're the best. But what we showed is a bunch of MCs can be together and win. Put them on your album, and get along without no egos, no issues, no problems. We showed them that ten was better than one. We made guys get on they business.

Look at Gucci Mane. A guy like him went from selling drugs and out here doing all types of shit, and we helped the South in that way. You know how many drug dealers and hustlers and some murderers became rappers because dem niggas from New Orleans is doing it? They left the streets alone. You know how much crime that took away? That's power making a man give up twenty thousand dollars a day being in the dope game, then starting a business, saying, "I'm done."

BROTHERS BRYAN "BIRDMAN" Williams and Ronald "Slim" Williams, from the Magnolia Projects and veterans of New Orleans's vibrant bounce scene, brought New Orleans hip-hop music to the next level of prominence. The two started Cash Money Records in 1991, quickly generating a buzz throughout the city with groups like U.N.L.V. (Uptown Niggas Living Violent), artists like Kilo-G, and beats provided by the talented Mannie Fresh, who honed and mainstreamed Cash Money's sound.

Cash Money signed Juvenile, who had already made a name for himself in the city and wanted to work with Mannie Fresh, and built around adolescent stars like Lil Wayne, B.G., and Turk. They moved thousands of units independently, garnering the attention of major companies.

Wendy Day (Rap Coalition): In 1997, I went to Peaches, which was the independent record store of note in downtown New Orleans, and I saw a bunch of music for sale there that I knew I couldn't get back in New York. I saw the Cash Money logo on a bunch of different CDs that I had bought and I'm like, *Who are these guys?*

I went back home, and I got a call from a street team guy in Houston called Lump. Lump said, "I'm here with these two guys. They're brothers. Baby and Slim, and they own Cash Money."

I said, "Oh my God. I was just looking for them like two months ago in New Orleans." So, he puts them on the phone. And then I learned that they had put out thirty-one albums over a six-year period. That's an amazing quantity.

The first thing I did was put a business plan together. The second thing I did was I started bringing their music outside of just the Houston–to–New Orleans corridor, into the Midwest. So, every time they put out a CD now, we were able to get their numbers up really high.

The attorneys that I chose to do the deal represented Three 6 Mafia. I asked them if Cash Money could open up for them when they went out on tour. They're like, "Yeah, absolutely."

Three 6 Mafia were pulling up to shows in the Mid-South in a van, and here would come Cash Money with all their artists in a tour bus. That was all part of their imaging and who they were as artists—not only was the music great and exactly what the fans wanted, but they were larger than life. The guys looked like millionaires.

For nine months, I shopped their deal to labels saying, "This is the next No Limit." By the time we had crossed over into the new year, we had three different labels and we were at somewhere between a million- and two-million-dollar advance for six artists.

Dino Delvaille (A&R, Universal): We had a division in Universal, where it was four or five guys, where they would sit in a room on computers, and look up all the records that were independent that were doing well. And one that kept coming up was a company called Cash Money Records. So, I went down to New Orleans, bought all of their releases. The owner of the store said to me, "This is outselling DMX." And that was the time when DMX was on fire. And he gave me these CDs, the Hot Boys and B.G.

There was a number on the back of the CD that said, *For bookings, call this number.* So I called the number, and that's how I initiated the first meeting with Baby and Slim. I remember the first thing that Baby said to me when he met me was, "I respect you because you're the only motherfucker from New York that came to my backyard."

When I went to see them, it was some nondescript house in the hood. They had a studio set up with a glass partition and Mannie was in there with a drummer, a bassist, and a guitar player, and he was instructing them how to play over the beat. The only thing that was electronic was the drum machine. That's it. Everything else, somebody was in there playing that shit.

Young Buck (artist, G-Unit, Nashville): I was around fourteen years old, and Baby had came to my city [and] he had brought Wayne, Juvenile, Turk, and all of those guys with him. The first thing Baby said to me was, "Spit something."

When I did, he immediately was like, "Hold on, man." He called Wayne in there. Wayne, he was a little younger than me and he went to going off. I had to step back and say, "Shit."

Wayne is a talented motherfucker from the gristle just like myself. He was born with it. When you hear him rap, just know you fucking with a real, real, real talented individual.

Wendy Day (Rap Coalition): In March of '98, the deal was done at Universal. It was an eighty-twenty split and the guys were able to walk with their masters at the end of the three-year deal, which is another thing that made it so extraordinary.

Dino Delvaille (A&R, Universal): So, we signed that deal. And the first release was the Big Tymers [the group featuring Birdman and Mannie Fresh] record. It didn't do that well and I started getting worried. And then they came with the Juvenile record and the rest was history.

JUVENILE'S *400 DEGREEZ,* produced entirely by Mannie Fresh, became a gargantuan success, driven by the singles "Ha" and the Southern anthem "Back That Azz Up."

Before his UGK collaboration on "Big Pimpin'," Jay-Z performed on the remix of "Ha," marking one of the first times that an East Coast rapper offered his cosign to a Southern artist.

Big Gipp (artist, Goodie Mob): And then here comes the new Ludacris and T.I. and Cash Money and Master P. The game just took a different turn. It was almost like Outkast and Goodie Mob had gained the respect that we needed, so then it opened the doors for people to do other things and represent other places out of the Southern culture.

I think if anybody really broke through in New York, it was Master P and Juvenile. They really fucked with Juvenile. And I knew that they did when I heard Jay on the remix of "Ha."

CASH MONEY FOLLOWED Juvenile's success in 1999 with B.G.'s *Chopper City in the Ghetto.* The album's popular lead single, "Bling Bling," featured Birdman and Mannie Fresh and the Hot Boys—B.G., Lil Wayne, Juvenile, and Turk. It ushered into canon—and even into the *Oxford English Dictionary*—a term first coined by the rap group Cash Money Millionaires, denoting a lifestyle of flashiness and luxury.

Dino Delvaille (A&R, Universal): "Bling Bling" single, that's when I saw that this kid [Lil Wayne] is a star. That's when I said to myself, *That kid is a bigger star than Juvenile.*

Mr. Serv-On (artist, No Limit): P's famous thing used to be like, "Man, I'm making music for the guy with one speaker in his Cutlass. You don't have to have a Benz." That's what made people love us, is we were talking about real stuff: *Mama ain't got the money for the rent. Lights off. Daddy gone to jail for thirty years.* People was experiencing that. We accepted that responsibility like, "We got y'all. We going to represent y'all."

That was the difference of us and Cash Money. Even though they artists were so hard—Juvenile, they were hard artists, gangsters— "Bling" gave them a new look. For [No Limit], we were the underdogs, the soldiers, the riders. For them, it was the stuntas—the people hustling that are showing rings and cars and jewelry. They gave life to that, but we were different.

> **THE ARTISTIC BACKBONE** of Cash Money Records' late 1990s success—Juvenile, Mannie Fresh, and others—complained about financial irregularities. Meanwhile, Turk and B.G. would experience legal issues.
>
> Still, Cash Money continued as one of hip-hop's most successful record labels. Lil Wayne grew as an elite lyricist by engineering a legendary mixtape run. In 2005, he founded Young Money Entertainment and played an integral role in the early careers of Drake and Nicki Minaj by signing them to the imprint label.

Dino Delvaille (A&R, Universal): It's incredible, seeing these guys pulling numbers down South—five thousand, ten thousand—to seeing them flying in on a helicopter onto the stage and performing in front of however many people the Meadowlands could hold. It was just mind-blowing. And I must say, Slim and Baby, they definitely have a knack for finding talent.

> **VIRGINIA BECAME AN** unlikely hip-hop hotbed for innovative production after Teddy Riley relocated to Virginia Beach from New York. Riley became a main architect of new jack swing, a genre that melded hip-hop with pop and R&B.
>
> In Virginia, Riley had associates combing high school talent shows for potential acts, and he came to know the Neptunes duo, Pharrell Williams and Chad Hugo, childhood friends who first met in a band class as youngsters. The Neptunes broke through by collaborating with Riley on writing Wreckx-n-Effect's 1992's hit "Rump Shaker," and later Noreaga's "Superthug."
>
> The pair, along with another Virginia duo, Timbaland and Missy Elliott, took over radio airwaves in the early 2000s, crafting hit after hit and changing the relationship between hip-hop and pop. The Neptunes became renowned for their use of synthesizers, voice modulation, and

internationally inspired samples, producing genre-defying hits for acts like Virginia's the Clipse, Jay-Z, and Snoop Dogg, and pop artists like Britney Spears and Justin Timberlake.

Skillz (artist, Virginia): I knew Teddy had a studio down there [in Virginia Beach]. And then I ended up meeting Pharrell outside of a Tribe Called Quest concert in a parking lot. Super-weird dude, but it was just something about him. He starts rapping, and it's all this space shit. And I was just like, *Wow, this dude is weird.* But I had a guy that rapped with me that was kind of on that same vibe, so they were kind of vibing.

I'm just beatboxing, listening to them rap and shit. And he told me his name was Magnum the Verb Lord. I still call him that shit to this day. That was his first rap name, Magnum the Verb Lord. Shit's crazy.

LONG BEFORE THE Neptunes broke through, back when Pharrell Williams was known as Magnum the Verb Lord, he participated in a group named S.B.I. (Surrounded by Idiots) with DJ Timmy Tim (Timbaland), Magoo, and Larry Live. Through Magoo, Timbaland met Missy Elliott and began crafting demo beats for her R&B group, Fayze.

Eventually, Timbaland and Magoo joined Missy Elliott at Da Bassment Crew under the no-frills stewardship of Jodeci's DeVanté Swing in upstate New York.

Jeff Sledge (A&R, Atlantic Records): [Missy] said that when they signed to Devanté and Devanté had flown them upstate, some isolated area, that they literally worked in a basement, which is why they were called Da Bassment Crew. Devanté would not allow any of them to watch TV or listen to the radio. They had no outside influences while making those records. Zero.

That's why those records sound the way they do, because they're not influenced by anything. They literally created their own genre of music because they just were doing what they thought sounded dope, and fortunately the world did, too.

DA BASSMENT'S SWING Mob collective disbanded in the mid-1990s. Timbaland and Missy Elliott continued working together as a production pair. In 1996, Timbaland's career took off following his production of Ginuwine's debut single, "Pony," which featured vocoded vocals and a slide whistle. The same year, both Timbaland and Missy heavily contributed to Aaliyah's sophomore album, *One in a Million*.

In 1997, Timbaland and Magoo released the lead single "Up Jumps da Boogie" from their debut album, *Welcome to Our World*. The song featured Missy and Aaliyah and climbed to the top of *Billboard*'s Hot Rap Songs chart. For Timbaland, it was the beginning of a career that helped shape hip-hop with his far-out sound effects and space-age elements.

Skillz (artist, Virginia): I would read Tim and Missy's name in *The Source* or in *Vibe* magazine: "Produced and written by Virginia Beach duo, Timbaland and Missy." I'm like, *Who the fuck is that?* And then one day, "Up Jumps da Boogie" comes on TV and it's Tim, Missy, Magoo, Aaliyah, Ginuwine, Playa. And I'm like, *Oh shit, they got a whole squad.*

I met Tim through Magoo. And the first day I went to the studio, we did like six songs together. And through Tim I met Missy, and we've been cool ever since. I knew that they were trying to get Missy to put out a record, but she just wanted to write songs and put out artists. Missy was dodging record deals, like, "No, I'm cool, dude."

Once, she pulled up in a fucking purple Lambo. That was the first time I saw a Lamborghini in person. I knew she was writing songs and I knew they did Aaliyah, but I'm like, *Goddamn, did they do the Beatles? What the fuck?*

And that's when I started paying attention to songwriting.

MISSY ELLIOT LAUNCHED her debut solo album, *Supa Dupa Fly*, at about the same time as "Up Jumps da Boogie," with Timbaland serving as producer.

Comfortable in her skin, dripping with charisma and creativity, Missy

> Elliott delivered anthem after anthem like "Get Ur Freak On," "Supa Dupa Fly," and "Pass That Dutch."
>
> She placed the bricks for successful artists like Nicki Minaj, Lizzo, and Megan Thee Stallion. Her influence on hip-hop—reaching well beyond Virginia—cannot be ignored.

Skillz (artist, Virginia): I believe that we didn't have a voice for so long, so, when we finally did get to a point where we had one, it couldn't just be a flash in the pan. We gave hope to a whole state of people. It's always been an underdog mindset in Virginia, because we got looked over so much. So when it finally happened for us, we knew we had to be loud and bright and different and original in order to stay. And I believe that's what made us have the type of voice that we have. I truly believe that we just cut from a different cloth down there.

19 THAT STUCK WITH ME

Oakland, Los Angeles, New York
1991–1997

Through their lyrics, both Tupac Shakur and the Notorious B.I.G. (born Christopher Wallace) deftly illuminated the hard truths of inner-city life, but also its moments of hope. Each of these onetime friends represented separate coastal regions, and their brief, impactful lives were parallel in many ways.

In climbing hip-hop's ranks, they were pitted against each other in the escalating East and West Coast hip-hop rivalry, and gunned down within months of each other in the mid-1990s. Neither made it past the age of twenty-five.

Their legacies have only grown in subsequent decades. Both earned inductions into the Rock and Roll Hall of Fame. The Library of Congress entered Shakur's "Dear Mama" into the National Recording Registry. *Billboard* named the Notorious B.I.G. the greatest rapper of all time. Both sit high on any list of top MCs to ever hold a mic. They are not only hip-hop icons, but global sensations whose impact still resonates.

In his music and life, Shakur examined the full spectrum of modern urban existence, from the plague of poverty to the beauty of Black women, and the challenges of teenage pregnancy, violence, and misogyny. His voice came to personify the struggle against oppression.

Afeni Shakur gave birth to Lesane Parish Crooks in 1971, a month after being acquitted in the Panther 21 criminal trial. She had spent two years incarcerated and represented herself against charges that she and others had planned to bomb two police stations and a New York City office. She renamed her son Tupac Amaru in honor of the Incan leader of the rebellion against the Spanish in Peru.

The family eventually moved to Baltimore. Tupac Shakur attended Dunbar High School before transferring to the Baltimore School for the Arts, where he called himself MC New York. He relocated to the San Francisco Bay Area in 1988.

Christopher Wallace, the son of Jamaican immigrants, grew up in Brooklyn on Bedford-Stuyvesant's St. James Place. Voletta Wallace, his mother, worked two jobs in order to afford her son's private school education. Tall and heavyset, Christopher dropped out of high school after gravitating toward the area's hustlers, drug dealers, and gamblers as the crack epidemic raged around him. On the streets, he enamored bystanders with his impressive rapping ability. Wallace started peddling drugs himself and drew nine months of incarceration in North Carolina before committing himself to music, first assuming the moniker of "Biggie Smalls," a nod to Calvin Lockhart's character in the 1975 film *Let's Do It Again*.

Leila Steinberg (Tupac's mentor and first manager): When Tupac came along, he was seventeen. I think I was twenty-five. He could've been older than me, he was so well read, and he was able to articulate everything that I had witnessed that people weren't putting words to yet.

Those first conversations that I had with Pac, we both felt that globally, everybody's hearts are fucked up. We were all damaged wherever we came from, but the power of money is at the core of most of these issues, and Black people weren't sitting at any tables. He was determined to change that.

From the minute that I talked to Tupac, I felt that he was the artist that could lead the conversation and challenge people in their ideas, their beliefs, that he could speak to race and poverty in a way nobody had before him in this specific genre. And I always had a vision for changing the hearts of people globally, and I felt that his music and his poems spoke to that.

I never planned on managing. I never was good at math, didn't even know that I had esteem issues. And here was this seventeen-year-old that came along and said, "You have everything it takes."

Atron Gregory (manager, executive producer): She did a show and she booked J.J. Fad. The show was just so incredible, and she took such good care of us.

Leila Steinberg (Tupac's mentor and first manager): I ended up doing shows that ten thousand kids would show up to. J.J. Fad came one year and Atron was tour-managing for them, and Atron was like, "How the hell did you capture this market? It's incredible."

And that was the first time I realized I was a promoter.

Atron Gregory (manager, executive producer): I just told Leila, "If you ever need anything, just hit me up." By the time she hit me up, I had left Ruthless [Records] and Digital [Underground] was doing good.

Leila Steinberg (Tupac's mentor and first manager): Atron pulled me to the side, and he said, "One day, there's going to be an artist that comes through here and you're going to know that you need some help. Keep my number. If you ever want to do something, call me."

A year went by. Two years went by. And I met Pac and I hit up Atron and I'm like, "I've got that kid that you were talking about. I need your help."

Atron Gregory (manager, executive producer): It wasn't just Tupac. It was [the group] Strictly Dope.

Leila Steinberg (Tupac's mentor and first manager): Strictly Dope was Ray Luv, Dize was the DJ, and then we had dancers. Ray was the artist before Tupac that I was going to put out. He's [jazz legend] Cab Calloway's grandson. He was fifteen and really an incredible writer.

Ray's father came over to my house and he said, "If you help my son, you are going to pay. This business ruined our family and I don't want you helping my son."

His dad scared the shit out of me. So then I met Tupac shortly after and I told Pac, "I can't just let him go, but you have to put him in the group with you. But I can't really be in the mix because his dad scared me." So that's how Strictly Dope got formed.

We had this little concert in my backyard, and I filmed it and I sent the tape to Atron.

Atron Gregory (manager, executive producer): She sent me a videotape and I liked it.

Leila Steinberg (Tupac's mentor and first manager): He was like, "Well, I don't know."

I was like, "Look, tell [Digital Underground's] Shock [G] I'm bringing him to the studio. I know [that] if Shock tells you that he's good, you're going to help me get him a deal."

Atron Gregory (manager, executive producer): I said, "Have them go by and see Shock, and if he likes it, we'll talk about doing a deal."

Tupac was the only one that showed up with Leila to Starlight Studios to meet Shock. Pac went in there and rapped for Shock. I think he did "Panther Power." And Shock loved it, and then I told Leila, "We'll do it."

Money-B (artist, Digital Underground): After [Tupac] auditioned for Shock, we all had to go over and see Strictly Dope audition—him, Ray Luv, and Dize. It was obvious off the bat that he was the guy that had the *it* thing about him. He commanded the room. It wasn't the rhyme skills, because I thought him and Ray Luv were equally talented as far as rhyming. But it was this extra thing about Tupac that made you pay attention to him. You definitely saw that he could be successful in it.

Greg Mack (KDAY): [Tupac] came by the radio station with Digital Underground. He was very inquisitive. He asked me a lot of questions. He wasn't your normal rap guy. He wasn't just coming in there to shuck and jive. Just a bright-eyed kid. He just seemed very, very intellectual. I liked him a lot.

TUPAC SHAKUR APPEARED in Digital Underground's "Same Song" for the soundtrack of 1991's *Nothing but Trouble*. In November of that year, a twenty-year-old Shakur released his debut album, *2Pacalypse Now,* through Interscope Records. The album reflected a young, emboldened Shakur, both politically and socially conscious, and illuminated the oppression and hurdles facing inner-city Blacks through songs like "Brenda's Got a Baby" and "Trapped."

Shakur encountered opposition and controversy before and after the album's release. In late 1991, he filed a $10 million claim against the Oakland Police Department after officers stopped him for jaywalking. Shakur alleged the officers slammed his head against the concrete several times and choked him. He eventually received a settlement for more than $40,000.

The album had only been out a few months when eighteen-year-old Houston native Ronald Ray Howard killed Bill Davidson, a Texas Highway Patrol officer who had pulled him over. Allen Tanner, Howard's defense attorney, argued that listening to Shakur's "Soulja's Story"—which detailed an officer being shot—had turned his client homicidal. The ploy failed, and a jury convicted Howard of capital murder. However, the attention from the trial drew condemnation for Shakur's album from politicians like then–vice president Dan Quayle and C. Delores Tucker, a former civil rights activist. Within the next two years, Shakur also faced a wrongful death suit following the killing of a six-year-old when he performed at an outdoor festival, and had charges dropped for a shooting incident involving two off-duty cops in Georgia.

Beyond hip-hop, Shakur earned recognition for his acting ability. In 1992, he costarred in Ernest Dickerson's *Juice,* a film that documented the lives of four Black youths in Harlem. In it, Shakur portrayed Roland Bishop, a teenager revealed as power-hungry and maniacal.

Leila Steinberg (Tupac's mentor and first manager): When [the jaywalking incident] happened, that was another turning point when I think of really significant moments that made a shift. He was already fighting the fight, but it became personal at that point, and it really fueled his rage and his dismay of the way [police] departments worked.

The birth of police in this country was policing slaves, so their whole institution has been built on racism and selective protecting. He talked about it all the time. He was fixated on how he felt police operated, how he felt the courts operated. That fueled his fire. He was really angry after that.

Money-B (artist, Digital Underground): Pac would write a song within five minutes and then two minutes later he's saying, "Listen to this," and he'll say it just as passionately as any of the records that he recorded, spitting in your face and everything.

And it just so happened that we were recording *Sons of the P*, *2Pacalypse Now*, *Live from the Styleetron*, all at the same time. So Atron blocked out two months of the studio, Starlight. So, it was just eight-hour shifts: Raw Fusion session for eight hours, then Tupac would come in for eight hours, then Gold Money, then Digital. The sessions will bleed into each other because whoever came in, they might come a little early and be a part of your session, and then when yours is over, you're still kicking it.

So, when he did "Brenda's Got a Baby," it was after one of my sessions and Pac asked me to say that line that I said, but then as we're in there just jamming to the beat, Roniece [Levias] started kind of freestyling, and then Dave [Hollister] chimed in and it sounded cool. And Pac was like, "Yeah, do that."

Fabian "Fade" Duvernay (rap promotion, Interscope): [Interscope's] Tom Whalley asked me to take Tupac on a promotional tour. We went to New York City, to WNWK, to the Special K and Teddy Tedd show. We have a really good show. Pac's on it for like an hour, talking, playing music, everything's great. They loved him, and then we go to take the cab home. No cab will pick us up. So, Pac gets mad, and he goes over to the trash can and he starts pulling out Snapple bottles and starts throwing them at every car that passes.

Meanwhile, I'm like, "Dude, what the fuck? You tripping."

He's like, "Man, these motherfuckers won't pick us up as if we about to rob them. I'll show these motherfuckers." And he throws another bottle.

I was like, "Dude. You really fucking tripping."

"Fuck these cats."

And then it started clicking with me. "Oh my God. My nigga's becoming Bishop [his character in *Juice*]."

Because Tupac, to me, is two very different people. There's Tupac pre-Bishop, and there's Tupac post-Bishop. The Tupac pre-Bishop was very conscious, had a firm understanding on what was taking place politically and socially in the neighborhoods. He was a very insightful, very positive brother.

I saw a dramatic change in Pac, but it didn't happen because of Pac. It happened because of how everybody started treating Pac. It wasn't an all of a sudden he's a gangster, he's got a temper problem, he's a thug—as much as people started treating him more like Bishop than like Tupac. Gangsters are calling up to him, giving him love, like, "You a G."

Leila Steinberg (Tupac's mentor and first manager): It excited him that [C.] Delores [Tucker] and [Dan] Quayle talked about him, that he was that visible and he was getting under their skin. He was very aware that he was making the kind of noise that they wanted to shut up, and he would scream louder.

Fabian "Fade" Duvernay (rap promotion, Interscope): Dan Quayle didn't bother me at all. What bothered me was C. Delores Tucker. She was speaking as if the music is creating the violence, rather than the violence in the street is what's creating the music. My point to her was, "This music is a reflection of the lifestyle and what is taking place in the urban community." She had it the other way around.

I really had more problems where C. Delores Tucker was going with the argument, because she was a Black woman. At the same time, I understood it. No, it's not positive to call a Black woman a bitch. No, it's not positive to glamorize violence in the inner-city community. No, it's not positive to glamorize your Glock, your gold teeth, your gold chain, and all the money you have because you're selling rocks and have a big sack. I'm in one hundred percent agreement with her: Yeah, that glorifies it a little bit. But at the same time, it's what's taking place in the community. There's nothing on any of those records that someone didn't root in some type of reality that they experienced.

Cold 187um (artist, producer, Above the Law): When Pac came in, he got lyrics. To where you can go from "I Get Around" to "Brenda's Got a Baby," like, how the fuck do you do that? It's his range and his audacity to put it on tape—that's special to have the motherfucking heart, the gumption to fucking just go do that shit.

Colin Wolfe (musician, songwriter): All you had to do was just hit record. All the stuff on that MC Breed album, he freestyled all that. Everything. So, I just hit record, and he'd just go in on it. He was that good and that quick with it.

Deadly Threat (artist, Los Angeles): You know what really tripped me out about Pac? Pac could write a song in maybe ten, fifteen minutes. That's the ability this dude had. You know what else I learned from hanging around with Pac? This guy is not a fucking rapper. This fucking guy is a musician. His voice was actually an instrument. It's like he found the beats that actually harmonized with his voice, and with those two combinations, this is how he was killing the game.

Rappers don't really harmonize. We're hardcore. We're cutthroat. So, he was able to sit in both lanes, and people couldn't tell the difference because he'll talk shit to you in the singing type of voice until you're like, *Man, this motherfucker cursed me out singing to me.*

Dupré "DoltAll" Kelly (artist, Lords of the Underground): We were in Florida on Tupac's tour. It was Lords of the Underground. Outkast was opening up. I think it was six groups in three vans, and Lords and Pac used to chill. He would come to my room and we would build.

Even as a twenty-year-old, you've got this youthful guy talking about going back to your cities, starting youth programs and being elected officials and buying property and talking about gathering our people and waking them up. So, I'm looking at him like he's crazy. Like, *Man, we're rappers. I'm not going to take my money and go back. I'm trying to get out the hood.*

So he just had a different mindset. But as I started to get older in the game, I would say that all of those conversations that I had with Pac started to become a reality in my world. Like, *Wow, this is what this man was talking about.* And I understood why he had that game so much, because he came out of that Black Panther system of Black and Brown people being woke early. [He wanted us to] keep making inroads politically by realizing our power, realizing our voice.

He's a very animated dude. Almost seem like he yelling when he talking to you when he gets excited about something. And he would say, "We sell a million records. Why can't we get a million votes? We can do it!" He said, "You go back to Newark and do what you supposed to do. Treach, go back to East Orange. Ice Cube, go back to L.A. Common, go back to Chicago."

If we just went back and handled our own community, locally, it would mean so much more and be so much powerful on a federal level because, if we can do that individually, nobody would be able to stop our voice. Hip-hop has to just realize that it's important, that what we say as a culture, as a community, should be taken seriously, because we are a powerful demographic.

BY THE TIME Tupac Shakur began work on his third studio album, *Me Against the World,* he had started traveling to New York more frequently. He established a relationship with the Notorious B.I.G., and the two appeared together at the 1993 Budweiser Superfest in Madison Square Garden. Shakur also filmed 1994's basketball drama *Above the Rim.*

In November of that year, Shakur was offered money to appear on a song with an artist named Little Shawn. Shakur, looking to offset mounting legal costs after being charged with sodomizing and sexually abusing a woman, agreed to record the verse at the Times Square–adjacent Quad Studios. In the lobby, three men ambushed Shakur, robbing him and shooting him five times.

Transported to Bellevue Hospital Center, Shakur quickly discharged himself and appeared in a wheelchair in court the following day, when a jury convicted him of felony sexual abuse for a November 1993 incident at his New York hotel, while acquitting him of sodomy and weapons charges. A judge sentenced Shakur to between eighteen months and four and a half years of imprisonment.

While at Clinton Correctional Facility, Shakur began communicating with Death Row's Suge Knight, and joined the label. He was released from prison in October 1995.

Shakur publicly blamed his shooting on Bad Boy Records and the Notorious B.I.G., who was recording at Quad Studios during the time of the attack. Shakur was also provoked by "Who Shot Ya?," a track recorded by the Notorious B.I.G. before Shakur's shooting, but released afterward, and which concluded with B.I.G. shooting a foe.

Easy Mo Bee (producer): I never would have met Tupac if it wasn't for Big Daddy Kane. He asked us [the group Rappin' Is Fundamental] to come with him to Madison Square Garden in 1993. I stood right there on stage during that famous freestyle, "Gonna do it like this. Where Brooklyn at? Where Brooklyn at?" He also brought out Biggie and he brought out Tupac. We're not realizing that this freestyle is going to be one of the most legendary freestyles that would end up on a record.

So, that's the day I met Tupac. And one of the first beats that I played for him ended up being the track for "Temptations." When I was leaving, I always like to ask artists, "Is there anything special you always wanted to flip?"

He was like, "Yeah, I want some Bootsy [Collins], man. I want some 'Munchies for Your Love' and 'What's a Telephone Bill?' See what you can do with them."

"Munchies for Your Love" ended up being "Runnin'." Very genius of Tupac, the way he would record songs and place them on different projects. Mastermind, genius, smart.

Leila Steinberg (Tupac's mentor and first manager): Right after he wrote "Dear Mama," I came out here to bring Mac Mall, because he wanted to take Mac Mall to the Soul Train Awards with him.

Mac Mall (artist, Bay Area): Leila hooked Pac up with Digital. And it just so happened that I meet Pac at the E-40 video, practice looking hard, I tell him who I am. He had already been a fan of my music. I tell him who my manager is, and he trip out like, "Man, I know Leila. What is you talking about?" And that's how we started our relationship. He took me to the Soul Train Awards and I'm coming straight from high school.

Leila Steinberg (Tupac's mentor and first manager): I was with Ray Luv and Mac Mall, and we were in his apartment, and he said, "Oh my God, I've got one for you, Lei." He played "Dear Mama." I swear, I cried. There's so many songs he'd play for me, and I was like, "You're the best ever. You're the greatest to pick up a pen." And he *was,* for me.

Mac Mall (artist, Bay Area): For me, it was just like another dope-ass Tupac song. That type of greatness I expected from Tupac. I was just like, "He fittin' to kill it."

Would I know how the song would resonate with the world? No. But I was very happy to even be there because the whole project was ambitious. It was more poetry. And the same goes for "Brenda's Got a Baby." That's what Tupac do.

Leila Steinberg (Tupac's mentor and first manager): I really felt like I was in the presence of the greatest to ever touch the mic—for the whole picture, not for just lyrical ability or delivery. It was what he was saying through his gift.

Atron Gregory (manager, executive producer): He was a hard worker. He was a beautiful person. Did he have his moments? Yeah, of course. Who doesn't who strives to be the best in what their chosen field is?

Cold 187um (artist, producer, Above the Law): Pac didn't want to be this special shit. He just wanted to be one of the homies, which was his demise. He didn't realize how special he was. He never came out of that mold of being the little homie on the come up, basically.

Wendy Day (Rap Coalition): Tupac was somebody who when I first saw him, I was repelled by him. I would see him in the VIP line at clubs and he would have thirty people with him, and they'd be raucous and pushing each other and joking. So he wasn't somebody that I had a lot of respect for. I loved what he stood for, but I didn't like how he was shooting at cops and making rap look bad.

And then when he was [shot and] pistol-whipped at Quad that night, I felt really sorry for him. He was convinced that there was a cabal of powerful music industry people in New York that were trying to kill him. I just felt like he was prey. And I had a relationship with the Nation of Islam, so I asked them if they would secure Tupac. Happily, they did so.

[Then] I got a letter from Rikers from Tupac after he was found guilty of sexual misconduct, thanking me. In this letter, he said, "It just really pleases me to know that my music touched somebody enough to do such a kind thing for me."

After I read that, I'm like, *No, motherfucker. I did not do this because I'm a fan. In fact, you're kind of a douchebag.* So, I wrote him back and I said, "I don't mean to disrespect you, but I'm not a fan of your music.

Every time I saw you in line, you were loud and obnoxious. Your antics are keeping other rappers from being able to make money and do shows, because they think that everybody's a troublemaker like you and you're a black eye on rap."

I mean, I went there. I thought, *There. I feel better.*

And of course, after I mailed it, I was like, *Oh my God. Why did I do that? I'm such an asshole. I should've been polite and just told him "you're welcome," or didn't respond.*

And back comes a letter from him and he was so cool, and he was so kind. He's like, "I totally get what you're saying. That's not what I'm about. I'm really a very peaceful guy." I got to see the vulnerable, sensitive side of him, and it actually made me like him.

He asked me what the Rap Coalition was and I sent him some of my favorite books, and we started writing back and forth. Tupac was my first board of adviser. Chuck D was my second. Vin [Rock] from Naughty by Nature was my third. Aside from the fact that they were cosigning me and giving me strength in the hip-hop community, they were able to tell me what their needs were. So it enabled me to be able to adapt and bring on other functions of Rap Coalition.

Atron Gregory (manager, executive producer): The biggest misnomer is that Tupac was sitting in jail waiting to get out on bail. That's just not true. Tupac was going to get out of jail, whether it was with Suge or not, because he had bail pending approval appeal. That was long before Suge. But that took several months to get through that process.

Fabian "Fade" Duvernay (rap promotion, Interscope): They called me into a meeting with Tom Whalley, Jimmy Iovine, and they say, "Hey, we're going to have Tupac go over to Death Row. We're going to let Suge bail him out."

I'm like, "Uh-uh. Tupac ain't going to Death Row. That's my artist. That's Interscope."

"No, no, no. You don't understand what we're doing, Fade. We're consolidating it."

I'm like, "No. Tupac is not Death Row. Death Row is not Tupac."

Meanwhile, we get in a whole discussion over that. Of course, I lose, and I give them my notice. I basically tell them, "I'm out of here.

I'm not going to deal with that violence with my artist over on their label." So, I quit.

Atron Gregory (manager, executive producer): He said he wanted to sign with Death Row because he wanted to be with the best, and Dre and Snoop were the best at that time. But Suge wouldn't let anyone work with Dre that wasn't part of Death Row, and Tupac wanted to work with Dre. That was part of Tupac's reasoning for wanting to go to Death Row. Another part of his reasoning, he felt like he needed protection and Suge could provide protection.

I don't begrudge him or have anything against him for feeling that way. Even though Pac had the Panthers. He had some pretty strong people behind him at that time. But you can't always beat the court system.

NO DISS TRACK before or since has carried the same vitriol and consequences as Tupac Shakur's blistering "Hit 'Em Up," released in the summer of 1996 as the B-Side to "How Do U Want It." The track featured the Outlawz, a group Shakur founded upon his prison release, and took direct, confrontational aim at a litany of East Coast rappers. Shakur reserved his most vicious and personal disparagement for the Notorious B.I.G., Puff Daddy (Sean Combs), and Bad Boy Records, whom he held responsible for his being ambushed in New York City.

The song escalated the already simmering East Coast/West Coast feud.

Big Gipp (artist, Goodie Mob): I was the first person to hear that record. Me and Lisa from TLC, Lisa Lopes, Left Eye. Pac knew that we all had a relationship with Big, and he loved it because we wasn't from the West or the East. So, he was playing it because he knew that we would give him an unbiased reaction.

I remember when he played me that record, I looked at him, like, *Pac, man.*

He was like, "Gipp, fuck that shit, man. Fuck that shit. We got to get 'em."

That's how he was in the studio. He was on ten all the time. And I just remember him playing the record and just being like, "Wow. Motherfuckers is gonna really, really get in they feelings when they hear this record." It was just the most raw shit I had heard at that time.

Leila Steinberg (Tupac's mentor and first manager): We had a fight about it. I didn't want him to release it. Some things you put out into the ecos, you can't ever get them back, and there's no return from that.

He got excited that it bothered me so much. He was like, "Man, you just gave me all the ammunition I need. I don't care if it can't be retracted."

At that point, I knew what was coming. It's hard, because my friend who I loved so dearly, who I wanted to see enjoy life a little bit, the more successful he became, the less he enjoyed being here, the more he hurt, the more desperate he was, and to me, he represented the fight for "Brenda's Baby."

Greg Mack (KDAY): I did see him right before he was killed. He was a totally different person. It's like the business had just really changed him. It was not the same Tupac.

I was walking into a convenience store. He had pulled up, had his top down. I said, "Pac, what's up, man?" He looked at me like I wanted to kill him. He just gave me the meanest look. The security guy that was with him said, "Man, that's Greg Mack. That's Greg Mack." And then he started smiling. He was like, "Oh hey, what's up, man?" He got out and gave me a hug, blah blah blah. But he just had that look.

I always tell people that you can sometimes look at a person's eyes before they're going to die. They just have this look that they're not going to be around much longer. He just looked real angry. Not the same kid I met in the beginning.

SHAKUR ATTENDED A boxing match featuring Mike Tyson and Bruce Seldon in Las Vegas on September 7, 1996. After the fight, Shakur spotted Orlando Anderson, an alleged member of the South-side Crips, in the lobby of the MGM Grand and took part in assaulting him. Later that evening, an assailant stopped at a light and shot into a sedan driven by Suge Knight. Shakur, a passenger, was struck four times, twice in his chest and once in his arm and thigh. Paramedics escorted Shakur to University Medical Center, where doctors removed his right lung in an effort to stop the internal bleeding.

Shakur died six days later. He was twenty-five.

While the murder remains officially unsolved, Anderson has long been assumed to be the perpetrator. He was killed in a gang-related shooting two years later.

Young Buck (artist, G-Unit): The whole Pac era was something that captivated from the beginning. As an artist, he was the first individual that I remember locking in on, and it really was a pure truth. I was probably a born Pac fan, because I started to understand the music and I was identifying with it because I was under these same conditions.

Mozzy (artist, Sacramento): My grandmother loved him. He was in my household *heavy*. It was just his whole upbringing and his whole background. That's the same hype my grandmother was on. She came from that era of Afeni Shakur. She considered Pac one of her children. His words, his teaching, his everything. My grandmother was sprung on him, so I naturally became sprung.

Leila Steinberg (Tupac's mentor and first manager): Tupac wanted to change things for Black people and all oppressed people, but primarily for Black people. He wanted to bring truth to circumstance. He always said, "I'm going to wake them up and leave them to you guys to figure it out." I was in such denial for so long that I wouldn't really acknowledge that he spent years letting us know he wouldn't be here after twenty-five.

THE NOTORIOUS B.I.G. had gotten his career started by recording a basement demo with 50 Grand, a Brooklyn DJ, that soon came to the attention of DJ Mister Cee.

Cheo Hodari Coker (journalist): Biggie was a stoop kid who became a corner kid. Voletta Wallace was strict—Jehovah's Witness, Jamaican,

"Do your homework." So, at home, that's what his life was. And then he would go out on the corner with his friends, and he basically had two different lives. Christopher Wallace was Peter Parker and on the streets he was Spider-Man. And his whole fear was that Aunt May would find out.

Mister Cee (DJ, producer): I got the same feeling that I got when I first heard [Big Daddy] Kane, the same feeling when I heard Biggie. That's the only two times I ever got that feeling of hearing greatness very early on.

50 Grand was Biggie's first DJ, and he was the first person who let me hear Biggie's demo. I came up with the idea about putting it into *The Source* magazine for its Unsigned Hype contest.

Matty C (journalist, *The Source*/A&R): [With B.I.G.], it was just the combination of the [KRS-One] and the Kane. The fact that Mister Cee is who brought it to me is just so crazy. I'm such a Kane fan. Then for him to come with this demo over the "Ain't No Half Steppin'" beat, it was like the second coming of Kane, but with a bigger voice—with a voice that's like KRS.

So, there was this massive potential to just take Big and then work with bigger producers. And this is why the whole thing with Puffy was so perfect, because everybody who brought Big to him didn't make beats.

SEAN COMBS HAS gone by many monikers throughout the years, and used the name of Puff Daddy as he gained momentum in the recording industry. He was born in Harlem in 1969 before his family moved north of the city, to Mount Vernon, following the murder of his father, Melvin Combs. Sean attended Howard University, where he became known for throwing popular parties, and served as a backup dancer for Heavy D, Doug E. Fresh, and Big Daddy Kane. He used his relationships to secure an internship at Uptown Records with Andre Harrell (once half of the pioneering rap duo Dr. Jeckyll & Mr. Hyde). Combs's strong work ethic enabled him to quickly climb the ranks to an executive position, and he steered the careers of popular

names like Jodeci and Mary J. Blige. He could also be brash, and, despite his adeptness at cultivating talent, Harrell fired him from Uptown
in 1993.

However, Harrell still believed in his protégé, and allowed him to
retain a Brooklyn artist he had recently signed: the Notorious B.I.G.
Soon, Combs launched his own label, Bad Boy Records, as a joint venture with Arista.

Cheo Hodari Coker (journalist): For a long period of time that it took to
finally close this deal, [B.I.G.] went to North Carolina to sell drugs.
And when Puff found out where he was, he said, "I got the paperwork.
Your deal is done. Get the fuck out of there. What are you doing? You
can get arrested."

Big left, and the morning that he left, he got on a six A.M. Grey-
hound; the spot got raided at nine. Had he not left that day, he
would've gone to jail. And he never forgot that. He always had that
love for Puff, that Puff to a certain extent rescued him.

Their relationship was like [Bill] Belichick and [Tom] Brady. They
brought things out of each other. Their tension is what made it work.
It was tension like, "You're a pain in my ass, but fine, I'll do it your
way"—on both sides. So, the same way that Belichick has a structure
and basically created the Patriot Way, in which it allows the 199th pick
of the draft to become the greatest quarterback of all time, at the same
time, the quarterback, his prodigious talent, is what makes the system
work. That's what Biggie and Puff were like.

Puff had this whole thing where he basically took his attitude about
R&B radio and applied it to hip-hop. He was the first person to start
experimenting with that on a mainstream level.

Nashiem Myrick (producer, Hitmen): I knew Puff was more of [an] R&B
producer, but he was a hip-hop producer in the same realm. Back then
in the '80s, early '90s, we had these things called "blends," blend tapes
where you would take R&B records—Luther Vandross or any R&B
singer—and mix them with hip-hop instrumentals. Puff basically took
that idea and structured records out of that format. And that's what
he did for Mary J. Blige and Jodeci and Father MC.

Cheo Hodari Coker (journalist): Jodeci, when he did that "Come and Talk to Me" remix, where he's taking these North Carolina 'Bamas and he dresses them Harlem chic and then puts breakbeats underneath their singing, that's really the birth of hip-hop soul. And then, with Mary J. Blige, he had his Aretha [Franklin] and he was able to take that attitude and give her a record that was as relevant as a hip-hop record as much as it was as an R&B record.

Easy Mo Bee (producer): When we recorded the "Party and Bullshit" song, [B.I.G.] had Junior M.A.F.I.A. in there and he was ordering food and his homeboys was visiting and maybe a girl would come by. So, he's doing all of this stuff, and I'm not really saying nothing because this is the first time we really around each other. But I was wondering like, *Yo, when is he going to rap and go in the booth?* And he kept telling me, "Yo, I got you, man." Ordering food, eating burgers.

And then he just jumped up and went right into the booth and just spat three verses. I was like, *Yo, who is this dude?* I thought he was playing the whole time. Because I'm one who when I go to the studio, I like to be real prepared. Like, "Yo, you know how much the studio time costs. So let's go in there knowing what we going to do, have everything down pat."

I just didn't see that with him. So then he went in the booth and did "Gimme the Loot," knocked it out, and then he came back out the booth and he just cut his eyes over at me, smiling. He said, "Told you."

So, after that I never ever questioned him no more. I'm like, "Order all the burgers you want and have all the girls, homeboys come by. I know you going to take care of business now."

Daddy-O (artist, producer, Stetsasonic): He didn't write. I'd never seen that before. When we came up, it was all about your rhyme books and your pads.

I put Lance "Un" Rivera in the business, and Un brought Big down to the studio because that's where we was putting together the Junior M.A.F.I.A. stuff. And Big sat on my phone in the lobby talking to some girl and then hangs up the phone to say, "I'm ready." And I look around and Un says to me, "He's ready."

I said, "So where's his pad and stuff?"

He said, "D, he don't write."

So, the whole time he was on the phone with this girl, he's composing, "I'm surrounded by criminals, heavy rollers, even the sheisty." He's doing that in his head while he's talking to her. Then he comes in and does it in one take.

And I'm like, "Okay, I'm done." Because I had never seen that before. I've now seen it twice after. I saw it with Jay-Z. And the only difference [between] Big and Jay is Jay will write two in his head, or three, and say, "Which one's better?"

And then I saw Styles P did it a few years ago. I say, "Hey, you need the pad?" He said, "No. I don't write, Daddy-O." I was like, "Okay. This is becoming a thing now."

Easy Mo Bee (producer): When you talk about me and Biggie's chemistry, the music was definitely the bond between us. I think maybe what Biggie liked about me is I think he appreciated my honesty. If I didn't like something, I would come out and I would say so. I tried to be like that big brother with the honesty. And I think maybe over time, he appreciated that because you got all these yes-men around you, they just there to smoke or drink or whatever. I was the one making sure that everything was getting handled. So I imagine that he had great confidence in me, because he knew I was very serious about the making of the records and the quality of everything, all the way down to the final product.

BY THE TIME he ran into Sean Combs outside of a New York nightclub, Craig Mack had experienced some starts and stops in the music industry, most notably as half of the duo MC EZ & Troup. Mack's impromptu rap impressed Combs enough that he placed Mack on the remix of Mary J. Blige's "You Don't Have to Worry" and signed him to his fledgling label.

Mack only released one album, *Project: Funk da World,* through Bad Boy. But "Flava in Ya Ear," produced by Easy Mo Bee, was pivotal in establishing Bad Boy's stranglehold on hip-hop. The song received a Grammy nomination in the Best Rap Solo Performance category and topped the Billboard rap songs chart. Its popular remix included the likes of the Notorious B.I.G., whom Combs broke next; LL Cool J; and Busta Rhymes.

Easy Mo Bee (producer): The Craig Mack "Flava in Ya Ear" session was my introduction to him. That was the first song that we ever recorded. When I made the beat, it was influenced by the Juice Crew. I was intending to make something, anything that sounded like the Craig G "Droppin' Science" remix.

Craig [Mack] was just one of the most gracious human beings. He was so humble, so happy. He loved hip-hop. You saw the smile on his face, and he'd start dancing and rapping. He was the same way every time. Just real happy about the music, and just loved doing his thing.

Monica Lynch (president, Tommy Boy Records): Puffy was really starting to come up with Bad Boy, and their offices were actually pretty close to the Tommy Boy offices, and I was friendly with Puffy. I asked him if he wanted to go to a [fashion] show with me. Oh my God. It was like a fish meeting water.

You know how Puffy is already so dramatic and has such an expressive face. When you walk into the big runway fashion show in Bryant Park, and flashes are going off, there's these fabulous people left, right, and center, and the music is going, I think it was like a fucking wet dream for this kid.

It was like you take somebody to the prom and then they end up dancing with everybody else.

READY TO DIE, the lone Notorious B.I.G. album released while he was alive, landed on September 13, 1994, and immediately propelled the Brooklyn MC to the top of the hip-hop hierarchy. In it, the Notorious B.I.G. harnessed his innate storytelling ability and keen eye for detail as he sourced from his life experience. *Ready to Die* sliced through the West Coast's grip on hip-hop, becoming a landmark album.

Ready to Die alternated between pop-oriented singles and gritty tracks, themes, and skits. "Juicy," the lead single, provided the ultimate rags-to-riches fairy tale. "Big Poppa" rose to number six on the Billboard Hot 100 and was nominated for a Grammy Award for Best Rap Solo Performance.

Cheo Hodari Coker (journalist): Big was fascinating. He was just as compelling as he was in terms of his record. He was nonchalant. He was funny. He was real chill.

But at the same time, you didn't really understand the significance of his quotes until you went home and listened to your tape recorder. And then you just realized he was dropping intellectual bombs left and right, and you're like, *Oh my God, this guy is the doorway to all this other shit.*

I was interviewing Big and in the middle of the interview, [members] from Junior M.A.F.I.A., they wanted to borrow a gun to rob somebody, and he basically shunned them off; didn't say go away, but he just basically bullshitted them. And then when they walked away, he said, "I know exactly where the gun is."

And he was talking about how this is what he was trying to change. He was trying to take these kids off the block to see the rest of the world. Basically, the whole point of him getting a record deal was that he was going to put other people on and take them out of this environment. He really was one of the first people to really think like that.

Mister Cee (DJ, producer): You got to look at what Big Daddy Kane did. [He] changed the game lyrically. Also, Kane changed the game as far as the style of dress. Big kind of did the same exact thing, changed the game lyrically and the style of dress—the whole Coogi sweaters and the Versace shades.

When you talk about changing the game with Big, you can't take away what Puff did as well—the whole sampling famous '80s records like "Juicy" from Mtume and "Between the Sheets" by the Isley Brothers. Telling a hardcore rapper, "This is what's going to make you be a superstar," you got to give Puffy that credit. You got to give Diddy the credit as well, sampling "Rise" by Herb Alpert to come up with "Hypnotize" [for *Life After Death*] and sampling Diana Ross.

It's those type of moves that Big and Puff did that really changed the whole complexity of how to make records in the '90s.

Cheo Hodari Coker (journalist): In Puff's mind, he's like, *I want to get that big, ra-ra, angry, Timberland boots, Carhartt, sipping 40s on the corner, wearing camouflage, Brooklyn vibe. But I also want to have a way I can sell it to Black females, because they're ultimately going to be the ones buying records en masse.*

That became the whole thing of him saying, "Yeah, you can do 'Machine Gun Funk.' You can do 'Warning' and all your hardcore records for your twenty friends in Flatbush. But I need you to do a commercial record like 'Juicy.' I need you to put on some nicer clothes and do this kind of playa thing, like the Isley Brothers, like some West Coast shit for 'Big Poppa.' "

And Big was always just like, "Whatever. Alright, I'll do it." He would make these commercial records that at the time he was making them, he was like, "Puff's on some shit, but fuck it." And then he'd make the record, and then of course the record would blow up, and then he would see, "Oh my God, Puff was right." They genuinely liked each other. They really did.

QUICKLY, THE NOTORIOUS B.I.G. began opening doors for his Bed-Stuy brethren. Junior M.A.F.I.A. (Masters At Finding Intelligent Attitudes) released its debut album, *Conspiracy,* in 1995. The album featured four appearances by the Notorious B.I.G., including on the lead single, "Player's Anthem."

Importantly, *Conspiracy* propelled the career of Lil' Kim, a brash and talented artist who had an outsized impact as a female hip-hop artist who embraced her sexuality in the face of an often misogynistic industry.

Chico Del Vec (artist, Junior M.A.F.I.A.): Big came up with the name Junior M.A.F.I.A. We was mafia because we used to watch movies like Al Capone and the mob movies. We used to be like, "We could be like that."

DJ Clark Kent (producer): I'm the first person to record [Lil' Kim]. I took her and did a solo record on a soundtrack called *Time to Shine*. I'm the first person to create solo shit for her, because we believed and understood she was gonna be that deal. She had it.

It's crazy because in the very beginning of Junior M.A.F.I.A., Foxy [Brown] might have been in Junior M.A.F.I.A. as well . . . she might have, 'cause they were all young and they were all little.

SEAN COMBS PLAYED a signifigant role in spearheading Mary J. Blige's seminal 1994 album, *My Life*. The album marked a continuation of their work from 1992's *What's the 411?* Blige earned her distinction as the Queen of Hip-Hop Soul during this time, simultaneously conveying extreme strength and sober vulnerability through her work.

The working relationship between Combs and Blige soon fractured. But not before Blige first alerted Combs to a group named the Warlocks from her native Yonkers, New York. He signed the trio and changed their name to the Lox. Jadakiss, Sheek Louch, and Styles P became staples of New York hip-hop in the late 1990s, crafting a lasting legacy.

Sheek Louch (artist, the Lox): First it was 'Kiss, he was little J and he used to rap at his grandmother's house around one turntable with this guy. And I used to be up there like, "Man, this is pretty dope how 'Kiss is doing this shit." I said, "I'ma try this, too." So I went and I got, like, a little black-and-white composition notebook. I started putting some words in. I was probably like eleven.

Styles P (artist, the Lox): We're all from Yonkers. We all rhyme. I met Sheek late, junior high, I met 'Kiss early high school, and it's just the level of what we do. It was very professional.

Originally, they was supposed to be a duo. They would have been like EPMD. I would have been like Redman. They would have been the Jungle Brothers. I would have been like Q-Tip. But it just ended up, we just all kept going hard.

Sheek Louch (artist, the Lox): Everybody's coming out of the Bronx, Queens, and for us, from Yonkers. They was also coming out of a town right next door to us called Mount Vernon, where Heavy D and all these people, Brand Nubian, and then we came later with the mixtape era. So we made our mark that way, rapping before the album.

Everybody else was making big noise, like Heav[y D] and Pete Rock and CL Smooth and all these guys that rocked right over in Mount Vernon, in New Rochelle. And then, Mary Blige came out and then it was all she wrote.

Styles P (artist, the Lox): We sold mixtapes that I stole from an odd job. We made a demo, pressed it, sold it. Somehow that demo got to Mary. She was playing it on tour, Puff heard us, and they wanted to hear us in person.

Sheek Louch (artist, the Lox): Imagine walking in and seeing Craig Mack, Total, Big, and all these people. It was like, *Oh, shit. Am I on the scene?*

Styles P (artist, the Lox): I thought Puff and the whole Bad Boy team at the time were like the Chicago Bulls of rap. It was a lot to take in back then. It was like, *Wow, we made it to the Bulls of rap.*

Sheek Louch (artist, the Lox): Musically, [Puff was] always honest in the studio. Like when we think it's done and we know this is a smash, he'll come in and say, "Nah, nah. That ain't it. We need to write another one."

Like, "What the fuck, nigga, did you hear these lyrics we spinned?"

And he'll come in and say, "Yo, but it sounds so personal. It sounds like you talking to homies on your block. It's not for the world. It ain't gonna bump in Texas. It ain't gonna bump in Little Rock, Arkansas."

He used to always say that kind of shit to us. And that's what made us workhorses. Leaving the studio, he said to us, "Y'all ain't got nowhere near the money I got and y'all always leave the studio earlier than me, every night. What the fuck?"

That stuck with me.

Styles P (artist, the Lox): [B.I.G.] was just a very rare dude; he's like a pure classy dude. Stuck out to me because he treated our homies the same way he treated us. He didn't have to, so that always stood out to me how classy the guy was.

Sheek Louch (artist, the Lox): I remember him asking us to get on ["Last Day"], like, "Yeah right, get the fuck outta here. We about to get on this project?" And we did it and Big played the beat and then he broke out.

Even when we did the song "You'll See," that shit was even [more] crazy. My first time hearing it [was] in the Palladium Club in Manhattan, like, *Man, is that our song that they're bumping to right now?* And this is fresh out of high school for us.

THE LOX'S BAD Boy tenure was brief. They soon signed with Ruff Ryders, a formative collective that helped reestablish a grittier New York hip-hop in the midst of Bad Boy's radio-designed singles. South Bronx siblings Darrin "Dee" Dean, Joaquin "Waah" Dean, and Chivon Dean founded Ruff Ryders first as an artist management firm that included acts like Eve and Drag-On.

DMX, born Earl Simmons, personified art birthed through pain, and evolved into the most noteworthy roster member. He found long-awaited success with Ruff Ryders in 1998, when he followed his debut, *It's Dark and Hell Is Hot,* with *Flesh of My Flesh, Blood of My Blood* through Def Jam and became the second rapper ever to release two number one albums in the same calendar year (Tupac Shakur had released *All Eyez on Me* and *The Don Killuminati: The 7 Day Theory* under the name Makaveli in 1996).

Swizz Beatz, a nephew of the Deans, honed Ruff Ryders' synth-production style.

Sheek Louch (artist, the Lox): Swizz paints the picture at all times. Besides making the beat, he's doing the dance, he's making these noises and the energetic shit, while you're there working on it. He's just real talented.

Styles P (artist, the Lox): When you're working along somebody and you are dedicating your lives to the same thing, working on a craft, it's just an organic raw energy that you're gonna produce that's gonna be fitting because you're sharing the dream, you're sharing the space, and the hunger. So you're bound to make something good.

BAD BOY RECORDS employed the Hitmen as its in-house production squad. The team featured Sean Combs as the head and included
Deric "D-Dot" Angelettie, Nashiem Myrick, Sean C & LV, Stevie J,
Chucky Thompson, Mario Winans, Carlos "Six July" Broady, and Younglord, among others. Most members possessed musical backgrounds
and they often worked in pairs, which increased internal competition.
The Hitmen became known for melding soulful R&B samples with hip-
hop. As the artist Mase once rapped: "Take hits from the '80s / But do
it sound so crazy."

Nashiem Myrick (producer, Hitmen): Puff was friends with a friend of
mine, Harve Pierre. When Harve introduced me to Puff at Howard,
he knew I was a DJ for Harve's group. And since we were from New
York, I used to meet him at the studio or pick him up from work and
go to sessions with them. And he knew I had records. He knew I had
all the breakbeats. So, he would say, "Yo, Nash, bring them breakbeats
of yours." 'Cause that's where he was getting into producing also.

Carlos "Six July" Broady (producer, Hitmen): I get a call from Bad Boy. It
might have been June [Ambrose], and she was like, "Yo, you got some
hot joints. I'm going to pass your number to my man—his name is
Nashiem [Myrick] and he's going to call you."

Nashiem's first conversation was like, "Yo, Big picked one of your
joints. You got to come to New York." That's the first shit he said to me.

I was like, "What?"

He was like, "Big like your shit. You got to come to New York.
When can you come?"

I'm like, "Shit, fucking right now. Let's go."

I had been out of Memphis once, that was to New Jersey on the
bus, and here it is, the following year, I'm on a plane to New York.
I'm like, *Damn.*

Soon as I got to the studio that night, Nash is like, "Yo, this my man
Carlos," and Big's like, "Yo, you got some shit. You bring that shit?"
I'm like, "Yeah."

My first official industry check came from Biggie for [Lil' Kim's]
"Queen Bitch" beat. Later on, I learned that Big wanted that beat for

himself, but Puffy didn't like the beat for Big. Big was like, "Yo, he not letting nobody else get that beat. Fuck it, I'ma buy it and use it for one of my artists."

Nashiem Myrick (producer, Hitmen): We [Myrick and Broady] had a lot in common as far as our choice in music. Big took to our samples 'cause we were different from the other producers that were giving him joints. We just had that hard, hard sound, me and Carlos. It was raw but then it was just undeniable.

Carlos "Six July" Broady (producer, Hitmen): People always talk about the crunk music and the Memphis sound, but if you pay attention to the records that I sampled on *Life After Death*, they were majority Memphis records. The Dramatics went for "Somebody's Gotta Die." "My Downfall" was Al Green—I chopped up "For the Good Times." The "What's Beef" drumbeat, I replayed the "So Glad You're Mine" drums. I can go on and on and on.

I thank RZA for putting that battery in my back, because the first few Wu-Tang Clan albums, they are a combination of Hi records and Stax records. The New York sound is a Memphis sound, if you ask me, because those soul records helps shape those joints.

Nashiem Myrick (producer, Hitmen): Sometimes I would chop up a sample and put it together and just give it to him without no drums, without nothing, just the sample, and we'll write a whole song to it. We had a bond musically.

Carlos "Six July" Broady (producer, Hitmen): I had brought a beat tape and Biggie played his "My Downfall" verse for me, and because I did the scratching on "Queen Bitch," he was like, "I need some scratching for this record of yours that I did."

When he played it for me, he was saying the hook to "My Downfall." I played Big the "Can't Nobody Hold Me Down" beat. He liked it, but he was saying Ice Cube had just did "Check Yo Self (The Message Remix)" [which also sampled "The Message"], [so] he ain't really want to do it. From there, Nashiem played it for Puffy and in an instant [he] was like, "Yo, this going to be the joint."

From my understanding, "What's Beef" wasn't a favorite beat of

Biggie's, but Puff liked it. It was that type of thing, whereas Puff might not like a beat, Big will like it. They just knew how to respect each other's space and creativity.

Shorty B (producer, Dangerous Crew): We had a studio in Atlanta, and [Too] $hort came in and said, "Hey, man. Puff Daddy's about to come in. They want to hear some beats for Lil' Kim." About an hour or two later, Puff and them came in. I played some beats, and they liked all the beats, right? He said, "Lil' Kim will be here tomorrow. We'll let her pick one of your beats."

I played, I'm guessing twelve, thirteen songs, and the last song I played was "Call Me," which is on the *Booty Call* soundtrack. As soon as I played that song, Lil' Kim said, "That's it. That's the one I want right there."

I spent the night at $hort's house and I'm sitting at $hort's kitchen table. I'm eating some eggs or something and the doorbell rings. It was Biggie. We set in there, chopped it up. . . . They picked Kim up from the airport and we all met back at the studio, picked out the beat. I think it was the same studio that Pac got shot at.

After the session was over, which was about four-thirty in the morning, me, Too $hort, my homeboy P.O., Lil' Cease, and Big, we coming down in the elevator, right? When the elevator gets to the bottom floor, Big looked at Cease. We go out to the front of the studio, Lil' Cease looks out to the right and he had a little flashlight, flashing. And about two blocks up the street, I saw a white van flash the lights. He came back and he said, "We ready, Big." So, Big jumped in the van and mashed on off.

Suge had them dudes spooked, man. I'm like, "$hort, did you see that shit? Suge's got them boys scared as shit." They were shook. That's when that East Coast/West Coast shit was going on.

After we finish the song, we fly back to Atlanta. At about nine o'clock in the morning, my phone rings. It's Big. He said, "Mary J. Blige is having a birthday party. I wanted to see if you and $hort wanted to come, man. I'll pick y'all up from the airport with limos."

I said, "Alright, Big. Let me call $hort and I'll find out what's happening. Let me call you back."

This is one of the realest conversations I've ever had with Too $hort, because there have not been many. $hort is not built like that. But I said, "$hort, man. Big just called and he's wondering if we want to go to Mary J. Blige's party with him."

$hort said, "Nah, I ain't gonna go."

I told $hort I'm going to go and fuck with Big and them, because I'm thinking in my mind, *Puff really want to fuck with me,* because he was really liking my music, right? But $hort said, "Man, you sure you want to do that?"

I said, "Why not?"

He said, "Man, what if they find out you, like, Pac's uncle or something? What if there's some undercover shit with the invitation? Maybe they found out who you are and how close you are to Pac."

I'm like, "Wow. I ain't think of that, $hort. That's real talk."

I called Biggie back and I said, "Nah, Big, we ain't going to be able to make it, man. But keep in touch and maybe we'll catch up on the next one."

I hung up the phone. I went to the bathroom, my phone rings again—I swear to God, five minutes later. Guess who it was? Tupac.

"Shorty B there?"

I said, "Pac? You home?" I think he had been out two or three days and had come to Atlanta to go to his mama's house.

He said, "Yeah."

I tell Pac, "I'll be there in about an hour."

He says, "Man, bring all the weed you got."

When I went over to the house, I knocked on Afeni's door, Jasmine Guy opened the door. Her hair was all over the place like she had been fucking all night. So I teased her. I was like, "Damn, my nephew home for real." She started laughing.

I spent the whole day with Afeni and Pac and his sister. So Pac said, "Shorty B, I want you to hear what I've been doing." So he let me hear this one song. "I'd rather be your N-I-G-G-A, so we can smoke weed. . . ."

I said, "Hold up, Pac. I just did that same song." Because it's like a Bootsy song, right? Which was "Gettin' It." And I had just recorded it the night before. I said, "I've got to let you hear this, because I don't want you to hear this later and think I heard your song and made this one."

Evidently, we were on the same page. He loved "Gettin' It" and I loved the song he was working on. He let me hear about forty songs. I sat over there with him, smoked weed, and just hung out with him all day at his mama's house.

Carlos "Six July" Broady (producer, Hitmen): I remember when Pac died. I remember vividly when I came to the studio, Jay Black was playing "Hit 'Em Up" real loud and shit. We like, "What the fuck is going on?"

Niggas like, "Yo, Pac just got killed."

We was waiting on Puff to come to the studio and they called like, "Yo, everybody got to leave. He about to shut the studio down." Everybody knew where Daddy's House was, so Puff didn't want nobody getting hurt. You just didn't know what was going to happen. It was just a crazy time.

> **AT THE HEIGHT** of the East Coast/West Coast rivalry, Sean Combs opted to work in isolation and shipped himself, members of the Hitmen, and their equipment to Maraval, Trinidad, for a series of pivotal sessions. The Bad Boy team coalesced at Caribbean Sound Basin, using the time to craft songs and sounds that came to dominate mainstream music. The sessions produced tracks used for Combs's debut, *No Way Out* (formerly titled *Hell Up in Harlem*), the Notorious B.I.G.'s sophomore offering, *Life After Death,* and other landmark albums.

Carlos "Six July" Broady (producer, Hitmen): What made the Hitmen work was when Puff formed it, he broke us off into teams of two. Me and Nash[iem Myrick] already had formed a partnership, Deric ["D-Dot" Angelettie] and Ron ["Amen-Ra" Lawrence] was already partners, and it was Puff and Stevie [J]. That was the core of the Trinidad trip, which is where everything popped off from.

Nashiem Myrick (producer, Hitmen): We got to really hone in on who we were as producers and see the similarity, but most of all see the differences in our abilities and what made each other special to the teamwork, to the outfit [during the trip to Trinidad]. It was a moment of clarity for us because it gave us time to reflect on things. Also [it] gave us time to be with each other to understand what Stevie J can add to what I do and what Ron Lawrence can add to what I do, what I can add to what they do.

Carlos "Six July" Broady (producer, Hitmen): The chemistry of the competition is what made it work. Me and Nashiem was on some hardcore hip-hop shit, like nasty-ass drums and crazy sample chops and shit. But you got Stevie J that knew how to refine records because he was a musician that can play every fucking thing, and he also was ill on the programming, him and Chucky Thompson. Prestige [Daven Vanderpool] and Younglord [Richard Frierson] was in there too. Ron is very intricate on his programming and how he does his drums in his records. D-Dot, he was new to making beats and he had an ill-ass record collection. His ear was just bananas, so his records was crazy and they was always upbeat.

That's really what made it stick. The competition was thick, and it was really brotherly, but the bar was set high. It's like, *Man, I got to either outdo my brother or be equal to him.*

Nashiem Myrick (producer, Hitmen): [The Hitmen] was the first hip-hop group that the individual talents were more a focus. Everyone in the crew was a producer by himself but had his own style. But we worked together as a team, and I think that was a first time that was done in hip-hop. Everyone in the crew had his own platform as a Hitman. We would do outside work on our own and then we'd have success there. But in-house, we'd collaborate, and you may see three or four of us on the same record and it just worked that way with us.

Just Blaze (producer): The producer's job is to deliver a product. You're there to make sure that the job gets done. The thing you have to remember is: Not every producer is a beat maker; not every beat maker is a producer.

You take somebody like Diddy. Diddy's a producer of the highest.

He knows how to create events. And when I say events, I don't just mean parties. I mean musically. He knows how to take a good idea and make it a great song. He doesn't touch a drum machine.

You look at his crew of Hitmen, he knew who to get for what job. Easy Mo Bee is on the drums. Stevie J is on the guitar and bass. Nashiem may be chopping up the samples. Chucky Thompson is doing some other overdubs. Carlos Broady just found a crazy loop. Now someone else is coming in to do overdubs on it. He was an orchestrator. He wasn't just a producer.

Matt Sonzala (journalist): I feel like there was a moment where Bad Boy took over everything. The radio from coast to coast began its descent from being regional and interesting to just all playing the same thing.

Bob Power (engineer): Puffy really had his finger on the pulse of social movement. Making the songs that he made in the ways that he made them really spoke to people at that time, really seriously. In part it was a nostalgia thing, and part of it was bringing back records—not just a little sound or a little piece of it, but a whole hook that had people say, "Oh, I love that. I listened to that when I was four years old." But then he had different people on top of it, like Mary. So Puffy, like it or not, really had something going on at that point.

THE NOTORIOUS B.I.G. visited Los Angeles to promote his second album, *Life After Death,* in March 1997. The East Coast/West Coast rivalry raged on as many still mourned the recent death of Tupac Shakur. The Notorious B.I.G. attended the Soul Train Music Awards at the Shrine Auditorium. He later went to a party co-hosted by Qwest Records and *Vibe* magazine at Miracle Mile's Petersen Automotive Museum.

In the early morning of March 9, the Notorious B.I.G. departed the party with an entourage. While stopped at a red light, an assailant fired into the SUV that carried him. B.I.G. was struck by four bullets. The final and fatal one entered through his hip and pierced his heart and lung. He died at the age of twenty-four. No one has ever been charged in his murder.

The double album *Life After Death* arrived at stores a little more than two weeks later and exhibited another gargantuan leap in the Notorious B.I.G.'s lyricism. But the affable person revealed on the record was now gone.

Nashiem Myrick (producer, Hitmen): Even if you look back on *Ready to Die,* and then listen to *Life After Death,* the step Big took as an artist was incredible.

DJ Clark Kent (producer): He still would have been the best rapper we've ever heard, because he couldn't do anything but get better with the company around him. His company was Jay[-Z]. And if you listen to his first album, which was perfect, and then you listen to his second album, which again, was perfect, the lines, the bars, the raps were better. He grew immensely after he met Jay-Z. He forced his pen to a different level.

They did it for each other. He forced Jay's style, the way he said rhymes, the way he thought about record-making, to a different level. They were perfect complements for each other. That's why I say Jay is the best MC, Biggie's the best rapper. Biggie's the second-best MC, Jay's the second-best rapper.

Cheo Hodari Coker (journalist): He wanted the life that Jay-Z now has. Big was the one that talked about having a clothing line, having businesses, in addition to also having a roster of artists, and also married an R&B diva. Jay-Z took Big's template and took it to another level.

They were having these long conversations about their ambitions and what they wanted to do once they had the money, and once things were going a certain way. That's why Jay, in his rhymes, he'll constantly have a little Biggie reference here and there because that was probably, on the creative level, his best friend, because they could talk about the intricacies of the music in ways that few people could understand. [Like] those conversations between Thelonious Monk and Miles Davis arguing—that's what they brought out of each other.

At the same time, there was also a certain entrepreneurial sense, because I think Big, had he been able to live up to his potential, he definitely would've been trying to do exactly what Jay-Z ended up doing, which is maintaining hip-hop relevance and making records when he wants to make records, but then at the same time, making business moves. Everybody thought for a long time that the money was in hip-hop. The money wasn't in hip-hop; the money was in monetizing the culture of hip-hop—that's what makes you a billionaire.

It's Dre doing Beats by Dre. It's Puffy doing Cîroc. And it's Jay-Z's attitude businesswise about everything else, from his nightclub to sports management to the streaming service. But when you talk specifically to Puffy and to Jay, Big was the one who was always talking about monetizing the culture in terms of what he wanted to do—and those guys got to do it.

20 THE CONSCIOUS-NESS

The Midwest
1988–2010

Near the dawn of the new millennium, hip-hop continued its march toward becoming music's top-selling genre. Some of the largest artists began to break from the Midwest in the form of Detroit's Eminem, St. Louis's Nelly, and Chicago's Kanye West. Each added their unique imprint to hip-hop music that penetrated the mainstream—Eminem through his ability to provoke, Nelly through his Midwestern twang, and West through his relatable lyrics and fine-tuned production.

Until those artists emerged, most Midwestern hip-hop took elements from both the East and West coasts. Chicago artists nurtured a hip-house scene that mixed hip-hop and house music, before the artist Common Sense established himself on a national platform.

In Detroit, Esham emerged as one of the first hip-hop artists to break out of the Midwest when he released his debut album, *Boomin' Words from Hell,* in 1989. Esham, influenced by the Geto Boys, documented a Detroit in the throes of the crack epidemic. Coining his style "acid rap," he influenced a subsequent generation of artists and later developed a large-selling independent hip-hop label, Reel Life Productions.

Esham (artist, Detroit): I made music to the stuff that I heard and had access to, which was a lot of punk rock and other stuff. For those that don't know, acid rap would be a happy punch in the face. It's all over the place.

At the time, being that young, I was just expressing myself and really pushing freedom of speech as far as I thought it could possibly go. So, I was unconsciously making those rhymes up. I really didn't know what the hell I was talking about. That stuff would just come up in my head and I would just record it.

It was crazy to do it like that, but I just so happened to record some of the stuff that a lot of people was feeling on the inside but didn't want to say out loud. Some of the rhymes I was making was banned. People started to identify themselves in the music, but it took a minute to do that.

Detroit, it was wild. Crack had just came out and it exploded in the streets of Detroit. It destroyed a lot of families. Detroit was literally like hell, fires burning on Devil's Night. People getting shot and killed. It wasn't a nice place to be at the time.

Nobody could even understand why we were talking like that or why people was making up rhymes like that. They never had a vivid picture of Detroit until people started coming in and started to see the plight and the decay and the desolation of it, that they really started to understand what I was talking about. Like, "Oh, shit, it really is fucked up out here."

IN CHICAGO, ARTISTS found it difficult to gain the attention of record labels in New York and California. Instead they developed their own sound, an extension of house music's regional popularity. The hip-house subgenre featured fast-paced tempos that bridged the gap between hip-hop and dance music. Early significant contributors included Fast Eddie, Vitamin C, JMD, and Kool Rock Steady.

Capital D (artist, Chicago): You would have parties at someone's house. Basement parties, and a lot of house music would be playing and then you'd have the hip-hop set and then you'd go back to house music. That was the first entry of hip-hop to a lot of young cats at these parties. And then everybody in Chicago was getting their hip-hop from a station on the South Side that was called WHPK, which was at the

University of Chicago. It was a late-night radio show by JP Chill that started around 1986.

I was living in the South Suburbs of Chicago and it would be hard to get WHPK. You'd have to sit with your little antenna pointing in a certain direction in order to catch WHPK. But that's where people got up on a lot of the new stuff that was dropping. Then local artists would get known by going on WHPK, by kicking freestyles or playing new stuff. JP Chill broke a lot of Chicago artists in the late '80s, early '90s.

CHICAGO'S COMMON SENSE, born Lonnie Lynn Jr., began his career by rapping with his friends Corey Crawley and Ernest Wilson. Their group, C.D.R., gained a following and even opened for Big Daddy Kane. Common Sense, who later shortened his moniker to Common, earned a feature in *The Source*'s Unsigned Hype column while he was a student at Florida A&M University.

As a solo artist, he debuted with the single "Take It EZ," followed by the 1992 album *Can I Borrow a Dollar?*

With 1994's *Resurrection,* Common provided Chicago with its first breakout hip-hop solo album, achieving critical acclaim nationally. (Chicago native Da Brat, born Shawntae Harris, had released *Funkdafied* earlier in the year through Atlanta's So So Def Recordings, and became the first female soloist to receive platinum certification.)

The single "I Used to Love H.E.R." showcased Common's cleverness in utilizing an extended metaphor. In this standout track, a woman—representing hip-hop—and her aimless mannerisms depict what Common saw as the waywardness of the genre—specifically, the decline of Afrocentric rap and the continuing rise of gangster rap.

Rhymefest (artist, Chicago): The first time I heard "I Used to Love H.E.R.," I'll never forget it. It was a picnic and he performed it for the first time at the park. It was Common and it was Twista, and Twista was a little bit bigger at this moment, so Common opened up at the park. He performed it and he was so hype and you could tell he knew he had something, but nobody that was watching at the park understood except for a few. And I was like, *Oh my God, that was brilliant. I want to be like that.*

I admire Common and I long for my path in music to lead me to be as good as that. The fact that I was like, *I see the value in this type of lyricism and this type of cleverness in music and this type of weaving of words.* And I didn't look around me and say, "Wait, you don't want to get the whole crowd jumping, nigga? You want to be like this?"

Yeah, I want to be like that. I put that in my mind. I also sent it up to the universe and here we are.

Capital D (artist, Chicago): It was, in a lot of ways, a validation for a lot of artists. In some ways, Common sat between the whole East Coast/West Coast thing. He probably leaned more East Coast, but he wasn't wrapped up in the whole thing. That kind of distance allowed him to write a song like that, for it to get the love everywhere that it got love, and to be the first Chicago artist to have that kind of acceptance. That whole Common album, to me, was the first great Chicago hip-hop album. He clearly represented the South Side of Chicago, and it was just fresh.

ERNEST DION WILSON assumed the pseudonym No I.D. (Dion spelled backward) and produced the bulk of Common's first three albums, including *Resurrection* along with The Twilite Tone. No I.D. became a foundational figure within both Chicago hip-hop and the entire genre by serving as mentor to a teenage Kanye West, working with Jermaine Dupri and Jay-Z, and becoming an executive at Def Jam.

Capital D (artist, Chicago): There wasn't a unified Chicago sound or scene in the same way you had in Houston or in Atlanta. To me, I think [No I.D.] is criminally slept-on just in terms of what he did as a producer, and then what he has done as a business person, and the influence he's had on the genre, the influence he had on Kanye, the way he helped launch Common's career, the influence he's had on Jay-Z's more recent work. The influence he's had on hip-hop is enormous. No I.D. doesn't get the love, just as a base level, that maybe he were to get if he was from New York.

Rhymefest (artist, Chicago): Anyone who knows No I.D., knows he's a hard man to get in contact with. That's because he's a shaman. He's a master. He's a sage. He lives in the mountains, and he comes down every once in a while to show us his wisdom.

No I.D. is a true living hip-hop shaman, and those people, they don't want the recognition you think they deserve. They know who they are, and they can come down to the city at any point and show you. But they love living in the mountains in obscurity. It's part of their meditation process.

THE MIDWEST BIRTHED "choppers," artists who expanded on the quick delivery that those like Kool Moe Dee had pioneered, delivering lyrics at a breakneck pace. The breakthrough groups and artists included Ohio's Bone Thugs-n-Harmony, who signed with Ruthless Records through Eazy-E, Missouri's Tech N9ne, and Chicago's Do or Die, Crucial Conflict, and Twista.

AK (artist, Do or Die, Chicago): There was no rap going on other than Common Sense and Twista in Chicago at the time. It was Do or Die and Crucial Conflict that broke big. It took something special from the music industry ear. Because you heard the East Coast and then you heard the West Coast, but you never heard it like we put it down from the Midwest. So, it took time to bring something different to the table for hip-hop.

"PO PIMP," DO or Die's debut single, featuring Twista and Johnny P, an R&B singer, became an independent sensation. The group signed to Houston's Rap-A-Lot Records, and Twista began a long-standing relationship with Atlantic Records. The song, produced by the Legendary Traxster, became a breakthrough on the Billboard charts.

AK (artist, Do or Die, Chicago): I remember having a tape, listening to this song, and me and [fellow Do or Die member] Belo took it to Traxster. And I said, "Man, we want to replay this over." So we sat there with Traxster and we molded the song. I started to make the hook and the next thing you know, I began to write. [Then] Twista came in and did his part. Then we got [R&B singer] Johnny P in for the hook. Next thing you know, boom, the song takes off. So that's when I knew, *Okay, something is up.*

MARSHALL MATHERS SPENT time in Missouri and Michigan as a youth before his mother planted roots in Detroit. Mathers, who adopted the moniker of Eminem, befriended a Detroit rapper named Proof and made his name in the city's underground battle circuit.

Eminem first linked with Jeff and Mark Bass's F.B.T. Productions, recording his debut album, *Infinite,* for their independent Web Entertainment label. The effort was a commercial flop upon its 1996 release.

After being let go from his job as a cook, Eminem caravanned, competing in competitions around the country in 1997, from Cincinnati's Scribble Jam against the likes of Rhymefest, to the Rap Olympics in Los Angeles. Eventually, Eminem earned the attention of Dr. Dre, who offered his coveted cosign and a deal with Interscope and Aftermath Entertainment.

As a white rapper, Eminem confronted and overcame the same accusations of appropriation that artists like Vanilla Ice had faced before him. With his outlandish lyrics, aimed to provoke, and his deft lyrical abilities, Eminem represented a blue-collar audience, becoming one of the genre's top-selling artists of all time.

Capital D (artist, Chicago): The Scribble Jam competition was around every July. It was just straight underground Midwest acts. Like Lone Catalysts from Columbus, and cats from Cleveland. Some independent acts from New York came every year. One of the highlights of Scribble Jam was a freestyle contest.

Rhymefest (artist, Chicago): It's interesting how one person will get as famous as Eminem, but Eminem was just a competitor like all the other competitors.

Capital D (artist, Chicago): No one knew who Eminem was. He was just some dude. He had a little mixtape that he was trying to sell. I was one of the judges. He actually went up against this guy from my crew named All Star. And All Star should have won, but then he tried to play the race card and Eminem was ready for him.

Rhymefest (artist, Chicago): Battle rapping now is like a sermon that you write. You study your opponent, and you write these five-minute sermons. Back then it was like, "We're gonna play a beat, any beat, and you've got to freestyle from the top of your head."

I remember Eminem said something that was so crazy, it fucked my self-esteem up for like two minutes. Because the whole thing was he was a white rapper, and that was an anomaly in the '90s. He was clearing the brush and paving the way for Mac Miller, for Logic, for all these people.

He said, "I'll let my razors split you until they have to staple-stitch you. This nigga took my facial tissue, turned it to a racial issue."

And I was like, *Oh, shit.*

Because the crowd went crazy, and the Black people were like, "We're gonna forgive that, because it was artfully done."

And then I realized the art in battle rapping was the art of controlling your emotions, it was the art of being in control. And ultimately, I prevailed in the battle, but goddammit Eminem won the war.

EMINEM TOOK SECOND to Juice (formerly J.U.I.C.E), an artist from Chicago, at the 1997 Scribble Jam competition. Through Rhymefest, Eminem came to the attention of Rap Coalition's Wendy Day, the organizer of that year's Rap Olympics.

Wendy Day (Rap Coalition): I was in Chicago working with Twista and Do or Die at the time. My plan was to drive to Detroit to speak on a panel, and I took Rhymefest with me. He was an amazing unsigned rapper from Chicago.

I come out of the panel and, outside, Rhymefest is in a cypher and they're freestyling and taking turns trying to impress each other. I come out and I'm starving, and I'm like, *God, I need something to eat.*

Rhymefest and I finally get into the car, and he hands me Eminem's demo. I'm like, "Cool." I tossed it nicely on the floor in front of him and I put on the radio and off we went. We were headed to Denny's. All I could think about was, *I want the Grand Slam. I'm so fucking hungry.* He completely turned around, staring at me with his back against the door with a look on his face like, *Oh my God.*

He's like, "I can't believe you just did that."

So I looked at him. "What?"

He's like, "Man, that was some foul shit."

I'm like, "What are you talking about?"

He's like, "Well, you're white. He's white. You know how hard this is."

I'm like, "'Fest, white boys can't rap."

He's like, "Wendy, he's amazing. I was just in a cypher with him."

So he totally peer-pressured me into listening to the demo, and I got through half of the first song and I made a U-turn across the grass and I went back, and I picked up Eminem. I'm like, "Get in."

NEWARK'S CLUB ZANZIBAR hosted the original Rap Olympics in 1993. Wendy Day's iteration was held outside of Los Angeles International Airport in 1997, with the winner receiving $500 and a watch. Day imagined teams pitted against one another; however, the event ended in a freestyle battle with the rapper Otherwize topping Eminem, who had shown enough to earn an invitation onto *The Wake Up Show,* Sway & King Tech's influential syndicated radio program.

Wendy Day (Rap Coalition): My plan was to have three or four different rounds. There would be a timed round where they would have to rap in a certain amount of time. Then they would have to freestyle off the top of their head. Then they would have to pick a piece of paper out of a hat, and that topic, they would have to rap about for thirty seconds.

I wanted to include famous rappers, as well as up-and-coming rappers. I created teams. Wu-Tang had a team. J-Smoov, which is Project Blowed, he had a team. I had a team. There were a couple other people on another team that I can't remember. But the prize was a bootlegged Rolex watch and a trip to *The Wake Up Show*, and my team won.

And then Eminem decided that he wanted to battle one of the guys from Project Blowed, and he won the battle. So, they got the Rolex, and he got to go to *The Wake Up Show*. That was how we divvied up the prize. When Eminem got to *The Wake Up Show*, Dr. Dre heard him and went up there and that's how they met.

ANOTHER MIDWESTERN HIP-HOP artist landed atop the Billboard charts a little more than a year after Eminem released his major-label debut album, *The Slim Shady LP*. Nelly's group, the St. Lunatics (with Murphy Lee, Ali, Kyjuan, City Spud, and Slo' Down), earned regional success through their 1997 single "Gimme What U Got." But no mainstream rappers had emerged from St. Louis, and the St. Lunatics had trouble securing a group deal. Instead, they pushed Nelly, born Cornell Haynes, to the forefront as a solo artist in helping him land a deal with Universal Music Group.

Nelly dropped his studio debut album, *Country Grammar,* in June 2000. Jason "Jay E" Epperson handled the bulk of the production, and the St. Lunatics were featured prominently. The album showcased Nelly's use of pop-rap sing-alongs and distinct Midwestern dialect, and introduced four successful singles: "Country Grammar (Hot Shit)," "E.I.," "Ride wit Me," and "Batter Up." *Country Grammar* topped the U.S. Billboard 200 chart for more than a month.

Jay E (producer, St. Louis): We always would give the beats to Nelly and the Lunatics. Sometimes we would go through beats, and they would write stuff then and there, but they were heavy smokers, and the skating-rink studio wouldn't allow smoking in there. So I would give them a beat tape, and they would go off and write in the car or whatever. Then they would come back, and we would do the songs that they wrote to them.

I just remembered Nelly really loved [the "Country Grammar" track] and pretty much made that his song. Nelly was part of that new culture of hip-hop of where, to me, it kind of birthed a lot of rappers

today with the singsongy sound. Even Drake, I feel like, has a lot of
Nelly influence in his stuff.

> **KANYE WEST MOVED** to Chicago from Georgia as a toddler in the
> early 1980s. West's mother, Donda West, was a college English pro-
> fessor who supported his interest in poetry and music. West appren-
> ticed under No I.D., and gained his first production credits for Grav's
> 1996 LP *Down to Earth*. West later joined a group, Go Getters, along
> with GLC, Timmy G, and Arrowstar.
>
> West signed to Gee Roberson and Kyambo "Hip-Hop" Joshua's
> management-production company, Hip Hop Since 1978, cultivating a
> production style that sped up the samples of renowned soul records.
> He received his first platinum album through his work on Jermaine
> Dupri's *Life in 1472*.
>
> West landed the break that propelled his career when he became an
> in-house producer for Roc-A-Fella Records and joined with Just Blaze
> in crafting some of Jay-Z's genre-defining tracks. But West had larger
> accomplishments in his sights.

Kyambo "Hip-Hop" Joshua (A&R, Roc-A-Fella): Wendy Day from Rap
Coalition was doing a convention in Chicago and asked me to be on a
panel, and I'm only eighteen years old. I had never been to Chicago
before. I go there thinking I'ma meet Common Sense and maybe
Twista. I loved Common's album at the time, and I liked Twista's
album. But I was on the panel with both of their producers, No I.D.
and Legendary Traxster.

Me, No I.D., Legendary Traxster go on a panel together, and basically I'm telling them, "I'm working with Jay[-Z]. I'm starting to work
on this new record."

And No I.D. is like, "I don't really got the Jay-Z type of beats, but I
got this kid I'm working with who definitely loves Jay and I think he
got the type of stuff you looking for. I'll have him come by tomorrow."

The next day, we did our panel and he brought Ye through.
It was very, very brief. But we exchanged numbers and he would
constantly—he would just talk. He'd send me music in the mail and

we would just talk about music. And the first couple songs wasn't that good. The beats was good, but the songs was real . . . corny, for lack of a better term.

He was making songs that always remind me of Tupac's early songs. He was making songs about fat girls liking him and weird crushes, and then a song like "Dear Mama" would pop up. And then a song like "Jesus Walks" pops up.

RHYMEFEST, A SKILLED Chicago lyricist who collaborated with West, introduced him to the Addicts Rehabilitation Center Gospel Choir's 1997 a cappella song "Walk with Me," a spiritual and cele-bratory song that eventually provided the anchor to "Jesus Walks." Rhymefest said he had planned to use the song for his debut album. Instead it landed on West's debut, *The College Dropout,* bridging a gulf between mainstream hip-hop and religion, and claiming the Grammy for Best Rap Song.

Rhymefest (artist, Chicago): We are chosen by a spirit to manifest some-thing together at a moment in time. Gospel ain't my thing, but some-body gave me a tape. It had the song "Jesus Walks with Me." And when I heard the original song, it brought tears to my eyes. I didn't even know why, but it was just overwhelming. It was powerful. You had ex–drug addicts that were pouring their souls into being forgiven, and the mercy of God, and being held by a spirit that was bigger than themselves. I felt it. I saw it, even at a spiritually immature state.

I gave it to Kanye, I said, "Bro, you've got to turn this into a track." And Kanye called me a few days later and said, "Yo, I'm gonna let you hear this, but, bro, it's got to be for my album, *The College Dropout.*"

So, I was like, "Alright, cool."

Because even at that age and level, my ego realized, *This is bigger than you. Kanye's got a record deal. He's up there with Jay-Z right now, man. If you really want the world to hear this, it don't have to be you to say it.*

We got together. It was really quick, because greatness usually happens fairly quickly. I think the process was a process of closeness, of brotherly-ness. Of trying to understand God together, of trying to work through the emotion of the beat together.

I'm like, "Bro, we're gonna talk about the Bible."

He said, "Nah, man, we're gonna talk about sinning. The verse is the sin, the chorus is the salvation."

And it made me think about God differently. The chorus is always salvation. The verse is always struggle.

The process of writing "Jesus Walks" is we're gonna talk about it in making songs in conversational tone, the conversation was more of a process of what is struggle and how does it lead to salvation? I think that not only did we write the song, but we lived it out afterwards.

Kyambo "Hip-Hop" Joshua (A&R, Roc-A-Fella): That was one of the records that convinced me to take him serious on a personal level. I remember him playing it for me and being like, *Oh, shit. This is the level that makes it special to me.* Just the beginning of it and how the whole song felt and the first line, "You know what the Midwest is?" It was just like, *This is it. If we can stay in this pocket and make more of these without talking about Jesus on every song.* That approach was definitely real genuine. It was a perfect record.

There was no "Jesus Walks" before "Jesus Walks." There's gospel rap, and we might have a little Doug E. Fresh, "All the Way to Heaven," but you don't really get too many records that openly did that and was that good without it being straight-up gospel, vocals and chants. I feel like all the elements were great, and that was when everything lined up as far as his skill set and the timing of it.

It'll be like the whole side of him, just him not being negative or him not selling drugs. And it was quirky at the time. It wasn't even like it was underground positive, like Mos Def. He was just being him—the same quirkiness, the intensity, the same comedic sly thing, like as if he was just doing stand-up verses of what he became famous for later.

But it was coming from a real place. "I don't really have a lot. I'm kind of dorky, but I want better girls and they don't like me, so I'ma talk about the girls that don't like me and why they should like me." But the good records—when they came—they was real good.

Just Blaze (producer, New Jersey): My relationship with Kanye was a little bit different in the sense that we were both kind of in the same position, just trying to break into the game. Both of our first major album placements were on *The Movement* [a Harlem World album]. And then a couple years in, we both find ourselves in this new situation with Roc-A-Fella. And we just had different goals. His was to be an artist. Mine was just to be the best producer that I could be. Because we shared a lot of the same concerns, struggles, and whatnot, at certain points in his life, I was his ear. Because I could relate to the struggle probably more so than a lot of his other friends.

The fact of the matter is, a lot of his early songs weren't really that great. I saw the potential in them because he was a producer, and great producers, they always make the songs work. But do I think he was the best rapper? No. But what I saw in him was the potential to make good songs.

Kyambo "Hip-Hop" Joshua (A&R, Roc-A-Fella): When he started to get with other writers and flush out ideas even more, the songs got better—just him getting with Consequence and Rhymefest and those guys. It started to shape the sound.

Roc-A-Fella was a last option. Basically, it was like we couldn't get nowhere else—nobody was interested. Even with "Jesus Walks" and "Hey Mama." They knew he could produce, but they probably thought that he was a producer-rapper. They didn't see a big upside in that. The breakthrough moment came when we was watching Tupac's documentary, *Resurrection.* I remember him saying, "I figured it out. I can be myself." And after he said that, everything kind of clicked. The whole *College Dropout* concept came right after that. The whole four albums, the whole teddy bear mascot, all of that was probably like within a day or two of watching the Tupac film. He had a good three records at the same time, and that's when he started getting taken seriously as an artist.

Just Blaze (producer, New Jersey): I felt like when I heard "Jesus Walks," it was the culmination of all that persistence—the same with "Hey Mama." As relatively simple as those songs were, when you look at the construction of them, there's not a whole lot going on. They were just really good songs.

Rhymefest (artist, Chicago): I could tell you about the nuances of making it and ideas we had, but I think the more important thing is what happened afterwards. After it's made, you know you've got something special, but you leave it up to the universe with no expectations. And you get a Grammy and you ain't even put an album out yet. To me, that was the brilliance of when people truly collaborate with no expectations and with pure intentions. When it's all for the song and not for, "Hey, man, how much am I gonna get on this? How much are you gonna get?"

KANYE WEST'S *THE College Dropout* debuted in February 2004 at number two on the U.S. Billboard 200 and kept rising. The seminal album went platinum four times over, and earned ten Grammy nominations. Beyond two co-production credits, West produced nearly the entire album on his own. Throughout his debut, West pushed aside themes like violence and consumerism, which dominated mainstream hip-hop music at the time. His lyrics expressed vulnerability and relatability, discussing topics like religion, and debating the value of a traditional education, with wit and emotion.

While *The College Dropout* took years to come to fruition, West released his highly anticipated sophomore album, *Late Registration,* in 2005. The album showcased West expanding on his cutting-edge production and included hit singles like "Gold Digger" and "Diamonds from Sierra Leone." West dissected topics like institutional racism and the blood diamond trade while featuring appearances from artists like Brandy, Nas, Common, Jay-Z, and Jamie Foxx.

"Drive Slow," the fifth and final single, included GLC and Houston's Paul Wall.

Paul Wall (artist, Houston): Plain Pat, he was Kanye's A&R for a long time. He was working with Def Jam. He wanted to sign me, but Def Jam didn't. We still remained cool.

Then, as I got my deal, shit picked up for me. So, before Plain Pat put ["Drive Slow"] together, I had met Kanye at a photo shoot. It was a very stiff, industry type of event. And Kanye just came in out of nowhere and he just bust out freestyling. This was before he was Yeezy and all that. He was successful, but he wasn't the huge icon that he is today.

And he was like, "Damn, ain't nobody going to follow me? This supposed to be a cypher. Ain't nobody going to come behind me?" And of course, I was from Houston—you can't call me out like that on some freestyling. I came right behind and started flowing, freestyling, kicked my shit. And I had some fire, so he respected it.

Then, when he was in Houston for the Kappa Beach Party, he was like, "Hey, I'm in town over here with Mike Dean. He's mixing down my new single." We went to Mike Dean's house, and he's sitting there, mixing "Diamonds from Sierra Leone." He listened to the song at least a hundred times while I was there.

And then I get a call from Plain Pat a couple of days later and he's like, "You know I'm A&R-ing [West's] album. He said he fuck with you. Right now, we've got this song. It's called 'Drive Slow.' We don't have nothing on it. It's just a beat. But I think you'll kill it. We're going to send it to you and just do something on it. And if he fuck with it, we going to have you come out here and lay it in the studio with him out here."

To work with Kanye, that was big. So I was just like, "Shit, I'm going to do my best and if you ain't fucking with it, it's all good. I really appreciate the opportunity."

[Before that,] I do a verse. It come out sounding kind of dope. Now, the tempo for "Drive Slow" and "Sittin' Sidewayz," they two completely different tempos, so it really didn't go for "Sittin' Sidewayz." So my boy, T. Farris, was like, "Damn. Man, your verse hard as fuck, but it's just something about it, it don't really go with the beat. It's too fast. Just try to write another verse."

And I went in and wrote two verses. And that's what "Sittin' Sidewayz" was, and it did come out better, because it came out more to the tempo of the beat. But the first verse, I always kept in my pocket. I wrote it on paper like, *One day I'm going to use this on something, because I know this is a hard-ass verse. I'm going to save it.*

When Plain Pat said, "If he like it, we going to have you come out here, and lay it out," I said, "Fuck it. This might be perfect for that."

I laid it. It was perfect for it.

> **OVER THE YEARS,** Kanye West established a reputation for stoking controversy as much as for his music. Upset over the federal government's Hurricane Katrina response, West declared in 2005 that "George Bush doesn't care about Black people" during a benefit concert on NBC. In 2009, West took to the stage to interrupt Taylor Swift—who was accepting the 2009 MTV Video Music Award for Best Female Video—and trumpeted that Beyoncé deserved the award. He has also occasionally shown a political interest, as in his controversial support of former president Donald Trump.

Kyambo "Hip-Hop" Joshua (A&R, Roc-A-Fella): He did it so well the first time out, and he did it being himself. If somebody goes and says, "I'm going to be myself," and it turns out to be *College Dropout,* it's going to be hard to tell them to do anything else. Him being who he is, his whole approach and the way he's wired never ever changed one bit. He's just doing it on different levels that I don't think everybody is ready for. So, at this point, it ain't nobody that can talk to him. This whole sense of "Man, yo. You're going too far," it's hard to tell him that with the stuff people told him in the past and how it turned out for him. The stubbornness, it's just within his DNA.

> **IN RECENT YEARS,** many Chicago hip-hop artists coalesced around the city's developing "drill" scene. This offshoot of trap music, often focused on violence, produced the likes of Chief Keef, Lil Durk, and G Herbo.
>
> The city's roots maintain the imprints of those like Common, Kanye West, Rhymefest, and Lupe Fiasco—those who explored their art through socially conscious expression.

Rhymefest (artist, Chicago): I would say that the city collectively doesn't get the label that it deserves. And that label is the consciousness of hip-hop. Why can't we put together Common, Vic Mensa, Lupe [Fiasco], Rhymefest, Chance the Rapper, Kanye? You know all these people individually, but it's never given as a collective.

Chicago is really a revolutionary conscious. But historically, what is Chicago? Dr. [Martin Luther] King [Jr.] lived here. Jesse Jackson lives here. Barack Obama comes from Chicago. Common, Kanye, Rhymefest. All of this, and then you wonder why don't we know about Chicago for what it is? Shit, because if we did, it might be a different world, if we put it together.

21 TAKE IT AND FLIP IT

The ability to take something that existed and transform it into something new is a foundational component of hip-hop music. The pioneering DJs constructed the genre by extending the breakbeats of both popular and occasionally obscure music that predated them.

In hip-hop's golden age, Marley Marl modernized hip-hop production by discovering how to sample drums from a record. The Bomb Squad and Public Enemy elevated sampling to a brilliant art, and linked the youthful genre with its cultural and musical heritage by repurposing the work of James Brown and others. Groups like De La Soul and A Tribe Called Quest, and producers like Pete Rock and DJ Premier, constructed dynamic sonic collages by lifting from jazz, funk, soul, and other musical genres.

Throughout hip-hop music's adolescence, producers didn't think twice about sampling. Few viewed the process as appropriation. Even fewer considered offering royalties for using somebody else's work. The idea that hip-hop could grow as large as it did—and that producers would one day need to seek clearances in order to repurpose music—had not yet been thought of.

Those freewheeling days ended abruptly once hip-hop displayed massive profitability and record companies became vulnerable to sampling lawsuits.

But the process of crafting hip-hop, whether it's the producer seeing a track through or an artist in search of the right words or cadence, involves a high level of artistry and mastery—at least for the music that will stand the test of time.

Mr. Mixx (DJ, producer, 2 Live Crew): Nobody really thought about [clearances]. I guess 'cause you don't have a understanding of how lawsuit stuff goes, and evidently the guys that ran the record companies, they had a understanding of it, so they weren't scared. They said that for the amount of money that they would end up making on one of these records, they were willing to take that risk.

THE CROSSROADS MOMENT for hip-hop music arrived in 1991. The singer-songwriter Gilbert O'Sullivan sued the influential artist Biz Markie for using a portion of Sullivan's "Alone Again (Naturally)." Biz Markie had originally tried clearing the sample through O'Sullivan and, once rebuffed, released "Alone Again" anyway on 1991's *I Need a Haircut.*

On December 17, 1991, a judge sided with O'Sullivan and awarded him $250,000 in damages, barring Biz Markie's Cold Chillin' and its parent company, Warner Bros. Records, from continuing to sell the single and the album. Around the same period, De La Soul reached a settlement with members of the 1960s group the Turtles, over sampling a few seconds of their music.

Biz Markie pointedly titled his next album *All Samples Cleared!,* but the court rulings permanently altered the use of sampling and effectively ended hip-hop's Wild West days. Labels mostly strayed from the practice to avoid similar prohibitive penalties, driving those like Easy Mo Bee to seek out innovative alternatives.

Easy Mo Bee (producer): Someone I consider my very first true manager, Francesca Spero, she called a meeting for all of the producers that was on the staff at RPM [Rush Producers Management]. She had this memo that she passed out to every last one of us with a long list of all kind of artists—all the way from Anita Baker to Prince to Steve Miller Band—and she said, "You see those names on there? Stay away from them. Don't touch their music. Don't sample it." This was right after the *3 Feet High and Rising*, De La Soul thing happened. And then after that, the Biz Markie suit.

DJ Marley Marl (producer, Juice Crew): When [Biz Markie] got sued, I was like, *Good for his ass. Stop trying to do what I do.*

Easy Mo Bee (producer): In my opinion, Marley Marl and Ced-Gee from Ultramagnetics are the first two real true hip-hop sampling innovators. Neither one, in my opinion, ever get the full credit and recognition that they deserve in terms of being responsible for the whole mechanics of sampling, something that's just standard today. But they were the first to really bring attention and mainstream it.

DJ Marley Marl (producer, Juice Crew): I used to make it look so easy to do. I used to take kick snares in little parts. What they did was like took a whole thirty-two bars of a damn record. Just being stupid with it.

Easy Mo Bee (producer): I had to really rethink my whole process in terms of sampling. Before that, we didn't really have to think too much about what we sampled, and we were free to create these collages, just about from anywhere that you felt like you wanted to sample. So I came up with the idea, *Why do you have to always rely on loops? Why can't you sample the instruments and play something back original, as opposed to all of these instruments contained in a loop?*

It forced me to be more creative, and that's how we got [Craig Mack's] "Flava in Ya Ear," and Busta Rhymes's "Everything Remains Raw." I mentioned those two in particular because those two right there are highly indicative of my style when it comes to sampling. It's all being put together harmonically. Everything is in tune. Just like when you listen to a loop, you're hearing it as a whole. Inside that whole [loop] is bass, strings, guitars, whole bunch of instruments.

So my idea was, *Why can't I do that with samples? Just as if they're like instruments in the bank of a keyboard and just play back something original.* Because my thing was: I love sampling and I'm not going to stop. So I got to find another, better way to do it.

Salaam Remi (producer, New York): [Every] hip-hop generation takes whatever they're given and then turns it into what they want. Black culture is like that: always being given the scraps, and then turn it into the thing that controls everything afterwards. Because that's what we do. We take it and flip it.

Carlos "Six July" Broady (producer, Hitmen): Me and Juicy [J of Three 6 Mafia] used to talk about how fun sampling was. It's just fun when you know how to chop it up and take a little piece of this and make this big beat and it just started from a little piece of an old record that you just love to play and you may catch a break that you can manipulate and flip and bounce and stretch.

Bud'da (producer, Aftermath): Hip-hop, it's like no other genre. We are trendsetters. It's important for us to do whatever we have to do to keep what we do alive.

Just Blaze (producer, New Jersey): Do I think [the lawsuits] hurt creativity? To a certain degree, yes. Because there's going to be certain sample sources that you're just going to stay away from because it's a really big artist, or an artist who traditionally doesn't allow those samples for hip-hop records. At the same time, was it a necessary evil? Yes. Because you're sampling somebody else's work. Do I think there should be certain exceptions or limitations on things? Definitely. It's a necessary evil because I'll be damned if somebody samples some of my original music in ten years and I don't get anything out of it.

Bud'da (producer, Aftermath): Sampling is an art. When I first started producing, the only tool I had was to be able to sample. The interesting thing about sampling is, I didn't respect any one genre. You're listening to gypsy records. You're listening to rock. You're listening to lounge. I would be overseas and buy records. It widens your range of musicality.

Zaytoven (producer, San Francisco, Atlanta): I think that's the thriving point that kept me in the game as long as I've been in the game. Being a musician, you never run out of melodies. You can always sit down at an instrument and come up with something. That's probably the biggest factor of me even still maintaining in this music right now.

THE RESPONSIBILITIES OF a producer go far beyond creating a track's instrumental component. They see a song through from conception to mastering. Sometimes they are coaches and confidants, as during efforts to coax an ideal performance from a lyricist. In other moments, they are mentors and motivators.

Just Blaze (producer, New Jersey): Aside from being the orchestrator, you're also the person who has to pull the best performance out of the artist possible. You may have the artist do twenty takes of one verse until they nail it the right way. Or they may do twenty takes, and you take different sections from different takes and put together the one best take.

Technically he's a psychiatrist, because part of being a producer is dealing with the artist, and if you want to bring the best out of them, you have to know how to speak to people, and being able to speak to people is not always a given, especially when every artist has a different personality. As creators, most of us are weird in one sense or another. You have some artists who are extreme introverts, or extreme extroverts and full of energy and they're bouncing all around the room. You have to be able to match that energy. You have some artists who live in their head. So, you have to learn how to deal with that personality type.

You have to know how to deal with the artist who changes his mind every five minutes. You have to know how to deal with the artist who's feeling depressed, or having to deliver a hit single to the label or else they're gonna get dropped.

Salaam Remi (producer, New York): I meet artists at the very beginning, and I meet them once they're superstars. But I also have to understand, *What are they trying to get out of this whole interaction?* And then, *What can I bring to it? How can I help fulfill their dreams in a way that still gives me something vocally, melodically, lyrically that I now can position back to whoever their financier is at the label?* It's a service job in a lot of ways. But if you work at any service desk, you know that you have to fulfill different people's wishes.

Easy Mo Bee (producer): You do have to be like a coach, a psychiatrist. You have to be the one that whips. Like, "Yo, come on, man. Let's get working. You wasting too much time."

Just Blaze (producer, New Jersey): A lot of times you have a vision, the artist has a vision, and your client, which is usually the record label, has a vision. You have to find a way to execute all those visions to the best of your ability while still maintaining your truth. Because if you simply just try to cater to the artist, for example, you might not really be happy with the end result.

If you try to cater completely to the label, now you have a disgruntled artist. Then, most times when you have a disgruntled artist, the end result never works because the artist ends up at odds with the label and the label doesn't get what they want out of the artist and the relationship turns sour.

And if you just one hundred percent stick to your guns and nobody else's opinions matter, then you become the guy that's labeled as difficult to work with. . . . If you're super hot and you've got ten records on the radio, but you're an asshole, people are only going to deal with you as long as they have to. And that's just in life in general.

EARLY DJS TRANSPORTED massive equipment, like turntables and speakers, to create their beats and scratches. Producers later utilized drum machines in working to meticulously define hip-hop's soundscape. Today, producers no longer need to work inside a studio, and can construct hit songs from their laptops.

Zaytoven (producer, San Francisco, Atlanta): Back in the day, it was definitely a quality thing. Like, "Okay, we're trying to make something that's great, that's going to last for years and years." But now I think with technology and the way the world is moving so fast now, that time has passed. Now, I think most people got ADD.

You can spend ten years on making an album right now, but that don't mean it's going to last for ten years. It might last for two months.

And a guy can be in his basement and come up with a song in ten minutes and it can be the biggest song in the last decade, when you done spent a year trying to perfect one song.

Just Blaze (producer, New Jersey): Look at the technology that is available now. People are making records on smartphones now. You can go buy a basic MacBook Air or a cheap PC for the cost of relatively nothing. The cost of entry twenty years ago is ten times as much as it is now. And the resources are so much more plentiful now.

But what you don't have and what technology can't replace, is somebody who's been through it, and is still doing it, to be able to give you a little bit of wisdom along the way.

Zaytoven (producer, San Francisco, Atlanta): That's another reason why you stay around so long, is because you mentor other guys. They keep you in the game and it's a responsibility. When I get to rock with these younger guys, as they got bigger, they put me on songs. They always talked about me in interviews. So, it did nothing but make me bigger and give me more longevity.

Just Blaze (producer, New Jersey): I think for a lot of us in the DJ and producer culture, traditionally it was always about hiding your secrets. It was about blacking out your records, so they couldn't see what it was. It was about disguising your sample sources or hoarding your drum sounds. And on one hand I get it, 'cause those sounds are what give you your sonic identity.

But at the same time, my brain doesn't work like your brain, doesn't work like his brain, doesn't work like her brain. We're not going to do all the same things with those sounds, and we're not all going to do the same thing with the technology that we have, or even with the knowledge that we have.

My twenty-fifth birthday, I met Timbaland. And as a birthday present, he said, "Listen, I'm going to do something for you for your birthday." This is really my first time meeting him. He's like, "Come back to the studio tomorrow. I got something for you."

He gave me a ten-DVD box set of all of his samples and all his drum sets. And he was like, "Normally this is not something that I would ever do, but I'd be curious to see what you do with it, because your brain doesn't work like mine."

That was one of the coolest things that somebody had ever done for me. But he's right. Nobody's brain works the same way, so there's really no point in hoarding all this access, all this knowledge, all this music, because everybody's going to be able to do something differently with it.

THE GOLDEN AGE produced an artistic and evolutionary leap in lyricism that witnessed techniques traveling far past the genre's party-rap roots. Artists like Rakim, KRS-One, and Big Daddy Kane evolved how artists rhymed, opening minds and doors for those like Jay-Z, Nas, the Notorious B.I.G., and a litany of others.

As hip-hop expanded beyond the five boroughs, different regions produced varying styles and cadences, with newer iterations sometimes contrasting with the efforts of those who had brought the music to prominence. Mumble rap, for example, which rose to prominence in the 2010s, was more about an overall vibe than digestible lyrics.

For many artists, lyricism still involves craft. Some jot down their words in elegant books of rhymes. Others compose on smartphones while sitting in traffic. The creative process of innovation varies. Some are sticklers for routine. Others lift poetry straight from their minds to the tip of their tongue through elaborate freestyles.

Subject matter can be as diverse. Some use their voice and platform to shine light on social inequalities. Others seek to provide an escape from reality, to simply keep the evening going and the party moving. Some do both.

For the pure spitters, the effort to become a better lyricist starts at a young age, and often the quest for the perfect verse never ends.

Ras Kass (artist, Los Angeles): I knew I could write. My family, they're all pretty articulate and great writers. I figured I was just as good as my family.

Khujo (artist, Goodie Mob): In middle school, I used to do a lot of writing. It started out as writing little stories. Then, being able to say the stories to the music. After high school, that's when I could really concentrate on it, and being able to get in the Dungeon and get around like minds that felt like me, I guess that's when I would say, "Well, shit, if they can do it, I could do it too."

J-Live (artist, New York): A lot of people refer to Malcolm Gladwell and the ten thousand hours, right? You don't count those hours. They just happen. You just look back at it like, *Holy shit. I've been here for years perfecting my craft and it wasn't arduous and it wasn't tedious, because I was just enjoying myself the whole time.* And it wasn't isolating or lonely, because I had a community of people that I was doing it with, and it wasn't rigorous because I'm really just applying my natural talents.

I've studied the storytellers in this music, from Slick Rick to Ghostface [Killah] and really just honed my own style. It's very much like martial arts, like the old Bruce Lee saying: "You don't fear the man that's done ten thousand kicks once. You fear the man that's done one kick ten thousand times." Even though verses aren't all the same, it's the fact that you put that time in to put so many verses in.

Bun B (artist, UGK): I look at sports and you see a running back that can find that hole in the line, and you look at the quarterback that can throw a pass and see a guy forty, fifty yards down the field and put it right in his chest, or like Steph Curry gets hot from behind the three, or even now, you see a guy like James Harden get into a rhythm where he can put in fifty points a night, it's about falling into a rhythm and you're like, *Okay, I think I'm in the zone right now.*

And you just keep writing and keep pushing yourself and stay as active in the moment as possible. It's about constantly giving yourself the opportunity to get better, and finding ways to get better and wanting to get better.

Cormega (artist, Queensbridge): I'm a prick when I write. I could write ten rhymes right now, but I might throw nine of them in the garbage. I'm a perfectionist. That is one of the reasons I lasted longer in the industry. But as far as giving jewels in songs, I got that from Slick Rick and from [MC] Shan.

MC Shan (Juice Crew, Queensbridge): I'm always running my mouth. I don't care, I'm going to say what I got to say.

Cormega (artist, Queensbridge): People like Slick Rick and Shan were the people who wrote jewels in their music. But at the same time, you got Chuck D and KRS-One, they are teaching you straight-up. They giving you a different kind of lesson. I think Public Enemy is the greatest social rappers in the history of hip-hop. But unfortunately, some people are so ignorant, they just want to shake their head and dance to the rhythm and not absorb the jewel.

Ice Cube (artist, N.W.A): When I heard the line "I don't rhyme for the sake of riddlin'" from Chuck D, now that line sticks with me, because to me it's like, "You got the mic. Rock the mic, but man, give us a little bit of medicine. Drop some jewels on us. You an MC. You're supposed to be spitting game or letting us know what time it is." I've always had that mentality that that's the mission: Rock the mic, spit game, tell the truth as I see it, don't pull no punches. That, to me, is what I'm supposed to be doing.

Ras Kass (artist, Los Angeles): Comedians, they tell the jokes and they say the things that people don't really want to talk about, but in a way where it's digestible. That always felt like I was trying to do that.

Khujo (artist, Goodie Mob): I always wanted to have some type of nugget or some type of jewel in my lyrics, in my bars. At least have something that people can relate to.

Rodney-O (artist, Compton): I've never been so much of a subject rapper, or storyteller. To me, if it sounds good on the beat, you deliver it how it's supposed to be delivered, then that's what it is.

Rhymefest (artist, Chicago): It's whatever the moment calls for. I love when I'm in the room with people and we're not trying to write anything, but we have a subject, and we start discussing that subject.

J-Live (artist, New York): I might go weeks or months without writing, and then go days and weeks and months just writing nonstop, and then that well will run dry. And when I was coming up and having rhyme books, composition books, and by the time I finished one and started a new one, another year passed, and when I looked back at the old rhyme books, I wouldn't feel right kicking those rhymes, because I had gotten better, so a lot of times I could see the growth.

Cormega (artist, Queensbridge): You should get better as you get older, because we using brain energy. When you're younger, you got more physical energy than brain energy. As you get older, you got more brain energy than physical energy.

What I've learned recently is there are people that are rappers and then there are people that are recording artists. There are some rappers that can write something that will blow your mind as an artist, but they might not be good battle rappers. And then there are battle rappers that will blow your mind as a battle rapper, but they might not make songs that will blow your mind.

There's different things about myself that I had to learn as a rapper. The Mega that I used to be as a battle MC, if I was to battle that guy right now, I would lose. But if I was to have an on-wax battle with that rapper, where I have to write my shit, I would most likely come out on top.

Styles P (artist, the Lox): I don't write, but I'm not going to say it out of a bragging point. Mine's just literally that I couldn't write when I was younger. I have an off-beat/on-beat flow.

I was always outside kind of hustlin'. So it was just difficult for me to kinda pen it, and as a young child, I could never get my rhythm off paper. Like, reading it, I could never read it back the way I wanted to.

I kind of look at it like I'm making my own essay. I just say what's on my mind, the thoughts that's in my head. I just formulate them in a rhythmic fashion. I just keep going over it. I kind of just say back what I think the beat is saying to me, mixed with what, how I'm feeling, what I want to say. It's like a combination of things happening all at once is my process and I just smoke, turn the lights off, try to meditate to the beat.

Sadat X (artist, Brand Nubian): Sometimes I write in the studio. Sometimes I write at home. Sometimes I'm writing in the car to the studio. Sometimes I'm finishing a verse in the booth. All my stuff relies on spontaneity. I talk in sporadic bursts. I have different quick thoughts and jot them down real quick. That's just the way my mind thinks.

Craig G (Juice Crew, Queensbridge): Sometimes ideas will pop in my head, and I'll put them down in the notes in my phone, but when it comes to writing, I generally like to have the track before I go into the studio. I might write two versions of a song and then decide which one I like better before I actually go in and record it. So, I still like the peace and quiet, and to be honest with you, I still like writing with pen and paper, old-school. ·

Murs (artist, Los Angeles): I used to write in my head. Because I started off freestyling, and then, when I started writing, I noticed that I didn't understand bar structure. And then, after I started learning you have to rap to the beat, I found it was better for me—because I was really good at freestyling—to write in my head. The writing just got in the way with my already poor rhythm. Still not great rhythmically, I don't have a great cadence. So writing used to get in the way of that. And then as I learned to write in my head, then I went back to paper.

And so, taking what I learned about being rhythmic and listening to the beat first, and now I can only write to the beat. And I really don't listen to the beat until I'm in a place where I can write something down or record it on paper. Because I don't want to lose the initial feeling.

Mozzy (artist, Sacramento): I still write all my raps. I mingle with other ways of rapping, but I really like writing. I've been writing since a kid. I turn the beat on. Whatever the beat tell me to say, I just vibe off it like that. I never really come with a concept before.

K-Rino (artist, South Park Coalition): Writer's block is self-imposed. That's something you inflict upon yourself, because of a lack of feeding information into your mind. If I reach a ceiling in my knowledge intake, where now all my thoughts are going in circles, then it's time to start doing some reading. It's time to start watching more documentaries.

It's time to start being more observant of your everyday surroundings because once you do that, there is always something to write about.

Bun B (artist, UGK): Every now and then you get to phrase something in a way that no one's ever phrased before, and you get to make the connection between different cultural references, and you create a line and it's like, *Oh shit, I can't believe nobody thought of that before.*

Punch (president, Top Dawg Entertainment): When you really think about it, nothing is new. It's all the same stuff. It's just a matter of perspective and how you see it that makes it different.

K-Rino (artist, South Park Coalition): It's semi-euphoric. It's almost as if you had an out-of-body experience, because you write things down and you connect words and phrases together that you would not express in normal conversation. Your mind goes into another realm, and you start to really formulate what you want to say in a way that makes perfect sense. It's a beautiful thing. It's almost like bustin' a nut.

Mozzy (artist, Sacramento): I ain't going to lie. It's like a orgasm. It's like you just excited. I get out of my seat. I start walking around. I just get animated. I know this is a score right here.

The D.O.C. (artist, Dallas): I don't know how I know it, but I know it. I think anybody that raps knows it. The difference is being able to know when it's not the shit. Knowing when it's the shit is easy. Knowing when it's not the shit is where it's at. You have to listen with your ears and not your emotions.

Craig G (Juice Crew, Queensbridge): I kind of know it once I record the song and I hear it back the next day. That's when I'd usually know. Like right after I'm done recording it, I'm kind of sick of it. So, I got to kind of take a day or two and go back and listen to it. And I'll be like, "Okay. This sounded just like I thought it would in my mind."

HISTORICALLY, THE ESSENCE of MCing is rooted in authenticity and innovation. However, the use of ghostwriting—an artist employing lyrics written by somebody else—has been around since Grandmaster Caz became an unknowing participant in "Rapper's Delight."

Big Daddy Kane penned lyrics for his fellow Juice Crew members. Dr. Dre tapped the likes of the D.O.C., Eminem, and others for some of his most memorable tracks. A feud was ignited when Philadelphia's Meek Mill stated that Drake used ghostwriters.

Record companies are known to pay lucratively for ghostwriters to assist some of their elite artists. Some, like Skillz and Deadly Threat, crafted their professional lives around ghostwriting jobs.

Many hold Meek Mill's view that ghostwriting contradicts hip-hop's foundational values. Others view the act as an extension of the craft, adding depth to an artist's work.

Rodney-O (artist, Compton): I don't feel like nothing's wrong with it. I don't care how I get songs to the beat, long as it gets there. But people, especially with rap, everybody takes it so personal, so they feel if somebody else writes your raps that you're whack, or you're not real. I always felt like well, [Al Pacino] wasn't Cuban, but he played a Cuban [Scarface]. So he has to be like his movies in real life? That's bullshit.

Deadly Threat (artist, Los Angeles): Writing my mindset is easy. Writing somebody else's mindset is totally different. You got to know the person or at least know what the person likes. Other than that, you're fitting to just writing some stuff that the person don't want. You kind of have to pay attention to that part of it.

22 THE RECOGNITION THAT IT DESERVES

Hip-hop has now served as a significant cultural and societal force for decades, but it crossed a new threshold in 2018 when Kendrick Lamar was awarded a Pulitzer Prize for his fourth studio album, *DAMN*. Yet the genre has for the most part gone without the mainstream accolades or acknowledgment to match its outsized influence. Traditionally, conventional awards shows like the Grammys or Academy Awards, and gatekeepers like the Rock and Roll Hall of Fame, have either shunned hip-hop or only belatedly acknowledged its creators and contributions.

Most notably, the Grammy Awards—music's "biggest night," aiming to celebrate and honor outstanding achievements within the industry—share a strained relationship with hip-hop. While the Soul Train Music Awards and the BET Hip Hop Awards offer evenings of celebration that revolve around Black music, artists have voiced frustration for decades over the neglect of Black artists at the Grammys, and the voting process for Recording Academy members.

This tension peaked in 2014, when white duo Macklemore & Ryan Lewis won three Grammys in the Rap category. Macklemore subsequently apologized to Lamar, whose heralded *Good Kid, M.A.A.D City* lost to *The Heist* for Best Rap Album.

The Grammys' recognition of hip-hop has been an arduous journey, but the awards show, somewhat unintentionally, expanded awareness of the mostly underground New York art form in 1984. More than a million viewers tuned in to that year's Grammy telecast, many to celebrate Michael Jackson's night-long victory walk for *Thriller*.

That evening, Herbie Hancock performed "Rockit," a seminal track that fused elements of electro, jazz, and hip-hop, and the winner for Best R&B Instrumental Performance. During the set, Grand Mixer DXT, perched at a DJ booth, introduced millions to scratching, while validating the commitment to hip-hop for others back home in New York City.

Paradise Gray (manager of the Latin Quarter, X Clan): A host of R&B male stars who were being phased out, when they started feeling threatened by hip-hop, there was a whole backlash against us. We were being called gangsters and thugs, and hip-hop was being called a fad, and they said that it would never last. It was kind of saddening that people that we looked up to as heroes were so disrespectful of us.

I remember the moment that I felt redemption, though. For me, the moment of redemption was the night that Grand Mixer DXT performed "Rockit" live on the Grammys with Herbie Hancock. That night was the first time I actually saw myself on TV. That's the first time I saw a DJ and b-boys perform. That night was the *aha* moment. I cried when I saw Michael Jackson and Quincy Jones and the rest of the whole entire entertainment industry give hip-hop a standing ovation the night that hip-hop won its first Grammy.

THOSE IN HIP-HOP originally viewed the announcement of a Grammy for Best Rap Performance as a welcome acknowledgment of the genre. That elation mostly dissolved when the nominees were told to arrive early to the Shrine Auditorium in Los Angeles, since the 1989 inaugural award would be presented prior to the main ceremony, and would not be televised live. That relegation sparked a boycott of the awards led by Def Jam and Rush Artist Management. DJ Jazzy Jeff & the Fresh Prince won the category for "Parents Just Don't Understand" but did not attend; neither did fellow nominees LL Cool J and Salt-N-Pepa, and other prominent hip-hop voices like Public Enemy and Slick Rick.

> The boycott was not unanimous. Kool Moe Dee, who earned a nom-
> ination for "Wild Wild West," replaced Jazzy Jeff & the Fresh Prince as
> presenter of the Best R&B Male Vocal award, and performed a quick
> rap to try and shine a positive light on the art.

Kool Moe Dee (artist, Treacherous Three): The other thing that Public
Enemy did, they came up with a catchphrase of "Who gives a F about
a goddamn Grammy." So, if that's the case and we're taking that man-
tra seriously, then there's no reason to be angry.

So they said they're going to give hip-hop a category, but going
to air it in the pre-air TV version. There's only five of us that were
nominated. It's Salt-N-Pepa, J.J. Fad, LL Cool J, Jazzy Jeff & the Fresh
Prince, and me. So, there's really five companies that have a vested
interest in it. Russell Simmons and the people at Def Jam, I guess him
and Lyor [Cohen] in particular, they said, "We are going to boycott
the Grammys because they're not going to put us on TV on the live-
air portion."

I was on Jive Records. Salt-N-Pepa was on Next Plateau. So we had
other little labels, but we were subsidiaries of the major companies.
Def Jam, although they did have a major company behind them at
some point, they functioned more like an independent than anybody
else.

So, by them calling a boycott without telling anybody, one, I
resented the fact that we didn't have a strategy conversation. I think
the biggest mistake among African Americans is we still don't strat-
egize. Not that we all have to agree, but let's hear some other voices
and see what we got to say.

So, Will Smith was nominated. He was supposed to do a rap because
he was the guy that mainstream America was very comfortable with.
He was the guy they could say was articulate. He had a very fun kind
of energy, same thing that follows him to where his success happened
in movies. They wanted him to do the presentation of the best R&B
artist of the year, and he said he wasn't going to do it because he was
going to join the Def Jam boycott.

I absolutely didn't join the Def Jam boycott.

Two reasons. One, you have me and LL Cool J as adversaries at the time, and we didn't have a chance to talk or even have a strategy of whether we would do that or do something bigger than just boycotting. Number two, I thought we said, "We don't care about the Grammys." Are we being consistent with not caring or are we saying we really do care and now because you're not putting us on TV, we're not coming? Which still could be a valid strategy, but at least let's talk out what would be the best strategy because my idea was, we all get up on stage [and] we make a stand at the Grammys. We can get way more out of being there than not being there, if we're trying to make a statement.

So, I started getting a whole lot of backlash from the Def Jam side of the equation. They're literally calling *Black Beat, Right On!, Ebony,* whatever Black and other mainstream publications, and are telling them to boycott me because I'm crossing the picket line. So I get on stage, do my thing, introduce the winner of the category, and I go downstairs, and I let them all have it in the moment with all of the world press there. I just tell them, again, the strategy was much better to get together and say we have a voice. There's no reason for us not to be on the mainstream telecast, but this is just the hip-hop bias that we've always been going through. This is how you break the doors down.

THE NEXT YEAR, CBS aired Young MC accepting the Grammy for Best Rap Performance for "Bust a Move." His crossover hit beat out Public Enemy's socially impactful "Fight the Power." Public Enemy, however, still figured into the evening when Flavor Flav, outfitted in a tux and glowing sunglasses, blitzed the stage to congratulate Young MC mid-speech.

Young MC (artist, New York City): I didn't know it was coming. And I looked up to all the other groups in my category. I want to say it was Public Enemy and De La Soul; I forget who else. But it's all groups that I looked up to and it's my first record, so I'm not thinking [I'm going to win]. I have one big single that people know, but I didn't think I would have any impact on a Grammy.

I wasn't expecting it, but it's something I'm very proud of. Some people say [it is] the first Grammy [for hip-hop]. Will Smith had won the year before me, but it was the first televised Grammy and, if you remember, Flavor Flav came up and tackled me on stage. I know Flav and I know he's wild and crazy, but I know he caught flak for that, and a lot of people were supportive of me.

I'm doing interviews with the foreign press the next day and this woman looks at me and I'm wearing a suit, and she said that she was surprised that I didn't have the Grammy around my neck on a chain, because that's what she saw hip-hop as. To go from that, to where it is now, is an amazing thing, but I think that the people who are benefiting from how strong of a genre hip-hop is now need to hear the stories of how it was back then.

EMINEM BECAME THE first hip-hop artist to capture an Oscar when *8 Mile*'s "Lose Yourself" won for Best Original Song at the Academy Awards in 2003. Three years later, Three 6 Mafia won for "It's Hard Out Here for a Pimp." Voters had been slow in recognizing hip-hop's cinematic impact, but the delay was probably also due to rules mandating that songs had to be entirely original to be nominated for the Best Original Song category, which eliminated those that sampled from others.

"Lose Yourself" was the lead single from *8 Mile,* Eminem's semi-autobiographical film that detailed a white rapper building his confidence to launch his hip-hop career through underground venues in Detroit.

Luis Resto (musician, producer, songwriter): Marshall was in the middle of filming *8 Mile* and there was a makeshift studio trailer that went from site to site, wherever they were shooting. I got the call to come in. They were working on the title track for the movie and Marshall had said that he was concerned with it being too rock and roll sounding. He wanted it to build from beginning to end.

I went orchestral. We replaced the guitar chords with orchestra hits and violins, cellos, French horns, and I used ranging techniques to make the verses switch up from one to another and to build the tension. That's how the result came up.

What I really remember is walking into the trailer the first time [and] I heard Marshall's lyrics. He hadn't really rapped liked this up 'til then. He hadn't written in such a positive vein, and I just figured that people were gonna be pretty flipped-out when they heard it, because of the real different side of Marshall up to that point.

EMINEM EARNED AN Academy Award nomination, along with Resto and Jeff Bass. Resto, the only attendee of the trio at the awards ceremony, witnessed "Lose Yourself" beat out songs from *Chicago, Frida, Gangs of New York,* and *The Wild Thornberrys Movie.*

Luis Resto (musician, producer, songwriter): Since none of us ever imagined winning an Oscar, Marshall didn't want to be sitting in the audience if we lost, and I think Jeff stayed home because he had just had a new baby. All of us of assumed *Chicago* was gonna get it. Or, on the bill, you had Paul Simon. You had U2. You had the cut from *Frida.* But I went for the hoot.

It was pretty weird [winning]. To have Barbra Streisand handing me the award, it was just really surreal. And then I thought the statuette was gonna be a fake plastic Oscar, and then they give you the real one later, but it's the real one, and it's like eighteen pounds. That caught me by surprise.

GRANDMASTER FLASH AND the Furious Five broke down another barrier in 2007 when the group became the first hip-hop act inducted into the Rock and Roll Hall of Fame. Their inclusion arrived twenty-five years after the release of "The Message."

Run-DMC (2009), Beastie Boys (2012), Public Enemy (2013), N.W.A (2016), Tupac Shakur (2017), the Notorious B.I.G. (2020), Jay-Z (2021), and Eminem (2022) have have also been enshrined in subsequent years.

Rahiem (Grandmaster Flash and the Furious Five): [The] Rock and Roll Hall of Fame induction was definitely a surreal moment. It was the exclamation point, as far as recognition is concerned, of my life. It was very fulfilling for me to be signing the same wall as my idols like James Brown, Michael Jackson, Prince, Al Green. I felt like our induction was necessary to further help hip-hop to gain the recognition that it deserves.

KENDRICK LAMAR'S 2018 Pulitzer Prize consummated his standing as a lyrical master craftsman. Terrence "Punch" Henderson helped cultivate Lamar after the prodigy known as K.Dot (Lamar's first stage name) joined Top Dawg Entertainment (TDE), the independent label founded by Henderson's cousin Anthony "Top Dawg" Tiffith.

Terrence "Punch" Henderson (president, Top Dawg Entertainment): First time I heard the very first mixtape he did, my immediate thought was, *Wow, this kid is amazing. Sounds like Jay-Z. He sound like Lil Wayne, mixed.* At that time, he was so young—he was like sixteen or seventeen.

And then maybe a month after, I caught him in the studio, and he was writing a song and he was laying the vocals for this chorus, and it was so layered. He was stacking the chorus so much, almost like a R&B singer would. So I knew at that moment, *Okay, this kid got it.*

THE PULITZER PRIZE administration board cited *DAMN* as a "virtuosic song collection unified by its vernacular authenticity and rhythmic dynamism that offers affecting vignettes capturing the complexity of modern African American life." By that measure, Public Enemy could just as easily have won the category three decades earlier, with the sonic heft and lyrical urgency of *It Takes a Nation of Millions* *to Hold Us Back.* Since the Pulitzer for music was established in 1943, the award had nearly always been given to a classical composer.

Murs (artist, Los Angeles): He's just a very humble, intelligent, quiet dude. I wish I had his tight-lipped demeanor. He's very smart. I never know what he's thinking. He's not on social media a lot. He's like a fucking young-ass Yoda.

Terrence "Punch" Henderson (president, Top Dawg Entertainment): You don't realize the weight or the gravity of what that really means, because that's so out of our realm as artists. You can understand what a Grammy means, because that's usually the goal. The goal was never a Pulitzer as a rapper coming from the Compton and Watts areas, to get it. He didn't really understand what it meant at the time he won. It's like, where do you go from there? That's the Nobel Peace Prize, right?

23 THANK GOD BECAUSE OF HIP-HOP

In 2017, Nielsen Music, which measures sales and streaming, coronated hip-hop as the most widely consumed music in the United States. The genre birthed by creative and neglected New York City teenagers had combined with R&B to officially surpass rock and roll in popularity for the first time. The news did not shock anyone with a passing interest in popular music and culture.

Throughout these last decades, hip-hop music has undergone various permutations and reached every corner of America and most of the world. It has produced countless progenies, ranging from boom bap and G-funk to auto-tune, drill, and mumble rap. It ricocheted from the parks to records, from basements to the radio, from cassettes and CDs to peer-to-peer file-sharing Internet software and streaming services and social media, from being ignored at awards shows to winning a Pulitzer Prize.

From the beginning, almost anyone could imagine and engineer the genre's next great shift, be it Marley Marl stumbling onto sampling, Rakim elevating lyricism, or Missy Elliott pushing creative boundaries. Hip-hop will continue traveling in different, spiraling directions. The genre is still driven by youth, making its evolution inevitable and eternal. And as hip-hop continues to be a dominant commercial force, internal struggles will also span onward—between industry and independence; and the art form as a means of enlightenment and education, versus it being a vessel for pure entertainment.

Dupré "DoItAll" Kelly (artist, Lords of the Underground): When I think about hip-hop, I look at it this way. Break the word down. "Hip" is being in the know, right? "Hop" is a form of movement. That's why it forever stays young. It's the now movement.

So, whoever the leaders of the now movement [are], entertainment-wise, if they realize that they are leading—like your Drakes, who is very powerful right now, your Meek Mills, who is starting to be a little woke now. Your Rick Ross. Jay[-Z] is doing it. If you had even the younger guys like Lil Uzi Vert, your Migos and all of them. I'm not saying they're just caring about themselves, but if they realize that they have a responsibility with having a platform, then it will change.

DMC (artist, Run-DMC): Let's say a group like Migos [started] making songs like Public Enemy. Imagine if you had a guy that looked like Lil Wayne right now but was rhyming like KRS-One. Imagine you have fully clothed women with names like Nicki Minaj and Cardi B, but they're making records like Monie Love and Queen Latifah. Something went wrong somewhere where our women used to call themselves queens and princesses and be fully clothed, and that was revolutionary. That changed the game. Now the young women thinking, *Damn, I've got to dress a certain way. I've got to call myself a bitch and a hoe to be accepted.* No, you don't. We didn't create this hip-hop shit for that.

Monie Love (artist, London): Female MCing has evolved over the decades the way it needs to. There was always tongue-in-cheek sexiness. There was always [the] Afrocentric sister. There was always the girl that had more fun, more dancing. Then there was always the more lyricist girl. There were always those varieties.

The only thing that has happened is the potential for the girls that are more sexualized, and that's not the girls' fault. That's more so the money-machine end of things. Like, "We're not going put our money in our marketing behind the lyricist girl so much. We're going to put our money and our marketing more so behind the sexualized girls, the girls that want to twerk."

Which is fine. My thing is there's so many talented girls that don't twerk. It's kind of unfair that they get no light, no attention, no opportunity.

Kool Moe Dee (artist, Treacherous Three): We've taken business over humans over and over and over again. That's the way we're being programmed. So, if you're making a record and you have a chance to make, say, "Fight the Power," or you have the chance to make this record called "Booty Shaking" and it'll sell a hundred million, nine times out of ten, most people will sign up to make "Booty Shaking" because they know it'll get pushed harder because of the lack of depth. Corporate America will back it and you won't offend anybody. So, when you get to that kind of thing, most artists have to make a choice. Which kind of artists are they going to be?

Cormega (artist, Queensbridge): I think every lyricist is faced with that question: How do I get my point across and make people want to listen? Because at the end of the day, being a lyricist is a blessing and a curse. It's a blessing because you are so gifted with words, and it's a curse because being so lyrical can tend to be boring. How can you draw people in?

People in the streets, they love me. Streets respect me, right? I was in jail, and everybody knows that. So, if I'm making a song about the street, people are going to tend to listen to it more because they know this guy's telling the truth. He really been there.

So that's why I tell people in certain songs: I was in jail, but I went to the law library, and I helped my case. Somebody might be in jail listening to my music and be like, *Wow, I need to go to a law library.* So, that's one of the things that I try to do with my music. I try to influence people, but I never knew that my music would get people through hard times. I never knew that there was people going through dark places in regular life that my music would affect.

Paris (artist, producer, San Francisco): You have everybody now making music to sell other things or to create other opportunities for themselves, because music doesn't sell anymore—not like it used to. If your objective is to have a liquor company or to have a clothing line or get a reality show or some other shit, then you're going to make music that'll appeal to the masses that's going to oftentimes have a lowest-common-denominator content, and that's what we see now.

It's an all-that-glitters type of a scene now. Definitely style over substance.

Kool Moe Dee (artist, Treacherous Three): We have a power struggle going on. The spiritual, ethical side of us wants to say something, wants to give people ideas of how to make moves. But we don't really trust that our people will gravitate to and respond to the highest social consciousness for those of us that have it.

On another level, I'm trying to make as much money as possible, because we have a litany of African American superstars that ended up broke and nobody wants to be a part of that story, and a social construct where capitalism turns to materialism—becomes the predominant thought process—because you're living in a construct that says it's actually money over humanity.

Schoolly D (artist, Philadelphia): It's sad, because you show up thinking, *I'm just doing this for money, not to further the art.* That's the saddest state of hip-hop. Everything is about money. Money, money, money.

J-Live (artist, New York): There's always a war between art and industry. Because industry needs routine and scalability and sameness and predictability, and art needs to push the envelope and do it in a way that's never been proven or tested. But somewhere in between the most industrious stuff and everything else is just this need to assembly-line it. Every car can't be unique. They're selling records. We're making music.

Kool Moe Dee (artist, Treacherous Three): What I do like about what's happening on the independent side, even though we're still wrapped in the paradigm of corporate America, a lot of us are taking our destinies in our own hands and starting our own production companies. Unfortunately, because of the infrastructure of that, even, you're still constantly making more business decisions than social decisions.

Sir Jinx (producer): Every generation that comes along has a new rap, has a new game. That's how I look at hip-hop. It was a way for people to express themselves in the way they do it. So, whether it goes to

China, whether it goes to Jamaica, the gay community, it's their way of rapping. You can't stop the giant when it keeps going.

Sheek Louch (artist, the Lox): Has the game changed as far as the sound of music and the sound of the beats and the lyrical content? Yes. But it's supposed to. It's gonna be a 360. It's gonna be that shit Big was talking. The shit M.O.P. was talking, Mobb Deep. It's gonna go back to Common and the conscious Talib [Kweli] sound. It's gonna go back to that trap sound. That's the game. When you realize that shit, you gonna be aight.

Sadat X (artist, Brand Nubian): It's still evolving. Classical music with compositions by Chopin, by Beethoven, Tchaikovsky—those are three, four hundred years old. Whereas on a whole, rap right now, as we know it, is fifty, sixty years old. So, chambers are still being made in rap.

People are saying there are no classics being made nowadays. I don't believe that. Because to my daughter, to my nephews, some of these songs are going to be their classics. Rap is still defining itself. It's still growing in potential.

Grandmaster Caz (Cold Crush Brothers): A lot of people have made contributions to this culture. I believe that anybody who has a passion for hip-hop and has taken it upon themselves to improve the culture, to enrich the lives of other people who take from your example and do positive things and move the culture period, I think that's what it's really all about.

FROM ITS INCEPTION, hip-hop represented more than just a genre. The music's many complexities forced contradictions as it became a subject taught in colleges and universities across the globe.

For many, hip-hop music stirred something that had been dormant in their youth. The genre provided a megaphone for the oppressed and ignored. It shaped and defined popular culture, providing a source of community, education, and continuity.

Young MC (artist, New York City): When I saw two turntables and heard a guy on the microphone, I'm like, *Not only is it cool to listen to, but it's a way of self-expression and also a way that I could use what I was learning as well.* A lot of my early stuff had a lot of multisyllable words, because I really wanted to incorporate my education in my rhymes.

Ras Kass (artist, Los Angeles): Honestly, it promoted reading, especially reading outside of just regular school curriculum, 'cause school curriculum doesn't teach you analytical thinking. It just teaches you a lot of misinformation. So they started definitely help me learning more collegiate-type books, more educational.

Ant Diddley Dog (artist, Bad-N-Fluenz): I realized that there was an empty space that needed to be filled in my life, and I don't know if it was I needed a sounding board. I don't know if I needed to be entertained. I don't know if I needed an outlet for expressing.

Mac Mall (artist, Bay Area): I used to stutter real bad, and the only time I didn't is when I cussed and when I rapped. So, it kind of steered me that way. Actually, it did give me confidence.

DJ EFN (Crazy Hood Productions, Miami): The culture did a lot for me growing up. My parents got divorced and it sounds corny, but it's almost like hip-hop replaced my father in the sense that it was that kind of macho voice I needed to balance out my mom's voice in my life as a young kid.

Killer Mike (artist, Dungeon Family): I originally wanted to be a break-dancer. That was the coolest shit in the world, because in Atlanta, if you could dance, girls would like you. As a kid [I was] firmly interested in Run-DMC and the Fat Boys, breakdancing and b-boying and *Beat Street* and shit like that.

It's like you come to a cultural choice. Some kids are into skateboarding. Some are into BMX. The rap shit, I loved the whole culture of hip-hop. But I couldn't do a headstand. My chubby ass just didn't have it in me.

Ant Diddley Dog (artist, Bad-N-Fluenz): At the time, as far as being a young person, it felt like this is meaningful for me, because I feel like it's not for adults. This is for me. This is for my creativity. When I first started rapping, this was a place where it felt like freedom.

Ras Kass (artist, Los Angeles): As much as I liked Duran Duran, Michael Jackson, and Whitney Houston, it wasn't theme music to my daily life. And then you started hearing everything from "My Adidas" to "Fuck Tha Police" to "Fight the Power," it just sounded like how I felt every day. I could emotionally relate in a way that no other music I had ever before and probably never will.

DJ EFN (Crazy Hood Productions, Miami): It taught me a lot, not just the macho side. It taught me about history. It taught me about the struggle that other people have in other cities. I'm learning about other places, other countries. I'm even learning vocabulary words through lyricists.

Killer Mike (artist, Dungeon Family): It awakened my curiosity, whether it was Public Enemy and learning about myself and knowledge itself, or Cypress Hill, learning about cannabis, shit like that.

Thirstin Howl III (Lo Life, Brooklyn): Growing up in the ghetto and the hood, my family were all gang members—my mother, her brother, sisters, everybody. So, no one actually ever taught me to pursue anything, to set goals, and that knowledge was the power to everything. So, through my travels in life and prison and all that, being introduced to hip-hop, I began getting a little more educated.

Cormega (artist, Queensbridge): When you in jail, you find out everything because they got radios. That is one of the only things you could do in jail. You listen to music and you watch TV. So you got to understand, music is powerful. Music is escapism. Music is inspirational.

Before championship fights, what do they come out to? They come out to music. Before wars, people come out to music. When people are stressed-out, they listen to music to calm down. So when you are in jail, you close your eyes, you put on some headphones, you are not even in jail no more.

Cold 187um (artist, producer, Above the Law): When we was hustling, we was young—nineteen, eighteen—basically fresh out of high school. We knew we had talent, but we were making a lot of money. But the shit that was going on in our lives made us really, really write [Above the Law's debut album] *Livin' Like Hustlers,* really dig down. The struggle made us really want hip-hop. Hip-hop was the savior. It saved us out of probably doing life in prison or something. It gave us that.

Thirstin Howl III (Lo Life, Brooklyn): When I became a hip-hop artist, my mind opened up entirely to everything. The more I got involved in my craft, the more my mind expanded and opened to every piece of information that was out there. Even things that had nothing to do with hip-hop. My mind was just broad now. Because it definitely triggered something. I'm experiencing so many different things that the ghetto doesn't offer me or show me. I live hip-hop like a religion.

Bun B (artist, UGK): Hip-hop and religion have both been forms of expression within the Black community. Music in general, and religion to be more specific, you look at the early times when Blacks were given freedom, the church and the gin joint were where Black people would go together and commune, and that's where they got their chosen worldviews and information from.

For many people in the world, hip-hop has become that stand-in for modernized religion. It's the way that they choose to contribute to society. It's what makes them want to be a better person, and makes them decide who they want to be around, and what kind of life they want to live.

Skillz (artist, Virginia): It's been the number one genre of music for the past thirty years. And if not number one, then very close behind it. So it's been huge, influential music from the time that it started 'til now. So it's embedded in our lives.

Ice-T (artist, Rhyme Syndicate): Music, as a whole, not just hip-hop, is the closest thing you're going to get to anything that'll desegregate people. Music has no color barriers. You can go back to the roots of R&B and jazz; white people have always embraced it.

Hip-hop really brought Black and white kids globally together, because as long as you don't know somebody's story, it's easy to hate them. But once you understand where they're coming from, then you might have some compassion for the situation. It's just another way of communicating, music. Unfortunately, we all can't communicate as well just [through] talking.

DJ EFN (Crazy Hood Productions, Miami): I think that it's inspiring across the world and it ties us all together that you can create something from nothing, and that is to me the hip-hop story, that you can take this something from nothing and you can morph it and adapt it and fuse what's you and what's a part of your culture.

Kokane (artist, producer): Thank God because of hip-hop.

ACKNOWLEDGMENTS

Hip-hop music has provided me with hope, motivation, and education. I hope that this book offers something in return. Bringing it to life was not without its hurdles. At times, attempting to report and organize an oral history book that captured generations' worth of impactful twists and turns in hip-hop's evolution felt, quite simply, insane. It is always difficult imaging something that doesn't yet exist and trying to will it into the physical world. My goal throughout that challenging process was to focus on the artistry and determination of hip-hop music's contributors above all else. I felt a responsibility to seek out their stories and see them through to the page.

Hip-hop is still a young musical genre. We are fortunate that many of its pioneers are still with us and able to provide their testimony. I am forever grateful to every person who lent their time, reflections, and memories to fill the pages of this book.

Many individuals saw value in this project, allowing me access where I would have otherwise had none. Chad Kiser is simply the gatekeeper to West Coast hip-hop, and was completely selfless in facilitating interviews and allowing me to pick his mind. Paris, the revolutionary artist and producer, equipped me with motivation to keep hammering away at this throughout the years. Bill Adler, one of the deans of hip-hop journalism, embraced this project and shared his recollections and extensive Rolodex with me. Jeff and Eric Rosenthal at ItsTheReal took my calls again and again, and thankfully vouched for me. Likewise, Wendy Day is the very definition of selflessness.

In a similar vein, those like Sama'an Ashrawi, Reed Baker, Russ Bengtson, Erik Blamoville, Nancy Byron, Eddie Gonzalez, Juan Guerrero, Jorge Hinojosa, Tamiko Hope, Tamar Juda, Erik Nielson, and Alex Stone served as conduits for interviews, oftentimes opening doors for more than one key figure.

I am indebted to Nathan Roberson, who steered my first two books into existence and encouraged me to tackle this one. The immensely talented Tricia Boczkowski probably worked on this book as much as I did. After acquiring it, she expertly edited down the initially unwieldy draft and offered words and messages of motivation throughout the process. Thanks to Crown's Paul Whitlatch for skillfully helping to bring the book home. Dart Adams is a reservoir of hip-hop knowledge, and his detailed eye saved the text from what would have been regrettable miscues. Three books in, Daniel Greenberg is more a friend than an agent at this point, someone at my side from the initial plan to the final printing.

A lot of great hip-hop journalism books already exist, and many served as roadmaps. I am appreciative to the authors who allowed me to pick their expansive minds during this reporting process. They include: Soren Baker, Dan Charnas, Brian Coleman, Joseph Ewoodzie Jr., Gerrick Kennedy, Kevin Powell, Jeff Weiss, and Ben Westhoff.

I could never list all of the friends and talented journalists whom I bounced ideas off for this book over the last few years. A sampling includes: Christopher A. Daniel, Michael Lee, Mark Lelinwalla, Mat Lewis, Shauntel Lowe, Adam Maya, Dave McMenamin, Jeff Pearlman, Joe Posnanski, Shea Serrano, Bill Simmons, Marcus Thompson, Tommy Tomlinson, and Tzvi Twersky.

I can do nothing without the support of my family. To my siblings, Diana, Danielle, and Matthew, thanks for your unflinching support. To my nieces and nephews: Whitney, Dannen, Danica, Cadence, and Jaxton, I love you guys with everything I've got. You don't choose your in-laws, but I lucked out in Angela, George, Dan, Jamaal, and Nicole.

Tanya, you are my forever confidante and motivator. You have the vision to see things when I don't. On the many days when this seemed too big a project to finish, you never doubted me and offered me strength to keep after it, one sentence, one quote, one page at a time. To my sons, Jayden and Aaron: I know Daddy worked on this book for a long time. You guys kept asking when it would be completed. The answer, finally, is *now,* and my goal is to make you guys proud every day. You are all, and all is for you.

Mom, I remember you snatching the album that I had discreetly purchased. That made an adolescent me want to seek out this genre even more. Look where it brought me.

SELECTED BIBLIOGRAPHY

The quotations that fill these pages were collected through my own firsthand interviews. However, I consulted a number of books that provided a roadmap of hip-hop music's winding and impactful history. They include:

Adler, Bill (1987, 2002): *Tougher Than Leather: The Rise of Run DMC.* Los Angeles. Consafos Press.

Ahearn, Charlie, and Jim Fricke (2001): *Yes Yes Y'all: The Experience Music Project Oral History of Hip-Hop's First Decade.* Boston. Da Capo Press.

Baker, Soren (2018): *The History of Gangster Rap.* New York. Abrams Image.

Campbell, Luther (2015): *The Book of Luke.* New York. HarperCollins Publishers.

Chang, Jeff (2005): *Can't Stop Won't Stop: A History of the Hip-Hop Generation.* New York. St. Martin's Press.

Charnas, Dan (2010): *The Big Payback: The History of the Business of Hip-Hop.* New York. New American Library.

Chuck D (2017): *Chuck D Presents This Day in Rap and Hip-Hop History* with Duke Eatmon, Ron Maskell, Lorrie Boula, and Jonathan Bernstein. New York. Hachette Book Group.

Coleman, Brian (2007): *Check the Technique: Liner Notes for Hip-Hop Junkies.* New York. Villard Books.

Coleman, Brian (2014): *Check The Technique, Volume 2: More Liner Notes for Hip-Hop Junkies.* Berkeley, Calif. Gingko Press.

Ewoodzie, Joseph C., Jr. (2017): *Break Beats in the Bronx: Rediscovering Hip-Hop's Early Years.* Chapel Hill. University of North Carolina Press.

George, Nelson (2005): *Hip Hop America.* New York. Penguin Group.

Grandmaster Flash, with David Ritz (2018): *The Adventures of Grandmaster Flash: My Life, My Beats.* New York. Broadway Books.

Greenburg, Zack O'Malley (2018): *3 Kings: Diddy, Dr. Dre, Jay-Z, and Hip-Hop's Multibillion-Dollar Rise.* New York. Little, Brown and Company.

Grierson, Tim (2015): *Public Enemy: Inside the Terrordome.* New York. Omnibus Press.

Hodari Coker, Cheo (2003): *Unbelievable: The Life, Death, and Afterlife of the Notorious B.I.G.* New York. VIBE Books.

Iandoli, Kathy (2019): *God Save the Queens: The Essential History of Women in Hip-Hop.* New York. HarperCollins Publishers.

Jay-Z (2010): *Decoded.* New York. Spiegel & Grau.

Jordan, Brad (Scarface), with Brandon Meadows-Ingram (2015): *Diary of a Madman: The Geto Boys, Life, Death, and the Roots of Southern Rap.* New York. Dey St. Books.

Kennedy, Gerrick D. (2017): *Parental Discretion Is Advised: The Rise of N.W.A and the Dawn of Gangsta Rap.* New York. Atria Books.

Light, Alan, ed. (1999): *The VIBE History of Hip Hop.* New York. Three Rivers Press.

Mane, Gucci, with Neil Martinez-Belkin (2017): *The Autobiography of Gucci Mane.* New York. Simon & Schuster.

Prince, James (2018): *The Art & Science of Respect: A Memoir by James Prince.* Houston, Tex. N-The-Water Publishing.

Rakim (2019): *Sweat the Technique: Revelations on Creativity from the Lyrical Genius.* New York. HarperCollins Publishers.

Sarig, Roni (2007): *Third Coast: OutKast, Timbaland & How Hip-Hop Became a Southern Thing.* Boston. Da Capo Press.

Serrano, Shea (2015): *The Rap Year Book: The Most Important Rap Song Every Year Since 1979, Discussed, Debated, and Deconstructed.* New York. Abrams Image.

Walker, Lance Scott (2018): *Houston Rap Tapes: An Oral History of Bayou City Hip-Hop.* Austin. University of Texas Press.

Westhoff, Ben (2011): *Dirty South: OutKast, Lil Wayne, Soulja Boy, and the Southern Rappers Who Reinvented Hip-Hop.* Chicago. Chicago Review Press.

Westhoff, Ben (2016): *Original Gangstas: Tupac Shakur, Dr. Dre, Eazy-E, Ice Cube, and the Birth of West Coast Rap.* New York. Hachette Book Group.

INDEX

JONATHAN ABRAMS is an award-winning staff reporter for *The New York Times*. He is the bestselling author of two previous books, *Boys Among Men* and *All the Pieces Matter*. A graduate of the University of Southern California, Abrams was formerly a staff writer at *Bleacher Report*, *Grantland*, and the *Los Angeles Times*.

ABOUT THE TYPE

This book was set in Walbaum, a typeface designed in 1810 by German punch cutter J. E. (Justus Erich) Walbaum (1768–1839). Walbaum's type is more French than German in appearance. Like Bodoni, it is a classical typeface, yet its openness and slight irregularities give it a human, romantic quality.

**AVAILABLE FROM *NEW YORK TIMES*
BESTSELLING AUTHOR**

JONATHAN ABRAMS

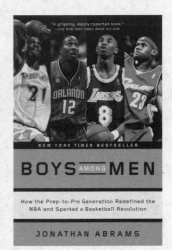

"Jonathan Abrams is a marvel."

—Shea Serrano, *New York Times* bestselling author
of *The Rap Year Book*